A Castle in Wartime

A Castle in Wartime

*One Family, Their Missing Sons,
and the Fight to Defeat the Nazis*

CATHERINE BAILEY

VIKING

VIKING
An imprint of Penguin Random House LLC
penguinrandomhouse.com

First published in Great Britain as *The Lost Boys: A Family Ripped Apart by War*
by Viking, an imprint of Penguin Books, a division of Penguin Random House Ltd., London, in 2019

Illustration credits on page vii

ISBN 9780525559290 (hardcover)
ISBN 9780525559306 (ebook)

Printed in Canada
1   3   5   7   9   10   8   6   4   2

Maps illustrated by Ian Moores

In memory of my father Martin, with love

List of Illustrations

On page 405

The majority of the photographs have been produced by kind permission of the Brazzà family archive. The author and publisher are also grateful to the following for permission to reproduce photographs: H. Huber for 1; The Gemeinde Museum, Absam for 2; Mike Foster for 5; Ullstein bild/Getty Images for 7, 11, 12 and 13; Toni Schneiders/Bundesarchiv for 21; ANPI Udine Photo Archive for 25; The German Federal Archives for 27 and 28; The Nationaal Archief for 29; Hulton Archive/ Getty Images for 30; Dr Gudula Knerr-Stauffenberg for 31 and 32; Popperfoto/Getty Images for 33; Zeitgeschichtsarchiv Pragser Wildsee for 34; Dea/S. Vannini/Getty Images for 35; Stutthof Museum for 37; Army Film and Photographic Unit for 38.

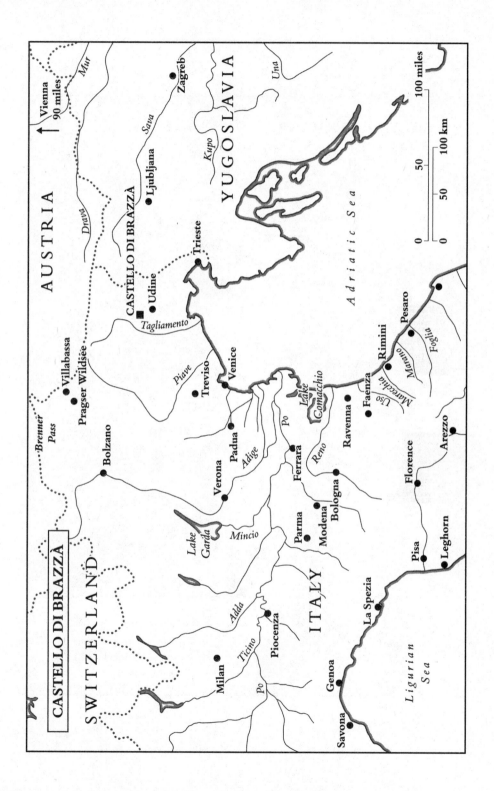

CASTELLO DI BRAZZÀ

SWITZERLAND

AUSTRIA

YUGOSLAVIA

ITALY

Adriatic Sea

Ligurian Sea

↑ Vienna
90 miles

CASTELLO DI BRAZZÀ

Zagreb

Ljubljana

Trieste

Udine

Tagliamento

Venice

Treviso

Piave

Villabassa
Pragser Wildsee

*Brenner
Pass*

Bolzano

*Lake
Garda*

Mincio

Adda

Ticino

Milan

Padua

Verona

Adige

Po

Ferrara

Piocenza

Parma

Modena

Bologna

Reno

Ravenna

*Lake
Comacchio*

Faenza

Uso

Rimini

Marecchia

Marano

Pesaro

Foglia

Arezzo

Florence

Pisa

Leghorn

La Spezia

Genoa

Savona

Mur

Drava

Sava

Kupo

Una

Po

100 miles

100 km

0   50   100 km

0   50   100 miles

GREATER GERMANY
15 APRIL 1945

SWEDEN

COURLAND

Riga

*Baltic
Sea*

Memel

LATVIA

*North
Sea*

SCHLESWIG-
HOLSTEIN

Danzig (Gdańsk)

Gdynia

Königsberg

EAST PRUSSIA

Hamburg

Stettin

POMERANIA

HOLLAND

WARTHELAND

Poznań

Warsaw

Berlin

Antwerp

Elbe

Oder

LOWER
SILESIA

Lodz

BELGIUM

Cologne

Dresden

Breslau

Lublin

Rhine

Frankfurt am Main

UPPER
SILESIA

LUXEMBOURG

Prague

Cracow

GERMANY

CZECHOSLOVAKIA

Strasbourg

Regensburg

Schönberg

FRANCE

BAVARIA

Vienna

Munich

Berne

Innsbruck

Salzburg

Brenner Pass

AUSTRIA

Budapest

SWITZERLAND

Bolzano

HUNGARY

Brazzà

Udine

ROMANIA

Milan

ITALY

Trieste

Danube

Padua

YUGOSLAVIA

0   100   200 miles

*Mediterranean
Sea*

Florence

0   100   200   300 km

CORSICA

Key

- - - - **Front line**

  German occupied territory

  Allied and liberated territories

  Neutral countries

SARDINIA

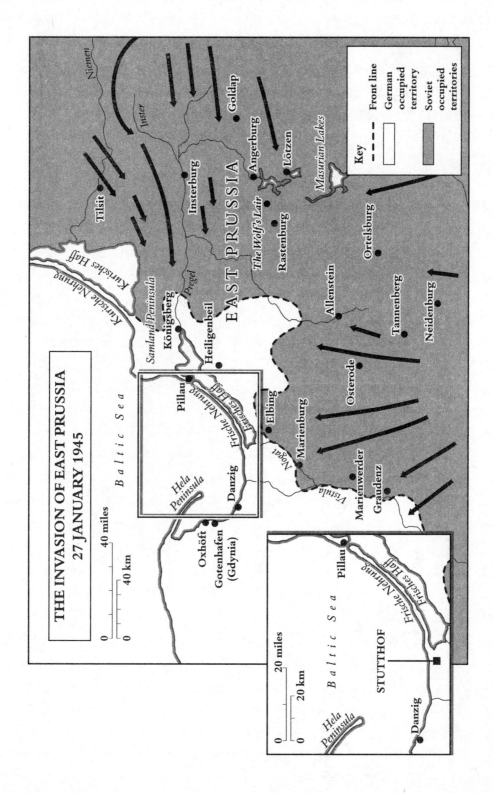

THE INVASION OF EAST PRUSSIA
27 JANUARY 1945

0   40 km
0   40 miles

Baltic Sea

Kurische Nehrung
Kurisches Haff
Niemen
Inster
Tilsit
Insterburg
Pregel
Samland Peninsula
Königsberg
Heiligenbeil
Goldap
Angerburg
Lötzen
Masurian Lakes
The Wolf's Lair
Rastenburg
EAST PRUSSIA
Ortelsburg
Allenstein
Tannenberg
Neidenburg
Osterode
Elbing
Marienburg
Frische Nehrung
Frisches Haff
Pillau
Hela Peninsula
Danzig
Nogat
Marienwerder
Graudenz
Vistula
Oxhöft
Gotenhafen
(Gdynia)

Key

- - - Front line
German occupied territory
Soviet occupied territories

0   20 km
0   20 miles

Baltic Sea

Hela Peninsula
Danzig
Frische Nehrung
Frisches Haff
Pillau
STUTTHOF

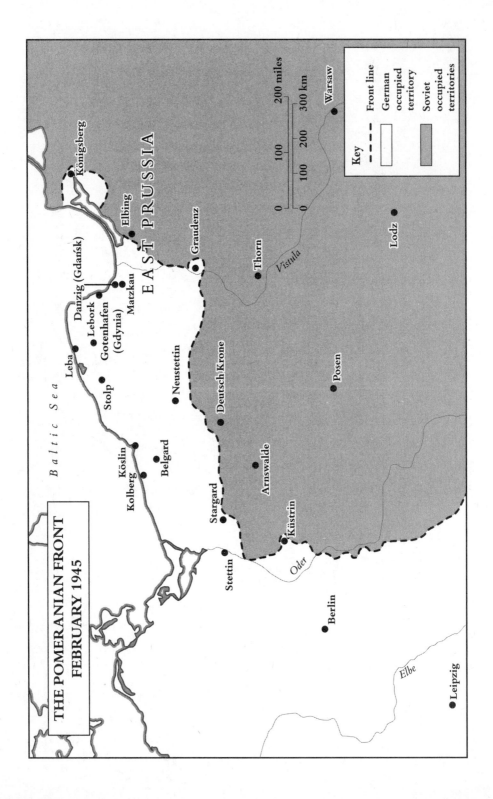

THE POMERANIAN FRONT
FEBRUARY 1945

Key

Front line — — —

German occupied territory ☐

Soviet occupied territories ▨

0   100   200 miles
0   100   200   300 km

Baltic Sea

EAST PRUSSIA

Königsberg
Elbing
Danzig (Gdańsk)
Matzkau
Gotenhafen (Gdynia)
Lebork
Leba
Stolp
Köslin
Kolberg
Belgard
Neustettin
Deutsch Krone
Graudenz
Thorn
Vistula
Warsaw
Lodz
Posen
Arnswalde
Stargard
Küstrin
Stettin
Oder
Berlin
Elbe
Leipzig

Prologue

Innsbruck, Austria, 16 December 1944
'Monika calling steamboat.'

This cryptic announcement, broadcast to Austria over the Voice of America, was received with relief by the handful of people able to decipher it. The coded message signalled that the Allies were still trying to infiltrate agents into Innsbruck to make contact with members of the Austrian Resistance.

It was seven o'clock on a winter's morning, the grey old city walled in by snow-covered mountains. A roof of dense cloud hung over the domes and spires, cutting out the sky and the summit of the Nordkette. Towering 7,000 feet above the city, the sheer face of the mountain rose like a wall, blocking the north end of the fine baroque streets. The illusion of being confined in a small space was maintained in the alleys and passageways in the medieval quarter. On a chill, gloomy day such as this, passing the tall, narrow-fronted Gothic houses, the sensation was of walking along the bottom of a ravine.

Thick wreaths of smoke spiralled beneath the clouds. The day before, American planes had bombed the city, killing 259 people. In Herzog-Friedrich-Strasse, a protective shroud covered the famous golden roof of the balcony, designed for Emperor Maximilian in 1500. Beneath the bombed-out buildings, parties of children, drafted in from the villages along the valley, worked to clear the rubble. They were watched by small groups of SS soldiers who stood on the street corners, guarding the defusing crews. Forcibly recruited from the nearby concentration camp at Reichenau, it was their job to deactivate the bombs that had failed to explode.

The Allies were now convinced that Innsbruck, rather than the Reich capital of Berlin, was where the war was likely to culminate. Recent intelligence reports indicated that Hitler was building an

Alpenfestung – an Alpine fortress – in the mountains that encircled the city. Blueprints obtained by OSS⋆ operatives pointed to a chain of underground factories and armouries. It was to this remote, impregnable fortress that Hitler, and a coterie of his most fanatical supporters, intended to retreat when the *Wehrmacht*† was beaten. From here, they would carry on the fight, defended by elite SS troops and sustained by huge stores of supplies that had been carefully stockpiled in bombproof caves.

With Hitler holding the high ground, Allied military commanders were predicting that the battle to take the fortress could extend the war by up to two years and exact more casualties than all the previous fighting on the Western Front.

In these circumstances, intelligence from Innsbruck, the capital of the Alpenfestung, was suddenly at a premium. Allen Dulles, the OSS station chief in Switzerland, hoped to recruit a network of agents from within the city. Their job would be to supply hard military intelligence and assist the passage of US and British forces when they reached the western borders of Austria. But, as Dulles recognized, Innsbruck was not fertile ground. That autumn, the Gestapo had arrested all known anti-Nazis. Moving from house to house, the mopping-up operation signalled their determination to suppress all resistance operations in an area they looked upon as their last bastion.

Soon after midday on 16 December, the US Air Force returned to bomb the city for the fourth time that month. 'A sharp left rally was executed immediately after bombs away and a course flown around Innsbruck,' the pilot reported. 'Due to undercast, no visual observations of results were possible.'

Some hours later, Frau Mutschlechner, a resident of forty-seven years, sat down to write her diary. 'It is a black day for Innsbruck,' she began. 'The old city centre has been hit as well as the graveyard. Everyone feared there would be another raid and sure enough the enemy bombers came and wreaked their evil.'

⋆ Office of Strategic Services, the forerunner to the Central Intelligence Agency (CIA).
† The armed forces of Nazi Germany.

There was no gas or water in the city and the cemetery was now closed for burials. In the flat, dingy light, the only colour was from the fires that had yet to be put out. 'Fräulein Kummer's photo studio is on fire,' Frau Mutschlechner reported. 'Warger's paper warehouse, the stained-glass factory in Müllerstrasse, Café Paul in Maximilian-strasse and Hellenstainer's Gasthaus are all burning . . . Showers of sparks and burning paper are falling from the warehouse. One would marvel at the eerie beauty of it were it not such a sad occasion.'

The raid marked a change of tactic. In addition to dropping 200 tons of bombs, the US planes had dropped thousands of propaganda leaflets. In the coming weeks, they would drop thousands more. These, and the messages broadcast on the BBC's Austrian Service, urged the city's inhabitants to rise up and prevent Hitler from making a last stand in the Tyrol: 'Tyroleans, we know that you will not permit it. You will see to it that none of the Nazi leaders can hide. We know that already Tyroleans are fighting the Nazis everywhere . . . Even if the Nazis still feel secure in your country, we know better; you are on our side.'

But the vast majority of Tyroleans were not on the Allies' side. In Innsbruck, the citizens were actively pro-Nazi. It was they who had informed on the burgeoning resistance networks. Protected as they were by the mountains, they did not fear the US raids. After the attack on 15 December, at the sound of four short blasts of a siren, they fled to the bombproof caves, deep beneath the Nordkette.

PART ONE

One night that December, in the bitterest of weather, a car inched its way along Herrengasse, past the burnt-out shells of houses that belonged to Innsbruck's wealthiest inhabitants. Sleek and black, with a long, low-slung bonnet, the number plate, and the blue glare from its headlamps, identified it as belonging to the Gestapo. At the corner with Rennweg, beneath a low arch, the car turned right, its wheels sliding on the snow.

At what hour precisely – even on which day – it is impossible to say. The official documents relating to the terrible purpose of its journey would be destroyed within months of its having taken place.

The car was heading east. Approaching the outskirts of the city, the driver, wearing the grey field uniform of the Waffen SS, took the Reichsstrasse 31, the main road up through the Inn Valley to the German border. So secret was his assignment, he had waited for darkness to fall before leaving the Gestapo's headquarters. With a blackout in force, there was no danger of other drivers, or people he passed, seeing two of his passengers. They were so small, not even the tops of their heads were visible through the window.

Craning his neck, the driver could see the children in his rear mirror. The boys were seated next to an SS nurse, their escort for the journey. Aged two and four, they had blue eyes and fair hair, which fell in tumbles of long blond curls. Both boys were dressed in home-made woollen overcoats that were many sizes too big, as if someone was expecting them to grow into them.

Leaving the city, on the long, straight road that ran through the centre of the valley, the car picked up speed. All around, the frozen landscape was visible, lit by the light from the moon on the snow. On either side, wide, flat fields stretched to the base of the mountains that rose thousands of feet above the valley. The road itself, a thin black stripe in the expanse of white, was clear of snow. After heavy falls,

tractors and snowploughs were deployed to keep it open. Staff officers attached to the Wehrmacht's High Command frequently used it.
It was the quickest route from northern Italy, where the German
Army had suffered a series of defeats, to Adolf Hitler's headquarters
at Berchtesgaden.

The two boys huddled in the back were brothers. Officially, they
belonged to no one. Three months earlier, after forcibly wrenching
them from their mother, the SS had altered their identities. On the
orders of Heinrich Himmler, the Reichsführer SS, the Ministry of
the Interior had supplied the necessary documents. New birth certifi-
cates, with false names, and invented dates and places of birth, had
been issued, enabling the SS to act as the stolen children's legal guard-
ian. They were the 'Vorhof' brothers now. The ministry had named
the elder boy 'Conrad'; the baby was 'Robert'.

Up ahead, strange snow-shrouded shapes loomed in the fields,
caught in the blue glare of the car's headlights. The railway line running parallel to the road was the main supply route to the German
Army in Italy and the Americans had been bombing it for weeks.
Wreckage from the raids was strewn across the fields. There were
upturned train carriages, spilling their snow-covered contents; the
wrecks of downed aircraft, identifiable by the tips of their propellers;
and, in this thinly populated area, the sudden, stark interiors of
houses that had lost a wall through shelling.

Earlier in the day, the order to pick up the children had been flashed
through to the Gestapo. Marked top secret, it had come from the
Reich Main Security Office, Himmler's headquarters in Berlin. The
boys were to be taken to a Nazi-run orphanage at Wiesenhof, a tiny
hamlet high in the Alps above Innsbruck.

It was not far to go. Turning off the valley road at Hall, a prosper-
ous medieval town some 8 miles from Innsbruck, the car headed up
into the mountains. From here, it was a five-minute drive to the
orphanage.

The road climbed steeply out of the town. On the right, behind
a long wall, was a former monastery, now used as a psychiatric
hospital. Within the grounds lay the recently dug graves of upwards
of 200 victims of the Nazis' euthanasia programme. Men, women

and children aged from fourteen to ninety, they had been murdered by the Gestapo because they were mentally or physically disabled.

Higher up the mountain, clusters of farmhouses stood on either side of the road. This was the outskirts of Absam, a village of some 1,200 inhabitants, 98 per cent of whom belonged to the Nazi Party. The houses were prettily decorated in the Alpine style. Wooden carvings, a centuries-old tradition in the Tyrol, hung beneath the gables, and murals of religious scenes were painted on the walls. Some were of the patron saint Maria Schutz, protector of families; she was shown with her arms around the children who were sheltered under her long cloak. In the centre of the village, two lime trees had recently been planted outside the school. They were a reward from Franz Hofer, the Nazi *Gauleiter** of the Tyrol, for the community's loyalty to the party. In the pagan mythology the Nazis embraced, the lime was a hallowed tree and a symbol of justice. Traditionally, judicial courts were held beneath its branches. It was believed that the tree would help unearth the truth.

Above Absam, the road wound up through a forest. Then, reaching a plateau of upland, where cattle were put out to grass in the summer, it narrowed to a single track. Here, the snow lay undisturbed in thick, undulating drifts formed by the wind blowing down the valley. On one side, sheer rock rose hundreds of feet to the summit of Mount Bettelwurf. The track twisted, following the contours of the rock until, rounding a bend – on which, in this isolated spot, someone had placed a shrine to the Virgin Mary – the orphanage lay directly ahead.

In the half-light of the moon, its silhouette was familiar to the Gestapo driver; he frequently delivered children after dark.

---

* Nazi Party regional leader.

The house was in darkness, the windows blacked out; standing four storeys high, its Gothic turret could be glimpsed at the back.

Despite its pretensions to grandeur, it sat uneasily in its surroundings. Hemmed by the mountain that towered above it, and the forest that enclosed it on three sides, its long, narrow shape was unappealing. Large black crosses, made from timber, were stamped in a pattern along the white-painted exterior, and the roof, which was gabled, hung low over the upper floors, obscuring the windows and lending the house an air of menace. The front door, made of thick dark oak, was small in proportion to the rest of it. Stencilled in large Gothic script above the door was the name of the orphanage. *Wiesenhof.* Meadow Court.

To the locals living in the isolated villages and farmhouses along the plateau, it was a 'cursed' and 'haunted house', one that brought misfortune to anyone associated with it. Formerly a hunting lodge, it was built in the early 1800s by a wealthy aristocrat whose fortune came from the nearby salt mines. In 1878, his family sold it to a property developer, who wanted to create a luxury spa resort. After laying a pipe from the mines to provide salt-spring baths, he extended the Wiesenhof and built a second hotel in the grounds. But he ran out of money before he could complete the work and in 1899, when the bank called in his debts, he committed suicide.

In the decade that followed, a succession of owners had tried – and failed – to resurrect the spa. Then, shortly before the First World War, it was sold to Siegmund Weiss, a wealthy Jewish businessman from Vienna, who leased it to the Viennese Anthroposophy Society, founded by the Austrian mystic and self-proclaimed clairvoyant Rudolf Steiner. Anthroposophy was a spiritual movement which sought to promote physical and mental well-being using natural means and, by the 1930s, the Wiesenhof had become one of the most fashionable resorts in Europe. Run by Steiner's disciples, it offered a range of alternative medical treatments and therapies, and was visited by international celebrities, aristocrats and prominent members of the Nazi Party.

But the 'curse' of the Wiesenhof had struck again in 1938 after Germany invaded Austria. In the months following the *Anschluss*, thousands of Jews were rounded up in Vienna, where the Weiss family was living. On the night of 10 November alone, 8,000 were arrested. That same night, 680 others committed suicide or were murdered. Walther Eidlitz, the grandson of Siegmund Weiss, remembered how 'the mobs came rolling in over all the bridges of the Danube, and how the men held up their clenched fists threateningly towards the dark walls of the houses and rhythmically shouted in chorus: "Death to Judah! Death to Judah!"' Soon after, he fled the country. But his mother, whose childhood had been spent at the Wiesenhof, was arrested and sent to the concentration camp at Theresienstadt, where she died in 1941.

In the absence of the spa's Jewish owners, high-ranking Nazis and wealthy guests from all over Europe continued to enjoy its sybaritic routine. Yet, as the manager, Rudolf Hauschka, recalled, the annexation of Austria placed the resort in 'serious danger': 'one was continually aware of living in an oasis which could at any moment be covered over with a sand storm.' He would turn out to be right.

An event which Hitler would come to regard as one of the worst personal blows of his life, and which his investigators linked back to the Wiesenhof, led to its transformation from a luxury spa to a Nazi-run orphanage.

It began with the controversy surrounding the Anthroposophists' tenancy after the Germans seized Austria.

Three years earlier, the anti-occult faction within the *Sicherheitsdienst* – the Nazi security service – had banned the Anthroposophy Society. Its opponents included Joseph Goebbels, Reich minister of propaganda; Gestapo chief Reinhard Heydrich; and Martin Bormann, the Führer's private secretary. Branding the society a menacing, Jewish-controlled

sect which, through its links to Communists and Freemasons, belonged
to a shadowy international conspiracy that threatened the German
people, they wanted to eliminate the movement entirely. But the
Anthroposophy Society had equally powerful supporters within the
Nazi Party – among them Rudolf Hess, Hitler's deputy, and SS General
Otto Ohlendorf.

Throughout the 1930s, both Hess and Ohlendorf – who would
later stand trial at Nuremberg for the murder of 90,000 Jews – were
regular guests at the Wiesenhof. Without formally endorsing Rudolf
Steiner's doctrines, both men considered aspects of anthroposophy to
be compatible with National Socialist principles, particularly Steiner's ideas on biodynamic farming. In the gardens and fields around
the Wiesenhof, the land was cultivated using these methods. Sowing
and harvesting were determined according to astrological principles
and, as an alternative to fertilizers and pesticides, a variety of homeo-
pathic treatments were used.

To Heydrich and Goebbels, this was 'occultist quackery'. But as
long as the Anthroposophy Society enjoyed Hess's protection, they
were unable to eliminate it. While continuing to peddle rumours of
the 'prominence of the Israelite element', and 'covert saboteurs and
antagonists', they instructed their agents to move cautiously. No
action was to be taken against the Wiesenhof; instead, it was to be
kept under close surveillance.

In keeping watch, the Gestapo relied on locals employed at the
house. A large number of the gardeners, maids and other staff necessary to maintain the luxurious standards at the spa came from Absam,
the nearby village rewarded by the Gauleiter of the Tyrol for its loyalty to the Nazi Party. Based on the villagers' reports, the Gestapo
placed its own agents inside the clinic. 'Despite the fact that we cultivated the best of relations with the neighbourhood, gossip continued,'
Rudolf Hauschka recalled. 'We felt mistrust come crawling out of
every corner, and we later heard that informers, passing themselves
off as patients, were watching what we did.'

It was the villagers' prejudice against the clinic's Jewish owners,
and their mistrust of the new-fangled ideas practised by the Anthroposophists, which led them to inform the Gestapo of the goings-on at

the Wiesenhof. 'Everything is wrong there,' they muttered. 'It does not belong to us.' A community of devout Catholics, whose families had worked in the salt mines since the fifteenth century, the anti-Semitism embedded in their culture was reinforced by the Nazis' propaganda. Every Sunday, at Mass, they were told that Jews had murdered their God. Across the valley, in the village of Rinn, the church was named after Anderl, a three-year-old boy 'murdered' by Jews in medieval times. His death, depicted in a gruesome painting that hung inside the church, was part of the folklore of the Tyrol. In the backward, inward-looking villages, many still believed the myth that the Jews had used the boy's blood to make matzohs for Passover.

With the connivance of the villagers, the Gestapo's final move against the Anthroposophy Society came in the spring of 1941.

On 18 April, Rudolph Hess arrived to spend the weekend at the Wiesenhof. In an attempt to evade the Gestapo, he had booked into the clinic under an assumed name. One night during his stay, Hess, who surrounded himself with astrologers and was interested in mysticism and the occult, convened a seance in his room. Conducted in the strictest secrecy, it was in direct contravention of Hitler's ban on occult practices. 'Mystically inclined occult investigators of the hereafter must not be tolerated,' the Führer had pronounced in the autumn of 1938. 'They are not National Socialists: they have nothing to do with us.' Via their informants, the Gestapo learned what had occurred during the seance. According to their files, the participants had summoned the ghost of Bismarck – the Prussian statesman who had unified Germany and built a powerful empire in the last decades of the nineteenth century. They had asked his ghost how the war would end. His reply, 'rapped out on the seance board', was that Hitler would lose the war and go to ground, and that Germany would be plunged into dire misfortune.

Three weeks later, on 9 May, Hess flew alone and unannounced to Scotland on a quixotic mission to negotiate peace with Britain. His flight – just weeks in advance of Operation Barbarossa, the planned invasion of the Soviet Union – came at a sensitive time for the regime and, as soon as it became known, the search for a plausible and face-saving explanation began.

The story, fuelled by the Gestapo's reports of the seance at the Wiesenhof and Hitler's shock at such a personal betrayal by one of his closest friends, centred on Hess's susceptibility to occult doctrines and practices. Reich minister Hans Frank was present at the meeting convened on 13 May to discuss the crisis. 'Hitler was evidently in torment. I had not seen him for some time and I was deeply shaken by his utter depression. In a very low voice, and hesitantly, he spoke to us . . . He described the flight as pure insanity, and believed an astrologer had put Hess up to it. "It is high time to destroy all this star-gazing nonsense," he said.'

The following day, Hitler's private secretary sent a telegram to Heydrich, the chief of the Gestapo: 'The Führer wishes that the strongest measures be directed against occultists, astrologists, medical quacks, and the like, who lead the people astray into stupidity and superstition.' The result was *Aktion Hess*, a purge of so-called 'practitioners of the occult'. Hundreds were arrested and interrogated — including faith healers, fortune-tellers, graphologists and Christian Scientists — and a ban placed on all 'occult' organizations, with special emphasis on the Anthroposophy Society.

On 9 June 1941, the Gestapo raided the Wiesenhof. 'Suddenly, police cars appeared and, in no time at all, the sanatorium was surrounded by Gestapo officials,' Rudolf Hauschka recalled. 'A thorough search of the house began, with the contents of the library, office and book-keeping room being carried off in lorry loads. My scientific library, which included ordinary scientific works on chemistry, botany and anatomy, was also seized. When I asked why books that were not prohibited were being taken away from me, I received the answer: "Everything you read is suspect as far as we are concerned." '

Later that day, Hauschka and his colleagues were arrested and taken to the Gestapo prison at Innsbruck.

Soon after, a notice was posted around the Wiesenhof estate: *In Dem Deutschen Reich Einverleibt* — 'Incorporated into the German Reich'. Within months, the estate became an SS stronghold; a barrack was built in the forest below the house to accommodate thousands of SS mountain troops and, for the purposes of rewarding party cronies, a number of properties were seized. One farmhouse, with spectacular views over the Inn Valley, was given to Franziska Kinz, a film actress much admired by Hitler and Goebbels.

After lying vacant for eight months, the Wiesenhof itself was used to house senior SS officers serving at the new barrack until, in the autumn of 1942, it was transferred to the *Nationalsozialistische Volks-wohlfahrt* (NSV) – the state organization for the people's welfare.

It was then that it became an orphanage for children aged between two and twelve.

Very little is known about the time when the Wiesenhof was a Nazi-run home for children. The suggestion is that there were upwards of sixty children, a significant proportion of whom the SS had stolen and given false identities. The local families, whose loyalty the Gestapo had counted on during the years when the house and its estate was leased to the Anthroposophy Society, had continued to work there. When the war ended, the fear of punishment led these same families to kick over the traces of all that had occurred. They destroyed the records relating to the orphanage.

For the rest of their lives, the villagers employed at the Wiesenhof remained tight-lipped about how they treated the children and what conditions were like there. They never spoke about it. Nor did the inhabitants of the nearby villages, who, at the very least, would have known of its existence, ever speak about it. It is as if the place never existed. In the 1960s, the building was taken over by the Austrian state and turned into a police academy. Today, in this tiny hamlet, there are people – residents of thirty years or more – living just yards from the academy who know nothing of its former history. As one woman said, 'No one ever told us it was an SS orphanage. We never knew it was there.'

But there is no doubt that many did know of its existence. In a number of the pretty, chalet-style houses dotted along the plateau beneath Mount Bettelwurf, and in the village of Absam, evidence of their knowledge can still be found. When the orphanage was closed down at the end of the war, the locals looted it. Some of their descendants still have the towels that were used to dry the children after their baths. Pale blue and pink in colour, they are inscribed with the initials 'NKWD' – the Nazi ministry that ran the Wiesenhof.

Just one glimpse of the interior remains. A local woman, who visited the house after the war, remembers seeing the beds the children had slept on. They were decorated with paintings of forests and flowers and arranged, dormitory-style, in the former dining salon at the back of the building. A large high-ceilinged room, with five bays of windows, it was here that the Wiesenhof's infamous guests, Hess and SS General Ohlendorf – the murderer of 90,000 Jews – had dined before the Gestapo closed the spa.

The names of the children who slept, night after night, in the rows of painted beds are lost. Their captors destroyed the files that contained their details – their ages, their SS aliases and their individual characteristics – because they wanted their stories to be forgotten.

The 'Vorhof' brothers are the one exception. In the face of the deliberate, collective amnesia that descended over this remote part of the Tyrol after the war ended, a fragment of memory survives. It comes from Frau Buri, who was the head nurse at the orphanage when the Gestapo delivered the boys.

In the weeks after their arrival, Frau Buri kept a close eye on the 'Vorhof' brothers.

Conrad, the four-year-old, she noted, was shy and rather nervous and always cried when he was put to bed. Whereas Robert, the two-year-old, seemed to adjust to the home with much less difficulty and after a while began to play happily with the other children. She and the other staff were impressed at how Conrad protected and looked after his little brother. In the mornings, he would help Robert dress, even tying his shoelaces for him.

Their angelic looks and impeccable manners marked them out from the other children. They always said 'please' and 'thank you'. As the weeks passed, Frau Buri grew more and more curious. She wondered who the boys could be. The entry in the register, filled in the night they arrived, simply said 'Vorhof brothers, Conrad and Robert: mother arrested'. She knew that 'Vorhof' was an alias; the SS always changed the smaller children's names and never gave any information about who they were or why they were being held. But she and the other staff found it hard to believe the mother was an ordinary criminal, since the boys had told them they lived in a 'big house' and had horses.

One day, she overheard the brothers chatting to each other. To her amazement, they seemed to switch effortlessly between three different languages – German, English and Italian. She had assumed German was their mother tongue; the boys spoke it fluently with no trace of an accent. It was possible, of course, that one of their parents was English or Italian, but to hear them speaking in *three* different languages was puzzling. There was one other thing: the boys' overcoats, which had obviously been remade from an adult's coat, struck her as most unusual. The fabric, which was a distinctive, deep Prussian blue, was of the same colour and texture as the greatcoats worn by officers in the German Navy.

She tried questioning the boys. What were their names? she asked. 'Robert' told her his name was Robertino; but Conrad said he had forgotten his. She did not believe him. *Any four-year-old boy would know his name.* 'Conrad', she concluded, was concealing the brothers' true identity. It was not that he had forgotten. He simply was not prepared to say.

PART TWO

3

'Secret. AHQ DAF proceed Castello di Brazzà 15:00 hrs. 5 miles NNE Udine. Ref C.3427.'

Above the noise of the engine, and the bangs and creaks of the jeep's suspension as it moved at speed along the unmetalled road, came the crackle of static, punctuated by bursts of voices, mostly unintelligible.

Robert Foster, Air Officer Commanding, Desert Air Force (DAF), was travelling in the lead vehicle. Following behind was a convoy of some fifteen lorries, escorted by motorcycle outriders.

They were heading north, towards the Alps. The road stretched ahead, white and straight, bordered on either side by low mulberry trees clipped in a fan shape. On the near horizon, the ridge of mountains, their peaks still covered in snow, stood up into the sky, rising out of the flat country like a great wave about to break.

It was 12 May 1945. Five days previously, when the Germans capitulated and the ceasefire was signalled, Foster's Advanced HQ had been halfway up the main road from Venice to Treviso side by side with General Army HQ. Now they were on their way to Udine, a medieval city in the province of Friuli, close to Italy's border with Yugoslavia.

The day had been still and warm and the heat rose off the dusty road. With the cooling evening air came the scent of wild thyme growing in the fields and of condensation forming on the dry earth.

Foster leaned back and breathed it in. This was the fourth time his Advanced HQ had moved in a month. But this time, the war in Europe was over.

His war had ended on a high. Six weeks earlier, he had overseen Operation Bowler, one of the most sensitive bombing missions of the Italian campaign. The target was a convoy of German shipping lying at anchor in the Venice lagoon. He himself had come up with the codename for the operation. Resigned to the high probability of failure, and prompted by a dark sense of humour, he had called it Bowler because he knew that if any part of Venice was damaged other than the harbour where the ships were docked, he would be 'given his bowler hat' – a popular euphemism for an ignominious return to civilian life.

At forty-seven, his career in the RAF had been long and distinguished. He had joined as a fighter pilot in the First World War, winning a DFC at the age of twenty after destroying five enemy aircraft. At the outbreak of the Second World War, he had been appointed station commander at RAF Wyton, where he had served during the Battle of Britain. Senior posts in the Mediterranean Command had followed, culminating in his appointment as AOC, Desert Air Force. His return to Italy had been something of a homecoming; though he had been educated at Winchester and the Royal Military College at Sandhurst, he had grown up in San Remo on the north-west coast of Italy, where his father, a doctor, had treated expatriates living in the fashionable resort.

Foster had spent weeks planning Operation Bowler. The question was, *how* to bomb Venice. While the Allies balked at such a drastic solution, the harbour had become a focal point for enemy traffic. The destruction of the road and rail network in the north of Italy meant that the Germans had resorted to transporting desperately needed supplies by ship to Venice. These were then transferred to barges for onward distribution via the canal and river network. The major difficulty was that the docks were located in the south-west corner of the island, 300 yards from the Grand Canal. Residential districts, and myriad important historic buildings and cultural monuments, lay close by. Somehow – if they were to be spared – a plan had to be devised whereby the bombs would land directly on the harbour, an area that was just 650 by 950 yards.

The planes took off on the afternoon of 21 March at 14:30 hours. The striking force consisted of forty-eight Mustangs and Kittyhawks, with a Spitfire squadron providing an escort. Once over the target, the bombers dived almost vertically from 10,000 feet, dropping their bombs at the last minute. The dramatic dive, followed by the low release, was the only way of ensuring that the bombs fell directly on the target. Four waves of planes flew over the city. So accurate were the pilots that crowds of Italians gathered on the roofs of the palaces along the Grand Canal to wave and cheer them on.

In London and Washington, the operation was hailed as a spectacular success. None of the city's historic buildings had been damaged, and the harbour had been completely destroyed, preventing the Germans from using it. A flood of telegrams had come in congratulating Foster. One was from the Air Chief Marshal, who had taken the unusual step of circulating a brochure of the 'neat little operation' to other military commanders in Whitehall.

Up ahead, the outriders were flagging the convoy to slow down. With the precision of a salute, their arms moved in unison, signalling to the right. Further on, set back from the road, an imposing arch loomed.

Foster peered through the clouds of dust churned up by the motorcycles, keen to get a glimpse of the castle that a month before he had made a split-second decision not to bomb. He remembered its footprint from the aerial reconnaissance photographs; the ruins of what appeared to be an old fortress, and the substantial house to one side. The barns and cottages, standing a little way off, and the sequestered position of the place – set amidst acres of woods and arable land – indicated a large country estate. It was evidently a grand establishment; landscaped paths, radiating from a lake cut in the shape of a shamrock, ran through the extensive gardens. He had even spotted a swimming pool in the grounds.

For an instant, he was back in the Operations Room outside Bologna, a fuggy, windowless room, thick with tension and cigarette smoke. In the last days of the Italian campaign (which began on 9 April when the Allies had launched their final offensive), DAF had flown a record 21,215 sorties. It was on one of those days – now merged into a blur – that an adjutant had shown him the photographs of the castle. Its name was Brazzà and a spotter plane had identified it as the HQ of a battalion of German troops. Seeing the photographs, something about the castle had captured Foster's imagination; if the

German retreat continued, it was possible that DAF could take it over. On a whim, he told his adjutant to take it off the target list, earmarking it as a potential Advance HQ on the move north to Austria.

The road leading up to the castle was over a mile long. It was impossible to see where it was leading; the overhanging boughs of the trees bordering the track lent the sensation of travelling through a long tunnel. As they progressed along it, Foster found it incredible to think that the castle was about to become his headquarters. Back in April, if someone had told him that he would be occupying it within a month, he would not have believed them. The speed of the German collapse had taken everyone by surprise. Just 30 miles away, up on the mountain passes leading into Austria, tens of thousands of Wehrmacht troops were being held in pens by the Allies.

A set of gates, surmounted by a pair of stone ball finials, marked the entrance to the castle. On rounding a line of ilex trees, a substantial villa, built in the Palladian style, came into view. Along the balconies and terraces, classical urns stood out white against the pale flint grey of the house and the deep greens of the trees around it. The castle itself, which dated from the Middle Ages, rose behind the villa and was considerably more ruinous than it had looked in the reconnaissance photographs. There were breaches in the high walls of the keep, and most of the fortified tower had crumbled away. Trails of ivy and wild clematis hung from the broken stonework, and in the gardens around the castle a profusion of roses – pale yellow, apricot and crimson in colour – were in flower.

Seeing it all, Foster could not help but smile. It was the nicest place imaginable. Once again, the advantages of air reconnaissance meant they had trumped General Army HQ in finding the best headquarters in the neighbourhood.

An hour or two of light remained. Leaving the officer in charge of the move to supervise the unloading of the vehicles, he set off to explore the castle and its grounds.

Walking briskly, keen to stretch his legs after the long car journey, Foster headed in the direction of the Home Farm. There was not a soul about. The whole place, with its barns and outbuildings, taking up some 100 acres – the size of a small village – had an empty, dilapidated air about it. Approaching the buildings, he could see they were in a poor state of repair; there were tiles missing from the roofs and broken panes of glass in the windows. Here and there, discarded farm machinery lay rusting in a corner. The place seemed long abandoned.

Yet, as he walked on through the courtyards and narrow passageways that connected the buildings, he had the uncomfortable sensation that there were people around. The doors to a number of the barns were open; farm tools stood propped up against the walls – scythes and hoes with gleaming blades, as if someone had just cleaned them. A row of chairs, sometimes a single chair, had been placed outside, indicating that a group of people or a single person had recently been sitting there. Passing a row of farm-workers' cottages, he noticed there were plants and kitchen utensils on the windowsills.

The ghostly presence of people he could not see unnerved him. Could they see him? Was he being watched? The situation was not one he had encountered before. He and his staff had occupied a number of large country houses as DAF had advanced through Italy. They had been made to feel welcome. Usually the owner of the property or a member of his family had shown them around. So where were the castle's owners? The odd emptiness and the dilapidation of the estate hinted at dark events in the recent past.

Retracing his route, Foster returned to the main house. As he passed the crescent-shaped flower bed that stood in the centre of the courtyard, he noticed that someone had driven through it. The imprints of the tyres were fresh, and the flowers lay crushed in the tread marks. He presumed the Germans had reversed their trucks up to the entrance of the house to load them as they were leaving.

The front door was ajar. Pushing it open, he found himself in a great hall. Hand-drawn maps dating from the sixteenth century, silver plate and the stuffed heads of spiral-horned antelopes adorned the walls. In one corner, approached through an arch, a stone staircase led up to the *piano nobile*, the principal floor.

The steps – a single flight – were wide and shallow. On the narrow landing at the top was a thick panelled door, its surround decorated with filigree stencil work. Foster expected the door to be locked, but it opened into a series of interconnecting rooms stretching the length of the villa. The first, he noted, was a perfect square. Yet, while it was well appointed, commanding views over the garden on three sides, it was sparsely furnished. The one significant item was a fine glass-fronted cabinet, the sort used to display porcelain and silver. Crossing over to it, he could see from the rings in the dust that the shelves had been emptied recently. By the Germans, looting the owners' possessions? he wondered. Or the owners themselves, anxious to remove their valuables? Pictures were also missing from the walls, the blank spaces suggesting where landscapes and family portraits had once hung.

The other rooms were all of large proportions, with polished wooden floors and magnificently carved chimneypieces. The walls were limewashed in bright colours – ochre, aquamarine and pistachio green. But there were no personal belongings of any kind; nothing to indicate who owned the house or what sort of life they lived. The silence of the place – almost reverential – and the perfunctory arrangement of the few items of furniture had the deadness of a museum.

Then, as Foster was passing along the gallery which connected the two wings of the house, a sudden noise startled him. A grating, scraping sound, it was coming from the floor above. A narrow staircase led off to the right and, as he climbed the stairs, the noise grew louder. He could not think what it was. The only time he had heard anything like it was in Africa; it reminded him of the sound of a carpet being brushed on the lawn after a sandstorm.

The stairs opened directly into a vast room. It was 200 feet long, taking up the entire area of the second floor. Immediately, the origin of the sound was apparent. With upwards of twenty tables positioned across it, the room had been turned into a makeshift silk factory and thousands of silkworms were feeding on mulberry leaves. Some of the cocoons had hatched and on the tables by the windows the moths fluttered against the lower panes, drawn by the light. Evidently, someone was feeding them; but again, there was no sign of their presence.

Inching his way around the tables, Foster went over to a window. The mountains were now blue, shot with gold from the last rays of sun. To the south, on the horizon, was the sea – the lagoons east of Venice. Looking over towards Tarcento, the bell towers of numerous hilltop villages were visible. Closer – about a mile off – a line of poplar trees marked the main road from Udine. Between the gaps in the trees, he could see the traffic moving. All the traffic was going from east to west.

Earlier that afternoon, he had passed along the road. The progress of the convoy had been slowed by a line of carts, piled high with furniture and grain sacks stuffed to overflowing with the possessions of the families following behind. There had been mothers carrying babies in their arms, and groups of tired children and elderly relatives, some laid out on beds on the carts or propped up in chairs. The carts had been of all shapes and sizes; pony traps and shooting brakes – even old wooden-wheeled barouches and curricles.

Foster had seen the situation reports compiled by General Army HQ. The families were fleeing their homes in the east of the province. A no man's land inhabited by both Italians and Slovenes, it was disputed territory granted to Italy by the Allies as a reward for switching sides during the First World War. Following years of persecution under Mussolini's Fascists, the Slovenes were calling for all Italians living in the disputed area to be denounced as Fascists, and for the land to become part of Yugoslavia.

Already, Yugoslav troops, commanded by Marshal Tito, had crossed the border and were terrorizing towns and villages. More than 1,000 Italians had disappeared without trace and hundreds had been arrested and deported to concentration camps that had been formerly run by the Fascists. In some towns, army patrols had rounded up almost the entire population. They were holding them in makeshift prisons where men between eighteen and fifty-six years of age were being systematically starved until they agreed to volunteer for Tito's army.

From where he was standing, Foster had a view over the landscaped gardens stretching up to the road. The beauty and tranquillity of it all was a world away from the horrors faced by the people passing beyond the line of poplar trees, and the spate of murders sweeping the north of Italy.

4.

There had been no let-up in the volume of top-secret telegrams flooding into Desert Air Force headquarters in the ten days since the Germans had surrendered. The recriminations following the defeat of Fascism had brought Italy close to civil war. Liberation had brought widespread killings, leaving hundreds dead on the streets of cities and towns throughout the north. 'Total of unidentified bodies at the mortuary since the liberation of Milan now amounts to over 400,' reported the British Ambassador in a telegram to the Foreign Office. 'The sinister feature of these killings is that all identification marks have been carefully removed before shooting. It is therefore difficult to say whether the victims are Fascists executed by Partisans, or Partisans executed by Fascists, or just victims of personal vendetta.'

In the province of Friuli, the situation was particularly acute. In the space of ten days, hundreds of Italians had been killed by other Italians, adding to the tally of atrocities committed by Tito's forces. At Ziracco, a small town on the plain 12 miles east of the castle, there had been a dozen murders. Further south, in the Manzano area, one partisan commander was reported to have killed forty-three people.

On the way through Udine that afternoon, Foster had attended an intelligence briefing at the regional headquarters of AMG,* the interim organization set up by the Allies to govern Italy. The Coolant Mission – the SOE† unit operating in the area – was reporting the discovery of another mass grave in Drenchia, close to Italy's border with Yugoslavia. The bodies were found in 'a ditch containing 30 corpses alleged to be Italians shot by the Slovenes'. Coolant's intelligence indicated that the Communist Garibaldi partisans, of which there were 4,000 in the Udine

* Allied Military Government.
† Special Operations Executive, the British unit formed in 1940 to conduct espionage, sabotage and reconnaissance in occupied Europe.

area, were about to join forces with the Yugoslavs to launch a Communist coup. The unit had learned that Mario Lizzero, 'perhaps the most dangerous of the Garibaldi leaders', was directing the operation: 'He is intelligent and unscrupulous and has complete control of the Communist Party. His present activity is to manoeuvre the penetration of all Municipal and Provincial offices, in and outside Udine, by Communist elements.' Coolant was also warning that a 'big net of Communist agents, lavishly supplied with funds' was active throughout the province. Their orders were to 'penetrate to Treviso and Venice to build up Communist centres'. While the Allies could count on the loyalty of the anti-Slav partisans, a force of some 8,000 men, their hatred of Communism had further escalated tension in the region.

In Udine itself, which was just 5 miles from the castle, the situation was becoming ugly. Garibaldi commanders, operating from secret hideouts around the city, were compiling lists of individuals whom they regarded as weak and fearful, and whom they believed could be bribed to join their units with gifts of money and food. Local girls were being told not to associate with Allied troops. Many had received anonymous letters warning that those caught doing so would have their heads shaved. In some districts, the Communists had daubed graffiti on the walls of the houses: '*Zivio* [Long live] *Tito*', '*Zivio Stalin*', '*Tukay je Jugoslavia*' (This is Yugoslavia).

During the briefing, a leaflet had been circulated. It was one of hundreds that had dropped from the skies over Udine on 2 May, the day peace was declared. With the ceasefire in operation, the Yugoslavs, who had fought on the side of the Allies, had stopped bombing the city; but their planes had returned to deliver a chilling message:

Citizens of Udine, Today you receive our visiting card: Terror accompanies our victorious march. Weep over the ruins of your homes and meditate upon your sins, you who in the secrecy of your hearts await the ENGLISH, the protectors of the Bourgeois and the well-to-do. Be it said once and for all, so that afterwards it may not seem strange to you: FRIULI BELONGS TO THE BOLSHEVIK ZONE OF INFLUENCE and consequently the patriots whom you must support are the communist patriots of the

Garibaldi. IF YOU ARE NOT WILLING TO DO IT FOR LOVE, YOU WILL DO IT BY COMPULSION.

Over the previous twenty-four hours, 200 Yugoslav troops had marched into the city. Simultaneously, 500 men from Gorizia, fleeing to avoid Slovene conscription, had arrived and were clamouring to be enrolled in the anti-Slav partisan brigades. Peace in Europe had lasted eleven days. The intensity with which the crisis had blown up, fanned by Tito's threat to seize the strategic port of Trieste, meant that the talk at the briefing was of one last battle or – if the Communists pressed their plans to seize the region – the first of a Third World War.

In this 'witches' cauldron of conflicting politics and nationalities' – as one army officer described the situation – Foster's Desert Air Force had a significant role. Besides flying sorties over the Alps to monitor the tens of thousands of Wehrmacht troops corralled on the main passes, the squadrons were to hunt down the SS stay-behind units that were hiding out in the mountains; further, they were to determine the strength and disposition of Yugoslav forces to the east of Udine, and pinpoint the positions of the Garibaldi partisan units that had retreated to the mountains with their weapons to prepare for a Communist coup.

A soft evening light flooded the house. Foster stood on the gravel drive outside the west wing, looking up. There were still a number of rooms that he had not seen, but he could not work out how to get to them.

He could see the windows. But inside, when he had tried the door leading into the wing, it had been locked. With operations resuming early the next morning, he wanted to see the rooms while he had time.

5.

The entrance to the wing was reached from the garden along a white stone path, bordered by low, tightly clipped hedges.

Stepping through the door, Foster entered a small hallway. Immediately, he was struck by the contrast to the empty rooms in the rest of the house. Along one side of it, outdoor garments were crammed on a coat rack and on the floor below was a row of riding boots. Beside them, sun hats of various shapes and sizes had been piled on the head of a marble bust. On the hall table, strewn around a pair of Chinese vases, were all sorts of items, among them bunches of keys, a dog lead, packets of seeds and rolls of gardening twine.

Despite the clutter, the room had a sense of order. The riding boots stood in a neat line, arranged according to size. The effect was curiously poignant. At the far end of the row, there were two tiny pairs of jodhpur boots. One looked as if it belonged to a child of four or five; the other was even smaller.

The passage beyond the hall was in semi-darkness. Stopping at the entrance to it, he switched on a light. Straight away, his attention was drawn to a small card pinned to the door on his right. A gold crown was embossed on the thick white paper; below it, written in black ink in a curlicued script, were the words: '*Camera del Victor Emmanuel III, S.M Il Re d'Italia*'.

The bedroom of Victor Emmanuel III, His Majesty the King of Italy.

It was a startling discovery. For an instant, all Foster could think was that the king owned the castle. But then if it belonged to him, why had it been necessary to pin a note to the door to signal that this was his bedroom? Rather, the presence of the card suggested that the king's stay at the castle had been a sudden, temporary arrangement. So what had brought him to this remote part of his country? Had he used the castle as a hideout earlier in the war? An unpopular figure, tainted by his support for Mussolini's regime, the king had been Italy's commander-in-chief until the autumn of 1943 when he had negotiated an armistice with the Allies. Nicknamed *Il Re Soldato* (the Soldier King) by the Italians or, more unfavourably, *Sciaboletta* (Little Sabre) – due to the fact he was only 5 feet tall – he had spent the remainder of the war under armed guard in a castle on the Amalfi Coast.

To Foster's surprise, the door was not locked. Pushing it open, he went inside, expecting to see a large room that was sumptuously furnished befitting a king. But the room, which was of modest size and plainly decorated, was unremarkable – except that it looked as if someone had lived in it recently. The card on the door was misleading; it was not a bedroom, but a sitting room. Books, with markers in them, were stacked on the tables and bundles of letters, which had been sorted, as if someone intended to file them, lay in piles on the floor. A jug of water and a glass, half full, stood on one of the side tables, and a well-worn cardigan hung over a chair.

By the window there was a large round table covered with a velvet cloth. Crossing over to it, Foster stopped in front of the photographs. Upwards of thirty were arranged on the table; photographs both large and small, all in silver frames. He could see they were family portraits as the same faces featured, though at different ages, and in different settings. One face drew his eye. It was that of a tall, middle-aged man with an aquiline profile and a neat moustache. He had two duelling scars on his left cheek. In one of the photographs, he was engrossed in conversation with Adolf Hitler; in another, he was shaking hands with Benito Mussolini.

There were other pictures of Hitler, taken in different locations. Always, the same tall man was discernible in the background, standing at a discreet distance, just a few steps behind the Führer. His close proximity to Hitler suggested he was a trusted adviser. But who was he? He was not dressed in uniform. Was he a diplomat, or a civil servant? Foster wondered. And was he the owner of the castle?

He picked up the photographs carefully and examined them, one by one. There were no inscriptions of any kind; nothing to say where or when they had been taken. There were just two informal portraits of the man. One was in a family group. He and his wife and their four children – two sons and two daughters – were posing for the camera on top of a mountain. In the second, he was standing on a jetty by a lake; wearing a pair of swimming trunks, he had his arms around a young girl, aged about twelve, and his head was tilted back, laughing. From the family portrait, Foster could see the girl was his daughter.

Then he turned to the other photographs. They were mostly of two young boys. There were pictures of them as babies, lying cradled in the arms of a pretty, fair-haired woman, and later, when they were a little older, of the boys together. They were angelic-looking, with long blond curls and bright, smiling eyes. In one photograph, they were sitting happily on the laps of two German soldiers. Foster recognized the setting: the picture had been taken on the bench in the walled garden outside. Curious, he spent some minutes trying to decipher the family relationships. The boys' mother – ten or so years on – was the young girl who featured in the photograph taken on the jetty by the lake. In which case, her father – the man with Hitler – was the boys' grandfather. The girl had married a dashing-looking Italian officer. In the photograph taken at their wedding, his distinctive hat, adorned with plumes and cockades, indicated that he was an officer in one of the smart cavalry regiments. Oddly, there were no photographs of the boys with their father.

Foster went over to the door, which connected to another room. It led into a nursery. It had two beds and a cot in it and he assumed it was where the two boys in the photographs had slept. Paper mobiles, decorated with baby elephants, hung from the ceiling. On one of the beds, a teddy bear lay, propped up on a pillow; the beads of its eyes were missing and it had a flattened, bedraggled look about it.

After a quick glance round, he went back into the main room. Among the hundreds of books lining its walls, he spotted a copy of Hitler's *Mein Kampf*. Taking it down off the shelf, he was surprised to see the pages were unread. He was also surprised to discover that many of the books were in English. There were volumes of Hansard and numerous editions of *Strand* magazine, one of which contained a prescient article by Winston Churchill, entitled 'The Truth About Hitler', published in 1935.

As Foster was leafing through a guidebook of historic towns in Germany – towns the British had obliterated – he heard a sound outside. Going over to the window, he saw a man working in the garden. He was getting on in years and wore mechanic's overalls which were blue and smeared with grease. He had a proprietorial air about him and was busy cutting back the ivy that had enveloped a wall of the house.

Straight away, Foster put the book aside and went out to talk to him. At last, here was someone who might be able to tell him about the castle's invisible inhabitants.

6.

The man introduced himself as Nonino. He came from a nearby village, he said, and he had been the butler at the castle for fifty-seven years. The old countess had taken him on when he was eleven years old. He had started out as a coachman, riding on the footplate of the family's Landau carriage. Then, in the 1880s, he had become head of the household. It was a time when many guests had stayed at the castle. Back then, he told Foster, his duties had included looking after the horses and the carriages, polishing the great Venetian chandeliers and, in the evening, after dinner, if there were no musicians to play from the battlements of the castle, he led a choir, singing old Friuli songs.

He announced proudly that he had served three generations of the family. His first name was Giuseppe, but the family called him by his surname. They said it was easier to pronounce and sounded more friendly. Foster was hoping this would lead to stories about the current generation, but the old man shied away from the present and returned to a yet more remote past. The family's name was Pirzio-Biroli, he said, and they were descended from the Savorgnans, one of the most powerful aristocratic families in northern Italy. After settling at the castle in the 1200s, they had ruled over Friuli for centuries, siding with the Venetian Republic against the Austrian Empire. They had owned many properties. The fortresses from which they had defended the region stretched in a 60-mile line, all the way to Venice. Then there were the palaces, where he had served as a young man. The Palazzo Savorgnan, overlooking the Cannaregio Canal in Venice; the Palazzo Brazzà in Udine; and another, a few steps from the Trevi Fountain, in Rome.

He stopped talking for a moment and looked up at the Union Jack flying above the ruins of the castle. Then, shaking his head, he said he was sorry to say that all sorts of flags had flown there in his time. In the last war, the Austrian Army had occupied the castle, which had been disastrous for the family. One night in the winter of 1917, after helping himself to the wine cellar, one of the officers had fallen asleep leaving a brazier burning and the house had burned to the ground. The Royal Standard of the House of Savoy had also flown above the castle. This was in 1941, when the King of Italy had briefly used Brazzà as a military headquarters. After that, the Germans had arrived and hoisted the swastika. But the old Countess Cora di Brazzà Slocomb had always flown the Stars and Stripes. She was American – a wealthy heiress from New Orleans. Gesturing towards the house, he said it was her money that had paid for the new villa after the old one had been destroyed in the fire.

An American countess? Foster was taken aback by this unexpected piece of information. Immediately, he wanted to know what her relationship was to the man he had seen in the photographs with Hitler and Mussolini. Had she betrayed her country by siding with the Fascists? But he did not want to quiz the old man. It would be inappropriate to ask awkward questions. Intelligence personnel from the War Crimes Branch of the US Army were already in the area and it was their job to investigate suspected war criminals and collaborators.

'Where is the family now?' he asked instead.

The old man looked away. A long silence followed before he answered. Then, quietly, his voice trembling, he said they were all gone now; that in recent years, a series of tragedies had befallen the family. Briefly, he told Foster what had happened. The old countess, who had taken him on when he was a boy, was dead. She had died the year before in a lunatic asylum in Rome. Her only daughter was also dead – from heart failure at the age of fifty. Count Detalmo, who had inherited Brazzà from his mother, had vanished in the autumn of 1943 when the German troops had occupied the castle. Then, on 27 September 1944, a date he would never forget, the Gestapo had arrested the count's wife and their two sons aged two and four.

He pointed to a window behind them and said it was where the countess and the children had been living when they were taken away. Then he beckoned Foster to follow him.

Crossing the garden in front of the house, he spoke fondly of the countess. Her name was Fey and she was beautiful. Slim, with fair hair and bright blue eyes, she was German, of course. But *una bella tedesca* – a lovely German. She had first come to the castle in the winter of 1940, after her marriage to Detalmo. A year later, Corrado – little Corradino – the eldest boy, was born. Then, in January 1943, Robertino. The boys were the spitting image of their mother – fair-haired and blue-eyed. *Beautiful boys.*

He paused in front of a wooden bench that stood in the shade of an umbrella pine. The bench looked towards the mountains and was framed by roses, which were trained against the white wall behind. He told Foster that it was where Fey liked to sit in the mornings. It was her favourite place in the garden. After the count left, he had helped her with the running of the estate. In the summer months, they had met here for an hour every morning to discuss the silk harvesting and the crops they were going to plant. They were a team, he said.

He walked on, heading towards the entrance to the castle. Returning to the story of her arrest, he became increasingly agitated. To begin with, there had been no trouble with the Germans. On the contrary, the soldiers occupying the castle adored the children. They were always playing with them. Then, one evening, the order had come through from Berlin. Immediately, the colonel in charge informed Fey that she and the boys were to be taken to Germany. They must be ready to leave at dawn the following day. But he said there was no need to worry. They were only going for a few weeks. They would be back soon.

At the main gate to the castle, with its stone ball finials and ornate fretwork, the old man stopped and drew a long line in the gravel with his foot. It was where everyone had gathered to say goodbye, he said: the household staff, friends and neighbours, and the farmhands and their families. Fey had only been given permission to bring along as much as she could carry, and he and the other staff had spent the night helping her prepare for the journey. They had packed salamis and hams, and tins of condensed milk for the boys. The army doctor, stationed with the German troops, even gave her 300 marks, which he told her to sew into the lining of her coat. At the memory of Fey struggling to the car with the cases, and the two boys, muffled up for the journey, his eyes filled with tears. They were lost now. He did not think he would ever see them again.

With tears now rolling down his face, he said that one of the German soldiers had told him what had happened to them after they left. Their first night had been spent at the railway station in Villach, sleeping on the floor with refugees. Then, when they got to Innsbruck, the SS had arrested Fey and taken the children from her. The soldier said they had given the boys false names and hidden them in a place where no one would find them – an orphanage somewhere in Germany, he thought. Fey had spent time in the Gestapo prison at Innsbruck, then the SS had moved her on. This was all the soldier could tell him. Six months had passed now and all trace of her had been lost.

Looking around at the idyllic scene, Foster found it hard to believe what he was hearing. Out in the fields, there was a light mist and the cypress trees rose through it, their tops lit by the last rays of the sun. Over by the barn, teams of oxen were bringing in sacks of meal. The cream-coloured beasts stood peacefully and patient-eyed while the carts were unloaded. What possible reason could the SS have had to arrest Fey and the children? The order had come from Berlin, indicating that someone of high rank had issued it. He had failed to establish the identity of the man with the duelling scars, pictured with Hitler and Mussolini. Was there a connection? he wondered. Yet, for the second time, Foster stopped himself from questioning the old man. He found his grief discomforting; he did not want to risk distressing him further. Instead, he changed the subject. The Desert Air Force had captured some fine horses, which he intended to bring to the castle. Would it be possible to see the stables? he asked.

They stood a little way off, in a low stone building behind the barn.

Stepping inside, Foster could see that there were rows of empty stalls. It was where the Germans had kept their horses and the smell of the animals' sweat still hung in the air.

As they walked past the line of empty stalls, Foster described the scene he had witnessed north of Ferrara after the Desert Air Force had bombed the bridges over the Po. Along the south bank of the river, thousands of horses, of all colours, shapes and sizes, had crammed the fields. A shortage of petrol meant the retreating German Army's transport had been largely horse-drawn. When they reached the great wide river, they had no means of getting the animals across and they had to abandon them. This was where DAF had captured the horses they wanted to stable at Brazzà.

They came to the last stall. It was in the far corner of the stables and was occupied by a small white pony. The old man stopped to stroke his muzzle. It was called Mirko, he said, and it was twenty-seven years old. He had taught the boys how to ride on the pony – and their father before them. The little one – Robertino – had adored it. Every morning, as soon as the boy started walking, he had brought him down here to give the pony an apple.

Again, a sharp sense of loss assailed the old man, and he turned abruptly and walked away, muttering that he had things he must be getting on with.

On his way back to the house, the story of the mother and her two boys kept turning through Foster's mind. His own son was six years old. Despite all that he had seen in the war, the thought that such a thing could have happened to him had the Germans reached Britain made a deep impression.

Where were these two Italian boys aged two and four? Nobody knew but, assuming they had in fact been sent to a Nazi orphanage in Germany, how could they be traced? The chaos in Germany was complete: the country had been invaded from both the east and the west and the damage and disruption caused by Allied bombing and by the extensive land battles was formidable. Movement for civilians around the country was difficult and hazardous, and starvation and general misery were rife. Upwards of 2 million displaced persons were surging through Germany, trying to get back to their homelands or fleeing from Communism in the east. The prospect of tracing two nameless children who had been swallowed up in the turmoil was indeed remote.

Moreover, they could be anywhere. There were a great many of these Nazi orphanages, not only in Germany, but in Austria, Poland and Czechoslovakia. Had the SS kept the boys in Germany or had they moved them to another orphanage in one of the countries the Nazis had occupied?

Most distressing of all, though, was the thought that no one would look for them. From all that the old man had said, it seemed likely that both their parents were dead.

PART THREE

7

Villa Glori, Rome, 19 October 1937

At exactly nine-thirty on a dull, humid morning, Benito Mussolini entered the vast piazza on a white horse. Behind him, mounted on black horses, followed the commanders of the Italian police force. A fanfare of trumpets sounded and the 6,000 *carabinieri* massed in the square raised their arms in the Fascist salute.

The ovation as Mussolini entered the piazza was deafening. Thousands of Romans lined the rails and crowded the terraces. It was National Police Day and they had come to the Villa Glori, a park on the banks of the Tiber, to watch the celebrations and to catch a glimpse of their idol. Following the conquest of Abyssinia, Mussolini's popularity was at its height. At his headquarters in the heart of the city, an entire department of fifty civil servants was devoted to fuelling the cult of personality the dictator encouraged. Shouts of *'Viva Il Duce'* and *'Viva l'Impero'* rang around the square, echoing the Roman shouts of *'Ave Imperator'* 2,000 years before.

Banners, 100 feet high, bearing the Nazi swastika and the colours of the Italian flag, hung from flagpoles and draped the sides of the covered stand reserved for dignitaries. Swathed in sashes and decorations and encrusted in gold and silver braid, they stood sweating in their uniforms: chiefs of police from all over Italy; ministers and civil servants; the Principe Colonna, Governor of Rome; and representatives from the Vatican in their long red robes.

The guest of honour was Heinrich Himmler, Reichsführer SS and chief of the German police.

Erect, inscrutable, a ceremonial sabre gleaming at his side, he stood, all in black, on a podium. Ostensibly, his presence was a goodwill gesture, a mark of the close relations between Italy and Germany. But the true purpose of his two-day visit to Rome was to urge Mussolini to use his police force to combat 'the totally destructive tyranny of Bolshevism . . . the Jew in his worst form'. That summer, Himmler had ordered the construction of a new concentration camp at Buchenwald to accommodate thousands of political prisoners, and more were in the pipeline. His aim was to persuade the Italian dictator to follow his example.

A hush fell over the arena as a military band played the German and Italian national anthems. Taking his cue from the final trumpet blast of the German anthem, Mussolini wheeled his horse round and spurred it into a gallop. As he rode up and down in front of the terraces, the display of machismo worked the crowd into a frenzy: '*Duce! Duce! Duce!*' men roared, raising their hats and lifting them high in the air. Women, waving handkerchiefs, screamed hysterically; some, overcome by the sight of their idol, fainted.

Two men stood alongside Himmler on the podium, unmoved by Mussolini's theatrics and the display of affection from the crowd. They were Reinhard Heydrich, Himmler's deputy and chief of the Gestapo, and Ulrich von Hassell, the German Ambassador to Italy.

Like Himmler's, Heydrich's rise to power had been meteoric. One of the darkest figures in the Nazi elite, a man who even Hitler acknowledged had an 'iron heart', he was the founding head of the Sicherheitsdienst, an intelligence organization charged with seeking out and neutralizing resistance to the Nazi Party. His murderous career was just beginning. Two years later, when the Nazis invaded Eastern Europe, he would be directly responsible for the *Einsatzgruppen*, the special task forces that travelled in the wake of the German armies, killing over 2 million people. Later, in the winter of 1942, he would chair the Wannsee Conference, where the plans for the Final Solution to the Jewish Question – the murder of millions of Jews in extermination camps – were agreed.

Ambassador von Hassell – Himmler and Heydrich's host for their short visit to Rome – cut an imposing figure. Tall, with a neat moustache and an aquiline profile, he wore the uniform of a major general in the NSKK.* A pale grey, it stood out against the black, silver-braided

---

* National Socialist Motor Corps.

uniforms of the police chiefs to his right. Two livid scars on Hassell's left cheek immediately signalled that he was of a different class and background. Known as 'Mensur scars' or 'the bragging scar', they were the preserve of the aristocracy. Won in fencing contests, popular among aristocratic students at Germany's elite universities before the First World War, they were prized marks of honour and courage. The victor in the contests was not the man who inflicted the wound, but the man who walked away with a scar, proving he was capable of taking a wound.

While the two police chiefs were unknown outside Germany, Hassell was a familiar figure to the crowds in the arena. Since 1932, when he was appointed Germany's Ambassador to Italy, he had shepherded the burgeoning friendship between the two countries. At the great state occasions, photographs of which appeared on page after page of the Italian newspapers, Hassell was the man in the background, hovering at the shoulder of the two dictators. In the spring of 1934, he helped broker their first meeting in Venice, when the two men had circled each other warily. A few months later, after Engelbert Dollfuss, the Austrian chancellor, was murdered, it had fallen to Hassell to patch up their uneasy friendship. Mussolini, who was close to Dollfuss and had personally broken the news of his death to his widow, held the Nazis responsible. With his blessing, an Italian journalist had branded the Germans a 'nation of murderers and pederasts'.

It was only after Hitler supported Mussolini's conquest of Abyssinia and Italy's withdrawal from the League of Nations that relations between the two dictators had been restored. Now they were approaching their apogee. A month before, Hassell had accompanied Hitler and Mussolini on a tour of Germany. Flattered by Hitler, dazzled by the armaments factories he visited, and the military parades put on for his benefit, the trip convinced Mussolini that Italy's future lay with Nazi Germany. The highlight was the rally he and the Führer attended in Berlin when a million people heard him deliver a speech in a thunderstorm. 'They are fanatical about me,' he boasted to his mistress on his return. 'The ordinary people were completely conquered. They have felt my force . . . The crowd for the speech was so big you could not see where it ended. They have never given such a reception before, not to kings, not to emperors, not to anyone. Yes, I have conquered them. They have felt the power . . . the red banners behind us, the rays of light, the torches . . . We passed like two gods on the clouds.'

The temperature dropped that night and a thick fog rolled through the streets of Rome; a night, one writer commented, when the smells of 'mould, mice and basements' hung in the dank passageways behind the Piazza Navona.

It took longer than usual for the cavalcade of Mercedes, flanked by police outriders on scarlet motorcycles, to push its way through the Rome traffic. Hassell was travelling in the lead vehicle with the two police chiefs. A retinue of SS officers and embassy officials followed in the vehicles behind. The Italian minister of propaganda was hosting a ball for Heydrich and Himmler, and they were heading for the Villa Madama on the other side of the Tiber.

The route from the German Embassy took them past the Colosseum, and through the Piazza della Repubblica; but the fog was so thick it was impossible to see more than a few yards. Even the graffiti that the Duce's supporters had scrawled in white paint on the walls of churches and palazzi was obscured. All that was visible were the tiny points of light from the headlamps of other cars on the road, and the dim orange glow from the braziers on the street corners. Shadowy figures, some of them small children, were gathered around the fires – families of peasants who had come into the city from the countryside, bringing the first harvest of chestnuts.

After crossing the Tiber, the cavalcade picked up speed on the Via di Villa Madama, the long, winding road up to the house. The air was clearer here, the fog now a thin mist. On either side of the road, ivy-covered walls and high, clipped hedges concealed the famous treasures in the villa's gardens: the curious elephant tomb, commemorating Annone, an Indian elephant given to the Pope by the King of Portugal in 1514, and Bandinelli's Giants, a pair of sculptures, each 14 feet tall, that guarded the entrance to the secret garden.

The villa, designed by Raphael for Cardinal Giulio de Medici in the early 1500s, stood on a hill overlooking the Vatican. One of the most glittering society venues in Rome, it had belonged to Count Frasso, whose wife was the wealthy American heiress Dorothy Caldwell-Taylor. Having inherited $15 million from her father in the 1920s, the countess had restored the villa from its dilapidated state and used it to host lavish parties for her Hollywood friends. Her guests included the leading film stars of the day, among them Marlene Dietrich, Cary Grant, Fred Astaire, Ginger Rogers and Clark Gable. Now, the villa was on loan to the Italian government as a venue for official parties.

It was almost nine o'clock and the forecourt was crowded with luxurious cars – Delahayes, Bugattis, Daimlers. It was customary for a servant to travel with the chauffeur and they stood smoking in groups, their liveries as resplendent as the gleaming vehicles. Small silver badges were pinned to their lapels on which were etched the coats of arms of the houses they served: Ruspoli, Colonna, Torlonia, families who owned swathes of Italy, akin to small kingdoms, and who belonged to the elite papal nobility.

For the most part, the Italian aristocracy had embraced Fascism. Mussolini's agricultural reforms had helped revive estates that had been hit by the depression at the turn of the century and, in towns and cities across Italy, he had been careful to bolster the landowners' authority by appointing them to senior positions within the party hierarchy. His strong stance against Communism further endeared him to families who feared losing their ancient castles and palaces in the event of a revolution. The relationship was symbiotic; Mussolini enjoyed the glamour and prestige his connections within the aristocracy conferred and they in turn – keen to curry favour with the regime – competed to host opulent Fascist gatherings.

As Himmler's cavalcade drew up, young men, carrying lighted torches and dressed as Medici pages, stepped forward to open the car doors. Hassell hung back discreetly as Arturo Bocchini, the Italian chief of police and the man responsible for Mussolini's personal safety, greeted his German counterparts. A dapper figure, famous for owning eighty suits by Saraceni – Rome's most expensive tailor – Bocchini was the son of a wealthy landowner. Anxious to impress Himmler and Heydrich, he had sought advice from well-connected

Germans living in Rome. Eugen Dollmann, a young academic, whom Himmler occasionally used as an interpreter, was one of the people he consulted: 'I advised him to make the most of the fortunate coincidence that his home was at Benevento, near the famous battlefield where the valiant Manfred, favourite son of the great Hohenstaufen emperor Frederick II, had forfeited life and throne . . . I further advised him against exaggerated courtesy and excessive friendliness. What was considered a prerequisite of social intercourse in his native land was only too readily construed by northerners as weakness, effeminacy, smarminess and lack of proper solemnity.'

The large entourage of SS officers and embassy officials waited behind as Bocchini escorted the two police chiefs and the ambassador up the steps to the villa. Ushering the three men across the stone-flagged hall, he led them into a large salon where the other guests were gathered.

An orchestra was playing Wagner's *Tannhäuser* in the background as the guests milled around, waiting for dinner to be announced. Italy's leading politicians and pro-Fascist aristocrats had been invited, and a large contingent of White Russians: men and women who had known the Tsar and Rasputin and who had fled Russia during the revolution with their jewels sewn into their clothes. Galeazzo Ciano, the newly appointed minister of foreign affairs, was also there. Just thirty-three years old, he was married to Mussolini's daughter. On his appointment, his father-in-law had conferred on him the highest decoration existing in Italy, that of '*Collare dell'Annunziata*', the possessors of which ranked as the king's cousins. Most of the assembled women dreaded being placed next to the arrogant and lascivious Ciano at dinner: 'his only method of conversation was a stream of clichéd chaff accompanied by a great deal of pawing,' one commented; 'in the case of women over "a certain age", he became absolutely dumb.'

Armies of servants had kept the fires in the villa burning for the previous few nights to take the chill off the rooms, but they were still cold, and the women, adorned with glittering necklaces and tiaras, wore fur stoles around their shoulders. As the German delegation entered, they craned their necks to catch a glimpse of the guests of honour. Heydrich, with 'his sharp, pale asymmetrical face', and Himmler, with his weak chin and puffy features, disappointed: 'We Italians enjoyed the statuesque blonds the Nazis usually sent over,' one woman remarked. Only Hassell, wearing white tie and tails, conformed to their high standards. 'The Ambassador looked superb and he knew it,' Himmler's interpreter noted. 'The eyes of Roman feminine society dwelt pleasurably on his aristocratic countenance, and he suffered their gaze with equal pleasure.'

A gong sounded – the signal to move through to dinner in the villa's magnificent *salone*. Crimson roses, sent by special train from San Remo, crowded the long table, their scent almost overpowering. Banners bearing the Nazi swastika and the black Italian Fascist flag, imprinted with the fasces, the ancient Roman symbol for power and governance, hung from the vaulted ceiling, next to exquisite religious scenes painted by Renaissance artist Giulio Romano.

Himmler and Heydrich were placed in the position of honour at the centre of the table, beside Ciano and Bocchini. Hassell, seated some distance from them, was next to Guido Buffarini Guidi, the Italian secretary of state for the interior – a man for whom, as one acquaintance described, 'politics, intrigue and the secret accumulation of power were his life and his ruling passion'.

Halfway through dinner, emboldened by several glasses of wine, Buffarini Guidi began to quiz the ambassador: 'We were just wondering what an educated and distinguished individual like you can possibly have to say to these, your compatriots, and how you can get on with them? Himmler? He is an idiot with no intelligence at all. And Heydrich?'

The answers Hassell gave to Buffarini Guidi's questions stuck in his craw. Later that evening, he noted the awkward conversation in his diary: 'When I insisted that Himmler was very clever, he remained sceptical and when I, as a diversionary tactic, extolled the "energetic personality" of Heydrich, he parried unfavourably: "We know his type well. He is a brutal man, a bloodhound."'

Among the pro-Fascist and predominantly pro-Nazi guests attending the dinner at the Villa Madama, Hassell's nickname was *Il Freno*

(The Brake); his opposition to a military alliance between Germany and Italy was widely known. But only a handful of people – among them Heydrich and Himmler – knew the extent of his contempt for the Nazi regime. For almost a year now, Heydrich's Gestapo spies had been watching him. Masquerading as servants, they were installed in the Villa Wolkonsky, the ambassador's residence, listening to his conversations, tapping his telephone and making lists of the 'anti-people' who visited.

The Gestapo's reports reflected the malevolent prejudice taking hold in Germany at that time: Hassell was observed to be too friendly with his Jewish dentist; his daughters' education in Britain was construed as proof that he was an Anglophile whose 'interests lay principally in England'; he had been overheard making derogatory remarks about the Italians; he associated with anti-Nazi German academics and intellectuals. This social circle came under close scrutiny. Primarily, his friends were anti-Fascist aristocrats: Principessa Santa Hercolani, the Borghese heiress; Marchese Misciattelli, whose palazzo in the Piazza Venezia he regularly visited; Contessa Pasolini, famous for the tea salons she hosted for prominent intellectuals; and Irene di Robilant, the rebellious daughter of Contessa Robilant, who ran a Fascist organization for women. Every morning, it was noted, Hassell rode out with the Hercolanis. Breakfast would follow at the Villa Wolkonsky, where they had been overheard discussing the dangers of their respective regimes.

Heydrich had circulated the reports to Mussolini and Ciano, the Italian foreign secretary. 'Unpleasant and treacherous' was Ciano's verdict; 'he fatally belongs to that world of Junkers, who cannot forget 1914 and who, being deep down hostile towards Nazism, does not feel solidarity towards the regime.'

Hitler had not sanctioned Hassell's appointment. Posted to Rome in 1932, he was one of the last ambassadors to represent the Weimar Republic. Born in Prussia in 1881, he came from an old Hanoverian family who belonged to the landed nobility. His upbringing was typical of a young man of his class. Attending the famous Prinz-Heinrich-Gymnasium in Berlin, a school for Prussian nobles, he was taught absolute fealty to the King of Prussia and to Prussian ideals, which implied service and, if needed, sacrifice for the greater good.

Yet, while Hitler despised men of Hassell's class, he depended on their expertise. In the early years of his regime, he was content to allow the ambassadors inherited from the Weimar Republic to hold on to their posts while he consolidated his power. Tipped as a future foreign secretary by his colleagues in the pre-Nazi Foreign Office, Hassell was held in high regard. 'A German nobleman from top to toe', as one described him, he was admired for his 'natural, often charming manner, his deep education, his excellent pen' and 'his cool, sharp mind'. Another praised his 'trenchant humour, his diplomatic finesse and his unshakeable political principles'.

Opposed to Hitler from the beginning, Hassell had used his position in Rome to fight for the ideals he believed in. After the debacle of the Treaty of Versailles, he was determined to build a bridge between Germany and the nations of Western Europe. Convinced that, for her own salvation and the security of her neighbours, a way had to be found to integrate Germany, he played an important part in the negotiations leading to the Four-Power Pact – an initiative between Britain, Italy, France and Germany to preserve the peace in Europe. Hitler, however, never ratified the pact and, as his aggressive foreign policy unfolded, Hassell found himself more and more at odds with the instructions issued to him from Berlin.

By the autumn of 1937, Hassell knew that he was being watched by Heydrich's spies and that Hitler and his circle wanted to replace him. Earlier that year, Mussolini, whom he was close to, had tipped him off during a conversation at the opera. Immediately, Hassell had asked Mussolini to intercede on his behalf, protesting his loyalty to the Nazi regime.

His protests were a bluff that would have been easily called had the Gestapo found the diaries he kept locked in a drawer in his desk. Dating back to the start of his posting, Hassell assigned codenames to individuals and countries – even to meetings and events. Sometimes he used several: Hitler was 'Inge' or 'Inges Chef'; Mussolini was '*Dein Tischherr*' (Table Companion) or 'Calvino'; Himmler, 'Zöllinger'; England, 'Lady Hay'; Göring, 'The Man with the Wineglass' or 'Sepp's Brother'; the Nazi Party, 'Inges family'. But the codenames were primarily for his own amusement; read in context, it would not have been difficult for the Gestapo to decipher them.

The diaries added up to a damning indictment; from his position at the heart of the German and Italian dictatorships, Hassell had charted the inexorable rise of Fascism, noting every deviation from the values he upheld – prudence, a firm moral outlook and a rigid adherence to the principles of law.

Yet his patriotic sense of duty, his natural reserve and the discretion instilled into him over the course of his many years as a diplomat prevented him from openly criticizing the Nazi regime. Aside from occasional outbursts, prompted by the boorish behaviour of visiting Nazi apparatchiks, the diaries tell us little about the man. He was careful to veil his criticism beneath dense, arid accounts of diplomatic discussions, internal manoeuvrings at Wilhelmstrasse – the German Foreign Ministry – and his own observations on European foreign policy. He never wrote about what he was actually feeling.

Far more revealing, however – and an irony, given the Gestapo's goal to expose Hassell's opposition to the Nazi regime – is the diary his daughter kept during the same period. Aged twelve when her father took up his post in Rome, Fey idolized him. Between 1933 and 1937, she noted his reaction to the rise of Nazism and the negative feelings he was unwilling to commit to paper, but which he confided to his family. Unlike her father, Fey wrote her diary in plain language. She did not hide it away; she left it lying around her bedroom at the Villa Wolkonsky – effortlessly accessible, had the Gestapo thought to read it.

A glance through the diary offers a far greater insight into Hassell than the dense, coded entries in his own diaries:

1 Feb 1933: Hindenburg has nominated Adolf Hitler as chancellor. My father is appalled . . .

2 May 1933: Today trade unions have been banned in Germany . . . at dinner my father said that Germany is going from bad to worse, and quickly.

2 Sept 1933: My father has returned from Berlin, where he met Hitler. He says that conversation with him is impossible. He never stops talking and always on whatever subject happens to interest him at that moment. Any kind of discussion is out of the question . . . Since Hitler abolished all other political parties last July, my father thinks that democracy is over in Germany . . .

7 July 1934: We heard about the massacre★ that Hitler organized with the help of the SS. My father is horrified; I have never seen him so pale. He says that the foreign newspapers are right to consider the whole lot a bunch of gangsters . . . He is in a state of turmoil and asks himself infinite questions. Can one avoid their domination? What can one do? Is it still useful to work with them to avoid worse things?

18 Sept 1935: My father has just come back from the Nuremberg rally and is horrified by the militaristic display of it all. But that is nothing in comparison to the anti-Semitic laws that have been announced. My father is terribly worried for his Jewish friends.

12 May 1937: We no longer talk about politics at table, since my father has found out that Reinecke† has been spying on him. That pig!

From a political and social perspective, 1937 had been a year 'the likes of which', Hassell admitted, 'I have never experienced before'. Following the declaration of the Rome–Berlin Axis in October 1936, an agreement informally linking the two Fascist countries, there had been a flood of official visits from Germany. Hermann Göring, the chief of the Luftwaffe, visited five times and Himmler twice. Rudolph Hess, Hitler's deputy, and Robert Ley, head of the Nazi labour movement and editor of a virulently anti-Semitic newspaper, had also stayed at the embassy, along with a host of government ministers and army generals. Entourages had to be accommodated;

★ The Night of the Long Knives.
† Second butler at the embassy and a Gestapo spy.

dinners, lunches and receptions hosted; sightseeing parties organized; and shopping expeditions arranged. 'There is no limit!' Hassell wrote in his diary.

Regardless of political differences, the overblown behaviour of the visitors offended Hassell's Prussian sensibilities. None more so than Göring. To Hassell's embarrassment, that January, at a ball held in his honour at the Palazzo Venezia, the Luftwaffe chief had toured the room tapping the emeralds on the tiaras of the assembled _principesse_, complaining that they were not as big as Frau Göring's. A few months later, passing through Rome on his way to Naples, he was back again: 'Göring will come in the next few days, totally privately, "with almost no retinue" – 5 railway carriages!' Hassell noted on 21 April. The visit got off to a bad start after he met him at the station in his official car: 'He found our car completely not up to scratch. We had to have a 200 horsepower Mercedes, like Ribbentrop. I told him I wasn't Ribbentrop.'

Later that day, he showed Göring around Rome, finishing at the Vatican, the highlight of the tour. Crossing the square in front of St Peter's, oblivious to its splendour, Göring outlined his and Hitler's foreign-policy objectives for the coming year. 'His remarks were in the style of a newly qualified cadet turned Caesar,' Hassell wrote. 'We had to swallow Austria soon, that was our priority, and also Czechoslovakia. He thought no one would complain!'

When at last he stopped to look up at St Peter's, Göring was unimpressed. 'It's just a toy compared to the Führer's new hall at Nürnberg,' he told Hassell. 'When it's finished the hall will be twice as tall and twice as wide. Big enough to dangle that cupola from the ceiling, like a chandelier.'

'These were the thoughts St Peter's Square inspired in him, displayed as it was in front of us in all its beauty and glory,' Hassell noted drily.

The strain of having to kowtow to the stream of unpleasant visitors from Berlin and to maintain the charade that he was loyal to the Nazi Party took its toll on Hassell. He was receiving medical treatment for stress-related digestive problems and his doctor had placed him on a special diet. Repeatedly, Hassell questioned whether it was right to serve such an immoral regime. But he always came back to the same conclusion; on the 'outside', it would be impossible to influence the Nazis' foreign policy. Keeping up the pretence of loyalty was a necessary compromise if he was to continue to fight for his principles and to pursue his dream of reviving Germany's fortunes in a United States of Europe. *'Pour moi l'Europe a le sens d'une patrie'* – a quite extraordinary statement for his time.

By the autumn of 1937, however, Hassell recognized that his dream was unobtainable. Mussolini's euphoria following his trip to Germany indicated that a formal alliance with Hitler was inevitable. Convinced that such an agreement would lead to war, particularly with two such unpredictable and explosive heads of government, Hassell tried to persuade Hitler to confine an alliance with Italy to cultural and economic cooperation. He continued to argue his case, even after both Mussolini and Göring warned him that if he persisted in his opposition Hitler would dismiss him.

His lone campaign also placed a strain on his family. Though Ilse, his wife, and their four children were staunchly anti-Nazi, they too were forced to lead a double life. The two boys, Hans Dieter and Wolf Ulli, were away at school and university, but the girls – Fey, aged nineteen, and Almuth, twenty-five – were living at the Villa Wolkonsky. With the Gestapo's spies installed at the embassy, the family no longer had any privacy or the opportunity to vent their feelings against the regime. After the Night of the Long Knives in 1934, Fey, then fifteen, had started having recurring nightmares about the Nazis, which she recorded in her diary. 'I saw the Bay of Naples, which was almost black, and above it, a yellow full moon. Gradually the moon turned into Hitler and became ashen coloured, like ice. Then it changed into a skull.' At sixteen, she was required to join the local branch of the Hitler Youth, where she would be bullied by one of the cadets who worked as a gardener at the embassy. He had wanted to oust the leader, a close friend of hers, and had complained to Berlin that the man was unsuitable as he took the group to church and to parties. Fey's response was to compose a letter to Berlin, stating her support for the leader, which she persuaded twenty people to sign. When the gardener found out, he asked her to hand over the letter and threatened to report her, saying that such activities now carried the death penalty in Germany. Fey found the threats absurd, but they were nonetheless upsetting.

Prior to the dinner at Villa Madama, there had been another unpleasant incident, involving her elder sister, Almuth. After drinks at the embassy, Hassell and his wife had taken Heydrich and Himmler to watch *Antony and Cleopatra*, which was being filmed at Cinecittà, the new studios built by Mussolini. Almuth went with them, travelling in one of the embassy cars with Heydrich and his deputy, Kurt Daluege. As soon as they arrived, she went over to her parents and quietly begged them to let her travel back in their car, as the Gestapo chiefs' 'crude and brutish jokes' were too much for her.

The inevitable move against Hassell came the day after Himmler and Heydrich left Rome. On the evening of 21 October, Joachim von Ribbentrop, the German Ambassador in London, landed at a military airport outside the city. The purpose of his visit was cloaked in secrecy; the press reported that it was a private trip with his daughter, who was recuperating after a car accident. In fact, Ribbentrop, acting as special envoy for the Führer, was in Rome for a secret meeting with Mussolini. His task was to persuade the dictator to agree to Italy becoming a signatory to the Anti-Comintern Pact, an agreement concluded between Germany and Japan to contain the spread of Communism.

Hassell was at the airport to meet him. When Ribbentrop stepped off the plane, he handed him a document, signed by Konstantin von Neurath, the German foreign secretary, granting Ribbentrop the right to conduct all negotiations with the Italian dictator. Hassell was even excluded from the meeting. He saw it as a personal betrayal; hours before, Neurath had told him that he had 'full authority to scupper Ribbentrop's plan'. By the end of the following day, Italy's inclusion in the anti-Communist alliance was a fait accompli. It signalled the reorientation of German foreign policy against Britain and France and, as Hassell believed, towards world conflict.

Mussolini did not sign the pact until 6 November. In the interim, in meetings with Ribbentrop and Neurath, Hassell continued to argue against it, condemning the alliance as 'block-building' and 'dangerous adventure politics'. Repeatedly, he asked for a private audience with Hitler to convince him to leave Italy out of the pact. But the Führer refused to see him.

Both in Germany and Italy, Hassell's enemies were already calling for his removal. On 27 October, Ciano saw Hess, Hitler's deputy, who was also in Rome. 'I took advantage to ask for von Hassell's head since he has been playing both ends against the middle for too long. I have documented the reasons for our mistrust in the man. Hess nodded and will speak to the Führer about it. He asked me for suggestions about a successor. I told him that a Party man would be fine. The alliance between the two countries is based, above all, on the identity of political systems that determines a common destiny. *Simul stabunt, simul cadent* [Together we stand, together we fall].'

Hassell was dismissed at the beginning of December. So great was his humiliation, he did not record the details in his diary. It was left to Fey to write about it in hers: 'My father says that it is already all over for him. Ciano and Ribbentrop are clamouring for his dismissal because he stands in the way of their warmongering policies.'

One of Hassell's last acts before leaving was to ask Himmler, who was in Rome on another visit, to stop persecuting Professor Werner Heisenberg, a Nobel Prize-winning German physicist. The professor had been publicly attacked in *Das Schwarze Korps*, the SS newspaper, for refusing to renounce Einstein's Theory of Relativity. Branding Heisenberg 'a White Jew',★ the editorial stated that he should be made to 'disappear'. During the meeting at the embassy, Himmler reiterated that he would only rehabilitate Heisenberg if he 'disassociated himself from Einstein's Theory'.

'Politics and diplomacy teach one a great deal about intrigue and lies. But I must confess that I never thought such an infernal mess possible,' Hassell wrote in January 1938. At the time, he was still expecting Hitler to offer him another posting. Flattered throughout his career by his Weimar contemporaries, who believed him to be the most promising diplomat of his generation, he was guilty of hubris.

★ The Nazi Party's term for Aryans sympathetic to Jews.

He could not believe that it was all over. He had also allowed his love for Germany to cloud his judgement; while the evidence was growing in plain sight – and he saw it – he could not believe that his country would ever fully embrace the Nazis. The 'gangsters', as he called them, were some sort of temporary aberration. Once they were removed, Germany would be handed back to its traditional Prussian ruling class.

Kristallnacht – Hitler's pogrom against the Jews in November 1938 – was a turning point for Hassell. Using the pretext of the murder by a young Polish Jew of Ernst von Rath, a German diplomat based in Paris, the SS and Gestapo carried out a wave of attacks against Jews across the Reich, assisted by civilians. On the night of 9 November, some 250 synagogues were set on fire; simultaneously, in excess of 7,000 Jewish shops and businesses were vandalized and Jewish cemeteries, hospitals, schools and homes looted, while police and fire brigades stood by. Dozens of Jews were killed and more than 30,000 Jewish men were arrested and taken to the newly built concentration camps at Buchenwald, Sachsenhausen and Dachau.

'I am writing under crushing emotions evoked by the vile persecution of the Jews after the murder of von Rath. Not since the world war have we lost so much credit in the world,' Hassell wrote in his diary on 25 November, two weeks after the riots. 'I am most deeply troubled about the effect on our national life, which is dominated ever more inexorably by a system capable of such things . . . There is no doubt that we are dealing with an officially organised anti-Jewish riot which broke out at the same hour of the night all over Germany! Truly a disgrace!'

Two days later, he saw Hugo Bruckmann, owner of a publishing conglomerate and an early supporter and promoter of Hitler: 'Conversations with B—— as to what one could do to give public expression to the general abhorrence of these methods. Unfortunately, without success: without office we have no effective weapon. Any action on our part would lead to our being gagged – or worse.'

In the coming months, Hassell would hold a series of secret meetings with two similarly minded men. They were General Ludwig Beck, who had just resigned from his position as Chief of the General Staff in protest against Hitler's policies, and Carl Friedrich Goerdeler, the former mayor of Leipzig and Reich commissioner for price control.

Together, led by General Beck, they would form the core of the German Resistance – a clandestine movement whose central object- ive was to kill Hitler and overthrow the Nazi regime.

8.

Ebenhausen, Bavaria, 6 March 1943

The house, once owned by Hassell's father-in-law, Grand Admiral von Tirpitz, stood on its own on the edge of the village. There was a church nearby, hidden by ancient yews. Otherwise, the house was situated in open country, the view stretching across the valley.

From the top floor, Hassell peered through the slats of the shutters. There was no one in sight but he could not throw off the sensation that he was being watched.

Retrieving a pair of binoculars from a drawer in his desk, he opened the shutters a fraction and focused on the ridge opposite. Trees ran along it and, when he had last looked, he was sure he had seen two men on the edge of the wood.

After some minutes, satisfied there was no one there, he put the binoculars back in his desk and took out a sheaf of papers, which he stuffed into his pocket. Then he went downstairs, and out into the garden. Stopping briefly to double-check there was no one about, he crossed the lawn to an old stone outhouse. The garden was well laid out and, to the casual observer, the building had the appearance of a carefully conceived grotto. But Hassell had purposely allowed the roses that climbed over the ruins to grow wild. Stooping down, he parted the undergrowth, looking for the foxhole.

It was a ritual he went through every time he returned to Ebenhausen. In his pocket were the latest pages of his diary. He did not make daily entries; it was not safe to travel around Germany with incriminating papers and far too risky to keep them in his flat in Berlin. Instead he would wait until he was at Ebenhausen to write up the events of a week or two, based on notes he had jotted down on scraps of paper and concealed in the lining of his jacket. Then he added the entries to the tea caddy that he had buried by the outhouse.

His entries had none of the reticence of his Rome diaries. Singularly focused on the conspiracy to overthrow Hitler, Hassell recorded every secret assignation, every rumour he heard regarding the Führer's health and mental well-being, and every whisper of an opposition move. His informants were among the most highly placed men in the Nazi regime: army generals, serving with the Wehrmacht's High Command; agents working for the *Abwehr*, German military intelligence; officials in the Foreign Office; men attached to the personal staff of Hitler's immediate entourage. There were reports, too, of Hassell's meetings with representatives of the US and British governments who, he and Beck hoped, might help precipitate a coup.

For Hassell, the diary was a dossier. He was working closely with Hans Oster and Hans von Dohnányi, leading conspirators in the Abwehr, who were also compiling material on the crimes of the regime: on atrocities committed by SS and Nazi leaders; on criminal and immoral practices in the Hitler Youth; on profiteering and infringements of the law; on the ill-treatment of prisoners in both Germany and Nazi-occupied countries; and on the pogroms against the Jews. The evidence was to be used not only to convince key individuals of the necessity of regime change but also subsequently for legal proceedings against the culprits.

So great was the danger to Hassell, so explosive the contents of the diary, that, in May 1942, he was forced to abandon it. Leaving the notebook buried in the foxhole, it was not until later that summer that he had the courage to resume. 'For several months I have been unable to write up my diary,' his entry on 1 August began. 'Certain information I received toward the end of April made it imperative to exercise more caution.'

The information came from Ernst von Weizsäcker, Hassell's mole in the Foreign Office. While he was state secretary, one of the highest-ranking officials, he met regularly with Hassell to keep him abreast of developments. They were close friends of long standing and Weizsäcker, though unwilling to resign his position, professed to support a coup against Hitler. On 29 April, he had asked Hassell to meet him at his house. Hassell assumed it was to discuss Hitler's recent reshuffle at the Foreign Office, yet to his dismay, despite many years of friendship, Weizsäcker had summoned him to break off contact. 'He carefully closed the windows and doors, and announced with some emphasis that he had a very serious matter to discuss with me,' Hassell wrote. 'For the time being, he had to ask me to spare him the embarrassment of my presence.'

Rumours had reached the state secretary that Hassell had been overheard criticizing the regime and calling for Hitler's removal, thereby placing Weizsäcker himself in great danger and costing him 'sleepless nights'. 'When I started to remonstrate he interrupted me harshly,' Hassell continued. 'He then proceeded to heap reproaches on me as he paced excitedly up and down. I had been unbelievably indiscreet, quite unheard of; as a matter of fact, "with all due deference", so had my wife. This was all known in certain places (the Gestapo), and they claimed even to have documents. He must demand, most emphatically, that I correct this behaviour. When I attempted to interrupt he became annoyed and said again and again: "Get this straight! If you do not want to understand me then I must break off" . . . I had no idea, he said, how people were after me (the Gestapo). Every step I took was observed. I should certainly burn everything I had in the way of notes which covered conversations in which one or another of us had said this or that.'

In August, when Hassell judged it safe to resume his diary, he was still smarting from the way his friend had behaved. 'The memory of my conversation with Weizsäcker torments me, because – even after taking into account the validity of all possible tactical considerations – there still remains his way of going about it, which, to put it mildly, is incomprehensible to me.' Struggling to excuse his friend's behaviour, he blamed the conditions under which the Nazi regime forced its critics to operate: 'the Cheka methods used by them . . . The fact that all opposition and all criticism, even those arising out of the most patriotic motives, are looked upon as punishable crimes . . . Their instinctive aversion to every person with real character . . . The consequent trembling fear on the part of everybody.'

His summary ended with a characteristic remark of defiance: 'According to confirmed rumour Hitler has a particular dislike for Ilse and me. In view of the character of the man I consider this a compliment . . .'

The pages Hassell deposited in the foxhole that cold March morning point to his frustration: 'I get fed up with Berlin (that is these futile attempts to overthrow the system) and long to settle for good at Ebenhausen and do only literary work. But that would certainly be wrong and cowardly.'

As Hassell and his circle recognized, orchestrating a *coup d'état* was not simply about replacing Hitler; it was about wresting control from the formidable Nazi apparatus, which was supported by hundreds of thousands of SS troops. The implementation and success of a coup therefore depended on the military: only the army had the weapons and power necessary to effect regime change.

Even before the war began, Beck, Goerdeler and Hassell had devoted their energies to bringing senior military commanders on board. But while a number were convinced of the necessity of a coup, they had failed to offer active support.

The obstacles were legion. Every soldier in the German Army had sworn a sacred oath of loyalty to Hitler. In strict legal terms, he was the Supreme Commander. Unless, therefore, he was removed, the army could not be counted on; yet without it, a coup could not be carried out. Additionally, irrespective of this oath of allegiance, the attitude of most officers was determined by the success of Hitler's war leadership. As long as the dictator continued to win battles, the conspirators saw little chance of persuading the military to cooperate. In the early years of the war, they recognized that the rapid military victories up to and including the first phase of the Russian campaign had strengthened Hitler's position. 'Nothing is to be hoped for now,' Hassell wrote in the summer of 1941. 'In wide circles, specifically in the army, Hitler's prestige is still great and has even increased as a result of the Russian campaign, especially among officers.'

Among the small group of generals sympathetic to the underground opposition's arguments, there was a further obstacle. None was pre-pared to make a move against Hitler and conclude peace with the Allies until they knew the terms of any settlement. The shameful defeat of 1918 and the subsequent peace treaty signed at Versailles had contributed to Hitler's rise, and no general would commit Germany to a second humiliation.

Hassell's principal role in the conspiracy, which was to explore the possibility of negotiating favourable peace terms with the Allies, was therefore of crucial importance. To convince the generals to precipi-tate a coup, his most pressing concern was to establish the conditions under which Germany's enemies would agree to an armistice or a separate peace with the 'other' Germany. In return for a change of regime, and the ending of the war, Hassell wanted to secure British agreement on the future borders of the German Reich and, in par-ticular, a promise not to exploit the void created by Hitler's removal for military purposes.

To this end, from 1939, he worked tirelessly and at great personal risk to further his connections abroad. On his return from Rome, he had joined an organization called the Central European Economic Conference, which had been set up to study European economic con-ditions. His job enabled him to travel freely and he used his trips as a cloak for his conspiratorial activities. While the passport stamps he was required to obtain meant the German authorities knew about his various movements, he managed to keep his meetings with repre-sentatives of the British government secret.

In February and May 1940, Hassell travelled to Arosa in Switzer-land, where he made contact with James Lonsdale-Bryans, an intermediary to the British foreign secretary, Lord Halifax. Believ-ing that Hitler's personal removal was a principal war aim, Halifax seemed willing to offer inducements to the conspirators for a reason-able peace. However, Sir Alexander Cadogan, the permanent under-secretary at the Foreign Office, took a different view. After meeting Lonsdale-Bryans, he noted: 'Ridiculous stale story of a Ger-man opposition ready to overthrow Hitler . . . this was the 100th time I had heard this story.'

Anthony Eden replaced Halifax in May 1940, and Cadogan's view prevailed. Senior officials at the Foreign Office did not believe a coup against Hitler was likely nor was Hassell regarded as credible. In their eyes, as the son-in-law of Grand Admiral von Tirpitz, Kaiser Wilhelm's naval chief, he was a typical representative of the influential Prussian caste that had been responsible for the First World War, the greatest military catastrophe of the twentieth century. Further, this caste had supported Hitler's policies in past years, as indeed – or at least on the face of it – had Hassell when he served as Ambassador to Rome, an important Axis posting.

The Foreign Office maintained this political line consistently. At the beginning of 1941, telegrams were sent to the British missions in Berne, Stockholm and Madrid with the express purpose of forbidding any response to further peace feelers from putative German coup leaders. Only when regime change had occurred was Britain willing to negotiate. 'I am sure,' Churchill wrote to Eden in September 1941, 'we should not depart from our position of absolute silence. Nothing would be more distressing to our friends in the United States or more dangerous with our new ally, Russia, than the suggestion that we are entertaining such ideas. I am absolutely opposed to the slightest contact.'

Hassell refused to give up. In January 1942, he met Carl Burckhardt, the vice president of the Red Cross, in Geneva. Burckhardt told him that leading circles in Britain were convinced that 'an arrangement with a decent Germany must be made'. This information was at odds with official British attitudes and policy. Yet in Hassell it fuelled the hope that an understanding was still within the bounds of possibility.

These hopes were dashed when, after meeting Roosevelt and Stalin at Casablanca in January 1943, Churchill announced that the Western powers were demanding Germany's 'unconditional surrender'.

Churchill would come to regret his failure to respond to the peace feelers put out by Germany's underground opposition. After the war, he admitted that he had underestimated the strength and size of the anti-Hitler resistance. 'In Germany there lived an opposition,' he wrote, 'which belongs to the noblest and greatest that the political history of any nation has ever produced. These men fought without help from within or from abroad driven forward only by the restlessness of their conscience.'

'If the generals had it in mind to withhold their intervention until it was absolutely clear that the corporal is leading us into disaster, they have had their dream fulfilled,' Hassell wrote in response to the Allies' insistence on unconditional surrender. 'The worst about it is that our own prophecy has been fulfilled; i.e. that it would then be too late and any new regime could be nothing more than a liquidation commission.'

Hassell and his circle now recognized that if the army would not overthrow Hitler then 'some sort of partial action' – his murder, in other words – was needed in the hope that 'the whole building would collapse like a house of cards'.

Assassination, however, presented problems of its own. While Hitler's whereabouts at any given moment was easy enough to establish, it was seldom possible to know his movements in advance. Prompted perhaps by his own acute sense of self-preservation, Hitler avoided fixed schedules and, insofar as he could, travelled only at the shortest possible notice. He wore a bulletproof waistcoat and a metal-plated bulletproof cap which, as his adjutant Schmundt testified, was of extraordinary weight. When Hitler did travel, the arrangements for his protection were all but impenetrable; he had his own security-service bodyguards, as well as a heavily armed SS escort; his doctor was constantly in attendance and he travelled with a cook, who prepared his food. His private aircraft, a Focke-Wulf Condor, was equipped with an armoured cabin, and a parachute was attached to his seat. He always used his own cars and four separate motorcades were kept in constant readiness at his various headquarters. The cars themselves had bulletproof tyres and windows, and extensive armour plating.

Crucially, therefore, Hitler's killer would have to be someone who had access to him. Given that an assassin was unlikely to come from within the security forces – to a man, fanatically loyal to the Führer – in the search for a potential candidate, Hassell and his circle were back at square one. The killer *had* to be a member of the armed forces – someone who could get close to Hitler on his visits to Wehrmacht headquarters or who saw him regularly at military briefings.

Hassell was pessimistic. 'In spite of all efforts,' he confided to his diary, 'what is still missing is a spark plug.' He was troubled too by the consequences of a failed attempt: 'Hitler's prestige is still great enough – if he can keep on his feet – to enable him to take counter-action which would mean at least chaos or civil war.'

Briefly, within days of the Casablanca Conference, his hopes were raised by the events on the Eastern Front. On 31 January, after one of the bitterest battles in military history, 91,000 German soldiers surrendered at Stalingrad – a dramatic and humiliating addition to the 200,000 casualties the Wehrmacht had already suffered.

While Germany had previously undergone reverses – in the Battle of Britain, for example, and at sea – Stalingrad was the first major setback on land. 'The last few weeks have brought the most serious crisis we have experienced thus far in the war,' Hassell noted in his diary on 14 February 1943. 'For the first time Hitler cannot deny his responsibility; for the first time the critical rumours are aimed directly at him. Exposed for all our eyes is the lack of military ability of the "most brilliant strategist of all time" – i.e. our megalomaniacal corporal . . . It is clear to all that precious blood has been shed foolishly or even criminally for purposes of prestige alone. Since strictly military affairs are involved this time, the eyes of the generals have been opened too so that they realise to which point the Wehrmacht has been brought and where Germany will soon be. In view of an event unique in German military history, even the most blind should now surely let the blinkers drop from their eyes.'

By mid March, after the coup he hoped for had not materialized, Hassell was fulminating: 'Sad to say the serious crisis mentioned at the beginning of my last notes did not precipitate the cleansing storm, the bitterly necessary, intensely longed-for change of regime . . . Vain are all efforts to pour iron into the bloodstream of the people, who are already supporting with all their might a half-insane, half-criminal policy. The military events alone, the irresponsible leadership of this megalomaniac and irresponsible corporal, should have induced them to act if the inner rot were not enough.'

Notwithstanding the defeat at Stalingrad, Hassell could not understand how the generals lived with their consciences. If they were not
convinced of the need for revolt by political or military arguments,
how could they have failed to respond to the brutality of Hitler's
Commissar Order, which required the Wehrmacht to kill Communists captured on the Eastern Front, and, most especially, to the
genocide of the Jews there?

Incredulous at the generals' insouciance, his verdict was damning:
'They have undoubted technical ability and physical courage, but little moral courage, absolutely no broad world vision, no inner spiritual
independence or that strength of resistance which rests on a genuine
cultural basis. For this reason, Hitler has been able to make them sub-
servient and bind them hand and foot. The majority, moreover, are
out to make careers in the basest sense. Gifts and Field Marshals'
batons are more important to them than the great historical issues
and moral values at stake. All those on whom we set our hopes are
failing, the more miserably so since they agree with all they have
been told and permit themselves to indulge in the most anti-Nazi
talk, but are unable to summon up the courage to act although all of
them *would* go along with it.'

Hassell was correct in his assessment of the generals collectively,
but he was wrong to believe that not a single one was willing to
risk an attempt on the Führer's life. At the time he was writing,
Major General Henning von Tresckow, backed by General Ludwig
Beck and senior officers in the Abwehr, was engaged in a conspiracy
to assassinate Hitler on the Russian Front. The fact that Hassell
was being watched by the Gestapo – and had been since March
1942 – meant that Beck, his great confidant and the acknowledged
leader of his resistance group, had no choice but to keep him out of
the loop.

Aged forty-three, Tresckow was chief of operations at Army Group
Centre, the Wehrmacht's headquarters on the Eastern Front. His
family, Prussian aristocrats, had a long military history. Over the
course of 300 years they had supplied the Prussian Army with twenty-
one generals. Tresckow himself had won the Iron Cross at the age of

sixteen, fighting in the Second Battle of the Marne in 1918. 'You, Tresckow,' his commanding officer told him at the time, 'will either become Chief of Staff or will die on the scaffold as a rebel.'

Before the Second World War began, Tresckow was a committed anti-Nazi. Like Hassell, Kristallnacht drove him into opposition. Regarding it as a personal humiliation, he believed that 'both duty and honour' bound him to do his best 'to bring about the downfall of Hitler and National Socialism to save Germany and Europe from barbarism'.

After cultivating a group of like-minded fellow officers, in October 1941, Tresckow sent his cousin and adjutant, Fabian von Schlabrendorff, to Berlin with a message for Beck to say that the staff at Army Group Centre were 'ready to act'. First, however, Tresckow wanted a guarantee that Britain would make peace soon after a change of regime – a guarantee that Beck and Hassell were unable to give him.

In the winter of 1942, as the war situation became more pressing, Tresckow sent a second message to Beck, telling him that his group were now willing to assassinate Hitler and thereby provide 'the spark' for the coup. They would take action at the first opportunity.

It did not come until a few months later when, in January 1943, Hitler was scheduled to visit Army Group Centre's HQ at Smolensk.

Tresckow's plan was to kill Hitler during lunch in the officers' mess. All two dozen officers seated around the table would shoot him – thus making the responsibility collective and ensuring that at least one bullet would get through the security entourage of SS and hit its target. It was necessary, however, to inform Field Marshal Günther von Kluge, commander of Army Group Centre, if only to prevent him from getting in the line of fire. While Kluge professed to be opposed to Hitler, he scotched the plan. Claiming that it insulted the tenets of the Officer Corps, he told Tresckow that 'it was not seemly to shoot a man at lunch'.

As it transpired, Hitler's visit was cancelled at the last minute and rescheduled for 13 March.

This time, Tresckow's plan was to assassinate him as he left the headquarters. Hand-picked troops lining the route were to open fire with their sub-machine guns. Again, Kluge had to be told and initially he gave his consent. But at the last minute he did not have the strength of character to follow through. As Schlabrendorff recalled, the field marshal 'brought up various arguments, claiming that neither the world, nor the German people, nor the German soldier would understand such an act at this time. He insisted that it would be much better to wait until the military situation had developed to a point that would force Hitler's elimination.'

It was a specious argument; as both Tresckow and Schlabrendorff recognized, the field marshal's opposition to the assassination attempt probably stemmed from the fact that Hitler had just given him 250,000 Reichsmarks as a birthday present.

Knowing that Kluge could not be relied on, they had a contingency plan to which the field marshal was not privy. 'Dropping the idea of shooting Hitler,' Schlabrendorff wrote, 'we planned instead to eliminate him by smuggling a time bomb aboard his plane. In this way, the stigma of an assassination would be avoided, and Hitler's death could be attributed – officially at least – to an accidental plane crash.'

Schlabrendorff had managed to obtain British explosives, seized from captured SOE agents – an important factor as British fuses were silent, whereas German fuses made a slight hissing noise. After placing the explosives in two bottles of cognac, Tresckow asked Colonel Brandt, who was travelling in Hitler's entourage, if he would deliver the bottles to a friend, based at the Führer's headquarters at Rastenburg in East Prussia. This apparently innocent request was granted.

Hitler left for Rastenburg later that day. Taking the parcel to the airfield, Schlabrendorff waited for a signal from Tresckow. He then activated the bomb and handed the package to Brandt. The aircraft took off, accompanied by a fighter escort. According to Tresckow's calculations, the bomb would explode thirty minutes after take-off. 'With mounting tension,' Schlabrendorff subsequently wrote, 'we waited at headquarters for news of the "accident", which we expected shortly before the plane was to pass over Minsk. We assumed that one of the escort fighters would report the crash by radio. But nothing happened.'

In 'a state of indescribable agitation', Schlabrendorff had to contrive an excuse to retrieve the package. 'The failure of our attempt was bad enough, but the thought of what discovery of the bomb would mean to us, and our fellow conspirators, friends and families, was infinitely worse.' To his relief, he established that the bottles of cognac were still with Colonel Brandt. Claiming that the wrong parcel had been sent by mistake, he flew to Rastenburg to collect it. It was only when he caught a train from the Führer's headquarters back to Berlin that he was finally able to dismantle the bomb. Locking the door to his sleeping compartment, he gingerly unwrapped the parcel. 'The reason for the failure immediately became clear. Everything but one small part had worked as expected. The bottle with the corrosive fluid had been broken, the chemical had eaten through the wire, the firing pin had been released and had struck forward – but the detonator had not ignited!' Schlabrendorff blamed it on the British, believing that it was 'one of the few duds that slipped past' an inspection. But it was possible that the fuse had failed to ignite due to the extreme cold over Russia.

A week later, on 21 March, Tresckow and Schlabrendorff made what was now their third attempt on Hitler's life. As part of the ceremonies to commemorate 'Heroes Memorial Day', Hitler was due to tour an exhibition of captured arms at the Zeughaus★ on Unter den Linden. To answer any queries, an officer from Army Group Centre was detailed to accompany him.

Tresckow assigned the role to Colonel Rudolf-Christoph von Gersdorff, an extraordinarily brave 38-year-old who, for the sake of saving Germany, had volunteered as a suicide bomber. Using explosives primed with a ten-minute British fuse, Gersdorff was to hide the bomb in his clothes and blow up Hitler and himself.

Hitler arrived at the exhibition at the scheduled time of 1 p.m., accompanied by Himmler, Göring and Field Marshal Wilhelm Keitel, the chief of staff of the armed forces. He made a short speech for German radio before moving towards the entrance of the exhibition hall. Here, Gersdorff greeted the Führer, saluting with his right hand, while setting off the chemical fuse with the other.

★ The Berlin Armoury.

As the acid ate through the wires, Gersdorff tried to keep as close
to Hitler as possible. But – almost as if he had some presentiment of
Gersdorff's intent – Hitler refused to stop and view any of the exhib-
its. Walking quickly through the hall, he emerged from the building
within two minutes. His early exit, throwing his schedule into confusion, was noted even in London, where the BBC was monitoring
the radio broadcast.

With only minutes to spare, Gersdorff rushed to a nearby cloakroom to disarm the suicide vest. Back at Army Group Centre HQ in
Smolensk, Tresckow was listening to the radio broadcast with a stop-
watch in his hand. When, almost as soon as Hitler entered the
exhibition hall, the commentator announced that he had departed for
the War Memorial, it was clear to Tresckow that this attempt, too,
had failed.

In Berlin, Hassell, unaware of General Tresckow's attempts to assassinate Hitler, had a new reason to despair. On 11 March, ten days
before Hitler's visit to the armoury on Unter den Linden, he learned
that his younger son, Hans Dieter, had been seriously wounded on
the Russian Front. A bullet had pierced his lung and there was a danger that the wound would prove fatal. He had been taken to a field
hospital and Hassell was hoping that he could be moved away from
the battlefield. He was also worried about his elder son, Wolf Ulli,
who was fighting in France. But at least Fey, and his two young
grandsons, Corrado and Roberto, were safe.

9.

When, at Ebenhausen in January 1940, Fey married Detalmo Pirzio-Biroli, a 25-year-old cavalry officer whom she had met several years before at a ball in Rome, she could not stop weeping. The celebrations were clouded by the family's awareness that, with Fey marrying, and her two brothers about to enrol on active service, separation was imminent. 'I was furious with myself,' Fey wrote in her diary, 'but the tears just ran down my cheeks. I later found out that my father had only just managed to finish his speech before leaving the drawing room in a hurry, because he too could not control his emotions. At the same time, Almuth and Hans Dieter had hidden in the cellar to cry their hearts out. It was too ridiculous!'

As newly-weds in wartime they knew they would not have long to spend together but, for the first five months of their marriage, the couple lived in Detalmo's family's palazzo in the centre of Rome. Then, in the spring of 1940, with Fey pregnant, they decided to escape the heat of the city and move to Brazzà.

The villa, with its twelfth-century castle and its vast estate, had been in the hands of Detalmo's mother's family, the di Brazzà Savorgnan, for over a thousand years. 'I had heard so much about this place that I was very curious to see it. Luckily, the reality is far lovelier!' Fey wrote excitedly to her parents. 'It stands on a hill far from all the troubles and the noise of the world. On one side, you look down over a great plain toward Venice. On the other, you can see the mountains, still tipped with snow. The ruins of the castle are in the grounds. The villa itself is enormous and is surrounded by many smaller houses where people attached to the estate live. Everything is in good taste. Detalmo and I have a bedroom and drawing room on the second floor – very airy and light, with a breath-taking view. This morning the gardener took me to the kitchen garden. It is huge and full of fig, pear, and apple trees.'

Fey also met Nonino, the family's much-loved servant: 'Nonino, coachman, butler and chauffeur at Brazzà for fifty-four years, arranges everything so perfectly that I find my main tasks are only to keep the twenty or so flower vases full and to discuss menus and shopping with the cook and the gardener.'

The couple had only been at the castle for a month when, in June 1940, Italy declared war on Britain and France and Detalmo left to join his cavalry regiment. Fey, however, stayed on to oversee the running of the estate and await the birth of Corrado. She loved the peace of Brazzà – 'the greenness, the great silence' – and, with its clean air and plentiful supplies of food, it was perfect for the baby. Yet, after Corrado was born in November, in contrast to the social whirl of Rome, she recognized the irony in her quiet, uneventful life. 'I'll just tell you in a few words what I do during the day,' she wrote to her sister, Almuth, in Munich. 'As soon as the little one is dressed and fed, I go out to check on the kitchen, the food, the laundry, and the housework to make sure everything is done as I want it. Then I go to the farm to talk to Bovolenta [the farm manager] about various problems – the pig, the hens, the rabbits and the pigeons. He is never very pleased when I arrive; at least that is the impression I get, because I keep discovering things that are managed to our disadvantage . . . In the afternoons, Corradino is put in his playpen. He talks a lot and is very athletic. I sit by, knitting, which I love, or mending, which I hate! After dinner I go to bed at about ten o'clock, and read.'

When Almuth visited Brazzà a few months later, Detalmo was home on leave. It was the first time she had seen the couple since their wedding and she was bowled over by their idyllic life, far away from the trauma and privations of the war. 'I feel as though I'm living through a dream,' she wrote to her parents. 'The journey was fine, and when I arrived at Udine station, I found Detalmo, thin but very charming in his uniform, waiting for me with Nonino and the carriage. We trotted slowly through the spectacular Italian countryside . . . Fey has become a beautiful woman; I had to keep looking at her anew. She seems to be in perfect health. We immediately went to look at Corrado. He really is the sweetest baby I've ever seen, and Detalmo is a very enthusiastic father.'

Soon after Almuth returned to Munich, Fey discovered she was expecting another child. 'You know if I should die now or after the second baby, I would feel immensely sad for leaving you,' she would later write to Detalmo. 'For the rest I would not be sad, for I have had so much happiness in these few years. I had a beautiful childhood, a lovely example in my parents for practically everything . . . and I came to know what real love between a man and a woman means, and what love for one's own child means.' Yet, cut off at Brazzà, her mood fluctuated and she was desperately anxious for her family in Germany and for her brother Hans Dieter, who was fighting on the Eastern Front. 'My mother wrote telling me my father is watched all the time by the Gestapo and the casualty lists in Russia are staggering,' she told Detalmo. 'I long for this war to be over and for you to come home.'

Detalmo was at Civitavecchia, a port on the west coast of Italy, waiting to hear whether he would be drafted to North Africa, where Italian forces and Rommel's Afrika Korps were fighting the British. He wrote to Fey to say that it was also possible that he would be posted to Udine, just 5 miles from Brazzà. Yet he felt it would be disloyal to leave his regiment. Fey urged him to accept the posting; aside from missing him, she needed his help in shouldering the responsibilities of managing the estate. Tired of a barrage of complaining letters, Detalmo wrote back firmly: 'I warn you once more, Fey darling: Do not complain. Complaining, besides being ungrateful toward providence, could also bring bad luck. Today news came that they must find some officers to serve on ships to North Africa. If I should be appointed to such a thing and cross the sea twice a week for months and months, you would then say: "How nice when he was in Civitavecchia. Why did it not stay like that?" Maybe I will try and come to Udine. However, even if this were not to take place, don't complain! I feel *so much* that complaining in our present position brings *bad luck*! You must do nothing but rejoice and be happy and thank God for what we have today, because so far we have been extremely lucky!'

Providence seemed to be on their side, however. At the beginning of 1942, just before the birth of Roberto, Detalmo was indeed posted to Udine. He was charged with overseeing the military forts that stretched across the plain to San Daniele, 10 miles north-west of Brazzà. Built to repel the many armies that had set out to conquer the north of Italy over the previous thousand years, most of the castles belonged to or stood on land owned by his ancestors.

Detalmo remained at Brazzà throughout 1942. The children were thriving, and both he and Fey wrote regularly to her parents in Berlin with details of their progress. 'The two boys are turning out well but are very different in character. Corrado is nervous and brilliant-minded; Roberto is slow and always half asleep,' Detalmo reported to his mother-in-law. For Fey, the children seemed an anchor of stability when the world was in turmoil. 'I love the little boys so much,' she wrote to her parents. 'They are all my joy in these uncertain times.'

As both Fey and Detalmo recognized, they continued to be 'extremely lucky'. Unlike almost anywhere in Europe, Brazzà remained untouched by the war. The nearest fighting was hundreds of miles away across the Alps, and it was one of the few regions that were not being bombed by the Allies or the Axis powers. Their idyll, however, was coming to an end. On a cold night in January 1943, sitting in front of a blazing fire in the library, Detalmo wrote what would turn out to be his last letter to his father-in-law from Brazzà:

> It's ten o'clock and we are alone. Fey is sitting at her writing desk, and you can tell the effect the hot wine, which she is drinking for her cold, is having on her speech . . .
>
> There's no doubt that the happiest people are Corradino and Robertino, who are lucky enough to be two years and one year old. They fall into utter despair about twenty times a day, but each time it never lasts more than twenty seconds. They are lucky to be in Brazzà, for the clean air as well as for the food. Brazzà is like a huge old hen protecting us with its broad wings.

A few weeks later, after being at home for over a year, Detalmo heard he was being posted elsewhere.

Detalmo's loyalties were not as straightforward as they appeared. Not only was he a committed anti-Fascist and an admirer of Ugo La Malfa, 'Cornali', the famous Italian Resistance leader, but he had many British relatives and friends to whom he felt nothing but warmth and admiration. He was also part-American, connected via his maternal grandmother, Cora Slocomb, to a wealthy New Orleans family.

He had therefore long hoped for a posting that would give him opportunities to extend his links with the Allies. Now, assigned as an interpreter to a prison camp for British and American POWs at Mortara, near Milan, he would have access to the Allies and the opportunity to work with 'Cornali', who was organizing clandestine resistance groups in the industrial areas of northern Italy.

Confined with his regiment and then at home at Brazzà, he had been prevented from using the connections to British intelligence which he had exploited on behalf of his father-in-law in the early years of the war. In February 1940, it was Detalmo who had set up the meetings between Hassell and Halifax's intermediary Lonsdale-Bryans, with whom he was acquainted. Since the meetings had to be strictly secret, Detalmo had arranged for Lonsdale-Bryans to travel to Arosa in Switzerland, masquerading as a specialist physician attending Hassell's elder son, who was being treated for a recurrent bronchial condition. Yet, despite setting up three meetings, nothing came of Detalmo's initiative. Clearly the British had no faith in the ability of the German Resistance to eliminate Hitler and establish a democratic government.

Parting with her husband was a wrench for Fey but she recognized that his posting at last gave him the opportunity to work secretly against Mussolini's regime. Her isolation at Brazzà meant that she felt safe in confiding anything to her diary: 'Detalmo is happy because he can dedicate himself to the undercover organization of Milan and at the same time avoid having to go and fight against the Allies,' she noted. She was also buoyed by his letters: 'Darling little Fey, be in good spirits and don't worry about anything,' he wrote a few days after he left. 'Give my love to the two little ones and have a big long kiss from me. I see you and the children as something so great and beautiful that it almost acquires the shape of a dream.'

Fey did not see Detalmo until June, when he obtained leave to take her and the boys to visit her parents at Ebenhausen. It was also an opportunity for him to brief his father-in-law on developments in Italy. Rumours were circulating among the British and American

POWs at Mortara that the Allies were preparing to invade southern Italy, and while they were staying at Ebenhausen it was announced that the British had occupied Pantelleria, a small island south of Sicily. Drawing on his conversations with senior figures in the Italian Resistance, Detalmo was convinced that, if an invasion were launched, it would precipitate Mussolini's fall. He also hoped that if the Fascist regime were overthrown in Italy, it would trigger a move against Hitler.

Fey did not take part in the political discussions between her father and her husband. While she supported their cause unreservedly, the children were her focus and she was thrilled to be home with her parents, who had not seen the boys since Roberto was born. 'We are all with my family at Ebenhausen,' she wrote on her first night home. 'I'm at the desk in the little drawing room looking out over the garden, which is in full bloom. I adore this view. The children have been a great success and – even though a mother should never say it – they are really beautiful and well behaved. This evening, Detalmo told me briefly what my father said to him: his position in Berlin is ever more difficult; they are reluctant to grant him trips abroad, and he's been informed that he is under constant surveillance. Furthermore, he is despairing about the army. With very few exceptions, no one is disposed to take any initiative against Hitler. They are frightened to risk their own position, in case of prison or death.'

A month after she and the boys returned to Brazzà, the rumours Detalmo had heard were confirmed when, on 10 July, the Allies invaded Sicily. As he had predicted, Mussolini fell shortly afterwards and was transported by the Allies to a secret prison in the Apennines.

Detalmo and Hassell, who were in touch via a secret courier, both hoped that Mussolini's arrest would precipitate Hitler's downfall. In early August, Detalmo wrote to Fey: 'I am rather expecting news from your father, not personal things but rather general, if you understand my point. There must be lots going on up there. Let us hope it is for the best and not for the worst.' Fey was on tenterhooks too. She replied to Detalmo: 'I had the same impression as you. My father must be rather busy, but I am, as always, pessimistic; it is so much more difficult for him than the Italians.' And she wrote again, two days later: 'As you can imagine my thoughts continue with my father, and I am nervous and impatient. Now I have the feeling that he is not achieving anything. I am sure that he is doing his best and tries, but I would feel so depressed if all his efforts were to remain without success.'

Fey remained at Brazzà during July and August, looking after her boys and the household while Detalmo was at Mortara. 'It feels so good to be able at last to write freely and not have to fear the censor and the political police,' he wrote on 2 August. 'I feel full of confidence. I know that the laws are now humane, just and reasonable. Not any more the oppressive and humiliating Fascist laws. I feel no affront is being made against my honour and dignity as a man . . . My darling Fey, I am sorry the events have been such that we haven't had a chance to concentrate on ourselves. Life is dynamic and whirls like a wind. The old days are gone . . .'

On 3 September, the Allies invaded the Italian mainland, landing at Salerno, 165 miles south of Rome. Detalmo could barely contain his excitement. 'Events are precipitating!' he wrote to Fey. 'The Eighth Army has landed in Calabria . . . With Russia pressing so steadily on the Eastern Front, the situation should deteriorate very rapidly. Germany will have to shrink inside her own territory, and it is not an impossibility that within two months the war in Europe will be over.' Not long before, he had also cautioned her to leave for Rome at the first sign of danger. 'Put your safety and the children's first; our property and our belongings second,' he urged. Reluctant to leave Brazzà and believing it to be the safest place for the boys, she had replied sharply: 'I am preparing everything so that I can leave if things deteriorate. But let me tell you this: I want to leave Brazzà as late as possible for the sake of the children. Here they eat well, and it is not hot. In Rome it is hot, and the food will be bad.'

Detalmo's long-held ambition was to participate in building a democratic future for Italy after twenty years of Fascism. The moment he had been waiting for came on 8 September when, following secret negotiations between the Allies and Marshal Badoglio, the new head of the Italian government, Italy surrendered to the Allies. As soon as the armistice was announced, Detalmo opened the gates of the prison camp at Mortara, enabling some 3,000 Allied prisoners of war to escape. He then left his regiment and went into hiding with the partisans.

At Brazzà, Fey's 'quiet and uneventful life' was drawing to a close.

Within hours of the armistice, German troops began to pour across the border as Hitler moved to occupy northern Italy.

As these momentous events unfolded, alone and cut off from Detalmo, Fey was forced to make the biggest decision of her life. Was it best to stay at Brazzà with the children or would it be safer to leave?

Inexorably, she and the boys were about to be drawn into the Nazi machine.

PART FOUR

10.

Fey described the events of 8 September 1943:

When the voice of General Badoglio came over the radio unexpectedly to announce that an armistice had been signed between Italy and
the Allies, I was lonely but living tranquilly at Brazzà with my two
little boys and my sister-in-law, Marina. The house and farm were
running smoothly and the war seemed very distant from us.

I remember that evening so well. I was having dinner with 'Uncle'
Augusto Rosmini, an old friend of Detalmo's mother. A distinguished old gentleman with grey hair and a pointed beard, Rosmini
was a widower who had made a habit of coming to Brazzà every
summer. Ever since his wife's death, he had worn all her jewellery
under his clothes, rings on various fingers and gold bracelets down
his arms. He was a funny man, 'a good sort', as Detalmo said.

After Badoglio's announcement, Rosmini and I looked at each
other in shock. We realized that this was by no means the end of
Italy's troubles. German troops were posted all over the country, and
the Nazis would never permit it to fall into Allied hands. A period of
disorder lay ahead and it was likely that Italy would become far more
of a battlefield than it had been. My heart sank when I thought of my
family in Germany; correspondence would certainly become more
difficult. And Detalmo in Mortara? What would happen to him?

Rosmini and I spent the next twenty-four hours glued to the radio.
The Germans had already surrounded Rome and were fighting the
Italian army for control of the city. At lunchtime, we heard that German troops had taken over Bologna, Venice and Florence. From time
to time, one of the farm workers came in to report the rumours
circulating in the neighbourhood. Convoys of Allied ships had been
sighted in the Bay of Naples and were preparing to land on the coast
north of Rome – a rumour that was later contradicted. Naples itself

was in ruins following an Allied bombardment. Closer to home, the Germans had commandeered the railway lines in and out of Udine, and trainloads of troops and war equipment were streaming south. Given the chaos on the railways, Rosmini was anxious to get home and he left later that day, leaving Marina and me on our own, wondering what to do.

The next morning, Fey asked Nonino to bring the pony and trap round to the front of the villa. Brazzà was completely cut off; no post, no papers, and the telephone was dead. Even the local tram service had stopped running. Anxious to know whether Detalmo thought she and the boys should leave Brazzà, Fey wanted Nonino to take her to Udine to see if she could telephone her husband from there.

Avoiding the main road, they took the back route to Udine – a journey they made twice a week on market days. As they trotted along the white gravel tracks, through fields of maize, skirting farms and pretty hilltop villages, Fey was reassured by the peace in contrast to the alarming reports on the radio. 'It was a still, lovely morning. The figs were out on the trees and the women were working in the fields and tending the vines along the side of the road. Everything seemed to be carrying on as normal. The only difference was that the fires lit by the *contadini* [peasant farmers] to celebrate the armistice were still smouldering outside the farms. We passed women on bicycles, taking the milk to the *latteria*, the great churns balanced on the handlebars. Some called out to say their men were back from the army.'

On the outskirts of Udine, the roads were crowded with Italian soldiers hurrying back to their villages. After deserting from their units, many had swapped their uniforms for civilian clothes and were identifiable only by their military-issue boots. Orders had gone out to deport Italian soldiers to work camps in Germany, and to evade capture those that were able to had paid the exorbitant prices now being charged for items of clothing. Fey spoke to some of the soldiers. They told stories of total confusion and disorganization in the Italian Army, particularly among the high-ranking officers whose priority was 'to disappear'.

Arriving in Udine, Fey went to her usual bar in the Piazza San Giacomo. It was where she liked to go on market days to catch up with the local gossip. The sixteenth-century square, with its tight cobbles and tall, pastel-coloured houses, was one of the finest in the city and as she walked across it the festive atmosphere struck her as incongruous; crowds of Italian soldiers, apparently indifferent to the approaching Germans, were celebrating the disbanding of their units. They stood chatting in groups, or strolling up and down with wives and girlfriends, clean-shaven and intent on showing off their new civilian clothes.

Fey quickly established that the Germans had taken over all the telephone lines in the north of Italy, preventing her from ringing Detalmo. The bar was packed with people exchanging rumours and information, many of whom she knew. Pia Tacoli, who lived on a neighbouring estate at Brazzà, had just arrived after a difficult journey from Milan. German soldiers had boarded the train at all the stops, asking young men for their papers, and she had seen a number of deserters disguised as women. Others reported that large numbers of Allied POWs – escapees from Fascist-run prison camps – were hiding in the woods outside the city. The main concern, however, was that the Communist partisans in the mountains around Udine would use the hiatus to take control of the area. Yet, as one man had heard, 'They're saying just give us your weapons, go home, and we'll take care of the Germans.'

On returning to Brazzà, Fey half-expected to find Detalmo there. There were so many soldiers in the area, she imagined she would see him coming up the drive at any moment. Reassured by her visit to Udine, there seemed no reason to leave Brazzà; the neighbourhood was quiet and aside from the truckloads of Wehrmacht troops on the main road – which was a good 3 miles from the house – she had not seen any Germans.

But then, on the morning of 12 September, four days after the armistice, Field Marshal Kesselring, the commander of German forces in Italy, made an announcement on the radio. All territory occupied by the Germans, which encompassed the whole of Italy north of Rome, was to be subject to martial law. Strikes or any other attempts at resistance would be tried by court martial. The railways and the postal service were to be placed under German control, meaning that private letters would be banned and telephone conversations severely restricted.

Fey was with her sister-in-law, Marina, when Kesselring made the announcement. Soon after the bulletin ended, one of the farm workers came rushing in to say that large numbers of German troops, equipped with tanks and anti-aircraft guns, had occupied Tarcento, 10 miles to the north; more troops were heading towards Udine. 'Marina, infected by the general panic, did everything to persuade me to leave Brazzà and flee south to the protection of Detalmo's relatives. I did not want to go. As the daughter of a diplomat, my childhood had been spent living in embassies and Brazzà was my first proper home. Also, I felt that since German was my mother tongue, I might be of use in protecting the house and our contadini in the event of a German occupation. Nevertheless, I was swayed by Marina and our manager, Marchetti,* who kept quoting Detalmo's injunction that I should not hesitate to leave immediately if danger threatened. Unable to contact Detalmo, I gave in.'

After packing a few essential things, they left that afternoon. 'It was a flight in the true sense of the word,' Fey remembered. 'We abandoned everything as it was, giving only the vaguest orders to Nonino to hide our linen and silverware with the contadini. I knew that detailed instructions were necessary in such situations, but there was simply no time to issue any. As we drove away, I was filled with misgivings. Abandoning the families who worked for us seemed like an act of cowardice.'

Twenty contadini families worked at Brazzà, many of whom had been there for generations. The mutually dependent relationship between the Pirzio-Birolis and their contadini was enshrined in a farming system that dated back to the Middle Ages. As in most of northern and central Italy, farm workers did not receive wages, nor

---

* Guido Marchetti was the estate overseer at Brazzà.

were they required to pay rent to the landowner for the right to work their land; instead, they were engaged under the *mezzadria* or share-cropping system. In return for a house and the use of fields, farm buildings, carts and plough animals, peasant farmers gave 50 per cent of every crop harvest, and half of any profit made from the sale of livestock, vegetables, eggs and milk, back to the *padrone*.

Besides cultivating the fields and tending livestock, the peasant *capofamiglia*, or head of the family, was required to maintain his parcel of land. During the winter months, he had to keep the ditches clean, mend walls and terraces, plant trees, prune vines, and repair farm tools worn down after the harvest. It was a contract that involved not just his own labour but that of his entire family; women in the household worked in the fields and milked the cows, and children as young as four worked too, feeding the animals, helping with the grape harvest, and pressing the hay down in the barns.

The relationship between landlord and peasant demanded a continuing personal interaction, which went far beyond the business of the farm. The padrone was expected to guide and protect his contadini; in the event of poor weather or crop failure, he was supposed to be a source of capital, someone the families could resort to in a crisis. Yet many landowners abused the relationship by tyrannizing their peasants or fiddling account books, thereby reducing the contadini's share. Poor capital investment and the landowner's right to summarily evict tenants were other sources of grievance and, after the First World War, the harshness of the mezzadria system led to strikes and uprisings throughout the north of Italy. In response, the Fascists supported the landowners, crushing the uprisings and bringing further suffering to oppressed contadini on estates where the system had broken down.

At Brazzà, however, the relationship between the Pirzio-Birolis and their tenants had remained on a harmonious footing. This was largely due to the efforts of Detalmo's American grandmother, Cora di Brazzà Slocomb. A wealthy heiress, her father, a New Orleans entrepreneur, had founded a chain of hardware stores in the mid nineteenth century. As a young girl, Cora had been sent to Europe for her education. Speaking French, German and Italian, she settled in Rome in her early twenties, becoming an accomplished painter and mixing with other artists and intellectuals.

In 1887, at the age of twenty-five, Cora met and married Count Detalmo, a scientist and engineer. Moving to Brazzà, she was shocked by the poverty in the neighbouring villages and the poor standard of education and hygiene. Cora's progressive ideas meant that, unusually for her time and class, she rejected the traditional view of charity, believing it was not enough to hand out money to the less fortunate, but that a means had to be found to raise their status and to give them greater dignity.

An early campaigner for female emancipation, Cora resolved to use a part of her fortune to change the position of women at Brazzà. Recognizing that their submissive role was accentuated by poverty, she sought to make them financially independent. Astutely, she found a way to do this within the framework of the existing silk industry, enabling the women to continue their labour on the farms. In the spring months, the contadini at Brazzà cultivated silkworms, selling the cocoons on to reelers at Tricesimo, Friuli's main silk market. Seeing an opportunity to create a local weaving industry, Cora established a lacemaking school in one of the villages on the estate. She oversaw the work of design and production herself and, after the success of the first school, she established six more, creating extra income for hundreds of women in the area. Additionally, she founded a toy factory in a nearby town, where women were employed making stuffed toys, and she also encouraged Delser, a local lady, to open a factory to produce the 'Brazzà biscuit', a type of shortbread.

Cora campaigned on other social issues and by the mid 1890s she had become a celebrity figure in America after taking up the cause of a young Italian woman convicted of killing her lover. Only the second woman to be sentenced to death in the US, Maria Barbella, an émigré to New York, had killed the man after he seduced her and reneged on a promise of marriage. Using her social standing, Cora successfully campaigned for a reprieve, saving Barbella from the electric chair. She also used her public profile to promote Brazzà lace and by the early twentieth century it had become world-famous, winning a gold medal at trade exhibitions in London, Paris and Chicago.

When Fey married Detalmo, Cora was still alive but the two women had not met. In 1906, at the age of forty-four, Cora suffered a mental breakdown from which she never recovered, and thereafter she was consigned to a private asylum. A much-loved figure, the memory of her was still strong among the contadini at Brazzà and, as the new custodian, Fey had a sense of obligation towards them which was in part motivated by a desire to honour Cora's reputation.

Cora would not have run away. This thought preoccupied Fey as she left Brazzà with Marina and the children. There were no delays at the station and they caught the first train to the south. It was hot and crowded and Roberto, then a twenty-month-old baby, cried throughout the journey. Fey thought it was because he sensed the fear and nervousness in the packed carriage, which was full of people fleeing from the Germans.

At Venice, Marina got off the train to stay with her cousin, Princess Pia Valmarana, who owned a large palazzo on the Grand Canal. But Fey decided to press on to Padua, where Detalmo's other cousins, the Papafavas, lived.

The Papafavas owned Frassanelle, one of the finest neoclassical villas in the Veneto. Situated 7 miles to the west of Padua, it was surrounded by a large estate which had been in the family's possession since the thirteenth century. Fey had not visited, but Detalmo had told her about the splendid villa, with its two private chapels and the famous ornamental staircase that ran down through the woods, linking the villa to the estate farm.

Descended from the family of Da Carrara, lords of Padua in the fourteenth century, Count Novello Papafava was a committed anti-Fascist and had repeatedly offered Detalmo the villa as a refuge. Knowing that the count had eight children, Fey chose to go there rather than to Princess Valmarana's palace, which, full of priceless objects and expensive furnishings, was less child-friendly. She was also keen to escape from her sister-in-law, whose indiscriminating fondness for grand society, including Fascist aristocrats, irritated her.

★

Fey and the boys had left Udine just in time. That evening, upwards of 2,000 Germans occupied the city. 'I arrived in Piazza Vittorio just as the bulk of the Germans were arriving,' one resident wrote. 'There was this big military parade of tanks and armoured vehicles – all being driven by kids of 18 or 20 years old. Some were even younger. They were wearing shorts and looked as if they had just been playing football. I feel sorry for them when I think that their parents and siblings must already have died in the war, and now they are taking their place and will probably suffer the same fate. The locals turned out in great numbers to watch this monstrous parade. I couldn't see any sign of anyone demonstrating any sympathy toward the Germans. Not a friendly crowd. No one waved, no one lifted a hand. Everyone was just a spectator. Very serious and silent. The Germans were nonplussed and even they seemed stunned by the terrible roar of these machines. At the barracks, our soldiers have surrendered and are being guarded by these kids. The Police have run off and thrown their pistols in the road. No one is standing up to the Germans.'

Within hours of the occupation, parties of German soldiers pasted flyers on the walls of the buildings in the centre of the city. Issued by the German High Command, the notices warned the citizens of the various penalties in operation under martial law:

Attention!

Italian troops resisting German orders will be treated like traitors! The officers and commanders of these troops will be made responsible for their actions and shot without mercy as traitors!

Orders to civilians!

– A Curfew is now in operation between 9 p.m. and 4 a.m.
– All weapons of war being held by Italian soldiers or civilians must be immediately handed in. The unlawful possession of any of these weapons, or any other object designed for military use, will be punishable by death. Looting and sabotage are also punishable with death.
– Those caught listening to British and American radio broadcasts will be subject to extreme punishment.

★

That same day, the SS launched an audacious raid on the hotel high up in the mountains in the Abruzzo region of central Italy in which Benito Mussolini was imprisoned. Since his arrest on 25 July, the Allies had moved the former dictator from prison to prison in an attempt to keep his whereabouts secret. But on 26 August, they settled on the Campo Imperatore Hotel, a ski resort, 7,000 feet above sea level in the Gran Sasso mountains. The hotel had been emptied of guests and 200 Italian carabinieri drafted in to guard the prisoner.

Hitler had been horrified by the humiliation of his ally and, the day after Mussolini's arrest, had personally charged Otto Skorzeny, a Waffen SS colonel, with his rescue. It had taken Skorzeny many weeks to find out where Mussolini was being held, and it was only by intercepting coded radio messages that he had been able to establish his exact location. How to rescue the man proved more challenging. The location of the Campo Imperatore, on the side of a mountain, ruled out a parachute drop. Aerial reconnaissance, however, revealed a small airfield nearby. Skorzeny decided to land a group of hand-picked commandos by glider – a risky option but the only one available.

In the early afternoon of 12 September, as the twelve gliders prepared to descend, Skorzeny realized that the airfield was not flat, as he believed, but on a steep hillside. It left him with no choice but to crash-land his commando team on the uneven but flatter ground in front of the hotel. With the loss of just one glider, the risk paid off and, despite being outnumbered by the carabinieri, the SS commandos quickly secured the area after the guards surrendered without a single shot being fired.

Radioing for assistance, Skorzeny asked for a small STOL (Short Take-Off and Landing) aircraft to be flown in. After it touched down on the short, rocky plateau, Mussolini was brought out of the hotel and bundled aboard. Although the plane was designed for just one passenger, Skorzeny insisted on accompanying him; twelve SS men held it back by its wings while the pilot revved the engine at full power. On a given signal, they let go and it took off, but the aircraft failed to gain enough height and one of its wheels hit a rock, causing it to veer off the plateau and down towards the valley below. Only the pilot's skill saved the situation; struggling to maintain control, he managed to pull the plane out of its dive and Mussolini was transferred safely to Rome.

Two days later he met Hitler at the Führer's headquarters near Rastenburg on the Eastern Front. They agreed that Mussolini would return to German-occupied northern Italy as the puppet head of the Italian Social Republic, based at Salò on Lake Garda.

Italy was now formally divided. The Allies and Marshal Badoglio's government controlled the area south of Salerno; the rest of the country, by far the greater part, was in the hands of Mussolini's puppet government – de facto, the Germans.

Fey had been at Frassanelle for ten days when she received a panicked telephone call from Marchetti, the estate overseer at Brazzà: 'He was at his wits' end because the villa had been requisitioned by SS troops. He said that the soldiers were behaving rather badly, treating the place as if it were their own. But he also had good news: a message had arrived from Detalmo, who was safe and hiding out with the partisans near Milan. Straight away, I decided to return to Brazzà to see if I could intervene. I was worried for the contadini working on the estate and for the house, and I felt that if I was there, being German, it might help the situation. I went alone, leaving the children with the Papafavas.'

The scene that greeted Fey at Udine station was chaotic. The Germans were now deporting thousands of Italian soldiers to work camps in Germany and three or four trainloads were passing through the station every day. The soldiers were locked into cattle wagons, without food or water, and the conditions on board were appalling. On the northbound platform, local women, fearing their own sons and husbands might be in the wagons, had set up a long table, laid out with bread, food and cigarettes. When the trains stopped, the women rushed to hand the provisions out. Other women collected the notes the soldiers dropped on the platform in the hope that someone would send them on to their relatives. Sometimes the trains did not stop and, as the long lines of wagons passed slowly through the station, a flurry of notes fell on the platform. Fifteen-year-old Rosanna Boratto, who worked as a shop assistant in the centre of town, collected the notes every morning: 'I did not live in Udine, but it was my stop on the train to work. So I could only collect the notes between 7.20 a.m. and 7.50 a.m. because I had to rush off to work . . . The soldiers threw them out. All you could see were their fingers because the bars in the windows of the wagons were so narrow, they couldn't get their hands through. The notes fluttered on to the platform and I picked them up without anyone stopping me. I didn't send them off immediately but kept them in my handbag. One evening at home, I told my parents and showed them the notes I had collected. We posted all of them.'

Nonino was waiting for Fey outside the station with the pony and trap. Driving through the centre of the city, it was a very different place from the one she had left ten days before. The Germans were everywhere and the locals, hurrying along with their heads down, looked anxious. Everywhere, the latest edicts from the German High Command were posted on the walls of churches and historic buildings. Notice after notice had been slapped haphazardly, one on top of the other as the number of offences punishable under martial law had grown. The most recent edict related to Allied prisoners of war: 'Any Allied POWs that are being harboured must be handed in. If Italians offer them shelter, food, or help of any kind, they will be subject to terrible punishment.' Another announced that 'the German authorities will immediately arrest those who do not obey an order and they will be dealt with severely.'

Outside the shops, parties of soldiers were loading vehicles with food and other supplies they had commandeered. Fascists, once again in charge of public institutions, strutted through the streets in their black uniforms, having been reappointed to the positions they held before Mussolini's fall. 'Generally, people are afraid they will carry out vendettas and reprisals against those who replaced them earlier in the summer,' one resident reported. He went on to describe the racket the Fascists were running at depots formerly belonging to the Italian Army: 'People are rolling home big barrels of olive oil and carrying away big sacks of coffee on their backs. They're even taking bales of leather, linen, furs, and shoes and boots from the depot in Via Grazzano . . . The people getting the stuff are people who know how to hold their own, speak German or who are friends of the Fascists. Or they are people who pay 20L at the entrance to get in . . . Anyone out of favour caught trying to loot the supplies is shot. Already, at one warehouse, three have been executed by the Fascists.'

Leaving Udine, Fey noticed the roads were empty except for women, children and the elderly. Over the course of the twenty-minute drive to Brazzà, Nonino told her what had been happening while she was away. On 15 September, three days after she left for Frassanelle, the Germans had issued an ultimatum: anyone between the ages of eighteen and forty-five, excluding married women with children, had four days to prove they were in gainful employment. Once the deadline expired, those without occupation would be arrested and deported to Germany. To escape deportation, hundreds of deserters had fled to the mountains to join the partisans. Others were hiding out in the woods and in farm buildings. Before fleeing, the men had thrown down their arms and ammunition, and there had been daily incidents of death and mutilation resulting from children finding and playing with the weapons. There had also been a number of murders, committed by partisans who had come down from the mountains to kill Fascists and those they suspected of collaborating with the Germans.

As they turned into the drive at Brazzà, Fey was dismayed to see that it was crammed with SS troops and military vehicles: 'As I had feared, they belonged to an elite corps and were therefore the worst imaginable soldiers. I rushed up and presented myself to the major in charge who, to my surprise, told me the unit was moving on.'

After the SS troops left, Fey was convinced that her original instinct to remain at Brazzà was right. With the neighbourhood in a state of lawlessness and the possibility of more German troops arriving, she needed to be *in situ* to protect the house and the families working on the farm. On the spur of the moment, she decided to return to Frassanelle to collect the boys. If she and the children were living there and she gathered round as many friends as possible, it would be difficult for other troops to occupy the place.

Her plan, however, proved short-lived: 'I was just boarding the train for Padua when Nonino suddenly arrived, panting, on the platform. He had frantically cycled the 12 kilometres from Brazzà to tell me that within minutes of my departure another contingent of German troops had occupied the house. Nonino had learned that the officers were dining at Al Monte, a well-known restaurant in the centre of Udine. As my heart was now set on staying at Brazzà, I jumped into a taxi. When I arrived at the restaurant the officers were still there and, hoping to win their sympathy, I made up a story. I told them that I had left my two small children in Padua temporarily, and we had nowhere to live for the winter. I said I would be infinitely grateful if they could put aside at least a couple of rooms for our use. Initially irritable and uncooperative, the officers agreed to discuss it at Brazzà the next day.'

Determined to hide as many things as she could while there was still time, Fey asked the officers for a car to take her home: 'To my surprise, they agreed, and I drove to Brazzà in a beautiful little Fiat 1500, which had almost certainly been requisitioned from some poor Italian.'

The officers were airmen from the *Luftnachrichten-Regiment 200*, which was responsible for the Luftwaffe's radar network in occupied Italy. At a meeting with the unit's quartermaster the next morning, it was agreed that she and the children would occupy three rooms on the first floor of the villa. They were some of the best rooms in the house; one, a spacious sitting room, led on to steps down to the garden; another led out to a magnificent terrace, with a view over the fields to Modotto, a picturesque village owned by Detalmo's family.

Satisfied with the outcome of her meeting, Fey returned to Padua to fetch the children.

In reaching her decision, she was unaware of the danger posed by her husband's activities in the Resistance. Not having heard from Detalmo since the armistice, she did not know that agents from the Sicherheitsdienst – the German security service – were searching for him throughout the north of Italy.

A warning note sounded on her return: 'An SS officer was waiting when I arrived back at the house with the boys. I was about to take the children indoors when he stopped me, asking if we could have a few words in private. He then proceeded to ask me all manner of questions, at first, fairly politely, but then as my answers proved unhelpful, he became more hostile. His main interest was Detalmo's family. He told me they had killed a partisan leader by the name of Pirzio-Biroli.* I knew it wasn't Detalmo because this had happened in Albania during an attack on the airport at Tirana. But then he said they suspected another member of the family, who had distributed anti-Nazi propaganda. Of course I thought of Detalmo at this point, but I didn't say anything and the officer was unable to get anything out of me. Finally, irritated by my unhelpful replies, he left.'

As soon as the unpleasant interrogation was over, Fey sat down to read two letters from Detalmo, which had arrived in her absence. They were signed 'Giuseppe', the alias they had agreed he would use if the need arose. She opened the letters with a heavy heart. While, evidently, the SS did not know that the man they were looking for was her husband, with the Germans in occupation at Brazzà it was now impossible for Detalmo to come home. The best she could hope was that he would join the local partisans and hide out in the nearby mountains:

12 Sept 1943

Dear Fey

Don't write to me until I give you a new address. At the moment, I am continually on the move. Writing is difficult, and I'm not even sure if the post works. Anyway, don't worry about me. I am well, and I am eating well. I'm leading a rather adventurous life, which is not without its attractions. After I have told you everything, you will never again be able to say that I'm not sporty.

Love and kisses,
Giuseppe

The second letter was dated three days later. Clearly, he had received her message asking whether she should leave Brazzà:

---

* This was Detalmo's cousin, Carlo, who had joined the partisans in Albania, where he was stationed as an Italian officer.

Dear Fey

I don't know if this letter will reach you. I also wrote a couple of days ago. I am writing to tell you that I'm going south. I'll write as soon as possible, but I can't say when that will be. From here I cannot advise what would be best for you and the little ones. Ask friends for advice and then decide. I hope that soon we'll be together again. Lots of love to Corradino and Robertino and thousands of kisses for you. I am totally in love with you, and you are continually in my thoughts.

Yours,
Giuseppe

Fey was shocked to see that Detalmo was 'going south'. It could only mean that, whatever he had done, it was too dangerous for him to remain in the north. Briefly, it occurred to her that his activities in the Resistance threatened her own safety and that of the boys. But then if this were the case, she reasoned, he would have told her to leave.

She and the boys quickly settled into their rooms. 'Then after only a very few days,' she wrote, 'I received a covert message from Detalmo, delivered by one of our contadini. To my great excitement, he was in Udine, hiding in the apartment of our dear friends, the Giacomuzzis, and wanted to see me. I passed the word to Nonino, who quietly prepared the carriage and our little white horse, Mirko. Soon we were rattling down to our secret appointment. Detalmo was a little ragged and thin, but otherwise in good shape. The emotion of seeing each other again was enormous.'

Fey spent the night with Detalmo at the Giacomuzzis'. It was then that he explained why he was on the run from the SS. Since the armistice, when he had opened the prison gates at Mortara, enabling thousands of Allied POWs to escape, he had used his connections in the Resistance to help a number of the men cross the Alps to Switzerland or to join the Allied forces in the south.

As it was impossible for Detalmo to return to Brazzà, they decided that he should try to reach Rome, where he could disappear and play an active role in the emerging underground movement. On her part, Fey was adamant that she should remain at Brazzà. It was the best environment for the children and she was confident that she could handle the occupying troops. Further, if she was there, she could protect the house and the contadini from the Germans. Reluctantly, Detalmo agreed. He told her the decision was hers, but again cautioned her to go to Frassanelle at the first sign of danger.

The next morning, Nonino returned with the carriage. Despite the risk of being discovered by the Germans, Detalmo was determined to sneak into Brazzà to say goodbye to the boys. 'Nonino dropped us on the small road that ran round the estate,' Fey remembered, 'and we stole in through a gate, praying we would not be seen. The gate opened into the vegetable garden and from there we were able to dash through a small wood to the house. As soon as we got inside, I went to look for Ernesta and Cilla, our maids.* "Remember, you have not seen Detalmo," I told them. "If the Germans ask about a strange man, tell them it was a travelling salesman." It was terribly dangerous but worth it. The children were delighted by the secrecy of the visit, and we all spent a happy day together, the doors and windows of our room tight shut. After dark, Detalmo slipped away through the garden, out to the road where Nonino was waiting for him with Mirko and the carriage. Carrying false documents, he left for Rome. I felt proud of him, even though it meant I was now on my own with the children.'

* There were three maids at Brazzà: Ernesta, Cilla and Mila.

In the interests of protecting her two small boys and the contadini working on the estate, Fey set about establishing a rapport with the Germans. Anxious to ensure that no suspicion should fall on her as a result of Detalmo's clandestine activities, she went out of her way to be as accommodating as possible.

There were some forty airmen living in the house and in make-shift barracks around the park. Stationed at Campoformido, a nearby airfield, their job was to monitor Allied aircraft flying over the region and to coordinate the distribution of planes and supplies to Luftwaffe bases further south.

Fey's primary contact was with the two senior officers, Major Ottokar Eisermann and Lieutenant Hans Kretschmann. In Major Eisermann she found a sympathetic figure. As she acknowledged, he made the day-to-day routine of life under German occupation easier than it might otherwise have been: 'It was my good luck that I had a commander with whom I got on. Middle-aged, stout and slow-moving, Eisermann had a soft spot for women. He considered it his bounden duty to help and protect me and would often pay me little compliments in the style of the last century. He regarded all social duties, including his afternoon and evening get-togethers with his fellow officers, as a boring obligation. What he liked best was his morning stroll through the park, sauntering along, hands behind his back, becoming overexcited at the sight of some exotic tree or an unfamiliar flower.'

Kretschmann, however, the major's much younger aide-de-camp, was a very different character. Tall, slim with deep-set blue eyes and prominent cheekbones, he was the unit's political officer. In this capacity, it was his job to indoctrinate the airmen in Nazi ideology and to reinforce combat morale through training lessons and weekly lectures. Like Eisermann, Kretschmann was scrupulously polite to Fey; yet, from the outset, she was wary of him: 'Educated by the Nazis and soaked in their propaganda, Kretschmann lacked flexibility of thought. I do not believe he had a single independent idea in his head. His opinions had been learned at school, in the Hitler Youth, and at military college. While he was socially adept, I felt his chivalry was a tool he had picked up and cultivated for his own advancement. Unlike Eisermann, it did not come naturally to him, nor had he learned it by example from his family. Thus, there was a danger that in a crisis Kretschmann would discard such virtues as quickly as he had acquired them.'

Clearly ambitious, Kretschmann had a close relationship with the men under his command. He was a heavy drinker, and would take them to local bars where, after dinner, he would leap on to a table and tap-dance to their wild applause. But he was also prone to depression and his volatile temperament was another reason for Fey to be suspicious of him.

While she quickly established good relations with the Germans, their animosity towards Italians placed her in an awkward position. Deeply resentful at having been drafted in to defend Italy after the Italians had betrayed them, their anger was compounded by the large numbers deserting from the Italian Army, content to leave it up to German forces to defeat the Allies. The airmen were further incensed by the partisans' actions against German military personnel. Following the armistice, snipers had killed a number of soldiers in the neighbourhood. Others had died in ambushes and random attacks on sentries' positions outside depots and along the main roads. The consequence was that, in Fey's presence, and in front of her domestic staff and farm workers, the airmen made derogatory remarks, repeating the racist jokes in circulation and dismissing Italy as a 'nation of donkey drivers and chestnut sellers'.

With the exception of Fascists who had benefited from Mussolini's return, the locals' animosity towards the Germans was equally visceral. The deportations, the commandeering of food and the threat of death or severe punishment if they contravened the edicts of martial rule provoked hatred, heightened by their fear.

Fey found herself caught in the middle: 'My position as a German was not that comfortable at Brazzà. On the one hand, I had people of my own nationality staying in the house. In spite of their faults, I could not fail to understand and frequently sympathize with them. On the other hand, I had to maintain the distance appropriate for an Italian towards an invader. I was, for instance, often tempted to accept offers of car rides to Udine from the Germans. But even when I was in the greatest hurry, I refused. I knew how such little things could create the wrong impression.'

Despite Fey's efforts to please both sides, word of her close relationship with the Germans quickly spread. To begin with, people trudged great distances to ask her to intervene with Nazi officials, either on their own behalf or more usually for a son or brother who was about to be deported. 'They came in the belief that I, being German, could obtain more than an Italian,' Fey wrote, 'but they were mistaken. I was often treated with more suspicion than the Italians by the German authorities in Udine. The little word "von" in my surname showed all too clearly that I came from an aristocratic family, and the Nazis had never liked aristocrats. Despite hours of running back and forth between German officials, I was not able to save anyone from being deported, which of course made the local people more sceptical about me.'

Brazzà lay in the parish of Santa Margherita, which consisted of nine villages, four of them no more than hamlets. For the population of 3,160, the way of life had changed little since medieval times and everyone knew each other's business. The poverty in the tight-knit communities, where nearly everyone was related and those who owned a bicycle or who could afford to buy wedding clothes were regarded as wealthy, meant that, with no other form of entertainment, the church and other people's lives were a central focus.

In these deeply devout communities, the priest kept a close eye on the moral behaviour of his parishioners, which he then reported to the Vatican. Once a year he was required to fill in a questionnaire – one that the Vatican sent out to every parish priest in Italy – enquiring about the moral and religious standing of his congregation. His answers for the year 1939, gleaned at confession and through his position as the leading authority in the parish, reveal how closely people's lives were observed:

What is the percentage of church attendance in the parish? – *99%*.

Are there any groups in the parish who are against Catholicism or circulating anti-Catholic propaganda? – *No, apart from two infantile old men who have become the object of ridicule.*

What is the moral behaviour of the parishioners? – *Among the young there is a spirit of indifference, which is a reflection of the times, and libertine behaviour is creeping in.*

Are women wearing provocative clothing? – *Yes.*

Are indecently dressed women staying away from church? – *A few.*

Are women entering church bare-headed? – *No.*

Are there any public or private scandals? – *Yes, because of lax virtues among women.*

How is this being dealt with? – *Their mothers are being talked to and it is being addressed in sermons.*

Is there any swearing or alcoholism? – *Some.*

Are there any concubine unions? – *Yes, three.*

What's the average annual illegitimate birth? – *4.*

Is the spirit of the family still extant? – *Yes.*

Are people still reciting the rosary? – *Yes, except when they are working in the fields.*

Are there any Jews in the parish? – *No.*

Are there superstitious practices and seances? – *No, but some local superstitions continue to exist.*

The culture of reporting meant that at Brazzà, knowing Fey's true loyalties, the contadini confided information that she then had to keep from the Germans. She knew where deserters were hiding; she knew which landowners were concealing Allied POWs in the woods on their estates; she even knew the names of local priests involved in organizing the burgeoning resistance groups in the area. While touched by her employees' trust, it meant lying to Eisermann and Kretschmann when they asked about particular individuals or questioned her about hideouts that could be used by deserters and Allied prisoners of war.

Yet the fact that the two officers took her into their confidence was proof that her strategy was working. Calculatingly, she had set out to convince them that she was simply a naïve young mother: 'Whenever the war or the Nazis were discussed, I was careful not to express an opinion. This was partly strategic and partly because I did not trust myself. I knew I had to avoid getting entangled in political discussions in case my hatred of the Nazis slipped out.'

Besides the strain of having to play a double game with Eisermann and Kretschmann, Fey had other worries. She was fighting constantly with Bovolenta, the farm manager at Brazzà, who disagreed with her methods. A shifty man in his late sixties, he resented taking instructions from a woman – particularly a German one – and Fey suspected that he was cheating her by doctoring the weight of crop yields in order to sell the estate's produce on the black market.

She was also worried about her parents in Germany. With private letters forbidden, she had not heard from them since the armistice. The Allies were bombing Berlin and Munich and she was desperate to know they were all right. Relaying her anxiety to Major Eisermann, he agreed to allow her to use the military post, providing she called herself Private August von Hassell and used a military postal number.

'All is in chaos here,' she wrote to her mother at the end of October. 'I think Brazzà needs my vigilant eye. The situation is fairly difficult; the Italians hate everything German. I have not heard from you, which worries me a lot, especially when I know of those terrifying air raids. Then there is the separation from my dear husband for who knows how long; and lastly, my house is occupied by troops, so I have become a guest in my own home, a most unpleasant feeling!'

Almuth, who was living with her parents in Ebenhausen, wrote back immediately. She began her letter with a cryptic message confirming that the 'official' post – i.e. the military post – was their only chance of remaining in touch: 'My dear little soldier. Officially, the post is working again, but only officially. Tell my sister [meaning Fey] that it is still pointless to write directly.' Almuth went on to describe the bombing raids in Munich and Berlin. While it was comforting to know that her family was alive, hearing their frightening experiences heightened Fey's anxiety, and she was also troubled by the fact that, overseen as the military post was by the censor, it was impossible to know what was really happening or what they really thought. She had no means of judging how close her father and his circle were to eliminating Hitler or the extent to which he was in danger from the Gestapo.

Above all else, Fey missed Detalmo. He had been gone for almost a month and in that time she had had just one message from him, delivered by a friend who was visiting Brazzà, to say he had arrived safely in Rome. Hand-delivered messages were the only means of communication and the opportunities were few and far between. During the long evenings alone at Brazzà after she had put the boys to bed, just to hear Detalmo's voice, she reread his letters from Mortara. 'Darling, I miss you and the children very much. The long period at Brazzà ended so suddenly that I haven't had much chance to feel it taken away . . . Darling little Fey, I want you to feel that I am very near to you, always behind you. So you must not be afraid and feel alone.'

Early in November, Fey learned from Major Eisermann that large numbers of troops were being drafted into the area. Following a crackdown in Gorizia in the eastern part of Friuli, thousands of men belonging to the Communist Garibaldi partisan brigades had fled west, and were hiding out in the mountains behind Brazzà. They now controlled a number of the roads and mountain passes, threatening the Wehrmacht's supply routes from Austria.

That evening, fearing the region was about to become a battle zone, Fey wrote a panicked note to Detalmo, suggesting that she and the children should leave Brazzà and join him in Rome. By chance, a neighbour was leaving for the capital the following day and she promised to deliver the note.

Fey was not expecting a quick reply, but some days later, as she was working in the garden, she saw a shabbily dressed man coming up the drive whom she did not recognize.

It was mid November, a crisp, bright morning, and the boys were playing beside her. She watched as the man strode up to the front door and heard him ask the soldier on duty if she was at home. Immediately, she sensed that he belonged to the Resistance and that, in brazenly approaching the house, he was risking his life. While the Germans allowed her to come and go as she liked and did not screen her visitors, she hurried across the lawn and greeted the man like an old friend so as not to arouse the sentry's suspicion.

As soon as they were alone, the stranger told her he had come from Rome and had a letter from Detalmo. Leading him through the house to her private quarters, she assured him that they were safe, and offered him a meal after his long, dangerous journey. 'He gave me to understand that he was in Friuli to contact the partisans. He stayed for a while and, after the strain of trying to keep on good terms with both the locals and the Germans, it was a relief to be able to talk frankly to someone from the "outside". We discussed the war, Detalmo, and whether I should move to Rome with the children. He said there was plenty of food in the city and that air raids were infrequent. He also said that Detalmo was missing us and was keen for us to join him there.'

Detalmo's letter, the first Fey had received in a month, revealed that he had become active in the city's underground movement:

I am so happy to have this opportunity to write. I have been thinking so much of you all this time, and our separation has weighed heavily on my heart.

I haven't seen any of our usual friends, and nobody knows of my existence here. My main job is going to be *diplomatic* and will probably necessitate journeys. Of course, it is too soon yet to establish anything for certain. We have been, and are being, very active in many sectors. As far as I can see, I am not going to do military business anymore. This is also because I do not feel very much like shooting German soldiers. I always think they wear the uniform of Hans Dieter.

We still have many doubts as to the ability of the Italian political ship to keep afloat by itself. At any rate, we are uniting our efforts in an out-and-out struggle to make things work. My closest friend is going to deal with the press, and I shall cope with contacts abroad. In my spare time I go on with political economics, a little article writing for the United States (propaganda), and other things.

Progress in southern Italy is slow, but we are expecting major operations rather soon, which should speed matters up. The crisis in Germany is extremely acute and may lead to anything – from now on – at any moment. In one word, I believe we will meet again before spring comes and that it shall be for *always*.

If you feel safer down here, this is a chance for you to come down by car with the children. But you alone can judge what is best. In your considerations please put *first* your personal safety and the children's; *second*, the safety of our house and belongings. Don't be dominated by laziness to move; the journey by car is *easy*. There is plenty of food in Rome . . .

Send me a reply without address, without my or your name or names of places or people. The bearer of this letter will tell you my second name.

My darling, I love you, and you stand out in my thoughts as something extremely great and important in life. I would like to be with you and console you a little. This is a great revolution, like the other great ones in history. We must make the new world. Let us only think of this difficult task and especially that we are going to work *together* with the children under the blessing of our great love. Put all other mournful thoughts aside . . .

Giuseppe

Still undecided as to what she should do, Fey remained at Brazzà for another week. Despite Eisermann's warning, the expected drive against the partisans had not happened and, while her position in regard to the Germans and Italians was awkward, she felt she could cope. Much as she missed Detalmo, she remained convinced that Brazzà, rather than Rome, was the best place for the children and she did not want to leave until she absolutely had to. Looking ahead, she also thought it unlikely that Brazzà would be bombed. 'Even if the front reached Udine, there was a good chance that Brazzà would not be touched, since it was not on the main road. I was sure the Germans would not stand and fight in the plain of Udine but withdraw to more defensible positions in the Alps.'

Then, on Radio London on 28 November, General Montgomery, the commander of the British 8th Army, broadcast a message to his troops. It was more than two months since the Allies had landed on the Italian mainland at Salerno and the much-vaunted 'two-week dash' up the coast to Rome had been thwarted by the Germans' defensive positions. Montgomery's message was a rallying call: 'The time has come to drive the Germans north of Rome. They have been outfought, and we can now go forward.'

Fearing she would lose touch with Detalmo entirely if the Allies occupied the city, Fey left for Rome a few days later. She did not take the children with her. If they were going to move there, her plan was to return to Brazzà to collect them.

The Germans had requisitioned all motor vehicles, including taxis, and Fey walked from Termini, the main railway station in the centre of the city. There had been no opportunity to send a message to Detalmo to say that she was coming, and when she arrived it was a complete surprise. 'He could hardly believe his eyes when he found me at the door. It was just wonderful to see him and we were so happy to be together again. So much had happened to both of us that it felt like years, not months, since we had parted in secrecy at the back of the park at Brazzà.'

Detalmo was living in a wing of the family's palazzo in the Via Panama with his sister, Marina, who had come down from Venice. A wide, tree-lined street, it was in an elegant quarter of the city, close to the Catacombs of Santa Priscilla. Marina, rather than Detalmo, was the official occupant and, with the Germans still searching for him in the north, he had kept his arrival in the city secret. He did not appear when she had visitors and saw only friends he could be sure of or people who, like himself, were hiding from the German authorities.

Fey found the apartment seething with conspiratorial activity. Detalmo was working for the *Partito d'Azione*, an underground centre-left political party. His job was to liaise with British and American intelligence agents, who were operating undercover in Rome. The work, which involved preparing the ground for the democratic government they hoped to establish once the Germans were defeated, was dangerous. Several of Detalmo's friends had already been arrested and were being held in the notorious Regina Coeli (Queen of Heaven) prison on the banks of the Tiber.

A succession of people moved in and out of the apartment at all times of the day and night and every room was used for some sort of clandestine purpose. The garage operated as a print room where maps, marking the fighting lines, were produced to help escaped prisoners of war rejoin the Allied forces in the south; the cellar was used as lodgings by two partisans, who slept behind bags of coal; upstairs, on the second floor, a small walled-up room had been built where people could hide in case of police raids. Other rooms, as Fey described, were used as meeting places: 'Much of the time was spent discussing the fine details for hiding such and such a person. There were so many people who needed to be hidden – partisans, Jews, and members of the underground political scene. Detalmo had close links to the Vatican and he was able to arrange for a large number to be concealed in convents and monasteries. As these properties belonged to the Holy See, they were extraterritorial and carried diplomatic immunity so were safe from the Germans.'*

Fey stayed in Rome for three weeks. During that time, the situation deteriorated. Despite Montgomery's message to the troops, neither the 8th Army nor the US 5th Army, whom they were fighting alongside, was able to break through the German lines. By the

---

* Some months later, in February 1944, several of these properties would be raided by the SS.

middle of December the two armies were digging in for the winter in a vulnerable position below the monastery of Monte Cassino.

It was clear to Fey and Detalmo that the Germans were unlikely to withdraw from Rome, as people had speculated earlier in the month. 'We spent hours discussing whether I should come to Rome with the children or remain in Friuli,' Fey wrote. 'It was so difficult to decide in the uncertainty that reigned; things could change dramatically from one minute to the next. The food situation in Rome was unstable and no one knew how much longer supplies would continue from the embattled countryside. Rome itself could turn into a war zone at any time. But what in the end decided us was Detalmo's secret activity, which, if discovered, would endanger us all if we were staying at Via Panama. So the idea of establishing a family base in Rome was dropped.'

Fey returned to Brazzà on 17 December. The situation in the neighbourhood was calm and she was thrilled to be back at home in time for Christmas with the boys: 'It was the first Corradino and Robertino were old enough to appreciate. The day after my arrival, to their great excitement, we began to make the decorations. On Christmas Eve I set up a large tree in our living room. When Nonino lit the candles, I threw the doors open, and in came the little boys, beaming with delight, followed by the maids, Mila and Ernesta, and finally the German officers. I felt sorry for them as they were so far away from home and I thought it would cheer them up to be included in our family circle. One of them even came dressed as Father Christmas, carrying the traditional bulging sack over his shoulder.'

From now on, contact with Detalmo would be intermittent. The Allies were bombing the trains in and out of Rome, making it difficult for couriers to deliver letters and messages. 'I don't know what's happening. No word from you for a long time,' he wrote a month after Fey left. 'It is v upsetting, as I long to know how you and the children are. Without news I feel so isolated . . . I had the negatives you gave me printed, which is a great consolation. The children's coats, made out of Grandfather Tirpitz's uniform, are still a bit big! Corradino shows a certain serenity, a self-confidence, while Robertino looks cross and unhappy about being photographed. It's very funny! A hug and kiss with all my heart.'

Fey was now resolved to remain at Brazzà for the duration of the war. All her fears were about the man she loved and the risks that came through her association with him. But, as the events of the coming year would prove, these fears were misplaced. The real danger lay in the one place in which she thought she and the boys would be safe.

12

The winter passed without incident. 'We never heard a gun or the whistle of a falling bomb whereas, for most of the rest of Europe, bombing raids and the apparatus of Nazi terror were the framework of people's daily lives,' Fey wrote.

Then, in the spring of 1944, Major General Ludolf von Alvensleben was appointed *Polizeiführer* (SS and police commander) in Udine. Previously attached to *Einsatzgruppe D*, the notorious SS paramilitary death squad, he had been implicated in some of the worst excesses of German rule in Russia. His unit's murderous activities in the Crimea were detailed in regular communiqués to Berlin. 'In the period under summary,' the reporting officer noted in the spring of 1942, 'further success was achieved concerning the arrest and the disposal of unreliable elements thanks to the extended network of secret informants . . . From 16 to 18 February 1,515 people were shot: 729 Jews, 271 Communists, 74 partisans, 421 Gypsies and asocial elements, and 20 saboteurs.'

At the beginning of the war, Alvensleben had served in Poland, where he was alleged to have murdered 4,247 Poles in the months after the Germans invaded.

Fey was not aware of his previous history, but he came from an old Prussian family known to her parents. In the hope that she could use the connection to gain a reprieve for Italians threatened with deportation, she invited him to tea. 'Knowing that he was in overall charge of the SS and Gestapo, I mentioned a man called Feliciano Nimis, a local lawyer, and told him that Nimis's deportation to Germany would have disastrous consequences for his family. To my surprise, Alvensleben acquiesced and the order was rescinded.'

Confident that the major general could be persuaded to reprieve others in the community, Fey issued further invitations. As it transpired, Nimis was her one success. However, the sight of the SS chief's car on the road to Brazzà was noted by the contadini working in the fields.

Within weeks of Alvensleben's appointment, the SS began to raid the villages around Brazzà. The locals called them *rastrellamenti* – rakings. Looking for men between the ages of eighteen and forty-five, the troops moved from house to house and combed woods and farm buildings.

Throughout the winter months, the Germans had been trying to conscript men of military age. Under pressure from the Allies in the south, reserves were needed for the Wehrmacht and for the labour battalions tasked with constructing defensive lines at strategic points across central Italy. Repeated orders went out for the men to volunteer at recruiting stations. But few had turned up and the raids were intended to flush out those in hiding.

The SS search parties set out from depots in Udine. 'Going past the barracks this morning, I saw ten trucks pulling out in convoy,' Umberto Paviotti, a resident of the city, noted in his diary on 10 May. 'Each one had about 10 Germans on board, armed to the teeth, and with a machine gun mounted on top of the vehicles. The backs of the trucks were empty.'

Paviotti, aged forty, was exempt from military service and his job as a water surveyor meant that he could move around freely on his bicycle. Some days later, he cycled past the school the SS had requisitioned to imprison men rounded up in the villages. 'There are about 500 of them,' he recorded. 'You can see them hanging out of the windows, all shouting. Outside, there are crowds of women, trying to see their sons and husbands. Three or four Germans and about twenty of these damned Fascists hold them back . . . I heard the men were seized by force – coming out of church and bars, and from their houses. The Germans helped themselves to anything they wanted as they dragged the men away . . . At Nimis and Qualso, a bunch of them, aided by Fascists, made all the villagers leave their homes. They kept them hostage while they went through all the houses, taking anything valuable – money, gold, silver, clothes etc.'

The villages lay within a 10-mile radius of Brazzà. At Feletto Umberto, the closest – just 2 miles across the fields – most of the young men in the tiny hamlet, twenty-six in total, were taken away.

With the SS manhunts in full flare, German armed forces became increasingly visible in the area. At Campoformido, the Luftwaffe base close to Brazzà, the peasants were banned from nearby fields. 'The Germans are building wooden aeroplanes and wooden anti-aircraft guns around the airfield to act as decoys for Allied reconnaissance planes now flying over the area,' Fey wrote to her friend, Santa Hercolani.[*] 'The locals say, what are they thinking? Do they expect the Allies to drop wooden bombs on these wooden planes?!'

The partisans were also stepping up their activities; railway bridges and electricity substations were attacked, and numerous Fascists murdered. In Povoletto, a small village 6 miles to the north-east of Udine, Communist partisans shaved the heads of seven local women for sleeping with German soldiers. In this febrile atmosphere, wild stories circulated. 'Mussolini is building a weapon of mass destruction in Venice, people say. One that is going to throw this terrible death ray, which will shoot 3,000 kilometres and will win him the war,' Paviotti reported. 'The news on the radio is that the Allied troops in the south have launched a big offensive. People are anxious for further news but we hear very little and understand even less.'

On the night of 14 May, Allied planes started bombing the region. 'At four in the morning we heard three loud explosions coming from Udine,' Fey wrote to Santa. 'The next day we heard the air-raid sirens and the sound of machine-gun fire coming from the direction of the airport. The English bombers were seen flying very low, close to Udine, and the accompanying fighters fired their machine guns at the ground. Some German planes went to attack them and we watched a dog fight, high above us. Luckily, none of the planes was downed but it was quite something. Passing through a village nearby, I saw that someone had written "God Curse the English" on a wall. After the bombings in the north and now this, people are turning against the British and the Americans in favour of the Russians and

---

[*] The daughter of Scipione Borghese, 10th Prince of Sulmona.

thousands are joining the Communist partisans here. To cap it all, the weather is hot and oppressive and thunderstorms threaten to destroy the hay harvest. Our contadini look tense and gloomy as they go about the fields.'

The contadini depended on the hay harvest to feed their animals throughout the year. Hail and thunderstorms frequently swept down from the mountains and at Brazzà the peasants still relied on the warning system that had been in use for centuries. In isolated villages, high up in the mountains, storms were announced by a pealing of bells. Lower down the slopes, hearing the warning, the villagers would ring their own church bells, a signal to the contadini to go out into the fields to do what they could to bring in the hay or protect the crops. In this way, the warning of an approaching storm was communicated from the mountains to the foothills and across the plain, the harsh clamour ringing out from every village campanile.

The weather broke on 16 May, the night Allied planes returned to bomb electricity substations near Trieste. 'The storm finally came last night,' Fey wrote to Santa. 'Very little rain but huge claps of thunder and a great deal of lightning. The children were already awake as the bells were going off in the villages before it started. In between the thunder we could hear loud explosions coming from the mountains. The boys, of course, were very frightened. I sat with them for several hours and eventually managed to get them off to sleep by singing their favourite lullaby.'

It was Brahms's 'Lullaby' that Fey sang, with its chorus: 'Lullaby and goodnight, you are Mother's delight / I'll protect you from harm and you'll wake in my arms.'

On 24 May, the shooting of two German soldiers outside the village of Premariacco, 5 miles from Brazzà, ratcheted up the tension in the neighbourhood. Umberto Paviotti spoke to the villagers the next day: 'It's unimaginable what consequences this is going to bring,' one resident reported. 'People are saying the Germans are going to shut the whole village down, seize all men and carry out pointless reprisals against the innocent.'

The SS descended on the village the following day and all the houses were searched. 'Some weapons were found in one house and they told the woman present to immediately find her husband and son,' Paviotti recorded. 'But she didn't know where they were. So they shot her twice, doused the house in petrol, set fire to it and threw the dying woman into the flames. People said they heard her screaming and then silence.'

Two days later, with the culprit for the murder of the two German soldiers still not found, Alvensleben judged that the time had come to set an example.

On 28 May – Pentecost Sunday – Lieutenant Kitzmüller was on duty at SS headquarters in Udine when his immediate superior, Major Moller, asked him to select thirty prisoners for execution from among those rounded up in the villages. 'I was speechless and even Moller, who was used to such things, seemed a bit perturbed. When I objected that we absolutely didn't have that many detainees who deserved to be executed for their crimes, he replied brusquely: "I hope that among 500 prisoners you will find 30 candidates for the death sentence." And he let me go. At first I couldn't resign myself to this terrible order and I leafed through the register from beginning to end at least twenty times without finding a single candidate. So then I decided to go to Moller again to tell him that I hadn't been able to identify anyone. I did this in the hope that he would ask someone else to do it. When I told him that I hadn't found anyone appropriate, he declared: "That's rubbish. Their crimes are irrelevant. I need people for an act of reprisal that will spread terror."'

Twenty-six prisoners were selected, of which thirteen came from the hamlet of Feletto Umberto on the border of the Brazzà estate – 'the Thirteen Martyrs of Feletto Umberto', as they would come to be known.

There were two twenty-one-year-olds, three twenty-year-olds, five boys of nineteen and three of eighteen. None of them had played any part in the murder of the German soldiers. Rounded up on 9 May, they had been in prison in Udine when the killings took place.

It was Alvensleben who made the final selection. In stripping Feletto Umberto of its young men, his aim was to send a warning to the neighbourhood. The hamlet had a long history of subversive actions against the Fascists and the boys belonged to the Youth Group, a Communist-run partisan organization. Further, when they were originally rounded up, an informer had betrayed their hiding places. The message Alvensleben wanted to communicate was that the SS were omnipotent: no hiding place was safe.

The number of prisoners selected, and the date and manner of their execution, were designed to incite maximum terror in a population whose daily lives revolved around their religious beliefs. The men were to be executed in two groups of thirteen: the first at Premariacco, where the German soldiers had been killed; the second at San Giovanni al Natisone, a village further south. Thirteen was a number of religious significance: there had been thirteen present at the Last Supper. The date Alvensleben chose for their execution was also symbolic – 29 May, Pentecost Monday. A holiday of great spiritual importance in the villages, Pentecost was when the Holy Spirit had descended to bestow the gift of tongues on the twelve Apostles so that they could go out and spread their faith. The festivities normally lasted the whole weekend. The village priests, wearing red vestments to signify the flame of the Holy Spirit, scattered rose petals through the streets, doves were released and there were outdoor feasts on long tables set up in the village squares. Above all, it was a time of renewal, when the villagers celebrated the new life the Holy Spirit breathed into their faith.

The Germans did not announce the executions. On the morning of 29 May, at Premariacco and San Giovanni al Natisone, they turned up out of the blue.

In the piazza in Premariacco – the site chosen for the execution of the thirteen men from Feletto Umberto – the rose petals were still strewn across the square. Situated 15 miles from Brazzà, the village, like so many in the region, was one of the poorest in Italy. The petals were the only splashes of colour in a place that poverty rendered monochrome. The roads through the village, mud-bound in the winter, dust-blown in the summer, were unmetalled; the houses, made of bleached white stones hauled from the bed of the nearby river, lacked plaster facades; the wooden shutters, rotting and hanging from their hinges, were unpainted. Inside the houses, but for crucifixes and embroidered pictures of the Sacred Heart, the rough walls were bare.

Vittorio Zanuttini, a farm labourer, lived in a house close to the square. 'At about 8 o'clock in the morning, I was stopped in the piazza by some German soldiers and they ordered me to oversee the works for a hanging. Full of terror, I ran to the village hall to ask for clarification from the secretary to the mayor, who advised me to obey their orders. A German lieutenant, carrying lengths of rope, took me to the *Osteria ai Cacciatori* – the village bar – where he taught me how to tie the knots for the nooses. He said that if they didn't hold, I would end up on the gallows myself. In the meantime, outside in the village square, soldiers were forcing passers-by to put up the beams they had taken from the mayor.'

Basic in structure, the gallows consisted of a single beam nailed to two pillars, like a goalpost. A bench then had to be found for the condemned men to stand on and someone was sent to the church to retrieve a pew. As one group of soldiers supervised the erection of the gallows, another combed the village. Only women, children and the elderly were left, and they were rounded up – out of the fields where they were working, and from their houses – and forcibly taken to the village square to watch the hangings.

Vittorio Zanuttini was in the square when the trucks carrying the thirteen men from Feletto Umberto arrived. 'At about half past nine, two trucks entered the village. One was civilian and painted in red. On board was a group of youths, dressed in civilian clothes. Following behind was a military truck, filled with German soldiers, heavily armed. The youths were told to get off the truck. I remember they were laughing and chatting among themselves, and smoking cigarettes. I don't know whether they thought they were a working party and the Germans were going to ask them to build something in the piazza or what, but they clearly had no idea what was about to happen to them. Suddenly, a German officer gave an order and the poor men had their hands tied behind their backs.'

'The boys arrived there quite happily,' another man wrote. 'They actually thought they were being taken home. Try and imagine how they felt when the lorry stopped in front of the gallows and the soldiers started tying their hands behind their backs. They shouted out that they were innocent. They invoked their mothers and their children. They begged for a moment so that they could write or pray.'

The village priest asked the Germans if he could give the men the last rites, but they refused and he retreated to a wall where he performed absolution, keeping in close eye contact with the men.

'They were all made to stand on the bench in a row,' Zanuttini continued. 'I know there were thirteen because that's how many nooses the Germans made me tie. They put the nooses around their necks and suddenly kicked the bench, leaving them suspended in space. It was a stomach-churning scene that lots of us had to witness because the Germans had marched us down to the piazza at gunpoint.'

On Alvensleben's orders, the SS left the bodies of the thirteen men on the gallows until five o'clock the following afternoon so that people could see what happened to partisans. Hundreds from all over the region came to view the macabre sight and to hear the stories circulating in the village. Umberto Paviotti cycled there a few days after the hangings: 'I heard from the local priest that he was barred from giving the boys a Christian burial. And I heard from someone who was present at the execution that after it happened the Germans walked around the bodies, sniggering. I also heard that once the bodies were removed, two partisans came and took the rope down and swore they would hang Germans with the same rope.'

On the night of the executions, a German plane clipped the bell tower in a nearby village and crashed in flames. The villagers interpreted it as an act of God in revenge for the hangings. 'The seven crew rose high into the sky without an aeroplane. What a shame!' Paviotti wrote.

Alvensleben's reprisals continued. On 30 May, the SS rounded up a further 600 men from villages close to Brazzà. As if the deaths of thirteen of their sons was not enough for the hamlet of Feletto Umberto, a force of 1,000 Germans and Fascists returned four days after the hangings and took more men away. Two villagers were shot dead – one for trying to run, the other for attempting to attack the troops.

As the partisans sought the informer who had given the men away, the finger of suspicion fell on Fey. A number of the contadini at Brazzà were related to families in Feletto Umberto and stories of Fey's fraternization with the Germans – the teas with Alvensleben, the Christmas lunch she hosted for the Luftwaffe officers, her entitlement to send letters through the military post – had leaked out. Her apparent failure to use her influence with the Germans, together with her knowledge of the whereabouts of local men hiding in the area, fuelled the speculation that she was a collaborator. The rumours were compounded by Brazzà's physical isolation from the community. As partisan attacks on German troops stationed in the region had increased, sentries were posted along the drive up to the villa, and trenches, fortified by high coils of barbed wire, dug around the perimeter of the park, lending the place the appearance of a fortress.

The situation was further complicated by the enmity between the various partisan groups. While Brazzà itself, and the area to the west of it, was controlled by the Osoppo, which was affiliated to liberal and right-wing political parties, the area to the east, including Feletto Umberto, was controlled by the Garibaldi partisans, who were largely Communist. The Garibaldi far outnumbered the Osoppo and were linked to Slav brigades that were also operating in the area and who had territorial ambitions over the Friuli-Venezia Giulia region.

Among the Osoppo, Fey's loyalty was unquestioned; Detalmo's cousin, Alvise di Brazzà, commanded one of the brigades, and the Tacoli brothers, Ferdinando and Federico, whose family owned the neighbouring estate to Brazzà, were also leading figures. 'The Osoppo's work is valuable and courageous, but I cannot help them,' Fey wrote to Santa; 'the German presence here means that I must be a passive resister. I cannot hide or feed the Osoppo, as other landowners are doing. The Garibaldi, on the other hand, frighten me. They are mostly Communists and want to expropriate all landed estates in Friuli, so I keep my distance.'

Soon after the Feletto Umberto hangings, Fey learned that she had been placed on the Garibaldi 'blacklist'. It meant that she was now a target in the attacks they were orchestrating against collaborators. Houses had been set on fire, property vandalized, and a number of people murdered. In an attempt to show the Garibaldi that her sympathies lay with the locals, she instructed her farm manager, Bovolenta, to sell the estate's produce in the markets at reduced prices. But it made no difference.

As the weeks went by, Fey found herself more and more out of her depth. Her one opportunity to prove her anti-Nazi credentials was to use her influence with the Germans to prevent deportations. But with the exception of the lawyer Nimis, she had failed. She considered leaving Brazzà and returning to the Papafavas' estate near Padua; but, without access to the military post, she would have no means of communicating with her family in Germany, and she could not bear the thought of losing touch.

Very quickly, the situation deteriorated. Collaborators and Germans were being killed on a daily basis and, in response to SS reprisals, thousands were joining the Garibaldi in the mountains to the east of Brazzà. Paviotti, whose job as a water surveyor meant that he visited remote villages high above the plain, noted the strengthening support for the Garibaldi movement: 'The word "partigiani" [partisans] is known even among the children and the partisans move around these villages day and night, well supplied by the locals. People are saying that the Communists will soon control the area. Even now, Garibaldi men, armed with machine guns, are manning roadblocks up in the mountains. In response, the Germans have started requisitioning bicycles. Someone said they need 20,000. The rumour is that they are gathering them in order to flee if they have to.'

Throughout this period, acutely aware of the increasing danger, Fey kept the children with her at all times. 'I held Corradino's little hand on one side and Robertino's still smaller one on the other. Whatever I was doing they came with me – seeing to the animals, going about the woods and fields, and to meetings with Bovolenta, the farm manager. If I went to see Alvise, Detalmo's cousin, he would tease me, saying, "Here comes Cornelia, mother of the Gracchi" – a reference to the Roman widow who dedicated her life entirely to the education of her sons.'

Inevitably, at Brazzà, the boys saw a lot of the Luftwaffe airmen and, for the most part, Fey was grateful for their kindness. They would bring the children treats and allow them to sit at the steering wheel in their trucks. There was one officer, however, whom Corrado saw more of than she would have liked – and sometimes even knew. This was Lieutenant Kretschmann, whose strong Nazi views she had mistrusted from the beginning. As the unit's political officer, he was based in the house during the day, rather than at the airfield at Campoformido, and his office overlooked the garden. Frequently, if Fey and the boys were passing, he would come out and invite Corrado into his office to 'use' the telephone, which was, as Fey recalled, 'a source of endless fascination' to the four-year-old. The children, especially Corrado, adored Kretschmann and, on the occasions when she had a meeting in town and it was necessary to leave them behind, they would beg to be left with him, rather than with Cilla and Ernesta, two of the maids.

If Corrado disappeared, Fey knew where to find him. 'Kretschmann once told me that if my back was turned Corradino would knock on his door asking if he could play with the odd bits of electrical apparatus lying about the office. If Kretschmann said, "I am busy now, could you come back later," Corradino would answer solemnly, "Of course, I'll come back in a while," and he invariably did. These were his private excursions. Robertino, on the other hand, hardly left my side. He was, after all, only two and a half years old. But if he did disappear, I knew he would be in the stables with Mirko, the little white horse. He would talk to Mirko for hours.'

Fey assumed that, as long as the Germans remained at Brazzà, she and the children were safe. But then, on 3 July, the Garibaldi attacked a villa belonging to a friend in the neighbouring village of Martignacco, which was also occupied by the Germans. After a gunfight that lasted a couple of hours, the villa was set on fire. That same day, 2 miles to the east on the road to Tavagnacco, the partisans killed a man because he was 'too pro-German'.

The next day, Fey wrote in panic to her mother:

The situation is becoming more and more complicated for me every
day. The Communist partisans have put me on their blacklist as they
say I'm too friendly with the Germans. On the other hand, the local
people appreciate me because they know that I help when I can . . .
But, if Communist partisans were to arrive here out of the blue, they
wouldn't for a moment think of asking how I behaved and what I did.
For this reason, I really don't know what I should do. My gut feeling
is to stay put and I'm sure this is what I will decide in the end. What
is certain, anyway, is that I don't know what I would do without
Nonino, my great and constant support.

Andreina's★ house was burned down yesterday during a partisan
attack. She had Germans in the house. These days, partisans with
Communist leanings frequently attack houses. It happened to some
peasants nearby. The partisans took away linen and books, saying
reading was unnecessary. They also wanted to set fire to the house,
but the peasants begged them not to do it because otherwise they
would be homeless. The partisans said, 'Well, you're not the landowners, you're only peasants, so we won't set fire to it.'

I continue to hide the most important things. I've buried the silver,
and Nonino helped me dig a hole in the park. Plates, glasses and linen
have been hidden with our peasants – all of this in the eventuality of
my having to leave or a fire caused by partisan attacks.

It was not just the attack on her friend's house and the knowledge
that she was on the Garibaldi blacklist that triggered Fey's anxiety.
However committed to eliminating collaborators and wealthy landowners, it was widely known that the Communist brigades were
inhibited by a lack of weapons. But a few days before she wrote to her
mother, Detalmo's cousin, Alvise di Brazzà, had told her that British
commandos were now in the area and that they were supplying and
arming the partisans.

The sound of the planes woke her at night – and always in the

★ Contessa Andreina di Caporiacco, a friend who lived in a nearby village.

minutes coming up to midnight. They flew low over the house and she could hear the change in the pitch of their engines as they turned and circled, searching for the drop zone. Yet, whenever she got up to look out of the window, she could not see them; but she could see a dim orange glow on the peak of Mount Joanaz, the closest in the chain of mountains that formed the foothills of the Alps.

The planes were Dakotas, used by British and American Special Forces. Painted black to reduce their visibility in the night sky, some had flame-arrester devices fitted to the engine exhaust vents to further obscure their position. Inside, special blackout curtains covered the windows so that the internal lights necessary for flight and navigation could continue to operate.

Flying from Foggia, an Allied airbase in the southern half of Italy, the planes were dropping weapons and other supplies to a brigade of partisans on the summit of Mount Joanaz. The orange glow Fey saw came from the fires the men lit to guide the planes in.

British SOE agents were on the ground to supervise the drops. Codenamed Coolant, the mission, consisting of two officers and a wireless operator, was the first to parachute into Friuli. Jumping from a height of 6,000 feet above the mountains to the east of Brazzà, they had landed on the night of 9 June.

'Body drops' depended on a clear, moonlit night to enable the teams to see where to touch down, and that night the sky had been cloudless and the moon full. To ensure their safe arrival, the partisans had sabotaged several miles of high-tension pylons, throwing the area into darkness.

Though operating behind enemy lines, the three-man team wore British uniforms – a precaution in case of capture. The Geneva Convention defined the rights of wartime prisoners: if caught in uniform, they would be treated as prisoners of war rather than spies liable to summary execution. Each man jumped with a hundredweight pack of weapons and supplies. Otherwise, they depended on their training for survival.

Rules for surviving in enemy territory, drawn from the experiences of previous missions, were circulated among all SOE operatives.

Major Duncan, attached to Mission Cisco Red,★ an operation based in central Italy, compiled a list of dos and don'ts for agents assigned to Italian operations:

1. Never remain static: one night and day in a house is ample.
2. Don't let children see you or, if they do, pretend to be a German if in uniform or an uncle if in mufti.
3. If the Partisans say there are 1,000 Germans coming up the road you are all right. But if they are laughing or happy, beware! They become easily overconfident.
4. Trust no one; there are spies everywhere.
5. The poorer the house, the safer it is: rich houses are invariably Fascist.
6. Women working in the fields are usually safe.
7. If a farmer sees you hiding in his fields, he will pass by where you are and pretend not to have seen you. Later, he will come back and, if he is sympathetic, will ask if you are hungry and produce food. If he doesn't produce food, go away quickly.
8. Any farm with young men walking about is safe; they are deserters either from the Army or Germany and are in as bad a spot as yourself.
9. Once you have stayed at a house and eaten there, you are safe; they will not tell the Germans as their house would be burnt down for having kept you there for the night.

Facing this unpredictable, dangerous environment, Captain Hedley Vincent, Coolant's 34-year-old commander, had briefed the team on its mission before taking off from Foggia. The objective was to secure partisan-held territory from which to attack the Wehrmacht's main supply lines from the Reich. The immediate priority, however, was to turn the partisans into an effective fighting force by supplying them with the arms, explosives, food and clothing they lacked. As Vincent later admitted, 'The execution of the mission depended

★ A mission to capture or kill an SS general who had carried out reprisals in central Italy, killing scores of villagers.

entirely on the safe receipt of stores in sufficient quantity. We could not just walk into towns and villages. We had in many cases to fight for them and then defend them.'

It was Vincent who selected Mount Joanaz as a dropping site. Some 3,000 feet above sea level, it offered security from surprise attack, the easy post-drop distribution of stores, and was acceptable to the RAF crew who had to pinpoint the site and make the perilous run to the drop.

Typically, a delivery would take place around midnight. Waiting in Canebola – a remote hamlet of just ten or twelve houses – Vincent and his team would listen out for the BBC 'crack', the coded announcement of an imminent drop. After climbing the 900 feet to the summit of Mount Joanaz, they laid out fires in the shape of a T. On hearing the drone of the approaching aircraft, a torch was used to flash the same letter in Morse code to guide the pilot to his target.

The success of the drops depended on the pilot's precision; on one side of Mount Joanaz, there was a sheer precipice, 3,000 feet down, and if the despatcher was a little early, the supplies were lost. As one SOE officer recalled, other factors also came into play. 'Not every package dropped from an aircraft gets gathered in to the central collecting point; if conditions are right a keen-eyed watcher will have counted the number of parachutes that opened and others will have marked where they landed – another argument for dropping by moonlight – but some may get caught in an air-current and be carried too far; with luck these may be found in the morning, not always by the partisans. A few seconds' mis-timing by the pilot or despatcher can spread the drop far and wide.'

The villagers turned out whenever a sortie was expected. Taking up position by the fires, they collected the packages as soon as they hit the ground. Bundles of clothing and boots came down without the aid of parachutes and, as one SOE agent recalled, 'with freefalling equipment, it became a dangerous operation'. But arms, ammunition and explosives floated down in containers. These were then unhooked from the parachutes and taken down to the village by men, women and children who frequently carried up to a hundredweight on their backs.

Living side by side with the partisans and dependent on their local knowledge and loyalty for their own survival, the SOE operatives came to admire their courage and commitment in fighting the Germans. 'One of my most vivid memories,' one agent recalled, 'is that of a long line of partisans and friendly village folk carrying enormous loads on their backs after gathering the equipment received from a parachute drop that had scattered itself all over Mount Joanaz, and seeing amongst all these people a little boy of barely four years of age carrying two pairs of heavy army binoculars up and down steep paths all the way to the village of Canebola.'

Throughout July and August, the drops continued on an almost daily basis. Only the dark nights in the moon's last quarter prevented them from taking place. During those summer months, four additional SOE teams parachuted into the region. The names of the missions were Sermon, Bakersfield, Ballonet and Tabella.

As Fey lay in bed, listening to the circling planes, all her anxiety centred on the threat from the partisans. She recognized that, in her eagerness to protect her children, her house and the families who worked on her husband's estate, she was embedded with the Germans.

13

Ulrich von Hassell's thoughts were never far from his youngest child and in early July he felt a longing again to see Fey, who, he believed, 'in her isolation needs help desperately'. He expressed this concern to a friend on one of the last occasions he and his fellow conspirators gathered. That evening, Hassell found General Beck, the leader of the group, in a negative frame of mind having lost hope of ever removing Hitler from power.

Since the spring of 1943, when Henning von Tresckow failed in his three attempts to kill the Führer, the chance of success was even more remote. The defeat at Stalingrad marked the start of the Wehrmacht's long retreat and, with every military setback, Hitler travelled less and less. He refused to visit hospitals for wounded soldiers or bomb-damaged cities, fearing such sights would induce pity and thereby make him weak. He now shunned the crowds that he had relied on to bolster his self-image. He made almost no public appearances and was virtually invisible, save to his personal entourage. His low state was noted by one of the few people who saw him regularly – Joseph Goebbels, his minister of propaganda. 'It is tragic that the Führer has become such a recluse and leads such an unhealthy life. He never gets out into the fresh air. He does not relax. He sits in his bunker and worries and broods.'

For some time, Hitler had not even visited Berlin. As the country's military might withered, so did he. A tremor developed in his hands. His left foot dragged behind him as he walked. His face took on a haunted look.

But the one ray of hope for Hassell and his circle was that it was no longer necessary to make 'desperately isolated attempts'. If they could only find a means of eliminating Hitler, an ingenious plan was now in place to overthrow his regime.

The plan was one that Hitler himself had requested to counter the threat of civil insurgency. Fearing that Germany's 4 million-plus foreign workers – the majority of whom had been forcibly deported from Nazi-occupied countries – might revolt, he and his senior commanders had devised a contingency plan, codenamed Operation Valkyrie. It hinged on mobilizing the Reserve Army throughout the Third Reich to quash an uprising.

Using this framework, Tresckow, in collaboration with General Olbricht, who had drawn up the plan for Hitler, adapted it for the purposes of engineering a coup. Once the Führer was dead, they would proclaim a state of emergency, blaming his death on an attempted putsch by the SS. This cover story would easily deceive unwitting members of the armed forces into believing that they were acting against a treacherous group of SS officers who had turned against their leader. Party officials and SS personnel would be arrested and only then would the operation reveal itself as a full-scale coup.

With Tresckow based at Army Group Centre on the Eastern Front, in the summer of 1943, the leadership of the conspiracy devolved almost entirely on Claus von Stauffenberg, a young lieutenant colonel who had served in the Afrika Korps as operations officer to Field Marshal Rommel, winning the German Cross in gold. Given Hitler's reluctance to travel, both his assassination and the planning of Valkyrie required someone on the ground in Germany and, after being seriously wounded in Tunisia, Stauffenberg had been appointed to General Olbricht's staff and was working at the headquarters of the Reserve Army in the centre of Berlin.

Aged thirty-six and strikingly good-looking, Stauffenberg was by all accounts an exceptionally courageous individual. As Ilse von Hassell wrote, he was 'the only one with access to Hitler who had the moral courage and the conscience to carry out the coup in order to prevent the total destruction of Germany'. Like Tresckow and Hassell, he too came from a Prussian noble family. While Stauffenberg had initially admired Hitler's military acumen and had been in favour of the invasion of Poland, he was outraged by Nazi atrocities against the Jews. A devout Catholic, he was also opposed to Hitler's suppression of Catholicism and other religions.

Stauffenberg's planning for Valkyrie was painstaking. Working late into the night from his house in a Berlin suburb, he put in place the civil and military measures which seizure of power would entail: the arrest of party officials, along with SS and Gestapo personnel; the occupation of ministries, railway depots, communication centres, strategic installations and access roads. Tirelessly, he moved through the upper military and administrative echelons of the Reich, searching out prospective recruits. But the one major obstacle remained: killing Hitler.

Already, in the first six months of 1944, Stauffenberg's assassins had made two attempts. Early in February, Hitler was scheduled to attend an exhibition of military uniforms at the Berlin Armoury – the same location as Colonel Gersdorff's attempt a year before. Knowing that 21-year-old Lieutenant Ewald-Heinrich von Kleist was due to show the Führer round the exhibition, Stauffenberg approached him to ask if he would volunteer as a suicide bomber. Kleist requested a day to think about it and to talk it over with his father, a vehement opponent of Hitler. The answer was categorical: under no circumstances must he miss this opportunity of fulfilling so vital a duty. 'A man who doesn't take such a chance will never be happy again in his life,' his father said. Kleist's chance, however, did not come. Repeatedly, Hitler rescheduled his visit to the exhibition, and in the end it did not take place.

The second attempt came a month later. This time, Stauffenberg recruited Eberhard von Breitenbuch, a young cavalry officer who had regular access to Hitler through his job as aide-de-camp to Field Marshal Busch.* Breitenbuch was due to attend a military conference at the Berghof, Hitler's home in the Bavarian Alps, on 11 March. Rather than use a suicide vest, Breitenbuch, who was a crack shot, chose instead to shoot Hitler with a 7.65mm Browning concealed in his pocket – an equally suicidal mission given that Hitler's security entourage would undoubtedly shoot back. As the doors to the conference room opened, he released the safety catch on the pistol, but at the very last minute he was barred from the meeting. The

---

* Ernst Busch replaced Field Marshal Günther von Kluge as commander, Army Group Centre, in October 1943.

SS-Sturmbannführer who had just announced Hitler's arrival stopped him with the words: 'Today, please, no ADCs!' Breitenbuch then had to endure a nerve-racking hour wondering whether his exclusion meant that his mission had been discovered.

The breakthrough Stauffenberg had long hoped for came on 1 July when he was appointed chief of staff to General Fromm, the commander-in-chief of the Reserve Army. It meant that from now on he would have regular meetings with the Führer. Stauffenberg had four children, aged between four and ten, and another one was on the way; but after countless assassination attempts had failed, he decided that, as one of the few people with access to the elusive Führer, he would have to do the job himself.

Hassell was not directly involved in the planning of the attempts on Hitler's life for the good reason that he did not have access to the target. But he was earmarked for the post of foreign minister or state secretary at the Foreign Office in the event the coup succeeded. At the end of 1943, he and Stauffenberg had discussed the composition of the post-coup government. Hassell's 'band of brothers', with whom he had conspired to remove Hitler since the summer of 1939, were to lead the government: General Ludwig Beck was to be the new president or head of state, and Carl Friedrich Goerdeler, chancellor. The names of all those in the future cabinet were written down – a list that would become a death warrant when it was found by the Gestapo.

At six in the morning on Thursday 20 July, a staff car arrived at Stauffenberg's house at Wannsee to take him to Rangsdorf, a military aerodrome south of Berlin. He was with his aide-de-camp, Lieutenant Werner von Haeften, and his brother, Berthold, a naval lieutenant. Berthold was only going as far as the airfield, but Stauffenberg wanted him there to ease the nervous tension; not a word could be said in front of the driver about the mission that filled their thoughts as they sped through the outskirts of the city.

The bomb, wrapped in a shirt in Stauffenberg's attaché case, weighed about two pounds. Of the same type used in previous assassination attempts, it had a British fuse, which was operated by breaking a glass capsule filled with acid. This then dissolved the fuse wire, releasing the firing pin. Stauffenberg had been at pains to ensure that the fuse was of the thinnest wire; the acid would burn through it in ten minutes. This estimate, however, was only approximate. The speed with which the acid consumed the wire would be, to some degree, affected by temperature and atmospheric pressure.

A second bomb was concealed in Haeften's briefcase.

The conference at the Führer's headquarters at Rastenburg in East Prussia was scheduled for one o'clock. Ordinarily, the flight from Berlin was of some two hours' duration, but there was a delay and Stauffenberg and Haeften did not land at Rastenburg until ten-fifteen.

At the airstrip, a car waited to convey them to Hitler's compound, known as the *Wolfsschanze* ('Wolf's Lair'). A gloomy, forbidding place, it was situated, deep in a forest, some 50 miles east of the old Teutonic Knights' capital at Königsberg. The low-lying swampy ground was the burial site for centuries of corpses. Here in 1410, the Battle of Tannenberg had been fought, and the Teutonic Knights, then at the height of their power, had suffered a shattering defeat. Napoleon's Grande Armée had retreated through these marshes in 1813 and, at the outbreak of the First World War, two complete Russian armies, encircled and outmanoeuvred, had been forced to surrender to Hindenburg.

For 9 miles, the road from the airport ran through dense forest. The day was hot, with the temperature in the upper eighties, and both Stauffenberg and Haeften were sweating profusely. On the way they had to stop at three successive security checkpoints controlled by the SS, and show the special passes issued to them for the visit. The first gate, some 2 miles from the centre of the headquarters, gave access to an extensive minefield and a ring of fortifications; the second led to a large compound surrounded by electrified barbed wire. From this gate, it was 800 yards to another checkpoint, and from there a further 200 yards or so to the entrance to the innermost compound, Security Ring A, where Hitler lived and worked. The bunkers here – cube-like, windowless blockhouses, disguised with camouflage paint – were said to have walls and ceilings 20 feet thick, and SS guards patrolled the area constantly.

While Stauffenberg and Haeften had no trouble getting into this menacing establishment, their concern was how they would bluff their way out once the bombs exploded. The plan was to depend on speed; Haeften was not attending the conference and his task was to make sure that their staff car was ready to leave as soon as the bombs went off.

Now, however, they had a two-hour wait to endure before the conference.

At eleven-thirty, Stauffenberg went over to Field Marshal Keitel's office. Keitel was Hitler's chief of staff and they went through the details of Stauffenberg's presentation. The official reason for his visit was to brief Hitler on the formation of two new East Prussian divisions which he had ordered on 19 July to help block the Red Army's advance. As Stauffenberg reported on the status of the divisions, Keitel suddenly informed him that the briefing had been brought forward by an hour and was now scheduled to take place at midday. With only fifteen minutes to spare, Stauffenberg, blaming the heat and the humidity, asked if there was somewhere he might wash and change his sodden shirt. A deferential officer directed him to a cloakroom.

Haeften was waiting in the corridor outside and both men went into the room to prime the bombs. Missing his right hand, and with only three fingers remaining on his left, Stauffenberg used a specially adapted set of pliers to break the glass phial and connect the fuse, while Haeften prepared the other bomb.

They had only been in there for a few minutes when they were interrupted by a sergeant major. The briefing with Hitler was about to begin and he had been sent to fetch Stauffenberg. He said he would wait while he finished what he was doing. Later, he would testify that the two men were 'busy with a wrapped parcel'.

The interruption was the first setback; with time running out and the sergeant major standing over them, Stauffenberg and Haeften were unable to prime both bombs, and it was only by quickly slipping the inert device into his briefcase that Haeften prevented the sergeant major from seeing anything.

With the only activated bomb now in his own briefcase, Stauffenberg followed his escort out of the room knowing that, within ten minutes, it would explode.

The second deviation from the plan came moments later. Usually, military conferences were held in the *Führerbunker*. But, due to the heat, the location had been switched and the conference was now taking place in an adjacent map room. Whereas the subterranean bunker was a concrete structure, the walls of which would contain and maximize the blast, the map room was a wooden structure with ten large windows, all of which were open. A blast here would be significantly less lethal.

As Stauffenberg approached the hut, he asked the escorting officer to place him as close to Hitler as possible. He told him that, after being wounded in North Africa, his hearing was impaired and he wanted to 'catch everything' the Führer said.

The conference had already begun when Stauffenberg arrived. The officer asked the men seated next to Hitler to move up and make room for him, then Keitel introduced him as the colonel who had come to report on the new divisions. After turning to acknowledge Stauffenberg's salute, Hitler resumed the meeting.

Taking his seat some 6 feet from the Führer, Stauffenberg placed his briefcase on the floor and nudged it under the heavy oak table with his boot. Three minutes had elapsed since he had primed the bomb and it was due to go off in seven minutes. After waiting for another minute or so, he excused himself. He had to telephone Berlin, he explained. It was urgent. But he would return as soon as the call was over.

Once outside the briefing hut, he hurried to an office across the compound where General Fellgiebel, chief of signals at Rastenburg and a fellow conspirator, was waiting. As soon as the explosion occurred, Fellgiebel was to telephone Berlin to activate Operation Valkyrie, and then cut all communications from Rastenburg. This would isolate the 'Wolf's Lair' from the *coup d'état* unfolding in the rest of Germany.

For three minutes, Stauffenberg and Fellgiebel waited in the office. Then came the single shattering explosion and a column of thick smoke rose into the air. Seconds later, Haeften appeared with the staff car. The priority now was to escape before the compound was sealed off. As they drove away, their car passed within 50 yards of the briefing hut; looking through the trees, it appeared to be gutted and stretcher-bearers were carrying bodies out.

By now, warning klaxons were sounding. A full security alert was in progress and sentries were being reinforced. Reaching the first gate, Stauffenberg and Haeften were in luck; they knew the sentry and, following a brief conversation, he raised the barrier and waved them through. At the second gate, after a short delay while their permits were checked, they were also allowed to proceed. But at the third and last checkpoint, an officious guard refused to let them pass: no one, he announced, was permitted to enter or leave the compound. Endeavouring to pull rank, Stauffenberg snapped at him in a 'parade ground' tone. Still the guard insisted he had to stick to orders. Desperate to get away, Stauffenberg snatched the telephone and rang the aide-de-camp to Rastenburg's commandant.

'Colonel Count Stauffenberg speaking from outer checkpoint south,' he said. 'Captain, you'll remember we had breakfast together this morning. Due to the explosion, the guard refuses to let me pass. I'm in a hurry. Colonel General Fromm is waiting for me at the airfield.'

Without waiting for a reply, he replaced the receiver and turned to the guard. 'You heard, Sergeant Major, I'm allowed through.' But the guard insisted on receiving the order personally and there was a further delay while he telephoned the commandant's aide. At last, on being told that Stauffenberg could pass, he raised the barrier. The car set off to the landing strip, Stauffenberg ordering the driver to hurry. As they drove through the forest, Haeften tossed the second bomb out of the window. By one-fifteen, they were airborne and on their way back to Berlin.

14.

Shock registered on all their faces. It was almost one o'clock in the morning and Fey and the forty-strong staff of the Luftnachrichten-Regiment 200 were gathered in the Grand Salon at Brazzà. Some hours before, to allay rumours of Hitler's death, Goebbels had transmitted an emergency broadcast, announcing that the Führer had narrowly escaped an attempt on his life. Now Hitler himself was due to make an announcement. The heat of the past week radiated from the walls of the airless room and sweat dripped off the men, who stood motionless in their grey uniforms. As they waited in silence, the only sounds were of the crickets in the garden, and the whine of mosquitoes, drawn by the light through the open windows.

Promptly, at the stroke of one, Hitler began his broadcast. Speaking in a low, faltering voice, he sounded tired and breathless. Fey could feel the men tense as they craned forward, struggling to catch his words, barely audible above the noise of the crickets outside.

'My comrades, men and women of Germany,' Hitler began. 'I don't know how many times plans and attempts have been made to assassinate me. If I speak to you today it is, first of all, so that you should hear my voice and know that I am unhurt and well and, secondly, that you should know of a crime unparalleled in German history.

'A very small clique of ambitious, unscrupulous, and at the same time criminal and stupid officers concocted a plot to remove me, and with me the entire staff of the High Command of the Wehrmacht.'

Fey studied the reactions of the airmen as Hitler described the impact of the bomb, which had exploded just 2 yards from where he had been sitting; caught in the glare from the glass chandelier that hung in the centre of the room, their faces were drawn and anxious.

Hitler's voice was stronger now and full of hatred. Repeatedly, spitting out the words, he denounced the conspirators. They were 'a tiny gang of traitors and destroyers', a small group of 'filthy, ambitious, despicable creatures' bent on 'sowing seeds of despair'. Listening to him raging, Fey felt a surge of elation; the plot had failed but it had so nearly killed him. 'A feeling of triumph stole over me. Here at last was a demonstration that there was still life in the heart of this nation of apparent slaves. There were still Germans with the courage and determination to sacrifice everything for a common cause.'

Hitler had escaped with a few minor burns and bruises. Within hours of the bomb exploding, he greeted Mussolini at the train halt below the 'Wolf's Lair' for a meeting which had been arranged long before. On the short walk from the station to the forest camp, he told Mussolini what had just happened. Wearing a black cape, his right arm in a sling, and with cotton wool protruding from his ears, he led him straight away to the wrecked conference building. The interpreter who accompanied them described the scene: 'The door was shattered and its broken parts were leaning against the opposite wall of the hut. The room itself presented a picture of destruction . . . tables and chairs lying in splinters all over the place. The beams from the ceiling had crashed down and the windows, complete with frames, had been blown out. The big map table was just a heap of cracked boards and broken legs.' Guiding Mussolini around the room, Hitler demonstrated how he was leaning over the table, resting his weight on his right elbow, when the bomb exploded. 'The bomb went off just in front of my feet,' he told him. He showed him the burnt trousers and the torn tunic of the uniform he had been wearing.

Mussolini, aghast that such a thing could occur in the heart of the Führer's own headquarters, congratulated him on his momentous escape. Yet, for Hitler, this was no mere escape. 'When I reflect on all this, it is obvious that nothing is going to happen to me,' he replied. 'Undoubtedly it is my fate to continue on my path and bring my task to completion. It is not the first time I have escaped death miraculously . . . What happened here is the climax! Having escaped death in so extraordinary a way, I am now more than ever convinced that the great cause which I serve will survive its present perils and everything be brought to a good end.'

It was the message Hitler wanted to convey to the German people.

At the close of his broadcast to the nation, he returned to the theme of Providence: 'Probably only a few can imagine what fate would have befallen Germany if the plot succeeded. I thank Providence and my Creator, but not because He has preserved me. My life is solely devoted to worry, to working for my people. I thank Him, rather, because He has made it possible for me to continue to shoulder these worries, and to pursue my work to the best of my abilities and according to my conscience. I see in it a sign from Providence that I must, and therefore shall, continue my work.'

Hitler used the broadcast to issue emergency orders. 'No military authority, no leader of any unit, no soldier is to obey any orders emanating from these usurpers; on the contrary, it is every German's duty to arrest or, if they resist, to kill at sight anyone issuing or handing on such orders . . . I am convinced that with the elimination of this very small clique of traitors and conspirators we shall at last create in the homeland the atmosphere which the fighters at the front need. For it is unthinkable that at the front hundreds of thousands, nay millions, of good men, should be giving their all, while a small gang of ambitious and miserable creatures here at home perpetually tries to sabotage them. This time we are going to settle accounts with them in the manner to which we National Socialists are accustomed.'

Meeting with senior Nazi leaders earlier, Hitler had elaborated on how he proposed to 'settle the accounts': 'I shall crush and destroy all the treacherous creatures who tried to stand in my path today. Traitors in the bosom of their own people deserve the most ignominious death – and they shall have it! I shall wreak vengeance – inexorable vengeance – on all who were involved in this, and on their families, if they aided them. I shall exterminate this whole brood of vipers once and for all! Exterminate them, yes, exterminate them . . .'

By the time Hitler's address to the nation ended – at ten minutes past one on the morning of 21 July – five of the leading conspirators had already been executed. Among them, Claus von Stauffenberg, who planted the bomb, and Colonel General Ludwig Beck, Ulrich von Hassell's closest friend and the man who would have been president had the plot succeeded.

★

Listening in the dead of that night to Hitler's broadcast, it did not occur to Fey that her father was one of the conspirators. Hitler had mentioned just one name: Colonel Claus von Stauffenberg. When her younger brother had visited at Christmas,* Stauffenberg's name had not cropped up in their conversations about their father's circle. Yet, as the days and weeks passed and it became evident that Hitler was taking advantage of the failure of the plot to arrest and liquidate anyone he thought opposed him, Fey grew increasingly anxious: 'As these events unfolded and more and more people were implicated, I became terribly worried about my father. The names of the men who had been executed, published in the papers, were all too familiar to me. Even though they were mainly army officers at that point, many were friends of my father. Maybe, I thought, the "civilian" opposition groups had not been discovered. Letters arrived regularly from my mother, but they carried no word about the attempt. Given the tight censorship, how could it have been otherwise? But she did refer to "one great preoccupation". This made me suspect something, but I did not give it much weight. Gradually, I found reassurance in the absence of bad news. I presumed that my father, if involved, had not been found out.'

In truth, as the summer wore on, Fey was beset with her own troubles. Tension in the region was escalating rapidly. With the help of the British SOE missions, the partisans now controlled the mountains to the north and east of Brazzà, encompassing an area of more than 1,000 square miles – right up to the Austrian border. Only one or two isolated German detachments remained. There had been fierce fighting on Monte Narat, which Fey could see from the house, and hundreds of German soldiers had been killed. In response, the SS were carrying out brutal reprisals, setting fire to houses and murdering indiscriminately. In the last week of July alone, it was reported that ninety had been killed at Sutrio, thirty at Arta, twenty-two at Pramosio and fifty-two at Paluzza. Down on the plain, the 'rakings' continued and, as all men of military age had fled the villages, the SS were now rounding up women, children and the elderly.

---

* Hans Dieter was convalescing from the wounds he had received on the Eastern Front in March 1943.

'Udine is paved with posters put up by the Garibaldi, calling for people to rise up and embrace Communism,' Fey wrote to Santa Hercolani at the end of July. 'Due to the dreadful SS "rakings" and reprisals, the Garibaldi brigades are getting bigger and bigger, and in order to feed the men hiding out in the mountains, the number of raids on local stores and shops has increased dramatically. Still no sign of D.'

Since 4 June, when the Allies liberated Rome, Fey had been waiting for Detalmo to come home. Thousands of members of the Resistance had made the perilous journey from Rome across enemy lines to join partisan forces in the north to continue the fight against the Germans. As the staff at Brazzà reported sightings of large numbers of men stealing through the villages on their way to the partisans' hideouts in the mountains, Fey could barely contain her excitement.

While she recognized that, with the Germans in occupation, it was impossible for Detalmo to return to Brazzà, she assumed he would join the Osoppo, many of whom were affiliated to the centre-left Partito d'Azione. Their hideouts were a fifteen-minute ride away, which meant she would be able to see Detalmo regularly. After the long months on her own, the thought that he would be close by and there to protect her and the boys in an emergency was a great comfort.

As the weeks passed, and there was no sign of Detalmo, Fey became increasingly anxious. In one respect her life was slightly easier now than it had been. Though, as the wife of a wealthy landowner and therefore a class enemy, she remained on the Garibaldi blacklist, the arrival of the British SOE missions had at least reduced the danger that she would be attacked for 'collaborating' with the Germans. Shocked by the extent to which the Garibaldi partisans' Communist goals prevented them from working with the Osoppo, Hedley Vincent, the commander of the Coolant Mission, had ordered the two groups to form a unified command. It was only by threatening to withdraw the mission – and thus the much-needed supplies – and by convincing the Osoppo of Winston Churchill's loathing of Communism – that Vincent had succeeded in persuading the two battalions to unite.

The Osoppo command had informed their Communist counter-parts that Fey was not a collaborator. However, she still feared that, with the Germans on the back foot, Brazzà itself would be attacked. As a leading figure in the Partito d'Azione and scion of a family that had been among the most powerful in Friuli for centuries, Detalmo's standing was high in the Osoppo and Fey hoped that, if he were home, he could use his influence to persuade the partisans to spare the house.

It was not until the first week in August that she finally received a message from him. It contained the devastating news that he had decided to remain in Rome. Sergio Fenoaltea, a senior minister in the newly formed democratic government, Italy's first in twenty years, had offered him a job as his political secretary and it was an oppor-tunity Detalmo felt he could not turn down. He knew that his proficiency in English and his contacts with the Allies were import-ant to the Partito d'Azione, and Fenoaltea, a close associate of Ugo La Malfa, was a man he admired.

Fey felt deeply betrayed by Detalmo's decision; that he had placed his political loyalties above his family upset her terribly. With the front straddling central Italy, they were now on opposite sides of the fighting line. It meant that she and the boys would be alone at Brazzà for the duration of the war.

In the ensuing months, Fey would come to look back at his 'deser-tion' as the moment when something in her marriage was broken.

A few days after Detalmo's message arrived, Fey received another blow. 'I was informed of something I had been dreading for some time,' she wrote. 'My protector, Major Eisermann, was leaving for a new posting. For almost a year he had supported and helped me with other less well-disposed officers and had made my life in the occupied house bearable. With his departure, I felt my position at Brazzà would be less secure.'

Before leaving, Eisermann introduced Fey to his successor, Col-onel Dannenberg. 'Tall and rather stiff in manner, he seemed a nice enough man, but I sensed that he was weak and would never oppose decisions made from above or by the political officer, Lieutenant

Kretschmann. Although Kretschmann was not hostile to me, he was far too fanatical a Nazi to be trusted.'

The strain of it all was affecting her health and at the end of August she spent several days in hospital in Udine having blood tests. From there, she wrote a guarded letter to Santa Hercolani, in which she summed up her worries:

> My guests are beginning to have strange people* around them, who come and steal things, and they're not safe any more. I keep coming across strangers in the corridor. The guests remain the same, but their boss has gone, and one [Kretschmann] is an <u>absolute thug</u>. This worries me, not so much for now but for the future. I can only hope that D is in good health and is doing something useful because it would have been much better if he had come back to give me a sense of protection. When will we see each other again? I'm fed up with all these separations without end and endless dangers. I can cope with living dangerously, but I don't want it to go on forever and ever.

In her list of concerns, Fey did not mention her father. She still had no idea that he had been arrested.

* The Germans were using troops of Cossacks to carry out reprisals in the area.

15

After the catastrophe of 20 July, Hassell could have run away; he could have gone to ground, hidden with friends or tried to escape with false papers, as a number of his fellow conspirators did. But he thought it dishonourable to flee. So he stayed in Berlin, waiting in plain sight for the Gestapo to come and get him.

On 24 July, he dined at the Adlon, a luxurious hotel close to the Reichstag, frequented by Nazi apparatchiks. On 26 July, Hans Gisevius spotted him, out walking in the peace of the Grunewald, a forest on the edge of Berlin. Gisevius, Beck's liaison officer to Allen Dulles, the head of US intelligence in Geneva, was himself wanted by the Gestapo and was hiding out in a house nearby. 'There goes someone who has death on his heels,' Gisevius wrote of his sighting of Hassell. 'His head was bent in a curious fashion . . . as if he were trying to hide from some terrible danger that was pursuing him.'

It was around three in the morning on 28 July that an insistent ringing of the doorbell woke Ilse von Hassell at Ebenhausen. She opened the door to two Gestapo officials and the local policemen. Almuth was with her. They asked where her husband was and, knowing that it had never been his intention to hide, she told them exactly where they would find him – at his office in Berlin. Before leaving, the Gestapo demanded to search his desk and papers. Ilse managed to divert their attention from a photograph album in which the last notes of his diary lay hidden. Despite her cooperation, she and her daughter Almuth were arrested and taken to the Gestapo headquarters in Munich and, after renewed interrogation, to a nearby prison.

A few hours later, Hassell was arrested in his office at the German Institute for Economic Research; he received the Gestapo agents, seated at his desk, as if they were official visitors.

He was taken immediately for interrogation at the Reich Main Security Office in Prinz-Albrecht-Strasse, where he remained briefly until his transfer to Ravensbrück. This notorious camp, set up to hold women, had a section in it for special prisoners or *Prominenten*, as the Gestapo referred to them. There Ulrich was treated humanely; in a letter to Ilse he reassured her that he was allowed out for walks in the courtyard and in fine weather could drink his soup on the steps of the block. The sculptress Puppi Sarre, also detained at Ravensbrück, saw him and was struck by 'his serenity, his confident mien and manner'.

But on 15 August he was brought back to Berlin in chains and interrogations at Gestapo HQ began. Hassell was held at the prison in Prinz-Albrecht-Strasse with others involved in the 20 July plot – among them members of the German intelligence service and senior military figures. Though they were forbidden to speak, they were able to have fragments of conversations in the communal bathroom at the end of the row of cells. Fabian von Schlabrendorff,* arrested for his part in the plot, remembered being told by Hassell: 'My death is certain. When you get out, please give a message to my wife. My last thought will be of her.'

Hassell did not leave a record of his sessions with Commissioner Habecker of the Criminal Police, who conducted the 'sharpened interrogations'.† But as Schlabrendorff describes in his detailed account of the methods the Gestapo used, the same treatment was meted out to all the conspirators:

> One method was to take the prisoner out of his cell for questioning and then let him wait endlessly in an anteroom. If this had no effect other means of influencing him were employed. Usually three officials worked together. One would threaten the prisoner and shower him with abuse, the second would talk to him in a soothing manner, urging him to calm down and have a cigarette, the third would then try and appeal to the prisoner's code of honour. In this way, the Gestapo provided for three different kinds of temperament in the hope that the prisoner would in the end succumb to one of these approaches or to the combination of all three.

* Schlabrendorff had also been involved in an earlier attempt to assassinate Hitler. He was the man who planted the explosives, concealed in bottles of cognac, on the plane carrying the Führer back from the Eastern Front in March 1943.
† Term used by the Gestapo.

If these methods failed to extort a confession or the names of others, yet to be arrested, torture was used. 'One night I was taken from my cell,' Schlabrendorff continued:

There were four people in the room: the Commissioner; his secretary, a girl of about twenty; a sergeant of the Security Police in uniform; and an assistant in civilian clothes. I was told that I was being given a last chance to confess. When I persisted in my denials, the Gestapo officials resorted to torture.

This torture was executed in four stages. First, my hands were chained behind my back, and a device, which gripped all the fingers separately, was fastened to my hands. The inner side of this mechanism was studded with pins, the points of which pressed against my fingertips. The turning of a screw caused the instrument to contract, thus forcing the points of the pins into my fingers.

When that did not achieve the desired confession, the second stage followed. I was strapped, face down, on a frame resembling a bedstead, and my head was covered with a blanket. Then cylinders, resembling stovepipes and studded with nails on the inner surface, were strapped to my bare legs. Here, too, a screw mechanism was used to contract these tubes so that the nails pierced my legs from ankle to thigh.

For the third stage of torture, the 'bedstead' itself was the main instrument. I was strapped down as described above, again with a blanket over my head. With the help of a special mechanism this medieval torture rack was then expanded – either in sudden jerks, or gradually – each time stretching my shackled body.

In the fourth and final stage I was tied in a bent position which did not allow me to move even slightly backward or sideways. Then the Police Commissioner and the Police sergeant together fell on me from behind, and beat me with heavy clubs. Each blow caused me to fall forward, and because my hands were chained behind my back, I crashed with full force on to my face . . . None of the brutalities succeeded in getting me to confess a word or to name one of my fellow anti-Nazis.

I am often asked how we were able to endure these brutalities. There are a number of sources from which a man can draw the strength to carry him through such ordeals. We all made the discovery that we could endure far more than we ever had believed possible. The two great polar forces of human emotions, love and hate, together formed a supporting structure on which we could rely when things became unbearable. Love, the positive force, included our faith in the moral worth of our actions, the knowledge that we had fought for humanity and decency, and the sense of having fulfilled a higher duty . . . Hate, the negative force, was just as important in sustaining us in our darkest hours of pain and need. The consuming, unqualified hatred, made up of equal parts of revulsion, contempt, and fury which we felt for the evil of Nazism, was so powerful a force that it helped us endure situations which would otherwise have been intolerable.

In the short periods of respite from interrogation, Hassell filled in the time left to him by writing his memoirs and such letters as he was allowed. 'A prison cell,' he said, 'is a good place to start one's memoirs . . . One sees one's life and one's self stripped of all illusions.' He typed as fast as he could, filling 150 pages using single-line spacing, but only managed to finish the period 1926–30, a happy time for him when the children were young. In letters to Ilse, he admitted that his recollection of the past gave him great comfort. His faith, too, upheld him; meditating on it, he had reached a sense of peace. Towards the end of the manuscript, visible in the margin, Ulrich copied out three lines from a well-known hymn: 'You can lead us dreaming through the gates of death and at once give us freedom.'

On 31 August, Ilse's widowed mother, Frau von Tirpitz, wrote directly to Hitler imploring him to show leniency towards her son-in-law. Martin Bormann, Hitler's secretary, replied that the Führer was unable to 'facilitate mercy' as 'von Hassell has himself confessed and cannot be released'.

A week later, together with nine other conspirators, Hassell was brought before the People's Court to face the notorious judge Roland Freisler. The retinue of lawyers and courtroom officials failed to create any semblance of a proper trial, with Freisler acting as prosecutor, jury and judge. Wearing a wing collar, white bow tie and a scarlet robe over his suit, he enjoyed playing the lead in the drama. His main props were the president's table and, behind it, a huge swastika, the folds of its drapery concealing a camera.

Freisler's modus operandi was singularly cruel; he interrupted the defendants, shouted them down, insulted them and swore at them. Made to appear like common criminals and stripped of their dignity, the cream of the Wehrmacht and the aristocracy came shuffling into the court with no laces in their shoes, and their belts and braces removed so that they were forced to hold up their trousers when they rose to be interrogated.

One of the German press representatives attending the trial recalled that Freisler's 'hatred' was directed primarily against the 'impressive Hassell': 'The shouting Freisler called him the father of lies, before he had even opened his mouth.'

Helmut Schmidt, later chancellor of Germany, also attended the trial, as a military observer. In his memoirs, *Was Ich Noch Sagen Wollte* (*What I Wanted to Add*), he recalled Hassell's graceful demeanour: 'When he was addressed by Freisler, he stood up and remained standing, and when Freisler had finished reading the charges, he sat down again. He remained expressionless and didn't make any gestures . . . After the war I wrote to his widow. I saw it as my duty to tell her what a huge impression her husband had made on me in his last hours.'

In this letter to Ilse, written in June 1946, Schmidt concluded: 'The whole trial was an example of Freisler's swagger, blending Goebbels' cleverness and loquacity with the jargon of the mob. That this process was full of mockery; that no witnesses were called to testify; that the official defence was only called the night before; that the defendants were not allowed to finish their sentences without being interrupted; that only what suited Freisler was brought up, was so depressing that I couldn't bring myself to return the following day.'

Of her husband, he said: 'He followed the trial with a distant look and a rigid expression, which told of his contempt for this court, and he gave his answers in the most sparing way without even glancing at

Freisler. I believe that the SS chiefs in the viewing room noticed who the real winner was . . . You will understand, dear lady, that, from this moment onwards, the conflict between the recognition of what we were heading towards and the notion of a fulfilment of our soldierly duty towards the Fatherland, for which we were raised, became unbearable in us young officers.'

Hassell's final statement in court was: 'If a government plunges its country and its people into the abyss of a fearful catastrophe, it has a duty to hand over the reins, forthwith. The government is not the same as the people. The people are permanent, the government fleeting, but nevertheless responsible.'

Hassell and the nine other conspirators were condemned to death on 8 September. The sentence was carried out at Plötzensee prison within two hours of its being handed down.

He had no time to write to his children. But to Ilse, his 'sunshine', he left the following lines:

My beloved Ilsechen

Thirty years ago today, I received the French bullet* which I carry about with me still. On this day, too, the People's Court pronounced its sentence and, if it is carried out, as I imagine it will be, it brings to an end the supreme happiness that I have known thanks to you. It was certainly too precious to last. At this moment I am filled with the deepest gratitude towards God and towards you. You are at my side and you give me peace and strength. This thought mitigates the searing agony of having to leave you and the children. May God grant that your soul and mine may one day be reunited. You are alive, however, and that is the great consolation I have amidst all my anxieties for you all, including the material ones; and, as regards the future of our children, knowing that you are strong and courageous – a rock, but a dear sweet rock, for them. Remain as you

---

* Exactly thirty years before – on 8 September 1914 – Hassell had received a near-fatal wound at the First Battle of the Marne. There were traces of the bullet still lodged in his heart.

are, good and kind, and do not grow embittered. God bless you and Germany . . .

In deepest love and gratitude, I embrace you.

Your Ulrich

Hitler's vengeance did not end with Freisler's verdict. He wanted the condemned men 'hanged like animals in the slaughterhouse' and he wanted them to die slowly. The widows would receive notification of their husbands' deaths through official channels followed by a bill for the execution of 585 Reichsmarks and 74 pfennigs.* They were forbidden to put announcements of the deaths in the papers.

The method of execution Hitler selected did not, as in conventional hangings, break the neck. It was a slow and painful death by strangulation. On his express orders, the hangings were filmed so that he could watch them over and over, at his leisure. According to his architect, Albert Speer, in the days after, Hitler spent entire evenings watching the footage. Speer himself was invited to a showing, but declined in revulsion. The audience, he noted, consisted primarily of civilians and junior SS personnel. 'Not a single Wehrmacht officer attended.'

The utter bleakness of the executions, as the ten men were brought out to die under the bright lights of the cameras, is revealed in an account by one of the prison warders:

> Imagine a room with a low ceiling and whitewashed walls. Below the ceiling a rail was fixed. From it hung six big hooks, like those butchers use to hang meat. In one corner stood a movie camera. Reflectors cast a dazzling, blinding light, like that in a studio. In this strange, small room were the Prosecutor General of the Reich, the hangman with his two assistants, two camera technicians, and I myself with a second prison warden. By the wall, there was a small table with a bottle of cognac and glasses for the witnesses to the execution.

---

* Approximately £2,500 in today's money.

The convicted men were led in. They were wearing their prison garb, and they were handcuffed. They were placed in a single row. Leering and making jokes, the hangman got busy. He was known in his circles for his 'humour'. No statement, no clergymen, no journalists.

One after another, all ten faced their turn. All showed the same courage. It took, in all, twenty-five minutes. The hangman wore a permanent leer, and made jokes unceasingly. The camera worked uninterruptedly, for Hitler wanted to see and hear how his enemies had died. He was able to watch the proceedings that same evening in the Reich Chancellery.

PART FIVE

16.

It was seven o'clock in the morning on Saturday 9 September – the day after Ulrich's trial. Fey was lying quietly in bed when she heard an urgent knock on the door. Without waiting for an answer, Lieutenant Kretschmann marched in. His face was pale and he seemed very disturbed. He did not say a word; he simply stood there, his eyes shifting nervously around the room. After some seconds, Fey broke the silence.

'For heaven's sake,' she said impatiently. 'What's happened?'

'Luckily you're at home' was his terse reply.

'But why shouldn't I be?'

'Didn't you listen to the radio last night or early this morning?' he asked.

'No, how could I? I have guests in the house,' she replied. 'For goodness' sake, tell me what's happened?'

'Your father has been arrested and executed. He has been hanged.'

Fey tried not to show any reaction, but as she struggled to retain her composure, her entire body began to shake. Without ceremony, speaking coldly and to the point, Kretschmann told her that, as the unit's political officer, it was his duty to report her to the authorities. At his suggestion, Colonel Dannenberg had driven into Udine earlier that morning to inform the Gestapo that Ulrich von Hassell's daughter was living nearby. She was to be kept under constant surveillance while they waited for instructions from Berlin.

Still shaking, Fey lay there, her mind racing. 'My thoughts flew to the children. Were they in danger too? My father . . . I couldn't allow myself to even think of it. I also realized at that moment that with Major Eisermann's departure I had lost my protection. Eisermann would certainly have done things differently; he might even have helped me to escape with the children. But Dannenberg was of a different temperament; he would never have the courage to take such a decision on his own.'

Kretschmann was unable to tell Fey how long it would take Berlin to respond; but she knew her priority must be to remove all incriminating evidence while there was still time. Immediately, she thought of Detalmo's letters from Rome; then she remembered he had been careful to write under the pseudonyms 'Giuseppe' and 'Isabella'. Her own diaries, however, were extremely problematic. There were more than seven volumes, going back to her childhood in Rome. 'I knew that if the SS found the diaries they would prove how much I hated the Nazis.'

Fey had some friends staying for the weekend. Pulling herself together, she told Kretschmann that, in the circumstances, it would be best if she asked her guests to leave. Allowing her a few minutes to dress, he walked out of the room. Straight away, Fey retrieved the diaries from a drawer in her desk, and put them into a bag.

Later that morning, as she said goodbye to her friends, she managed to hide the diaries in their luggage while Kretschmann's back was turned.

In Berlin, Hitler had charged Himmler with the task of wreaking vengeance on the families of the July plotters – 'this brood of vipers'.

It did not take long for the man in control of the terror machine to invoke *Sippenhaft* – the doctrine of 'blood guilt'. A principle of ancient Germanic law, obsolete since the Middle Ages, it was specifically revived by Himmler to punish the families of the conspirators. According to this doctrine, treachery was a manifestation of diseased blood, not only in the culprit himself but in his relatives too. They, therefore, were also guilty of the crime committed. 'In consequence all are to be exterminated, to the last member of the clan,' he announced in a speech to Nazi regional leaders on 3 August.

The following weeks saw the mass arrest of the relatives of those involved in the attempt on Hitler's life. This even extended to grandparents, parents-in-law, brothers, sisters and children.

By the end of August the round-ups were complete. More than 180 *Sippenhäftlinge* – prisoners of kin – were in custody.

Living under her married name in Italy, Fey, however, had escaped Himmler's net. At the Reich Main Security Office in Berlin, the officials charged with identifying relatives of the key conspirators had failed to link her to Ulrich von Hassell.

It had taken the zealous young Lieutenant Kretschmann to bring her to the Gestapo's attention. Once alerted, their response was immediate.

Shortly after ten o'clock – just three hours after Fey learned of her father's execution – Colonel Dannenberg, accompanied by an SS official, arrived to take her away. As she gathered her things, Roberto and Corrado clung to her, sensing something was wrong. 'I was horrified and desperate at the thought of having to leave the children, who were looking at me silently with frightened eyes. My only consolation was the presence of Ernesta and Mila, who I knew would look after them well, and with love. I told Ernesta to sleep in my bed in the children's room, and I told Corradino and Robertino that I would be back in a few hours.'

Outside in the courtyard, the household staff and soldiers stationed at the castle had gathered to say goodbye. A little way off, over by the farm buildings, Fey noticed the estate workers were there too. 'As I walked towards Dannenberg's car escorted by the SS official, I passed the terrified faces of the Bovolenta family who were hanging out of their windows watching the scene. Other contadini families watched silently from doorways. Nonino was crying, as was Mila. The German soldiers looked on, their faces grave and disbelieving. Ernesta was not there as I had asked her to stay in the house with the children so they would not see me leave.'

Colonel Dannenberg drove Fey to Udine – a fifteen-minute journey during which neither of them, nor the SS official, exchanged a word. In the centre of the city, the car turned into a side street and drew up in front of a large palazzo, appropriated by the Gestapo for use as a headquarters. Situated behind the cathedral, it was a fine eighteenth-century building, ochre in colour, with carved stone balconies. Clouds of red geraniums spilled through the pillars of the balustrades. Looking up at the facade, Fey recognized it immediately as the home of long-standing friends of Detalmo's family; she had dined there in the early years of her marriage.

As the SS official escorted her up the steps to the entrance of the building, a woman approached her. She was the wife of one of Udine's leading lawyers and she was asking for help for her husband, who the Gestapo had recently arrested for defending a group of Jews. Roughly, the SS official pushed her aside, telling Fey that she was forbidden to speak to anyone. Helpless, and feeling humiliated by the woman's initial assumption that she was in league with the Germans, Fey could only gesture that she was now a prisoner too.

Inside the palazzo, the Gestapo made Fey wait while they discussed what to do. The orders from Berlin were to hold her in solitary confinement in the local gaol. But in recent weeks the SS had arrested hundreds of men and women and the single cells were full. At this point – or indeed before she was detained – SS Police Chief Ludolf von Alvensleben, whom Fey had invited to tea on numerous occasions, could have revoked the order for her arrest. A fanatical Nazi, however, he had no sympathy for the July plotters, and after a long wait, the Gestapo drove her to the prison, where they handed her over to the nuns in charge of the women's section.

Fey described the conditions: 'There were 150 women prisoners in a space made for forty or fifty. The nuns who supervised us belonged to the order Ancelle della Carità (Handmaids of Charity) and had run the women's section of the prison for years. As they had only dealt with criminals until a few months earlier, they were surly and rude. The "political" prisoners were indignant at being forced to share cells with ordinary criminals: in one of the larger rooms there were about forty women who had to sleep without blankets on the wooden floors. Luckily, I was put into a cell with just two others. There was only one toilet for all 150 women, which we were only allowed to use twice a day – and all of us together. For this purpose, the cell doors were opened and we had to form a long queue, waiting our turn on the filthy, primitive bowl.'

Saint Maria di Rosa, the daughter of a wealthy aristocrat, had founded the Handmaids of Charity in 1840. Born in Brescia, an industrial town at the foot of the Alps, she had devoted herself since her youth to the care of the sick and the needy, turning down offers of marriage to look after the workers in her father's textile mills. She ministered to them during the cholera epidemic of 1836 and established a women's guild and a home for deaf children on her family's estate. 'I can't go to bed with a quiet conscience,' she once said, 'if during the day I've missed any chance, however slight, of preventing wrongdoing, or of helping to bring about some good.'

One hundred years on, the Handmaids of Charity failed to observe their founder's principles. Pastoral care was kept to a minimum. The nuns neglected to clean the cells and the prison was overrun with mice and vermin. The one meal handed out each day was a meagre bowl of soup. To spare the nuns the effort of having to provide anything more substantial, prisoners were allowed to receive food from relatives and friends and to order in from nearby restaurants. Nor did the Handmaids appear concerned for the souls of those under their care. Most of the women in the wing had been imprisoned because their neighbours had denounced them; they had little or no idea why they were there. In founding the order, Saint Maria's aim had been to 'prevent wrongdoing' and to offer spiritual guidance. Yet the nuns made no attempt to intervene with the Gestapo on the women's behalf, nor did they offer spiritual counselling.

'The job the nuns did best was pray,' Fey recalled. 'They began in the morning and prayed incessantly, before and after the meal, while going to the toilet, during daily "recreation" in the courtyard, in the afternoon – always praying. At eight o'clock in the evening, the Handmaids went from cell to cell, opening the small windows in the doors and mechanically intoning "*Sia lodato Gesù Cristo*" [Praised be Jesus Christ], to which we would answer, "*Sempre sia lodato*" [Always be praised]. There was a small chapel where, every morning, we gathered to celebrate Mass. Everyone attended the Mass; it marked a change from the tedium of our routine as we were able to leave our cells. While the continuous and mechanical praying got on one's nerves, the Mass itself was beautiful and it soothed the heart and lifted one's spirits.'

To Fey's surprise, Lieutenant Kretschmann came to visit her on her first day in the prison. He brought with him some bread and a roast chicken sent by Nonino. His manner was unctuous, his courtesy disarming. He was keen to impress upon her how much she was missed at Brazzà; straight-faced, without betraying a hint of guilt at his own culpability, he told her that his soldiers were so shocked and saddened by her arrest that they had stopped working and had all got drunk. He also told her that he and Colonel Dannenberg were doing everything they could to secure her release.

Almost every day, one or the other visited. They brought food and books, and assured her that they would get her out of 'this hell' before too long. To begin with, she found their attention infuriating. They were responsible for her incarceration. So how could they dare to visit proffering false comfort? But as the days passed, she was convinced by their concern. The two officers appeared to be working hard on her behalf, and their efforts to secure her release seemed to be genuinely motivated by remorse. Further, no one else was allowed to visit her, and it was consoling to be able to speak to someone from the 'outside'.

On 19 September, after Fey had been imprisoned for ten days, Kretschmann and Dannenberg succeeded in persuading the Gestapo to allow her to return to Brazzà. It was on the condition that she would be kept under close surveillance until further orders were received from Berlin.

When Fey arrived home, the airmen and servants were lined up on the drive. Corrado and Roberto were there too. As the car pulled up, they rushed forward to greet her. Straight away, Kretschmann escorted them inside, allowing Fey to spend the rest of the day alone with the boys: 'The elation of seeing the children was indescribable. Corradino was quiet but kept hugging me and crawling into my arms. When I began to cry at the joy of being with them again, he said: "Mama is crying. Corradino wants to help Mama." Robertino, wanting in some way to express his own happiness, rushed crazily on all fours from one corner of the room to the other. That evening, as I was saying prayers with them, Corradino said, "Mama must never go away again without telling Corradino where she is going and when she is coming back." I promised with all my heart never to leave them again.'

It was a promise the events of the coming days would force her to break.

17

Kretschmann kept Fey and the children prisoner. Scrupulously adhering to the Gestapo's orders, the young lieutenant locked them in at night and did not allow them out during the day. He had allocated a new set of rooms for their confinement. Situated on the ground floor in the east wing of the villa, they were more secure; the windows were barred, making escape impossible.

It was the same suite of rooms the King of Italy had occupied during his brief stay at Brazzà in April 1941. On one side, they looked out over the ruins of the castle; on the other, to a beautiful chapel, which Detalmo's ancestors had used for family weddings, christenings and funerals since taking ownership of the castle in the thirteenth century. The rooms, however, were smaller than those in the west wing, and Fey missed the view of the garden. With the prospect of 'further orders from Berlin' hanging over her, and the children fidgety as a result of being cooped in, the days dragged. But she was with them – this was the main thing.

News of her return spread quickly, and Kretschmann allowed her to receive visitors, which relieved the tedium of the long hours spent inside. Friends and neighbours rallied around and she barely had a minute alone. She was relieved to hear that her imprisonment had removed any suspicion that she was collaborating with the Germans. While she was in prison, the contadini had prayed for her, and were continuing to pray for her – proof they considered her to be on their side.

Her visitors updated her on developments in the neighbourhood during her absence. Large numbers of troops had moved into the area and it was feared the Germans were gearing up to launch an offensive. Along the ridge between Faedis and Nimis – mountain villages 7 miles to the east of Brazzà – the partisans were shoring up their defences. Trenches had been dug, and barbed wire and barriers placed along the road. In Udine, the German were requisitioning scores of villas and taking the city's supply of pasta, meat and flour from the warehouses. Simultaneously, the Fascists appeared to have found a new confidence and were swaggering around in their black uniforms, their belts bristling with handguns, daggers and grenades.

But it was news from Detalmo that Fey longed for. She had not heard from him since June, when he had written to say that he was staying in Rome. On the morning of her arrest, she had sent a message via the Red Cross to tell him that the SS were taking her to Udine and that her father was dead. Had he received it? Or had his reply been delayed or lost? His silence reinforced the sense of abandonment she had felt ever since she had learned that he wasn't coming home.

There was no word from her family in Germany either. Two weeks had passed since her father had been executed and they had not written. To be so far away from her mother, her brothers and her sister at such a time was deeply upsetting. Every part of her ached to be with them, to be able to console them and to share her own grief. Not knowing what had happened to them, she worried constantly.

Alone and cut off from those she loved, Fey was comforted by the one letter that was waiting for her on her return. It was from Santa Hercolani, to whom she had confided her disappointment at Detalmo's decision to remain in Rome. Ten years older than Fey, Santa was also close to Ilse, her mother. They had become friends in the early 1930s, when Hassell was posted to Rome. While Santa, evidently fearful of the German censors, had been careful in her choice of words, reading between the lines, Fey could tell that she too was desperate for news of Ilse:

Dearest Fey

I only wanted to tell you that I stand by you. You will certainly understand my state of mind and know my feelings. Remember that you can always think of me as an old, very old, sister, and I consider you much more than a friend . . .

If you can, write again, and if you know something, anything, tell me . . . Now we really are in the midst of the hurricane, and I think of your mother, of Wolf Ulli, and of the true value of many things that may be destroyed.

★

Fey had been home for two days when her neighbour, Pia Tacoli, the sister of Ferdinando, an Osoppo brigade leader, came to visit. In recent weeks, the Germans had also occupied the Tacolis' house; it was being used as a field hospital to treat soldiers wounded in the fighting with the partisans, an irony that amused Pia and her brother as the house was a stronghold of partisan activity.

It was just half a mile across the fields to Brazzà. But, that morning, Pia was careful to take a circuitous route. Reaching the ruins of the castle, she waited behind a wall until the guards, patrolling the path that ran past Fey's rooms, were out of sight.

Pia had come to propose a rescue plan, which she had drawn up with the help of a group of Osoppo partisans. Outside Fey's rooms, a path led through the woods to a small wooden gate which opened on to the main road. If Fey could manage to slip out with the boys, Pia would be waiting with a trap to spirit them away to the partisans' hideout in the mountains. To guard against the risk of German reprisals, the men and women working in the woods at Brazzà had sworn a vow of silence. Fey recognized that the plan was fraught with danger. 'The German guards who paced around the castle day and night had to be eluded. I was also afraid for Pia, since the Germans would connect her absence with my disappearance. However, my main reason for refusing her courageous offer was that I feared the terrible and indiscriminate reprisals on my family if I escaped. I could not take the risk that my mother and sister would be imprisoned, even taken to a concentration camp on my account.'

The day before, Fey had finally received a letter from her mother. She and Almuth were under house arrest at the family home near Munich. The letter was undated, but Fey was buoyed by its contents: 'She wrote of a small ray of hope regarding my father's fate. Relief flooded through me. Had the radio account of my father's death been wrong? I had already closed a chapter of my life as I had lain in prison in Udine, haunted by images of his brutal death. Although it seemed nonsensical that the radio should broadcast such a lie, I could believe anything of the Nazis. This idea, the remote possibility that my father had not been executed along with the others, gave me renewed hope.'

The news from her mother and the deceptive comfort of the

routine at Brazzà with its familiar rhythms, and the stalwart support of Nonino and Ernesta, meant that Fey allowed herself to disregard the danger inherent in her situation. 'I knew the SS was thorough, but I had little idea then just how thorough.'

On the evening of 25 September – six days after Fey returned to Brazzà – Colonel Dannenberg received a call from the Gestapo in Udine. Berlin had responded to their query. Fey and the children were to be deported to Austria: she had thirty-six hours to prepare for their departure.

The call came through shortly before Dannenberg was due to host a drinks party for Lieutenant Kretschmann, who was leaving the next day for another posting. The colonel invited Fey to join them; yet, after they had raised their glasses to the lieutenant's future, neither he nor Kretschmann had the courage to tell her that she and the children were about to be deported. Instead, Dannenberg wrote her a letter early the next morning before leaving for an appointment, and asked his adjutant to deliver it.

Fey, who was asleep in her bedroom, was woken by the sound of the adjutant slipping the letter under the door.

Dear Frau Pirzio-Biroli [the colonel began]

It is most embarrassing for me to have to write this letter, but I can only use this formal and crude method – that is, a letter – because I was suddenly called away to Verona. But I will hurry with my business there so as to be able to return in time for your departure tomorrow morning.

In a few words, I have been informed that you are to prepare for a journey that, for the moment, will take you to Innsbruck. The children will go with you. You are only permitted to take luggage that you strictly need.

I will drive you personally to Udine station, where you will be entrusted to a man in civilian clothes who will accompany you. I have tried to obtain more precise information but unfortunately without success. I can only tell you as consolation that I got the impression that it will not be long until we meet here again; of course, as long as the regiment is not posted elsewhere.

So, Frau Pirzio-Biroli, hold your head up, even if everything is very difficult for you. One must never lose courage. After all, you have nothing to do with the known facts. Have faith and don't show your distress. I don't yet know the hour that the train leaves. All I know is that you leave tomorrow morning. The exact time will be told you in my absence. Now, dear lady, courage.

With my respectful regards,
Col. H. Dannenberg

Quickly, Fey reread the letter to be sure she had understood it correctly. Reeling from its contents, courage was the last thing she felt: 'A feeling of total despair swept over me. I had been aware of the frightening possibility of deportation, but I had also hoped that the Gestapo in Berlin would dismiss a marginal case like mine – a single woman with two small children, alone in a foreign country. Now I was confronted with a fait accompli; I was being helplessly sucked into the Nazi terror machine.'

Her despair was compounded by anger; she blamed herself. If only she had listened to Detalmo and taken the boys to Rome after the armistice or, at the very least, accepted his cousins' offer to stay at Frassanelle, their estate outside Padua. With a stab of guilt, she recognized that, however much she had persuaded herself that she had stayed at Brazzà to protect the house and the families working on the estate, the truth was she had been afraid to leave. Brazzà was *her* protector. It was her cocoon from the world; it made her feel safe. Through her own weakness, she had endangered the children. If anything were to happen to them, it would be her fault.

Some minutes later, the colonel's adjutant returned to tell her that she and the boys would be leaving at dawn the next day.

With less than twenty-four hours to go before their departure, Fey had a great deal to do: 'The children had neither shoes nor clothes for a northern winter. Nonino was sent with an urgent appeal to the shoe-maker. The woman who knitted for us started to knit two jerseys. She worked far into the night producing two warm pullovers. At four o'clock the following morning, Nonino picked up the shoes. The cobbler had also worked through the night. I asked Alvise di Brazzà to look after the estate and to help Bovolenta wherever possible. The kind army doctor attached to the Engineer Corps gave me 300 marks, which he advised me to sew into the lining of my coat together with the 3,000 lire I already had. My baggage consisted mainly of things to eat. Overcoming my opposition, Nonino packed an entire ham and several large salamis. Alvise's wife, Anna, brought 600 cigarettes, which turned out to be a most precious gift. Our great friends and neighbours, the Stringhers, brought biscuits, tins of meat, tea, and condensed milk.'

Late that night, Pia Tacoli returned for the second time in a week. Earlier, after hearing Fey's news, she had ridden up to the Osoppo hideouts in the mountains – a dangerous journey that had involved skirting numerous German checkpoints. Making contact with the partisans high on the slopes of Mount Joanaz, she had begged them to come up with one last rescue plan. The plan, which they were now primed to execute, was risky; at dawn the following morning, as Fey and the boys were being driven to Udine, the Osoppo would ambush the car and kill their German escorts. As much as she wanted to, Fey could not bring herself to go along with it; the danger of the children being caught in the gunfire was too great, and while Colonel Dannenberg had proved himself to be a weak and cowardly man, he would be driving them to the station at Udine and she did not want to be responsible for his death. Pia left in the early hours of the morning, facing another long and dangerous journey into the mountains, to tell the partisans to stand down.

After she left, Fey wrote a letter to Lotti, her old governess. Her overriding fear was that she and the children would simply 'disappear'. Her father had warned her about Hitler's *Nacht und Nebel* (Night and Fog) directive. Purposefully targeted at the families of political opponents in the occupied countries, the decree was designed to quell resistance by promoting an atmosphere of mystery and fear. The directive stated that those arrested were to be secretly transported to concentration camps in Germany and no information was to be given out to their relatives. The Nazis had even coined a term for those who 'vanished'; they were *vernebelt* – transformed into mist.

Fey was writing to Lotti in case of this eventuality. Colonel

Dannenberg had told her that 'for the moment' she and the children were being taken to Innsbruck; he was confident that they would not be detained for long. But it was quite possible that he was wrong. The Gestapo were hardly likely to communicate their true intentions to a regular soldier. As she composed the letter, Fey forced herself to imagine the worst. If she *was* going to Germany, she could not be sure the children would go with her. She knew that if she 'disappeared', there was a danger they would be lost forever. Detalmo had not seen the boys since the summer of 1943 and the only photographs he had of them were ten months out of date. They were growing so fast, and changing so much, if she died in the camps and Detalmo had to go in search of them, would he ever recognize them? The same was true of her mother; she had last seen the children in the winter of 1942, when Roberto was just fourteen months old. It was imperative that someone should have the most up-to-date photographs, and Lotti was the obvious choice. While she had been part of the family since the 1920s, she had escaped the Gestapo's net and was now living quietly in Hamburg with her sister, Anni.

Writing the letter, Fey was circumspect about her reason for sending the photographs, but she knew Lotti would understand:

Dear Lotti

A few lines in a great hurry. Today I was informed that I would be 'accompanied' to Innsbruck tomorrow morning together with the children. You can imagine my feelings. But even in the darkest moments one must continue to hope for a better future and not lose courage.

I am afraid that I might be out of contact for a long time. So I am sending the latest photographs of the children, which have come out particularly well. I still have a lot to do before my departure as I want to leave the estate in good hands. I have much to think about, so I'll finish here. Think of us, dear Lotti and Anni.

Lots and lots of love,
your desperate and worried Li★

★

★ Fey's nickname.

The next morning, Fey was up before dawn. The weather had changed and it was a chilly 10 degrees and raining. Waking the children at 4 a.m., she dressed them in their new shoes and sweaters, telling them they were 'going on an adventure'. Two hours later, Colonel Dannenberg, accompanied by an SS officer, appeared to take them to the station. As they were escorted out of the house, Fey was overwhelmed to see the servants – most of whom had been up all night – waiting on the drive: 'Everyone had stayed awake to watch me go. Nonino, Pina,* Ernesta, Mila and Bovolenta, along with his enormous family. All were crying desperately. I did all I could to control myself for fear of upsetting the children still further . . . Taking a last look at assembled friends and neighbours and hugging the children close to me, I got into Dannenberg's car, unable to believe that I was really being taken away.'

* Nonino's wife.

18.

At Udine station, Colonel Dannenberg handed Fey and the children over to a Gestapo agent. The forecourt was packed with troops. Dressed in battle fatigue, they stood, formed up in long lines, waiting to board the military trains that were pulling into and out of the station in quick succession. Some of the carriages were armoured, the swastika clearly visible beneath the huge gun turrets. Cossacks, mounted on horses, guns slung over their shoulders and ammunition belts spilling from their saddlebags, were also queuing to board the troop carriers. The noise was deafening; the shouting of orders by company sergeants, and the cursing of soldiers, directed at the Cossacks when their horses reared and kicked out.

It was 6.20 a.m. and this was the launch of the long-anticipated *rastrellamento* against the partisans. 'The blow which we felt was always coming, but which we vaguely hoped to escape, fell on Sept 27th when the enemy opened a full-scale offensive,' the SOE commander in the area reported back to London on 4 October 1944. 'Sooner or later it was felt that if the partisans made sufficient nuisance of themselves, the enemy would retaliate. It was also felt that his retaliation could be countered until the time came when he was able to muster sufficient forces and equipment to launch a large-scale offensive.'

For almost three months now, the SOE-trained partisans had controlled the mountains above Brazzà, an area of crucial strategic importance to the Germans. The road leading up to the Plöcken Pass was one of the main supply routes from Germany; it was also one of the few lines of retreat available to the Wehrmacht if the war in Italy were to be lost. Only by deploying a huge force could the Germans hope to break up the partisans' positions and drive them out of the mountains. To the west of Udine, some 10,000 troops had been mustered, including formations of SS and squads of commandos. The soldiers boarding the trains at the station were to spearhead the offensive.

Shepherding Fey and the children through the melee, the Gestapo agent led them to a platform on the other side of the station, where they were to wait for a train to Villach. He said it would be a long wait. Villach, in Austria, was 17 miles from the Plöcken Pass and the Germans were using the railway to attack the partisans' positions. While the *rastrellamento* was in progress, no civilian traffic was permitted along the line. After the early start and the excitement of seeing the departing troops, the boys immediately fell asleep on a bench. It gave Fey time to think, and a break from the charade of the 'adventure'.

The Gestapo officer left her alone with her thoughts. Hour after hour, she paced up and down the platform; past the propaganda posters, pasted on the walls by the Germans, up to the blank departure board, and back to the bench where the children were sleeping. There was nothing else to look at; the troop trains had left and the station was now deserted. In both directions, the empty rail tracks stretched into the distance.

The long wait compounded her misery. She knew the train would arrive eventually, but she kept wishing it would never come. As she paced up and down, she tried to contain her panic; but there were too many uncertainties. On the way to the station, Colonel Dannenberg had admitted that, after Innsbruck, the Gestapo might send her to Germany. Her best hope was that it would be to Ebenhausen, where her mother was under house arrest. But if not there, where? Again, she found herself thinking about the possibility that she and the children might simply disappear. A cousin of Detalmo's, with contacts in the Red Cross, had promised to send a message to him, explaining what had happened. But would it be handed on? The thought that he might never get it made her feel even bleaker; at least if he knew she and the boys had been arrested, she could imagine him there in spirit.

After several hours, a close friend, Maria Nigris, appeared. A neighbour at Brazzà, she had heard of Fey's deportation and had come to say goodbye. 'I was very grateful for this demonstration of affection at a moment when I felt that even God had abandoned me,' Fey remembered. 'Especially since in associating with me, she inevitably risked arrest herself. We tried to ignore the uncertainty hanging over me and talked instead of Brazzà and what we would do at the end of the war.'

Maria kept her company for a few hours. Not long after she left, another friend – Luciano Giacomuzzi – came rushing on to the platform. He was out of breath and relieved to see Fey; after hearing of her situation, he had cycled to Brazzà in search of her – and back again to Udine – a distance of 18 miles. It was Luciano who had hidden Detalmo when he had returned from Mortara to say goodbye before leaving to join the Resistance in Rome. The memory of the precious night they had spent together at the Giacomuzzis' house in Udine was too much for Fey: 'At the sight of Luciano, the sensation of being on the verge of losing everything overwhelmed me. For the first time since the shock of my departure, I cried.'

Even Fey was not aware of the huge risk Luciano was taking in coming to the station. The director of the Udine Electricity Company, he was working for British intelligence. In recent months, he had supplied Hedley Vincent, the Coolant Mission leader, with plans of the regional electricity network, enabling the partisans to sabotage the Germans' supply by blowing up a number of substations in the mountains. In Udine itself, Luciano was working with the Adlestrop Mission, also under Vincent's command. Named after an airbase in Gloucestershire, Adlestrop was a covert SIS* operation whose agents had been infiltrated into Udine to work with 'certain reliable individuals' – of whom Luciano was one. RAF planes had dropped the three men on to Mount Joanaz in the small hours of the morning of 17 August. Dressed in civilian clothes, as opposed to the uniforms worn by SOE agents, after making their way down to the city, they had established a potentially important network. 'It seems possible,' Vincent reported to London, 'that many thousands of Allied supporters can be brought together under a central controlling body to form the civilian striking force in support of, and in close collaboration with, both the Allied Armies and the Partisan formations in the

* Secret Intelligence Service.

nearby hills.' The Gestapo's own network of informers in Udine meant there was always a danger that Luciano's work for the British would be exposed. While he was known to Adlestrop and Coolant under an alias, if his true identity was discovered, he faced the death penalty. Yet there he was coolly chatting to Fey on the platform under the gaze of the Gestapo official.

At midday, the train to Villach finally arrived – almost six hours after it was due. It was the first civilian train to be allowed through following the start of the *rastrellamento* and the platform was jammed with people. Holding the children tightly by the hand, Fey followed the Gestapo official, who, waving his police ID, cleared a passage through the crowds: 'He led us into a private compartment, where, almost immediately, the children went to sleep. They were good as they had never been good before, as though they realised that on this particular journey they absolutely had to be calm and quiet.'

It was just 60 miles to Villach, but it would take thirteen hours to get there. Further up the line, the Germans were using armoured wagons to bomb the partisans' positions and, a few miles outside Udine, the train came to a halt in a tunnel. When, several hours later, it finally emerged, the air was thick with smoke from the guns. Up in the hills to the east, plumes of black smoke marked the partisans' positions, close to the village of Nimis. This was Osoppo country; it was where Fey and her sons would have been taken had she agreed to the plan to ambush Dannenberg's car earlier that morning.

For the partisans, and the SOE agents who had armed and trained them, the offensive would prove catastrophic. After two days of non-stop fighting, they were completely surrounded. Forced to withdraw to escape annihilation, they fled east, pursued by the Germans. From the shelter of a monastery, high in the Julian Alps, Hedley Vincent sent a garbled cable to London:

WE ARE AT CRAVERO 10 KM E.N.E. OF CIVIDALE. ALL EQUIPMENT SAFE. ALL DOCUMENTS AND MESSAGES DESTROYED. ENEMY EMPLOY SEVERAL THOUSAND TROOPS. BROKEN THROUGH ON ALL FRONTS, NOW OCCUPY ZONE WHERE WHOLESALE MURDER AND BURNING

IN PROCESS. OUR LOSSES SEVERAL HUNDRED. AM TRYING REGAIN
CONTACT REMAINING PARTISAN FORCES. MEANWHILE WE ARE OUT
OF BUSINESS. WILL REVERT WHEN POSITION CLEARER.

German losses had also been heavy – over 500 dead, wounded or
missing. After the partisans withdrew from Nimis, SS troops and
detachments of Cossacks moved in to avenge the casualties. They
were led by two of the most hated, most brutal men in the region –
SS-Sturmbannführer Ludolf von Alvensleben, the police commander
in Udine, and 'Patriarca', the leader of the Fascist militia in Tolmezzo.
Moving from house to house, they rounded up the occupants and
corralled them to the end of the village. Thirty-six men were singled
out for deportation to Germany; twelve others were summarily
executed, shot one by one in front of their neighbours and relatives.
Leaving their bodies uncovered on the ground, the troops set about
looting the village. They killed all the livestock, loading the car-
casses, together with furniture and other possessions, into a convoy
of trucks. Then, on Alvensleben's orders, they set fire to their houses.
While they burned to the ground, the surviving inhabitants – women
and the elderly – were forced to watch as children, who had hidden
from the Germans, were thrown back into the flames by the Fascist
commander, 'Patriarca'.

It was almost dark when the train carrying Fey and the boys reached
the wall of mountains that bordered the edge of the plain. North of
here, the line to Villach wound through a ravine carved by the River
Fella; it was desolate country, the sheer faces of rock rising hundreds
of feet on either side of the track. With the *rastrellamento* still in progress, military traffic took priority and there were endless halts in
cuttings and tunnels.

Over the interminable hours, the enforced intimacy of the small
compartment meant that Fey had to talk to the Gestapo official. To
her surprise, he led her to understand that he considered her deportation absurd. She pressed him to tell her exactly where she and the
children were being taken. Would it be to Ebenhausen, where her
mother was living? He was unable to say. His instructions were solely

to escort them to Innsbruck, where he was to hand them over to a different branch of the Gestapo.

By the time they got to Villach, it was one o'clock in the morning and they had missed their connection to Innsbruck. The next train was not until dawn and the station was heaving with people, who were also stranded. The Gestapo official led Fey and the boys into a large hall, where hundreds of women and children were sleeping on the floor. The emergency accommodation was segregated and he left them there, saying he would return at first light. With the constant murmur of voices, Fey lay awake for hours: 'My mind was filled with worry about the next day, and I was haunted by images of my father, Detalmo and Brazzà and all I knew and loved. Luckily, the children, without a single complaint, curled up at my side. Their innocent, trusting faces seemed the only good thing left to me.'

A Gestapo official was there on the platform when their train pulled into Innsbruck the following afternoon. After taking them to a police station, where they were made to wait for several hours, he drove them to an interrogation centre on the outskirts of the city.

Inside the building, Fey and the children were ushered up a flight of stairs, and along a corridor, which seemed never-ending. The cells on either side were exposed, and the sight of the gaunt, frightened faces peering out through the bars alarmed Fey:

> My grip instinctively tightened on the hands of the boys, who said not a word, asked no questions, but trotted along beside me, solemn-faced.
>
> Beyond the iron bars, at the end of a second corridor, two other Gestapo men approached us, one in plain clothes and the other in uniform. After a couple of routine questions, which I answered without much enthusiasm, the uniformed official suddenly screamed, 'You are the daughter of that criminal whose head we cut off: that dog, that pig! Do you expect to be treated with kid gloves?' Then he laughed.
>
> Before I had time to recover, the first Gestapo agent, who had brought us as far as Innsbruck and who had, throughout the journey,

been relatively kind, was saying goodbye. Without noticing it, tears started to pour down my cheeks. Even though this man belonged to the Gestapo, he was my last tangible link with Italy and home. Unfortunately, the agent in uniform saw the tears I was trying to hold back and again shouted at me. 'Why are you snivelling? Don't be so stupid!' It was the best I could do to stop myself from collapsing as I tried to hide my fear and worry for the sake of the children. Although they must have been shocked to see their mother crying and being yelled at, they showed no reaction. I braced myself for an interrogation, but after a few minutes, the officer ordered his assistant to take us to a hotel in the centre of Innsbruck.

The Albergerhof – a fashionable hotel with 110 rooms – was located in Südtiroler Platz, next to the main railway station. Built for travellers at the height of the Austro-Hungarian Empire, it was an imposing four-storey building, the roof of which was topped by a decorative minaret. Inside, it was cosily furnished; chintz-covered sofas were arranged around the large fireplaces in the main salons, and pictures of skiing and hunting scenes decorated the oak-panelled walls.

To her amazement, Fey was shown up to a large, comfortable room, with a chambermaid on hand. From her window, she could see the mountains and the busy square below. There was even a garden at the back of the hotel where she could sit with the boys. 'After the dreadful things I had been expecting, it felt like paradise. I found the luxury of it hard to believe. But thinking about it as I unpacked, I interpreted it as a good sign. The Gestapo had not interrogated me: perhaps I was only required to attend one more session to answer some routine questions and then I could go back to Brazzà with the boys.'

The next morning, after a good night's sleep, Fey took the children down to breakfast. Years later, she remembered how proud she felt sitting with her two impeccably behaved 'little princes' in the dining salon. They spent a happy morning sightseeing and playing in the garden. Then she took the boys back to the hotel room for their afternoon nap.

She had only just settled the children when there was a knock at the door. Opening it, she was confronted by two Gestapo agents, neither of whom she had seen before:

> The two officials said that I would have to go with them for a few days to 'clear up' some 'outstanding questions'. The children would naturally have to stay behind. They would be sent to a good children's home, and some SS 'nurses' would arrive in a few minutes to take them away.
>
> Corradino must have understood or at least sensed what was going on. He became agitated and kept asking if I was going away. I did not believe the two agents and I wanted to tell him the truth. 'Please tell me,' I pleaded. 'Is it just for a few days or for much longer?' Smiling, one of them said, 'I assure you, it is only a question of a few days; you can relax, Madame.'
>
> The two SS 'nurses' arrived, both large blonde women without the slightest hint of gentleness. They enquired about the children's habits but made no effort to be friendly with them. I put on their little coats and told Corradino, as calmly as I could, 'Mama will follow you very soon, but first you will go for a nice walk.' Robertino thought this was a wonderful idea and confidently took the nurse's hand. But Corradino suddenly gave way to panic, flinging himself backward and howling wildly. He tried desperately to escape from the SS woman, tearing at the hand she had clamped around his little wrist. She managed with great difficulty to drag him away from me and out of the room. I wanted to scream out loud, but it would have served no purpose. I had to stand there like a statue listening to Corradino's wails growing fainter and fainter as he and little Robertino were dragged down the stairs.

Fey could still hear Corrado screaming when – as if the scene he had just witnessed had not taken place – one of the Gestapo agents asked her if she would be kind enough to pack up her things. He would look after them while she was held for questioning. They would be quite safe, he promised.

Some minutes later, the two men ushered her out. There were

forty rooms on this floor of the hotel; but the corridor was deserted, the doors to the rooms closed. Evidently, the other guests had heard Corrado's screams; yet not one of them had come out to see what was going on. Walking along the corridor, Fey had the feeling that the people inside were standing, listening out behind the doors, holding their breath. She felt a similar sensation as she passed the old man who was busy polishing the banister rails on the stairs to the lobby. A member of the hotel's staff, he had greeted her and the children on the way to breakfast that morning. Concentrating fixedly on his polishing, his movements exaggerated, as the three of them clattered by, he did not look up.

A car was waiting outside the hotel. As the Gestapo drove her through the centre of the city, Fey remembered that her jacket, with the money stitched into the lining, was in one of the suitcases. All her possessions had been confiscated; she had nothing except the clothes she was wearing. Peering out at the unfamiliar streets, she was desperate to know where the children had been taken. If only she could believe that she would have them back in a few days, as the agent had promised. Frightened and terribly shaken, she begged him for more information. He would not divulge their location; it was forbidden, he replied. Then – contrary to his earlier promise – he assured her that it would only be a matter of 'one or two weeks' before she was released and reunited with her boys.

19

At Adamgasse 1, a Gestapo prison in the centre of Innsbruck, the agents handed Fey over to a guard. Shouting at her, he marched her down a long, windowless corridor, lit by the fluorescent glare from the bulbs overhead. As they passed rows of cells with metal doors, each with a spyhole, their footsteps echoed on the tiled floor. At the end of the corridor, the guard shoved her into a tiny cell. The door slammed behind her.

The cell measured 9 feet by 6. Layers of straw were piled on the floor, lending it the appearance of an animal pen. Three bunk beds were crammed into it and messages – scratched into the brickwork by previous inmates – covered every inch of the walls. It was unseasonably cold and there was no heating and the cell was freezing. High up in one corner, there was a small window. It faced east overlooking the railway tracks and the River Sill. Fey could hear the trains and the distant horns of the barges, but all she could see was a small patch of sky.

The Gestapo headquarters, taking up an entire block, was situated in the heart of the old city, directly opposite the Archbishop's Palace. For much of the day, its austere facade lay deep in the shadow cast by the spire of the cathedral, which stood directly behind the palace. SS soldiers patrolled the stretch of pavement outside. To deter friends and relatives from throwing notes to the prisoners, or shouting out messages, they were under orders to shoot anyone caught loitering.

Upwards of 6,800 men and women had passed through the building since the start of the war. Of these, the Gestapo had sent only a fraction for trial; the vast majority had been transferred to Dachau, or to other concentration camps. Answering directly to Berlin, the Innsbruck Gestapo employed a staff of 120. They included chauffeurs, interpreters, telephonists and a large number of female secretaries – mostly young, unmarried women, conscripted for emergency war work. The various departments were organized according to the perceived threat. There was one for enemy agents, and one for foreign workers and saboteurs; another was devoted entirely to industrial and radio security. But the bulk of the Gestapo's work was focused on the detention and deportation of 'undesirables' and 'political opponents'. Jews, Gypsies, homosexuals, and people with physical and mental disabilities came into the first category; the second included Communists, Socialists, Monarchists, Catholic priests, and *Rundfunk Sünder* (radio sinners) and *Meckerer* (moaners) – people caught listening to the BBC and the Voice of America, or who had been overheard expressing negative opinions about the Nazi regime or the progress of the war. Consisting of forty male agents, the operative core – the investigators and interrogators charged with rounding up these individuals – was comparatively small. As one agent remarked, 'There was no need for a big outfit; we depended on the Tyroleans to denounce their neighbours and relatives, which they did with great willingness.'

The chief of the Innsbruck branch of the Gestapo was Werner Hilliges. Aged forty-one in the autumn of 1944, he was a corrupt, hard-drinking man, who had made a fortune profiteering on the black market. His ruthlessness was legendary. In the summer of 1943, at Reichenau, the SS-run work camp outside Innsbruck, Hilliges had shot a prisoner in the face at point-blank range after the man had questioned his orders. His deputy was SS-Hauptsturmführer Friedrich Busch, who supervised interrogations. Aged forty, he had been transferred to Innsbruck from Gestapo headquarters in Paris, where he was alleged to have tortured and murdered French nationals. Beneath these two men, the investigative agents were drawn from the ranks of the SS and the border police. The majority were Austrians, born in the backward, isolated villages of the Tyrol, or in the working-class districts of the industrial towns along the Inn Valley. A large number were illegitimate and had grown up as outcasts in the devoutly Catholic communities, where illegitimacy carried a huge stigma. To school leavers, with no formal qualifications, a career in the Gestapo conferred power and status, offering a step up the ladder for men who would otherwise have remained labourers.

Interrogations, lasting up to four hours, were conducted daily. Prisoners were brought to the headquarters in Herrengasse from Adamgasse 1, the prison where Fey was held. The interrogation rooms were sparsely furnished, containing just two tables and the implements of torture the Gestapo used to force the prisoners to talk.

One of the chief interrogators was Kriminalsekretär Walter Guettner. Five foot four inches tall, thin, nervous and shifty-eyed, he was known as 'The Little Rat'. His technique was to start with gentle persuasion: 'Don't be stupid. We know everything,' he would tell his victims. 'Think of your family, of your parents, make it easier on yourself.' If this did not produce results, other officers were called in and the prisoners were beaten. Wooden staves were used to club them about the body and the face. Then, stripping them naked, the officers used bullwhips, made from cowhide, to strike them across the genitals. They also used pistols, which they rammed sideways into the prisoners' mouths, breaking their teeth. If this 'ordinary' beating failed, 'extreme measures' were applied. Trussing the prisoner up by tying his hands around his ankles, they shoved a double-barrelled rifle through the space between his arms and knees. With two SS men lifting on either side, they placed the rifle ends between the two tables so that the prisoner hung between them, his head facing down. Water was then poured into his mouth and nostrils.

Fey could hear the guards bringing the prisoners back to their cells after the interrogations. If she looked through the spyhole in the metal door, she could see them passing along the corridor before they disappeared out of the narrow view. Six days had passed since she had first entered the cell and still the Gestapo had not called her for questioning. The sight of the broken bodies, and the moans and screams of those still conscious, haunted her. It was the same feeling she had after witnessing some terrible road accident; except she could not drive by and forget it. In all probability, it would be her turn next.

Day and night, the machinery of terror never stopped. Periodically, the Gestapo would transfer groups of prisoners to concentration camps in Germany and further east. They were chosen at random to free up space or to meet quotas set by Berlin. Fey had known about the camps for many years; in the mid 1930s, when Himmler first introduced them, her father told her they were being used to imprison Jews and anti-Nazis. But it was only now, listening to the stories circulating on the prison grapevine, that she realized the scale of the atrocities taking place.

At Adamgasse, transfers were heralded by the shouts of a guard in the corridor outside and Fey would listen anxiously as the list of names was called. Then came the hurried footsteps, the opening and slamming of cell doors, the sound of running engines in the court-yard, and the frightened voices of prisoners as they were dragged out to the waiting trucks.

To begin with, she shared the cell with one other woman: a pretty, young Austrian, with a kind smile, her name was Emma. Her story was mundane, but no less terrible for that. The Gestapo had impris-oned her for selling pork on the black market and for refusing to work at a hotel where she had been badly treated. When they first brought her into the prison, they had given her a severe beating and she lost the child she had been carrying for seven months.

With the constant flow of new arrivals, three Yugoslav women joined Fey and Emma. Ordinary petty criminals, one of them had been imprisoned fourteen times. Their obscene language, and their poor physical condition, shocked Fey: 'They were incredibly dirty; their skin was covered in blisters and pustules, and their hair crawling with lice. They were vulgar, and their talk was very obscene. Every morning, one of the women begged me to spread some lotion on her pockmarked shoulders, which I did as best I could. Another was suf-fering from crippling stomach pains, which I thought was appendicitis. I repeatedly tried to convince the guard that she needed an operation urgently or at least that a doctor should be called. My pleading would generally end in a tremendous quarrel, with the guard screaming and telling me to mind my own business and not to be impertinent. Slam-ming the door, he would shout, "Stupid bitch, be careful, or I'll have you sent to Ravensbrück!" '

Conditions in the overcrowded cell were primitive. There was no washbasin; but a reeking bucket – emptied just once every twenty-four hours – served as a toilet for the five women. There was nothing to do, nothing to read and very little to eat. Meals consisted of pumpernickel bread and a watery soup, which tasted of mould. Every day, Fey dreamed of the hams and salamis rotting away in her suitcases, or more likely being devoured by the Gestapo. She and the other women were only allowed out of the cell twice a day – for a thirty-minute exercise break in the courtyard behind the prison, and for a wash in the bathhouse, which was a short distance along the corridor. The washing arrangements were basic; the women bathed in a long, communal trough – similar to a pig trough – with five or six cold-water taps. Gawking at their naked bodies, the guards watched, making lewd and abusive comments.

As Fey quickly learned, the guards, all of whom were Austrian, had a reputation for being the most brutal in the Nazi prison system – more brutal even than the German gaolers in the north of the Reich. 'They relished tormenting and abusing us. One of their favourite taunts was to stand outside the cell doors jangling their keys. This maddening behaviour drove home the fact that one was a prisoner, locked in and totally hopeless.' At all times, she was conscious of an eye leering at her through the spyhole. Often, in the dead of night, the lights in the cell would suddenly come on. The switch was out in the corridor, and it amused the guards to see the women's startled faces as they woke, fearing they were about to be called for questioning. Sometimes the guards remained outside, flicking the switch on and off, making sleep impossible under the strobing light; at other times, they would enter the cell and roughly strip the blankets off the women. They claimed to be on suicide watch since a number of prisoners had tried to kill themselves with concealed knives, but it was just another instance of their prurience.

Throughout that first week, however ghastly the conditions in the prison, however much she longed for and worried about the children, Fey remained convinced that she would be released soon. She only had to hold out for one or two weeks, she kept telling herself. Then – as the Gestapo agent had promised – she would be reunited with the boys.

Regardless of her hunger, and the horrors of the overcrowded cell, with its smell of sweat mingled with excrement, the greatest difficulty she faced was in finding ways to pass the time: 'Sometimes I would think about the clever answers I would give when I was interrogated, but my main activity was pacing up and down the cell, reciting all the Goethe poems I knew by heart; it was the best way not to think of the children. I also took to giving fortune-telling sessions in the evenings. I designed tarot cards with which to tell everybody's future. I often "read" on the cards that one of my fellow prisoners would be released in the next couple of days. Of course, it never happened, but everyone loved to hear me say it, and some even half-believed it. I also set about learning Serbo-Croat, but it was too difficult, and my teachers were not the best. Still, it passed the time.'

20.

It was the morning of 10 October – midway through Fey's second week in the prison – and the Gestapo still had not called her for questioning.

Panic gripped her as she paced up and down in the cell: from the door to the wall opposite, between the bunks and the reeking bucket. At the door, she turned to the right; at the wall, to the left. It was an old prison trick which one of the Yugoslav women had taught her: if you did not change the direction of the turn, you soon became giddy.

Her thoughts were focused on her situation, not on lines from Goethe. The fact that the Gestapo had forgotten her and did not care about a mother separated from her children filled her with a helpless anger, so overwhelming she thought she would lose her mind. Where were the boys? How were the SS nurses treating them? And Detalmo and her family in Germany? Did they know she was here? *Did anyone know she was here?*

Two more days went by. Then, on the afternoon of 12 October – almost two weeks after her incarceration – a Gestapo official appeared. Fey recognized him straight away: he was one of the agents who had brought her to the prison. Motioning her to accompany him, he took her to an office at the front of the building. Desperate for news of the children, Fey was taken aback when, as soon as they were seated, he began with a prosaic detail: 'First, he asked me to pay the hotel bill for the night I'd spent with the children at the Albergerhof. I thought that was a bit much! He also informed me that he had taken the ham and salamis from my suitcases to prevent them from rotting. "Unfortunately", some had already become inedible and he had had to throw them away. Probably he had eaten them himself! When I pleaded for news of my children, he assured me that they were well and being cared for in a nearby "institute". Instructions to free me were expected any day from Berlin, in which case we could all go home. I did not know whether to believe him.'

Then the agent handed her two letters. The first was from her brother in Berlin:

Dear Fey

Yesterday I learned of your arrest. You can imagine how horrified I was. I rushed to Gestapo headquarters at once to find out where you were. They said, 'Staatspolizeistelle, Innsbruck.' I've given your address to Mutti [Mummy] and Almuth, and I'm sure they'll write immediately. If you can write to us, send your letters to my address in Berlin.

They assured me that the children are in a good children's home and will be given back to you as soon as you are freed. I feel sure that you'll soon be back in Brazzà. Mutti already knew about your arrest, because on the very day I got the news, she received a note from the Italian consul enclosing a letter from Dannenberg, the German commander at Brazzà. I send you his letter, which is doubtless a sign of the times. I think of you.

With love,
Wolf Ulli

Seeing her brother's letter, a wave of relief swept over Fey; if the Gestapo in Berlin were saying she would have the children back as soon as she was released, it must be true. The letter was dated 9 October. Only a few days had gone by since Wolf Ulli had spoken to them, and he was confident that she would be back at Brazzà soon.

Barely able to contain her excitement, she reread the letter carefully. It was the first she had heard from her brother since their father had been executed; the fact that he had not referred to his death was puzzling. Evidently, when writing, Wolf Ulli had known the Gestapo would read the letter, yet it struck her as odd that he had not expressed his grief, or offered words of commiseration, however veiled. It was so unlike him. She was also amazed that he had 'rushed to Gestapo headquarters' on hearing of her arrest. Surely the entire family had been arrested once her father's part in the plot to assassinate Hitler had become known? So why hadn't Wolf Ulli been arrested? There seemed to be just one possible explanation: it was proof that her father had not been executed after all.

Turning to Colonel Dannenberg's letter, she remembered all the times he had played with the children at Brazzà, spoiling them with little treats, and letting them sit in the soldiers' trucks; yet the moment her father's execution had been announced, he had driven into Udine and informed the Gestapo that Ulrich von Hassell's daughter was living nearby. Dannenberg had written the letter on 29 September – two days after he had personally handed her and the children over to the Gestapo. Reading it, his unctuous duplicity astounded her:

Dear Frau von Hassell

I am sorry to have to return your letter as well as one from Hamburg that arrived here! I beg you to return the letter from Hamburg to its proper address, which I do not know. I must apologise that both letters have been opened but I was given the embarrassing order to read your daughter's mail.

I feel it is my duty to inform you of what happened here at Brazzà. Your daughter was taken to prison in Udine when the sentence in connection with the known and unhappy affair was pronounced. I did what I could to make her stay in prison as bearable as possible.

For your information, I am Major Eisermann's successor. I was allowed to pay your daughter a visit every day, so either I, my aide-de-camp or another officer went to see her. I managed to have her brought back to the castle on my own personal guarantee. She had to be guarded night and day, but at least she was with the children and able to look after the estate. Then an order came from Berlin. She and the children had to take a train to Innsbruck in the care of a Gestapo official. I personally drove her to the station. I do not know her exact address or what will happen to her next.

As far as I could find out, they intend to interrogate her on what she knows about what happened. It is certainly a disadvantage that she is married to an Italian officer who seems to be working with the enemy.* As soon as I get more detailed information, I will pass it on to you. I very much doubt that she will be allowed to write, but I advised her, if she could, to address any letters to me and then I could send the news to you.

I will spare you a description of the farewells at Brazzà. I only note that the servants and the people living on the estate cared exceptionally for her.

With my respectful regards
Dannenberg, Colonel and Commander

After the interview, Fey was escorted to her cell by a prison guard. Believing that she would soon be back at Brazzà, she found the days that followed hardest of all. Whereas before, for the sake of her sanity, she had tried to ration her thoughts about the children, now she allowed herself to think about them all of the time. She spent hours daydreaming of holding the boys in her arms and waking up beside them; she worried endlessly about how they were sleeping at night, and whether, without her, they were able to cuddle up together.

Fey had expected to be released within days of her interview with the Gestapo agent. But it did not happen. In the absence of news, she became increasingly agitated. 'The weight of suffering and misery existing in that prison had its inevitable effect on me, and I began to get more and more depressed and anxious as the days wore on without news of the children. They had become such a part of my existence, my very being, that I felt only half a person without them.'

The end of her second week in the prison came and went, and a third; still there was no news from the Gestapo. Then, twenty-three days after she first entered the cell, she sensed that – at last – something was about to happen:

The Gestapo unexpectedly sent my suitcases over to the prison. A guard took me to a sort of garret, where I was allowed to open them in his presence. First, I put on some clean underclothes, since my old

---

* Detalmo's work for the new anti-Fascist government in the south of Italy was known to the Germans.

ones were absolutely stinking. I was furious to see that of the 600 cigarettes I had brought, 300 were missing, as well as the tea. However, the money had not been found. I bribed the guard with one pack of cigarettes to allow me to take two packs to my cell.

The following day, 22 October, was my twenty-sixth birthday. Again, the cell door opened, and I was called out. A prison guard announced, 'You're free.' I could have imagined no better birthday present! Instead, it was to turn into one of the bitterest days of my life.

I gathered my few belongings and took leave of my companions, who were overcome with envy. I felt especially sad in saying goodbye to poor Emma. I followed the guard down to the prison entrance, where my suitcases were waiting for me. A serious-looking SS official, in plain clothes, then walked up to me and said, 'We're going on a little trip.'

Immediately suspicious, I asked nervously, 'Where to?' To which he answered, 'I only know that I'm to take you to Germany.'

My heart hammering, I asked, 'And my children?'

'You've got children?'

'Of course I have! I've got two little boys who were taken away when I was imprisoned here.'

'It's the first I've heard of any children, and I don't know where they are. Anyway, I only ask you to be sensible on this trip. Don't make scenes or call attention to yourself. Please act as if we are old friends.'

My only desire at that moment was to fly at the man screaming, 'Where are my children? Give me my children!' Act as if we were old friends, my God! Where were they? Where on earth were they? The official just shrugged his shoulders as if he wasn't at all interested. I stood there in stunned silence, unable and unwilling to believe what I had just been told.

After escorting Fey out of the prison, the SS officer, accompanied by a female colleague, drove her to the railway station. 'We had to wait hours for the train. My desperation at that point was unbearable. There I was utterly powerless, in the hands of these criminals, without news from home and now forced to leave my children alone in a strange country without friends or family. I do not think I have ever been so utterly wretched in my life as I was on that platform at Innsbruck.'

The train, when it finally left, was crammed with people. It was of the type used to transport animals; there were no seats in the metal wagons and the floors were covered in straw. Two days previously, the Allies had bombed Innsbruck, hitting the poor working-class districts on the outskirts of the city. The men and women packed into the wagons, like so many heads of cattle, were mostly refugees. Hungry and exhausted after picking through the rubble of their homes, they were weighed down with the few possessions they had managed to salvage.

Fey, still in a state of shock and flanked by the SS guards, took her place among them. As the train pulled out of Innsbruck, she had no idea where in Germany she was being taken; her escorts had refused to divulge their destination. Peering out through the gaps in the metal slats, she could see the mountains rising on either side of the track. But she was unable to read the names of the stations they were passing: the Nazis had blacked them out – a precaution against an Allied invasion. Her one hope was that she was being taken to her mother's house at Ebenhausen, which was 90 miles or so away on the other side of the Alps.

A few hours into the journey, the SS guards allowed her to stand on the footboard of the carriage for a breath of fresh air. Looking out at the landscape, she was disorientated by the unfamiliar country. She knew the southern part of Germany as her mother's house was close to the Austrian border. She could see the Alps receding into the distance yet, on either side of the track, there was dense forest where there should have been rolling fields. Anxiously, she studied the houses in the tiny hamlets slipping past. Instead of the white chalets favoured by the Bavarians, with their gabled roofs and pretty wooden decorations, they were built of brick or poorly constructed from a primitive sort of wattle and daub. Then, seeing the sun setting in the west, she realized the train was heading due east, away from

Germany: 'I felt numb and in a daze as I struggled to get my mind in order and decide what could be done. In my confusion, I asked a kind woman, who was standing amid what looked like all her worldly possessions, for a pen and a piece of paper. After some difficulty, she found them, and I hurriedly scribbled down my mother's address. I wrote that I was being escorted to the east and that the children had been taken from me at Innsbruck. I had no idea where they were, or where I was headed. I then dropped the paper on to the tracks of some small station in the hope that it might be passed on.'

For hour after hour, the train continued through dense forest. Staring out at the same, monotonous landscape, it seemed to Fey that the journey would never end. She struggled to visualize a map of central Europe. Were these the ancient forests of Bohemia? Or was she somewhere else entirely? Silesia or Galicia, perhaps?

After two days on the train, they began passing through towns and villages that the Soviets had bombed. In the space of nine months, the Russians had advanced 1,200 miles and were now outside Warsaw. Tens of thousands of refugees were fleeing west, ahead of the Red Army. Fey could see them from the footboard: lines and lines of them, coming towards her, walking alongside the tracks. She was shocked by the lack of hope or happiness in their faces, and the absence of conversation as they trudged onwards. Frequently, the train was shunted into a siding to allow troop carriers to pass. The sight of crowds of young German boys destined for the Russian Front horrified her: 'I felt I could see branded across their unknowing foreheads the slogan that met the eye wherever one looked; on roads, in stations, in squares and shops: *"Alle Räder müssen rollen für den Sieg"* ("All Wheels Must Turn for Victory").'

There were long stops at bombed-out stations where Fey, watched closely by her minders, would sit, slumped on her suitcases, as they waited for a connection: 'During the stops at these desolate stations, frequently no more than piles of rubble and ash, I tried to keep my thoughts off the children by observing the life of men and women who had been at war for over four years. At first sight, everything seemed to be collapsing. People had shabby clothes and strained, nervous faces. There were few men around; all the station officials were women. Great crowds were shifting in one direction or another, entire cities moving, a thing not seen for centuries. Although the scene gave the impression of total disorder and chaos, on closer inspection this was not the case. While there were incredible delays (all trains were running twenty hours late), everything was functioning. Amazed, I watched soldiers and officers go off on leave according to plan, as if all were well on the two fronts . . . This astonishing efficiency in the midst of death and destruction surprised me again and again.'

The train rumbled slowly on under frequent air attacks until, 'after three days of constant travel,' she recorded, 'we arrived at a small town called Bad Reinerz, deep in the forests of Lower Silesia. It was a pretty place, quiet, orderly, and surrounded by mountains. This, then, was the mysterious destination that, for reasons of their own, my SS escorts had kept secret from me.'

21

An SS officer was waiting on the platform as the train pulled in. He was dressed in an immaculate black uniform and a silver-grey skull and crossbones glinted above the peak of his cap. As Fey stepped down from the train, he greeted her with exaggerated courtesy; placing his right hand across his abdomen, he bowed stiffly and with his left hand took hers and raised it to his lips. For an instant, his lips brushed against her fingertips; coming from a man like him, she found the gesture unbearable.

Following a brief exchange of paperwork, the SS escorts left, and the 'gentleman' officer led her to a small, unmarked car. Exiting the station, he took the valley road, heading south out of the town. Seated in the front next to him, Fey could smell the polish on his leather pistol holster and his long black boots. 'We did not utter a word. I was still beside myself with grief for having lost the children and I felt anxious and confused. Where was he driving me to? To another prison? But then the fact that he was treating me with such respect made me think not.'

A few miles outside Bad Reinerz, he turned right on to a single-track road. They continued in silence as they climbed higher and higher, the road twisting in a series of hairpins around the mountain. Thick forest obscured the view on either side. A few hundred feet below the summit, they reached a small track, marked by a wooden sign. 'Halt! This hotel is closed,' it warned. The words were printed in large Gothic script; beneath them, Fey could see the double Siegrune — the chilling lightning bolts of the SS.

Ignoring the warning, her driver veered down the track.

Some minutes later, they pulled up outside a large, imposing chalet. Four storeys high, with a gabled roof, it was both grand and homely. Hand-painted wooden shutters adorned the windows, and there was a wide terrace from which to admire the view. Stepping out of the car, the beauty of it all stunned Fey: 'I felt completely dis-orientated. I had suddenly returned to the civilized world. Looking at the scenery all around me, I felt as if I was dreaming.'

The Hindenburg Baude, as the hotel was called, stood on a plateau. To the east, the view stretched for miles, over the Kladsko Valley; in the near distance, the spire of a church rose from the fields, ringed by the sloping roofs of isolated farmhouses. The one blot in the other-wise picture-postcard landscape was the swastika that flew high on a flagpole outside the entrance to the hotel. Fey shuddered at the sight of the familiar colours, vibrant in the pale winter sun.

Taking her suitcases, the SS officer showed her into the lobby. With the same formal manners as before – as if, she recalled, 'we were at some grand society party' – he introduced her to a handsome boy in his late teens. He was with his sister, a striking woman, aged around thirty. Hearing their names, Fey realized that, unless the SS intended to liquidate her, she would be kept prisoner until the end of the war. They were Otto Philipp and Gagi von Stauffenberg, and they were cousins of Claus von Stauffenberg, the man who had planted the bomb at Hitler's headquarters.

No sooner had she begun to talk to the couple than a porter appeared to carry her luggage upstairs. She followed him up to a room on the first floor of the hotel. It was light and spacious and prettily decorated, with a large bed, a washbasin, and a mahogany wardrobe and dresser. Seeing the room made her feel sadder still; it reminded her of skiing holidays with Detalmo. It was now five months since she had heard from him; thinking about him, she felt only emptiness.

Before leaving her to unpack, the porter handed her two letters. One was a note from her grandmother, Marie von Tirpitz, which had been forwarded on from the prison at Innsbruck:

My dearest Fey

Thank you for your letter of 2 Oct. I was really touched that, despite everything, you thought about my birthday. I wish I could do some-thing for you. For example, send you some medicines to give you strength? Write to me if this is allowed. Did you know that Almuth and Hans Dieter obtained permission to come and see you in the prison at Innsbruck, but unfortunately, when they got there, they were told that you had been taken away somewhere else? I wonder where they have taken you? I hope to God that I will have news of you and the children soon. Bless you – and all love – from your old Grandma.

Tears of frustration welled as she read the letter. She knew she had been at the prison when her brother and sister had visited. If only the Gestapo had allowed her to see them – even for a few minutes.

The one consolation was that there was no mention of her father. It was almost two months since Kretschmann had told her that he had been executed; since then, she had received letters from her mother, her brother, and now this one from her grandmother. Not one of them had referred to his death.

Buoyed by the conviction that her father was still alive, Fey turned to the second letter. It was from Lotti, who was replying to the letter she had sent from Brazzà, enclosing the photographs of the boys:

You are alone and abandoned! But you are not on your own! All those who love you are with you every day. I am sending you all my best wishes from the bottom of my heart and never forget that God protects us all, although it is hard to believe this in such tragic times. My little brave fighter – I think of you and pray for you.

Fey put the precious letters carefully away and, steeling herself to be the 'fighter' her old governess remembered, she went downstairs to meet the other guests. She found Gagi and Otto Philipp von Stauffenberg, to whom she had been introduced earlier in the lobby. They were talking to an older couple, and a gaunt boy in his early twenties, whose shaven head made him look disfigured. Straight away, Fey could tell from the way they were laughing and teasing each other that they belonged to the same family. Evidently, they had not seen each other for some time.

As she chatted to them, their story emerged. While they were cousins of Claus von Stauffenberg, the family had not been involved in the coup; they had been imprisoned only because they shared the same surname. The parents' names were Clemens and Elisabeth. A slim, stylish woman in her early sixties, Elisabeth had been arrested soon after the attempt on Hitler's life. The Gestapo had taken her to Stadelheim prison in Munich, where she had been held for almost three months. In mid August, their three children – Otto Philipp, Gagi and Markwart – had also been arrested. Eighteen-year-old Otto Philipp and his elder sister, Gagi, had been imprisoned at Nördlingen in Bavaria. Markwart, who was twenty-three, had been sent to Dachau, where the SS had put him to work in the block for medical experiments. Clemens, a gentle and clearly very frail man, had only been arrested the day before. Arriving at the clinic where he was being treated for a heart condition, the SS had dragged him from his hospital bed and brought him directly to the hotel. It was the first time the family had been reunited following their terrible experiences.

Fey was moved by their story. Yet she could not help envying their joy at being together again. Their closeness, and the easy way they related to each other, reminded her of her own family. The relationship between Clemens and Elisabeth was particularly touching; while Elisabeth fussed and teased, saying that her husband, for the sake of his health, would have been better off staying at the clinic, Clemens whispered to Fey that for the three months he had been apart from his wife, he had felt completely lost without her and doubted whether he could have survived for much longer.

While they were talking, other prisoners were arriving. As they were brought into the lobby, the guards shouted out their names to an SS officer, who stood over by the entrance, ticking off the new arrivals on a list. Hearing the names, Fey caught herself scanning the drawn faces, her heart racing with anticipation. 'Goerdeler', 'Gisevius', 'Hofacker'. These were the leading families of the German Resistance – people her father had mentioned and with whom he had worked closely. At any moment, she expected members of her own family to walk through the door.

More prisoners were brought in that afternoon and in the early evening. Fey spent much of that time in the lobby, returning once or twice an hour, hoping that her mother and her siblings would be among the new arrivals. But this did not happen.

Seventeen of the twenty-two prisoners the SS brought to the Hindenburg Baude came from three families: the Stauffenbergs, the Hofackers and the Goerdelers.

The composition of the family groups pointed to the terrifying reach of Himmler's Sippenhaft directive – the concept that a traitor's family was also guilty.

The Goerdelers, of whom there were six at the hotel, were the immediate relations of Carl Friedrich Goerdeler – the man who would have become chancellor of Germany had the coup succeeded. They included his wife, his two daughters, his daughter-in-law, his niece and his elder brother. Goerdeler himself was in Plötzensee prison in Berlin, awaiting execution. A few days before 20 July, after finalizing the list of the men who would form his cabinet, he had gone into hiding, but had been arrested in mid August after a woman recognized him and denounced him to the Gestapo.

Cäsar von Hofacker, a high-ranking Luftwaffe officer and a cousin of Claus von Stauffenberg, had been arrested in Paris five days after the attempted coup. The right-hand man of Carl Stülpnagel, the military governor of Paris, Hofacker was deeply implicated in the plot. Hours after the bomb exploded, he and Stülpnagel had been responsible for the arrest of over 1,000 Gestapo and SS. When it became clear that the coup had failed, Hofacker had had every chance to escape, but he had chosen instead to remain at his office, saying it would be better if the world knew what had happened. A few days later, as he was being brutally tortured, the SS had rounded up his family. His wife and two of their children – a boy and a girl, aged sixteen and fifteen – were among the prisoners at the Hindenburg Baude.

The Stauffenbergs, the relatives of coup leader Claus von Stauffenberg, were the largest family group. In addition to the cousins Fey met when she arrived, they included Claus's 72-year-old mother-in-law, his sister-in-law, his brother and another distant cousin. This was Markwart, Count Schenk von Stauffenberg, known as Onkel (Uncle) Moppel in the family. A colonel in the German Army, he had arrived still wearing his uniform.

The remaining three prisoners were a middle-aged couple, named Arthur and Hildegard Kuhn, and Annelise Gisevius, an unmarried teacher in her early forties. The Kuhns' son, Joachim, an infantry officer on the Eastern Front and a recipient of the Iron Cross, had been drawn into the conspiracy early on. A close friend of General Henning von Tresckow, he had been trusted with obtaining the British-made explosives for the bomb. After the coup failed and Tresckow committed suicide, Kuhn had endeavoured to protect the general's reputation. He brought his body back from the forest where Tresckow had blown himself up with a hand grenade, reporting to the German High Command that he had been killed as a result of a partisan attack. Subsequently, Kuhn was captured by the Red Army and transferred to a prison in the Soviet Union, where he remained until 1956.

Annelise Gisevius was the sister of Hans Bernd, a senior officer in German military intelligence. A covert opponent of the Nazi regime, he had worked closely with Ulrich von Hassell, acting as a secret liaison to the Vatican and to US spy chief Allen Dulles. Annelise had been arrested in lieu of her brother, who had used his contacts to elude the SS following the coup.

Apart from Annelise, Fey was the only prisoner on her own at the hotel: the others were there with their families. Further, with the exception of two in the group, they had received privileged treatment in the months following their arrest. Accorded special status by the Gestapo, they had been entitled to individual cells and extra food rations. As an 'ordinary' prisoner at Innsbruck, Fey's experiences had been far more traumatic.

22

Fey was formally introduced to the other prisoners as they gathered for dinner in the dining room at the hotel. It was the first time the cousins had seen each other since their arrest and a loud hubbub of excited, happy voices filled the room. Feeling excluded, and desperately anxious about her own family, Fey took her place at one of the tables.

The room, which was oak-panelled with a low, half-timbered ceiling, looked as if it had changed little since the last century. The panelling was coated with a rich, dark brown patina and a fire blazed in the large hearth. The tables were covered with crisp white linen cloths and the walls were decorated with antlers, and pretty ornamental porcelain plates. The effect might have been described as charming were it not for the ubiquitous portraits of Hitler, and the Nazi posters and emblems that hung beside them.

Since her arrest, Fey had lost over a stone in weight. Glancing around the room, it was not difficult to spot the other prisoners who had been as harshly treated. They were 23-year-old Markwart von Stauffenberg, who had spent two months at Dachau, and Baroness Anni von Lerchenfeld, who had been imprisoned at Ravensbrück concentration camp. The cousins called the baroness 'Aunt Anni'. A redoubtable woman in her early seventies, and a famous beauty in her youth, her hair was unkempt and her shabby black dress hung off her thin shoulders. No one could explain why Markwart had been sent to Dachau, but Fey was told that Aunt Anni was especially hated by the Nazis. Not only was she Claus von Stauffenberg's mother-in-law, but her husband, Hugo von Lerchenfeld, had been one of the people responsible for Hitler's imprisonment following the Munich putsch in 1923.

Over dinner, the talk, unsurprisingly, was of the assassination attempt. Seated next to Alexander von Stauffenberg, Claus's elder brother, Fey listened in silence, agog: 'Everyone was swapping information, gleaned from friends and relatives, and people they had met in prison. Most of the details were new to me. Cut off at Brazzà, my only source of information had come from the radio. Then, at Innsbruck, I was not with the families involved in the plot. Every detail of the assassination attempt was discussed – the background to it, and its failure. Towards the end of the evening, the conversation turned to the fate of the participants – the executions and the thousands of arrests. I sat there with a feeling of dread, expecting my father's name to come up at any minute. But no one mentioned him and I was too nervous to ask.'

There was news, however, regarding other members of her family: 'One of the new arrivals explained the mystery behind my brother's contact with the Gestapo. Apparently, soon after the coup, my mother and my sister, Almuth, had been arrested and imprisoned in Munich. Immediately Wolf Ulli, who was in Berlin, had rushed to Gestapo headquarters, offering himself in their place. He said that he, not they, had been with my father when the bomb was planted. Wolf Ulli's persistence and courage so surprised the Gestapo that they sent him to Munich with a letter authorizing my mother's release to house arrest. It was a unique case. Even more extraordinary, Wolf Ulli himself was allowed to remain free. It all seemed so illogical given what had happened to me.'

Fey heard this from Lotte* von Hofacker, the wife of Colonel Cäsar von Hofacker, who had been arrested in Paris. She was with her two eldest children – a boy of sixteen and a girl aged fifteen. The others – a boy aged nine and two girls, aged twelve and six – had been seized by the SS. Later that night, Lotte introduced Fey to two other women whose young children had also been taken, and an intuitive understanding quickly developed between them: 'While each person in the group was suffering and grieving for one reason or another, we four women, Lotte, Mika, Irma and I, were brought close to each other in our terrible worry. Each of us knew that, whatever we might be saying or doing, thoughts of our children were always just below the surface.'

---

* Her name was actually Ilse-Lotte but the group called her Lotte.

'Mika' was Countess Maria von Stauffenberg, the wife of Berthold, Claus's eldest brother. She had last seen her children on the night of 22 July when the SS had arrived at Lautlingen, the family's castle in southern Germany. After ransacking and sealing the castle, they had taken her away, leaving her son and daughter, aged five and four, in the care of the Gestapo. Branded a 'Bolshevist' by the Nazis, Mika, who was in her mid forties, had grown up in Tsarist Russia. She had worked closely with her husband on the details of the Valkyrie plan, editing the draft of the proclamation that would announce Hitler's death to the German people. Berthold had been executed on 10 August, a few weeks after Mika had been arrested. Fey was overawed by her courage in bearing the loss of both her husband and her children: 'She was a glamorous woman, with a deep, languorous voice. As a child, she had already lived through one brutal period, the Russian Revolution, after which her family had escaped to Germany. Perhaps this accounted for her strength in facing her loss.'

Irma Goerdeler, married to Carl Friedrich's eldest son, had been separated from her sons – a three-year-old, and a baby of just nine months – in mid August. When the SS arrived to seize the children, all she was told was that they would be taken to 'an estate in the country'. She had heard nothing since. Nor did she know what had become of her husband, who had disappeared without trace.

Of the three women, it was to Lotte that Fey was most drawn: 'Full of energy, with a heart of gold, she was to become one of my closest companions in the period ahead. Added to her worry for her husband, of whom she had heard no official news, was her anxiety for her three youngest children. They had been taken from the family home in Berlin in early August. This preoccupation with our lost children bound us together. It was a tremendous relief to be with someone who could understand the constant torment that such separation caused. However, Lotte would never let her suffering show. She always remained outwardly cheerful so as not to upset the two older children still with her. I, on the other hand, felt somehow crippled by what had happened and could scarcely disguise my anguish.'

★

Comforted by Lotte and the other mothers whose children were missing, Fey began to recover her strength. The food at the Hindenburg Baude was good and the mountain air restorative. The staff looked after the prisoners well, cleaning their rooms and waiting on them at meals. But for the isolation, and the permanent presence of the SS guards, it was, as Fey described, like staying at a 'luxury hotel'.

Far away from people who might be drawn by idle curiosity, the hotel had been carefully chosen by the SS. Situated 3,500 feet above the Kladsko Valley, it was surrounded by pine forests. Aside from a few isolated farms, there were no houses for miles around. Two SS officers watched the prisoners around the clock. Walks, however, were permitted, and they were allowed to send and receive letters. At mealtimes, the guards left them to talk freely, sitting discreetly at their own table in a corner of the dining room. The lax security meant the group discussed the possibility of escape; but they had no official papers, and they dared not run the risk of reprisals as it was clear they would all pay if anyone did get away.

The owner of the hotel was a 'cunning, crafty woman', disliked by Fey. 'She was obviously a shrewd character. She cooperated amicably with the SS, though she would have got on just as well with anybody else if things had been different. She gave us to understand that she was personally opposed to the Nazis, but we did not dare talk to her openly for fear that she was a spy. Those working for her, mostly Poles and Russians, wore high boots and thick fur jackets. We wondered if they were prisoners, too, but we were unable to find out. Mika and Tante Anni would occasionally speak to them in Russian, but they did not reveal much.'

All contact with the local population was forbidden. Nevertheless, rumours of the SS-run hideout spread and, from time to time, parties of hikers could be seen at the edge of the woods, trying to get a glimpse of the hotel. One morning, Fey was looking out of her window when a man suddenly appeared below. 'He shook his fist up at me, saying "It's time to get rid of these criminals." He spoke in a low voice, and was looking around furtively, so he must have meant the Nazis, rather than us.'

Cut off from the outside world, the group quickly established a routine. Prayers were held after breakfast, followed by long walks in the surrounding woods with everyone telling each other their own story. In the afternoons, they read books, played bridge and organized group activities – musical evenings, drawing classes and lectures, given by Alex von Stauffenberg, who had been a professor of ancient history at Würzburg before the war.

Thrown together into such enforced intimacy, a special bond developed between the prisoners. While different in character and experience, they were united by grief and worry. Torn from children and other family members whose fate they did not know, they worried constantly. Denied information, they could only imagine their loved ones' physical and emotional pain. The lack of logic in the Gestapo's methods compounded their anxiety; there were no satisfying answers to the questions of why one person had ended up in a concentration camp and another in a prison, or indeed why they were now being held in a comfortable hotel.

Yet, inevitably, Fey noticed, cliques developed as the prisoners got to know each other's foibles, and individuals were singled out and whispered about: 'We never seemed to tire of talking about Miss Gisevius, who brought us no end of amusement. Single and of a "certain age", when arrested she had been wearing the lightest of summer frocks and so was of course now freezing cold. Everyone gave her things to wear, most of which did not fit, so she looked quite odd. On top of this, the poor woman had a round face with a prominent nose tilted upward at an impossible angle, crowned by an enormous pair of spectacles. She had a knot at the back of her head to hold her hair and her mouth was set in an eternal smile. She clearly felt lonely and her method of being kind to people was somewhat embarrassing. She would shower us with little expressions of affection, and was constantly offering favours of one sort or another so that we would talk to her. People did not like to spend too long in her company because she would not stop chattering.'

Aunt Anni, who circled the corridors 'in a pair of gigantic slippers', was also to be avoided: 'She would tell us in endless detail about her time in Russia during the revolution when her husband was a prisoner in a Russian fortress, and how she would wait day and night to help him escape, which he eventually did. She had a fertile imagination and you never knew what was true or not. Like Miss Gisevius, people tended to avoid her because she was too talkative.'

By the end of the first week, the group had divided into subgroups, and 'clan rooms' emerged as relatives sought refuge with their families. With no relatives of her own, Fey spent her time with the Stauffenbergs. 'I was steadily drawn into their close family circle, soon calling them by their nicknames and spending most of my day with one or another of them. They gave me back a sense of comfort and security that I had altogether lost that terrible day in Innsbruck when the children had been taken.'

Of all the Stauffenbergs, it was Alex, the elder brother of Claus, who held the greatest fascination for Fey. 'I noticed him from the very first moment he walked into the lobby. He was still wearing his uniform as he had been arrested while serving with his regiment in Greece. He was so full of charm and warmth, he stood out – even though he wasn't classically good-looking. He gave the impression of being a very strong, composed man. Aged about forty, he was very tall. His hair was dark and ruffled, and there were streaks of grey around his temples. He had a fine, well-drawn profile and clear blue eyes and an endearing sort of tic that made his eye twitch. Though I was hugely drawn to him, I felt awkward in his presence. His breezy manner was so far removed from the way I felt. Losing the children had left me with a constant, raw feeling, and he seemed so worldly, so confident.'

To keep her mind off the children, Fey gave Italian lessons to some of the prisoners. Towards the end of her first week, Alex joined the classes. 'Because of Alex's knowledge of Greek and Latin, he understood much more about the structure of language than the others, and frequently more than I did. I felt rather shy when he came to the lessons, not just because he was so clever but also because he was constantly amused at my way of expressing myself. Of course, he picked up the language much faster than the others. As we were allowed to go for daily walks through the woods, Alex and I developed a habit of walking along together and speaking only Italian. At the beginning, he spoke haltingly, but as the days passed not only did his Italian improve, but I found out much more about him.'

Alex had been seriously wounded at the Battle of Stalingrad in January 1943. After being declared unfit for active service, he was posted to Athens, where he served as an officer in the Reserve Army. Aged thirty when Hitler first came to power, he had opposed the Nazis from the beginning. As Professor of Ancient History at Würzburg University, he refused to lend legitimacy to the Nazis' official line on history, questioning the ideals of power-seeking emperors, and attacking the deliberate glorification of ancient Germanic peoples as a bogus means to support fanciful and objectionable racial theories. The SS had arrested him the morning after the coup. In the intervening hours, friends had offered him the opportunity to flee to Egypt, but he had honourably refused.

Soon, Fey and Alex were spending most of their time together; they sat next to each other at meals, and went for long walks in the mornings and afternoons. The awkwardness Fey felt in his company quickly vanished. For the first time in weeks, he made her laugh: 'His great untidiness, his vagueness, his nonchalance, was typical of the "distracted professor" that one reads about in books. Nevertheless his manner was boyish and playful; above all, he had a wonderful sense of humour. During meals he would whisper little jokes and comments to amuse me, mainly about our *"compagni di sventura"* [companions in misfortune]. The solemn-faced Kuhns, our two table companions, whom we sat next to at every meal, would have no idea what we were laughing about and would give us disapproving looks.'

Over the long hours spent in each other's company, Fey came to see another side of Alex, which contradicted her first impression of a composed, confident man. As she discovered, the death of Claus, and of Berthold, his twin brother, had affected him profoundly: 'He had been very close to both of them and he spoke about their times together as they were growing up. All three brothers had been musical; one played the violin, another the viola, and Alex the piano. Alex said they had made quite a successful trio. He talked a lot about his younger brother Claus, whose talents as an officer had led to fast promotion in the Wehrmacht. He was tremendously proud of the fact that he was one of the few top army officers with the courage and decisiveness to organize an attempt on Hitler's life.'

Yet Fey sensed that Alex was haunted by the failure of the plot – and not only because Claus and Berthold had been executed. To her surprise, he confided that his brothers had told him nothing of the planned coup and it had come as a great shock. The realization that they had kept it secret, feeling they could not trust him, was deeply painful. As Alex explained, it was not because they suspected he might betray them; rather, it was because he was too incautious. Repeatedly, Claus and Berthold had warned him that his hot-headed opposition to Hitler risked drawing too much attention to the family; potentially, it threatened to jeopardize their own work with the German Resistance. He understood why they had excluded him, but he felt his brothers had underestimated him; he also felt that, in some way, he had fallen short of the mark.

Alex also spoke of his wife, Litta.* She was a test pilot for the Luftwaffe who had been awarded the Iron Cross and the gold Front Flying Clasp with diamonds, two of the highest military decorations. They had met in the spring of 1931 when she had flown him to a mutual friend's wedding in Berlin. They had not married until the summer of 1937. Litta's father was Jewish and, under the Nuremberg race laws, she was required to obtain an 'Aryan certificate' to marry a non-Jew. It was only after the Luftwaffe recognized the importance of her work that they had risked applying for the certificate. The work, testing the calibration of cockpit instruments in combat aircraft, was dangerous. It entailed diving vertically from a height of over 15,000 feet and pulling out at the last possible second. Flying up to fifteen missions a day, Litta was proud of her ability to withstand the incredible g-forces generated in this manoeuvre without experiencing the 'haze' that affected most pilots. Her work, and his long tours of duty in the army, meant they had seen little of each other since the start of the war, and he missed her terribly. Litta had also been arrested following the coup, but the Gestapo had freed her after Göring personally endorsed her release on the grounds of 'war necessity'.

In turn, Alex asked Fey about her life. 'At first, I didn't want to talk about it. I found it too painful to remember the time before the

---

* Countess Melitta Schenk von Stauffenberg.

children were taken. I also felt ashamed of what had happened, that I was to blame. I didn't want anyone to see the extent of my pain and I was frightened that if I talked openly to Alex, he would think less of me. But then, under his gentle questioning, I found myself pouring out the story of my life at the embassy in Rome and at Brazzà, describing my father and his ideals, Detalmo, and my anguish over my missing children. As I did so, his support and sympathy made me realize there was no need to be frightened and, for the first time since Innsbruck, I felt able to come to terms with myself and all that had happened.'

As the weeks went by, winter set in and the snow came. During the day, they continued to spend hours together, walking for miles across the white, empty fields, and through forests festooned with icicles. In this frost-bound landscape, which Fey described as 'ethereal', she found herself more and more drawn to Alex. 'During our long walks, I gradually came to realize what it was about him that I found so attractive and compelling. I had spent my childhood outside Germany and grown up and married in Italy. My family aside, I had known only the worst and most tragic sides of my native land; Nazism, the Hitler Youth, the SS, prison, separation from my children and family. Alex was the first person who gave me back all the positive and good aspects of the German nation: culture, intellectualism, moral integrity. He symbolized that side of Germany for which I had been unconsciously homesick in Italy. Here was a man who personified the "perfect" German of my imagination: tall, attractive, very much the gentleman. And then his character; on the one hand, cheerful, with a great sense of humour, and on the other, melancholic, almost sad. After all that he had been through and all that he had lost, Alex had reacted with courage and faced the future with optimism. He was an outstandingly well-read man and, apart from history, loved poetry and could recite many of Goethe's poems, which I loved. In the uncertainty of our days at the Hindenburg Baude, those walks and conversations helped me forget our helplessness, our grief for those who had died, and my fear for the children. In the unreal and difficult situation in which we found ourselves, I had fallen in love with him. I sensed he felt the same, but I wasn't sure, and I didn't have the courage to say anything. I didn't know how to tell him.'

Their time alone together came to an abrupt end on 30 November, five weeks after they arrived at the Hindenburg Baude.

Early that morning, Fey was woken by shouts and the sound of heavy footsteps pounding up the stairs from the lobby. Seconds later, the SS came marching along the corridor, thumping on her door with their fists: '*Schutzstaffel! Alle aufstehen! Abtransport! Packen Sie sofort Ihre Koffer!*' 'SS! Get up! You're moving! Pack your bags immediately!' Stunned, she lay there listening as they moved systematically along the corridor, waking the other prisoners. '*Alle aufstehen! Alle aufstehen! Sie bis sieben Uhr bereit!*' 'Get up! Get up! You must be ready by seven o'clock!'

After dressing hurriedly, Fey found the others in the lobby. 'No one was happy to hear the word *transport*, since we had all secretly hoped to stay indefinitely at the Hindenburg Baude. We were naturally not told why we were being moved so abruptly or where we were going. Some of the group became extremely upset about the sudden order, and several actually broke down crying.'

Once everyone was packed, the SS corralled them on to the forecourt outside. An army truck stood waiting, its engine running. The exhaust fumes drifted in black clouds over the snow banked up around the entrance to the hotel. It was dawn and above the deep shadows of the lower slopes, the peaks of the mountains, lit by the rising sun, were the colour of rose gold. Fey thought how incongruous the belching lorry and the black uniforms looked in the otherwise beautiful setting. Despite the order to hurry, they stood for hours in the cold. There was not enough room in the lorry for all twenty-two of them and a second truck had to be ordered from Bad Reinerz to transport their luggage. Finally, at midday they set off down the winding road to the valley.

Outside Bad Reinerz station, a squad of soldiers ordered them off the trucks; it brought home the fact that they were no longer privileged hotel guests and were once again ordinary prisoners. More than the rough manner with which the soldiers hurried her along, it was the lack of information that weighed on Fey: 'The SS still refused to tell us where we were going. The hope of being transferred to another hotel vanished rapidly as we were marched through the station yard. To reach the third-class carriage assigned to us, we had to cross several railway tracks, dragging our luggage behind. Two lines of soldiers, with rifles at the ready, formed a corridor for us to pass through. I thought it more comical than frightening. All this fuss for twenty-two people! The carriage was much too small and, once we were all seated, practically one on top of another, we could hardly move. The windows in the carriage were barred and tightly closed, so the whole place soon became suffocating.'

The soldiers, who were travelling in the wagon behind with the luggage, took it in turns, two at a time, to stand guard over the group. Regular Wehrmacht troops rather than SS men, Fey found them 'fairly human' and, as the journey progressed, they began to chat. They gave her news of the war, telling her of the appalling German casualties on the Eastern Front. Between 1 June and the end of August, almost a million men had been listed as dead, missing or wounded. In the space of six months, the Russians had advanced 500 miles and now threatened to take East Prussia: if they succeeded, from the border with West Prussia it was just 300 miles to Berlin.

As they were talking, one of the soldiers finally admitted to Fey that their destination was Danzig. 'After what I'd just heard this was the worst place possible, since it meant we were heading straight towards the Russian Front. Danzig lay between East and West Prussia. In the event of a German collapse, the chances of which seemed to be increasing fast, we would fall into Russian hands. It would be better to be shot outright by the Nazis than to disappear forever into Siberia, where our families would lose all trace of us.'

It was dark by the time the train reached Breslau, where it came to a halt. So great was the Wehrmacht's need to rush troops to the front that all civilian traffic was being held there for the night. After the long and uncomfortable journey, Fey assumed they would be taken to a hotel where they could wash and rest. Instead, the soldiers herded them into a cavernous, windowless hall. 'The place was icy cold and seemed to have been specially constructed for prisoners in transit. They threw us a few pieces of wood for the tiny stove, then the door slammed shut and we heard the key turning in the lock.' The facilities in the hall were primitive. There were no beds to sleep on, only the cold stone floor and a few wooden benches. 'At least we could lie down,' Fey recalled. 'But what a change to the night before when we had slept in our rooms in a comfortable hotel! There was a toilet, open for all to see, shamefully placed against one of the walls. It had simply been put there, in the open space, without even the barest of partitions. Lotte and I tied some covers in front of it in an attempt to make it a little more private and dignified. But since the "curtain" was not high enough, one could still see who was behind it because the head remained visible, which was embarrassing for the user, but at least it made us all laugh.'

At four o'clock the next morning, in the pitch dark, they were escorted back through the freezing station to their carriage. The guards had changed, and instead of Wehrmacht soldiers, they were now in the hands of the SS.

It would take thirty-six hours to travel the 235 miles to Danzig. By squeezing up together, the group managed to free up space in the compartment, taking it in turns to sleep. Periodically, the guards came in to taunt them, hinting that the journey was to be their last: 'You had better eat up all your provisions now. You never know what might happen'; 'Please stay calm, remain seated, and try and get some sleep. It will be easier that way.'

Fey could not tell whether the taunts were a game the guards were playing for their own amusement: 'They wanted us to think that we were about to be executed. But since we had been kept alive for so long, I found it hard to believe that they meant to do away with us at the next stop. Even so, it was frightening. Everyone was on edge – though we tried not to let it show.'

Midway through the journey an unpleasant incident occurred, raising the tension in the cramped compartment. At one of the frequent stops at small country stations, two SS officers boarded the carriage and roughly ordered Alex and Uncle Moppel* – still in their

---

* Markwart, Count Schenk von Stauffenberg.

uniforms – to hand over their epaulettes, collar tabs and other marks of rank. Both men refused. While they no longer felt any loyalty to the Wehrmacht, their regimental uniforms symbolized the values that they and the 20 July plotters had sought to uphold: honour, decency and courage. A heated argument ensued, which quickly escalated into a vicious shouting match. Squeezed between Lotte and Otto Philipp, Fey looked on, horrified: 'Very quickly the SS officers became furious – almost to the point of hysteria. They were scream-ing at the tops of their voices, hurling threats and insults at Alex, who was shouting back. I was terrified they were going to shoot Alex. Some of the women in our group began to cry. It was the first time they had witnessed the brutality that lurked behind the suave, pol-ished manners so typical of the Gestapo and the SS. I had seen it at the Gestapo's headquarters in Innsbruck when the officer had yelled at me in front of the children, referring to my father as "that criminal whose head we cut off". Thankfully, the argument ended with a compromise. The SS men agreed to procure civilian clothes for Alex and Onkel Moppel so they did not have to defile their uniforms. I felt terribly shaken; it brought back those last days in Innsbruck with the children.'

There was another reason why Fey was so upset, which she could not confide to anyone. The stripping of the uniforms signalled that their most likely destination was a concentration camp. Removing marks of rank from soldiers destined for the camps was standard SS practice; the authorities did not want the other inmates to know that German officers were also being imprisoned. Fey knew that men and women were segregated in the camps, and she was terrified of being separated from Alex.

As soon as the SS officers left, the families in the group rushed to console one another, realizing they were about to be split up. Fey, feeling desperately alone, watched in silence as they embraced. The thought of losing Alex was unbearable. Since leaving the Hinden-burg Baude, there had been no opportunity to escape from the others. Yet throughout the long journey, when their eyes met across the packed carriage, he had held her gaze and smiled. Now she would not even have the chance to say goodbye to him alone.

As the train crept slowly on, Fey was unable to think of anything else. She wondered what she would say if by some miracle they were able to snatch a few minutes together. Knowing she was unlikely to see him again, would she have the courage to tell him how she felt? But then how could she? Her belief in the sanctity of marriage meant that an affair was unthinkable. At the same time, the force of her attraction to him was so strong, she longed for the smallest word or gesture from him to show that he felt the same.

Late on the afternoon of 2 December, the group finally arrived at Danzig. They had been travelling for fifty-five hours. The journey was not over. Another train was waiting to take them on to their destination, the location of which the SS were still withholding.

Two hours later, they drew into a small country station, where they were told they would have to wait in the carriage until a police van arrived. Outside, the flat, featureless landscape stretched into the darkness; but they could see sand dunes, suggesting they were some-where near the coast.

'As we sat there, none of us said a word,' Fey remembered. 'Those with loved ones wanted to cherish their last moments together. Lotte was comforting her son, telling him that everything would be all right and that he had to be brave and strong; Hildegard Kuhn was weeping quietly with her head on her husband's shoulder; and Gagi and the two young Stauffenberg boys were in a group with their parents, holding hands. Alex looked as desperate as I felt. There had been no opportunity for us to have a private conversation. This was it. We had reached our destination. All of us were worn out by sleep-less nights, lack of food, and nervous tension. We had no idea where we had stopped, but it seemed cold and desolate outside. Ignorant of what was to happen next, we had to wait in the stationary train, with the windows barred, for hours on end. At last we were ordered off into the cold night and pushed into a police van. It was dark inside, but after a short ride I could see through a crack near my seat that we were passing along an enormous net of barbed wire, lit by huge searchlights.'

As the van passed through the gates of the camp, Alex slipped a piece of paper into Fey's hand. On it, he had written out the poem 'Love Song' by Rainer Maria Rilke.

> How shall I keep my soul from touching yours?
> How shall I lift it up, above you, to other things?
> O wouldst that I could find a shelter for it in some dark
>   forsaken place, somewhere strange and quiet that does
>   not reverberate with your deepest feelings.
> But everything that touches us, you and me, does so, as with
>   one stroke of the bow two strings make a single sound.
> On which instrument are we strung? And which player holds
>   us in his hand?
> O sweet song.

23

The van came to a halt and they heard voices approaching outside. Seconds later, the camp guards slid the bolts on the rear tailgate and rolled up the tarpaulin cover, revealing a floodlit courtyard about a hundred yards square. Startled by the bright light and the blast of freezing air, the group shielded their faces. Then, from somewhere in the shadows, a voice barked, 'Disperse! Quick march!', and the guards disappeared at a trot.

Clambering down from the van, they found themselves in front of a long, low building. The wind smelled of the sea and the ground was sandy, like beach sand. A high wall ran along one side of the yard, which was enclosed by a double line of barbed-wire fencing; the columns of white porcelain insulators set at regular intervals indicated that the entire structure was primed to administer a lethal charge. On the other side of the wall, the camp was now shrouded in darkness; they could dimly make out the silhouettes of watchtowers, cutting menacingly into the sky.

A solitary figure paced up and down in the centre of the yard, caught in the glare of the searchlights. He was swaddled in a long black greatcoat, his collar turned up against the freezing cold. Of medium height, he had the physique and face of a fighter; square-jawed with wide cheekbones, and a flattened nose that looked as if it had been broken several times. Raising his hand for silence, he addressed the group in a high, staccato voice:

'I am SS-Sturmbannführer Hoppe, the commandant of Stutthof Camp. You are the so-called *Sippenhäftlinge*.* You all have relations who were involved in the attempted assassination of the Führer. Until your fate is decided, this barrack is at your disposal. You are permitted to walk around this yard until nine o'clock in the evening. If you

---

* The prisoners of kin.

go out later, the guards have orders to shoot. You are not allowed to speak to the guards, nor are you permitted to say your names out loud.

'There will be an inspection at eight o'clock every morning. You must cook for yourselves and do your own laundry. You must chop the wood and look after the stoves. You do not have to wear prison uniforms, nor will you wear any form of identification. You can entertain yourselves as you like, and you can divide up the rooms as you like. I will see to it that you get books from the camp library. If you have any special requests, address them to Oberscharführer Foth. He is the sergeant in charge and will be responsible for you. You may write home once a fortnight.'

With these words, the commandant swung around and marched off, leaving the sergeant to show the group to their quarters. Emerging from the shadows of the barrack, he introduced himself politely and ushered them into the building. As they went up the steps into the blockhouse, they were so overcome with relief, everyone was laughing and hugging each other. Fey felt as if she was walking on air: 'To my complete astonishment, we hadn't been split up. I was so happy I didn't care what the accommodation was like. The main thing was that I was still with Alex and I knew, from the poem, that he felt as I did.'

Stepping inside the barrack, they entered an enormous hall that took up the whole width of the building. In one corner, there was a wood-burning stove; next to it, there was a cooking area, with cupboards full of crockery, and pots and pans. On either side of the hall, there were four huge rooms, each capable of sleeping up to fifteen people, and a smaller room for storing wood and coal. There was also a large bathroom, with hot and cold running water. The whole place was scrupulously clean and smelled of fresh paint and raw timber. Some of the rooms even had a pleasant outlook over the forest that surrounded the camp.

As he showed the group around, Sergeant Foth, a short, pasty-faced man, wearing the black uniform of the Allgemeine SS, seemed eager to please, stressing both his and their importance. The barrack, he explained, had been specially built for them, and they were now 'special prisoners' in a 'special' division of the Stutthof camp. The order had come from 'high up' – 'very high up' – and the building had been assigned the codename Warhorse 1. The commandant had personally selected him to take care of their needs. They were to have no contact with anyone else. It was an honour, he said, to have been chosen.

Fey and the others were stunned by the revelation that the barrack had been specially commissioned. 'It didn't make sense to us. As relatives of those who had conspired to kill Hitler, we knew that high-ranking Nazis reviled us. At the back of our minds was always the thought that at any moment they would order us to be killed. So why had we been given these spacious barracks? Who had issued the order? And for what purpose? Whatever the reasoning behind it, there was nothing we could do, and we set about making our new quarters as comfortable as possible.'

The two small storage rooms at either end of the barrack were allocated to Miss Gisevius and Aunt Anni; as Fey recalled, 'none of us wanted to suffer under their avalanche of words'. The other rooms were divided into male and female quarters, or allocated to family groups. The six Goerdelers shared two rooms; the Kuhns and Clemens and Elisabeth von Stauffenberg had rooms of their own. Fey chose to share with Lotte, Gagi, Mika and Ännerle – Lotte's fifteen-year-old daughter.

As she went to fetch her luggage from the hall, Fey ran into Alex in the corridor. Their conversation was fleeting: 'Alex quickly asked me if I was all right, then he offered to take my suitcases. As I bent to put them down, he whispered in my ear. The room he was sharing with his cousins was next door to the room I was sharing with the girls. The walls were paper thin and you could hear every word. If I chose the bed on the other side of the wall from his, we would be able to talk to each other last thing at night and first thing every morning. In the coming weeks, this is what we did. We always spoke in Italian. It had become our private language.'

Living cheek by jowl with the others, it was the only opportunity Fey and Alex had to communicate. There was very little to do and the time passed slowly. Despite the commandant's promises, there was virtually nothing to eat and the group did not prepare their own meals. Instead, at noon, Sergeant Foth brought over a large vat of unappetizing soup. It consisted of a thin gruel on which floated a few pieces of potato and carrot, except on Sundays when it also contained bits of unidentifiable meat. Sometimes the soup had sand in it, blown in by the wind as it was brought over from the camp kitchens. At night, Foth came back with their second and last meal – a piece of black bread with some watery coffee, and occasionally some cheese.

During the day, Fey sat with the others in the large hall, which had the one stove that gave off any real heat. The groups formed at the Hindenburg Baude remained together, except the cold now confined them to the same room. Increasingly, Fey found herself on edge: 'The Goerdelers would talk among themselves about all kinds of intellectual subjects. They were particularly keen on Rilke, and they would recite his poems endlessly. Of course, it was one of Rilke's poems that Alex had written out for me and hearing that particular poem somehow jarred. Dr Goerdeler, who had assumed the role of head of the family, would lead the recitals. Aged about sixty, he was a rather irritable and irritating grumbler who, when not complaining about something, or reciting poetry, sat sullen and silent. While the Goerdelers held their discussions, an assortment of us would sit over by the stove, chatting. Onkel Moppel and Markwart would tell jokes, sometimes roaring with laughter for hours. Often, I felt awkward, as I didn't understand them and I had to pretend to laugh. Then in the afternoons, Alex and I would play bridge with Markwart and Otto Philipp, which I loved.'

Cocooned in Warhorse 1, the Sippenhäftlinge had no means of knowing what was taking place a few hundred yards from their barrack. The 13-foot-high wall that separated them from the rest of the camp blocked their view of the huge complex: the scores of barracks and factories, the gallows, the gas chambers, the network of roads, and the single, narrow-gauge railway line that disappeared ominously into the forest. It also prevented them from communicating with the other inmates. So strict were the rules governing their detention that they were not allowed to see, or be seen by, anyone. The camp guards were banned from entering Warhorse 1; they were forbidden even to look at the 'special prisoners'. It meant that whenever Fey and the others went out to exercise in the yard, the guards in the watchtowers would turn their backs. This eerie sight mystified them; they could not understand why they were being kept so secretly.

Throughout those first weeks, Foth was the only person the prisoners of kin saw. He brought cakes and sweets on Ännerle von Hofacker's birthday, and he arranged for them to receive packages of warm clothing. They found him 'decent and obliging'. But his duties in Warhorse 1 took up only a fraction of his day. Outside those times, he carried on with his job as head of the Jewish section at the camp. There, he had earned the reputation of being the most sadistic of all the SS officers at Stutthof. As one prisoner would later testify, 'This man felt sick if he had not killed one inmate during the course of a day's work.'

Occasionally, voices, speaking a Slav language, drifted over the high wall; the Sippenhäftlinge could hear the bang and clank of industry and the wail of sirens summoning the camp inmates to work. Then – as the days went by – they began to hear sounds that filled them with dread. A week after they arrived, they were woken at 4 a.m. by the crackle of flames. Looking out of the windows of their barrack, they could see the glow from the fire, burning a hundred yards away in the forest. Showers of sparks rose into the freezing air and, as the fire gathered momentum and the wind blew the smoke in their direction, there was a sickening smell, which they knew could only be the smell of burning flesh. Other sounds came from the direction of the forest. 'Every night, as in a horrible nightmare, I could hear dogs baying,' Fey recalled. 'I knew that it meant some poor prisoner had tried to escape.'

24

Tens of thousands of men, women and children were imprisoned at Stutthof, which was situated on the coast, 25 miles east of Danzig. 'It was a gigantic place,' one prisoner recalled. 'You couldn't take it all in with your eyes. It seemed to go on and on indefinitely.'

On most days during the cold winter months, a sea mist rolled in from the Baltic, shutting out the light and heightening the sensation of being in an ice-bound, locked-in place. Surrounded by water on all sides and staffed by 1,000 SS guards, the 300-acre site had been carefully chosen by the Nazis. The Vistula River to the west, and the canals running up to the sea through swamps and marshland, made escape almost impossible, and German nationals living in the nearby fishing villages could be relied on to betray any prisoners who succeeded in breaking out.

The camp had opened in 1939 after the Nazis invaded Poland. Originally built to house 4,500 Polish men, among them teachers, priests and other members of the intelligentsia considered politically unreliable, the numbers of prisoners quickly swelled as the German Army advanced east. Following a visit from Himmler in the winter of 1942, thirty new barracks were commissioned to accommodate Russian POWs. Built by the inmates, the foundations were laid using the bones of prisoners who had died from epidemics of typhoid and other diseases then sweeping the camp. 'There were so many corpses the ovens were working 24 hours a day,' one prisoner recalled. 'Because the bodies were piling up, the burning was hurried and the bones were still hard. We had to empty the ovens, pile the bones on to wagons and drive them to the construction sites. They slotted in between the little stones and made the surfaces of the roads smoother and more stable.'

Once the barracks had been completed, and a sprawl of work camps and factories constructed to employ the new prisoners, Stutthof could accommodate 25,000 inmates. Yet by December 1944, when the Sippenhäftlinge arrived, 60,000 were crammed into the camp.

These were not the Soviet POWs that Himmler had anticipated in 1942. Following a succession of military defeats on the Eastern Front, the labour shortage in the Reich had assumed desperate proportions, and the German war effort now depended on the huge reserves of forced labour in SS-run camps and ghettos throughout the occupied countries. From the summer of 1944, as the Red Army threatened to liberate these camps, tens of thousands of inmates were evacuated. Some 47,000 prisoners had arrived at Stutthof between June and October, many of them from Auschwitz. 'They stretched the camp to the limit, which couldn't even cope with the people already there,' SS-Hauptsturmführer Meyer, a senior camp official, recalled. 'Berlin was told, but did nothing. The only response was to put the prisoners to work.'

When it became clear that a large number of the new arrivals were in no fit state to work, Berlin issued a second edict: to spare the cost of feeding the prisoners, they were to be killed.

The mass killings of inmates had begun in June under the codename *Sonderbehandlung* (special treatment). To determine which of the new arrivals would live or die, Sergeant Foth, together with other senior SS officers, presided over a selection procedure, which began the moment the transports arrived.

In the four months between June and the end of October, twenty-six trains pulled into the small station outside the camp, each carrying an average of between 1,500 and 2,000 prisoners. The trains came from the Kovno ghetto, from Kaiserwald – a concentration camp in Latvia – and from Auschwitz. In October, following the Red Army's Baltic offensive, the numbers had rocketed: then, the trains had carried in excess of 4,000 prisoners.

Of the 47,000 people who arrived in the transports, over 60 per cent were Jewish and more than half were women. Their journey in the packed cattle wagons, often in searing temperatures, had taken many days: 'We reeked of sweat that had dried on our bodies and of urine and faeces that we couldn't clean off,' one woman recalled.

Crowd control and the need to avoid mass panic was a dominant concern for the SS guards, who, in the case of a large transport, were hugely outnumbered. For this reason, they attempted to conceal the prisoners' destination. When the trains arrived at Stutthof station, the sign read 'Woodland Camp', and bands of musicians, playing chamber music, were lined up on the platform.

From the station, the prisoners were marched through the gates of the camp, past Commandant Hoppe's villa, with its well-tended garden, to a large parade ground. Men and women were immediately separated from each other, as were mothers from young children. On most transports, a number of prisoners arrived with a death sentence for 'offences' against the Nazis. These were singled out by the SS – including Sergeant Foth – and taken to the crematoria, where they were shot in the back of the head or hanged.*

Standing on the packed earth of the parade ground, trodden down by the multitudes herded through the place before them, the others lined up to be counted. Thirteen-year-old Schoschana Rabinovici arrived in a transport of 3,155 prisoners from Kaiserwald. 'After they had counted us again and again, an officer stepped forward and gave a speech in German. His voice screamed and barked at the same time: "From now on you are no longer people; you are numbers, only numbers. That is how we will call you and that is how you must answer – with your own number, and in German. From the moment you stepped through the gates, you lost every right; the only right remaining to you is work for the German Reich. The only possibility you have of leaving here is to fly through that chimney." With those words he pointed his finger at a chimney that could be seen at the end of the camp. Out of it rose black, stinking smoke. We now noticed, too, the peculiar sweetish smell of burning flesh, a smell that immediately stuck to us and never left us until the end.'

The procedure that followed was the same for every transport. After the roll call, the prisoners were driven forward into a large hangar, where they were made to strip and hand over their personal

---

* According to one estimate, between 10,000 and 20,000 prisoners were murdered immediately on arrival.

possessions to the camp store. Then the guards shaved their hair – including their pubic hair. This was followed by a body-cavity search for hidden valuables – mouths, ears, nostrils, rectum and genitalia. Finally, a number was scratched on their arms and they were issued prison clothing. Whereas political prisoners wore striped uniforms, Jews were given civilian clothes with their number and a yellow star sewn on the back. Second-, third-, sometimes fourth-hand, the clothes had been stripped from those who had died in the camp – whether by execution or from illness.

The prisoners were then marched back out to the parade ground, where they were again made to form up in a line. Then came the selection process to determine whether they were worth keeping alive. Sergeant Foth, together with a doctor and other senior SS officers, stood at the head of the line as, one by one, the guards called the prisoners forward.

Trudi Birger, who was sixteen in the summer of 1944, arrived with her mother in a transport of 2,169 women from the Kovno ghetto. 'No one wanted to move forward,' she recalled. 'We were forced forward by the crush of women behind us, harried along by the Kapos* with their switches and by the guards who stood along the barbed-wire fence with their dogs . . . All my attention focused on the doctor. He was going to decide my fate in a moment. He was a tall, handsome, blond man in a Nazi uniform . . . For myself, I wasn't concerned about his verdict. I knew I would pass. I had had plenty of practice at making it through selections. I had learned to look cheerful and stand as straight as I could, to show that I was full of energy and goodwill. But I wasn't sure about my mother . . . She looked closer to sixty than to forty . . . And the dress they had given her, a shapeless black thing, did nothing to make her look younger.'

As the women queued up to see the doctor, the guards went up and down the line picking out those who were pregnant and those evidently too weak to work. A large number of the prisoners suffered from oedema caused by years of malnourishment. 'We had to show them our legs,' one woman remembered; 'whoever had lots of ulcers on their legs was immediately chased away.' Political prisoner

---

* Prisoners who had been appointed by the Nazis as guards.

Krzysztof Dunin-Wąsowicz was assigned to process the new arrivals with the SS guards. He described how, in some instances, many of the women were too weak to stand: 'There was one transport of 150 women from Thorn sub-camp. They were in a miserable condition. Some of them could not get up off the ground, they were just lying there, moaning. Many of them were pregnant or had just given birth. All of them were very thin and had wounds on their legs.'

The doctor examined those who reached the head of the line. After feeling their arm muscles, he asked whether they were suffering from any diseases. 'He looked intently and impersonally at each woman as she stood before him, inspecting her for flaws that would make her useless as a labourer,' Trudi Birger wrote. 'With small, cold gestures, barely a word, he sent some to the left, others to the right. There wasn't one of us who didn't know what that meant.'

Trudi and her mother passed the selection process, but thousands of women failed. Those deemed unfit for work were crammed into segregated blocks where they died from illness, or were summarily killed by the camp guards. A variety of methods were used: gas, death by lethal injection, drowning.

In the barracks housing Jewish women, Sergeant Foth determined which were to be killed. 'The death sentences were arbitrarily handed down by Oberscharführer Foth,' Dunin-Wąsowicz wrote. 'The guards and Kapos were as zealous, but when it came to killing Jews, Foth was without doubt the most depraved and ruthless. One time, when the gas chamber wasn't working, this bloodthirsty sadist beat the women to death with his own hands.'

Dunin-Wąsowicz described how Foth, a father of eight, particularly sought out pregnant women. 'Once it happened that one of the young Jewish women, who was pregnant, fled from a group he had condemned to death and managed to hide on the top floor of the barracks. Foth led a search party, found her, and brought her triumphantly back to the group.' As SS officer Hans Rach testified after the war, Foth would also scour the barracks housing women whom the doctor had judged fit for work, looking for his next victims: 'Every day, he ordered a roll call lasting several hours, picking out the sick and weak women. He judged their state of health according to their legs, forcing the Jewish women to run races against each other. Anyone who could not run was loaded on to a wagon and taken to the gas chamber. When the chamber was full, the door was shut. Otto Knott, who had undergone special training at Lublin concentration camp, climbed on to the roof and poured Zyklon B through a special opening into the chamber . . . Foth also did this.'

'I don't want anyone to forget the pure cruelty of the camps,' Trudi Birger wrote in her memoir of her time at Stutthof. 'They weren't just impersonal death factories, where people were processed in gas chambers and crematoria, like products on some kind of macabre conveyor belt. They were places where sadistic, barbaric criminals were able to carry out their cruellest and most grotesque fantasies.'

While camp regulations prevented the guards from flogging the prisoners, there were no rules against murder, arbitrary acts of maltreatment or everyday harassment. Prisoners were shot for insignificant reasons – smoking in the latrines or singing carols – and for the guards' own amusement. One of their favourite pastimes was to open the gates to the camp and cajole inmates to leave; then they would shoot them on the grounds that they had tried to escape. At other times, the guards used specially trained German shepherd dogs to attack the prisoners. Former SS members admitted that, 'for the fun of it', the dog handlers would set their animals on working parties returning to the camp to 'liven up the inmates a bit'. Prisoners were expected to stand to attention and doff their caps when a guard passed. At night, teenage girls were dragged out of their bunks to the SS barracks and made to parade, as if on a catwalk, so the guards could choose those they wanted to sexually abuse.

The *Kapos* exercised their own regime of terror. These were prisoners assigned by the SS to supervise working parties and to run the blockhouses. Exempt from hard labour, and allocated extra food rations, they made it easier for the SS to control the camps. The system – employed in all the Nazi concentration camps – was designed to allow the camp to function with fewer SS personnel; without the Kapos, it would have been impossible for the authorities to maintain day-to-day operations. In 1941, a number of Category A prisoners from civilian gaols in Germany had been transferred to Stutthof, and it was from their ranks, rather than the numerous political and religious prisoners, that the Kapos had been recruited. Convicted murderers, child abusers and members of violent criminal gangs, they were chosen for their cruelty.

Speaking to a group of generals in June 1944, Himmler boasted that the Kapos explained the 'success' of the concentration-camp system. Outlining this 'ingenious scheme' for 'holding down sub-humans', he explained their role in relation to other prisoners: 'The moment he becomes a Kapo, he no longer sleeps with them. He is held accountable for the performance of the prisoners' work, and for their cleanliness . . . The moment we become dissatisfied with him, he is no longer a Kapo – he's back to sleeping with his men. And he knows that, on that very first night, they will beat him to death.'

The Kapos would go to any lengths to convince the guards of their suitability for the job. According to the testimonies of survivors, they would sometimes bludgeon and whip prisoners to death. Beatings, according to Schoschana Rabinovici, an evacuee from the Vilnius ghetto, were an everyday occurrence: 'From experience we learned to keep silent when getting a beating. When you kept silent, those doing the beating calmed down faster.' Genowefa Larysz, the Kapo of Barrack 23 – a blockhouse for female Jewish prisoners – was one of the most notorious. Every morning at roll call, she forced her charges to stand naked in front of her for several hours with their hands in the air. She poured soup over any who failed this endurance test or who needed to go to the toilet. Then she would kick them, and beat them about the head with an iron-rimmed bucket, before passing their names to the SS guards to add to the list of women earmarked for execution.

Many of the prisoners sought to curry favour with the Kapos. Schoschana's mother, Raja, used her skill as a seamstress to make a pair of satin pyjamas out of the lining of a quilt for Anna, her Kapo. In return, Raja requested to be assigned to the barrack toilets, which would entitle her to extra rations: 'The toilets were situated in a large room at the back of the barracks – ten in a row, without cubicles . . . Most of the women suffered from diarrhoea and dysentery, and the toilets were very dirty. The toilet attendant had to sit in the toilet area the whole time, paying attention to their cleanliness, cleaning the ten bowls, and making sure the women were orderly in their use of them. When Anna went to the bathroom, the toilet attendant had to bump all the women waiting in the line to keep the toilet free for Anna's sole usage. At those times, Anna herself would walk imperiously down the line saying, "Make way, the Queen is going to shit." '

Whether fit for work or sick, the prisoners lived in the same conditions. Originally designed for 450 occupants, each blockhouse accommodated more than 1,000 people. They slept, three to a bed, in three-tiered wooden bunks – two sleeping in one direction, and one between them, lying the other way. The beds were less than 3 feet wide; yet many of the inmates thought themselves lucky to have them: some barracks were so overcrowded, the prisoners had to sleep on the floor. Food was almost non-existent and nearly all the inmates suffered from symptoms of starvation – dizziness, hallucinations and muscle atrophy, making any movement painful. In the mornings, they were given a bowl of soup: 'The guards had taken the spoons away so the only thing we could do was fish out bits of potato and carrot with our fingers,' one woman recalled. In the evenings, they received a small piece of bread spread with fat. To stave off hunger, as another inmate remembered, the working parties carried human bones in their pockets, which they 'sucked on like candy'.

Shifts, for those prisoners able to work, lasted eight and a half hours. The work was varied. There were numerous factories at Stutthof, including an armaments factory owned by Focke-Wulf, which made aeroplane parts, and a clothing factory, where uniforms belonging to German soldiers killed on the Eastern Front were recycled. A number of women worked as seamstresses in the fur section, repairing the collars on greatcoats that arrived, ripped by shells and bullets, and often spattered with blood. Most prisoners, however, were assigned to outdoor duties. On her first day at Stutthof, Maria Rolnikaite, an evacuee from Kaiserwald, was sent to work on a farm owned by a German. 'There were several of us in the work party. All women. They tied our hands behind our backs, and joined us together with a rope fastened to the farmer's cart. The farmer and the accompanying guard got into the cart and off we went. The pony pulling the cart built up to a trot and we had to run to keep up.'

Trudi Birger and her mother were sent to build tank emplacements. In December 1944, the front was less than 150 miles from Stutthof, and the Germans were frantically constructing defences around towns and cities in the area. 'This was harder work than we had ever done before,' Trudi wrote. 'Using picks and shovels, we had to dig deep pits in the earth and smooth them around the edges . . . The tank emplacements were three to four metres deep . . . I had to stand at the bottom of the pits and throw shovelfuls of dirt far above my head. Only a young girl, I worked in the shadow of those high walls, with the guard, armed with his machine gun, standing on top, grinning to see what a strain it was.'

That November, typhoid struck the camp. Due to the overcrowding, and the appalling sanitary conditions, it quickly developed into an epidemic. As SS medic Otto Knott testified, the rapid spread of the disease obviated the need to gas prisoners: 'I would say 3,000–4,000 at most were killed [by gas] . . . because many of the camp's inmates died of typhus, a continuous gassing operation was not at all necessary.'

By mid December, 7,000 had died from the illness. 'The camp doctors didn't bother with us. People just died in their beds,' Maria Rolnikaite recalled. 'One night, I came back from work. I was freezing cold. I got into bed and nestled right up against my neighbour's back, pushing my hands under her armpits. I didn't notice anything in the night. I thought she was moving and squeezing my fingers. But in the morning, I found out that she was dead. There were so many dead.'*

To begin with, the bodies were left lying in the barracks for days. But as more and more prisoners died, the guards, who did not want to come into contact with the dead themselves, appointed 'funeral commandos' to remove the bodies. Maria was one of eight appointed

* So terrible were the conditions at Stutthof, it is thought that 47,000 registered inmates died during its existence, the vast majority from illness.

from her barrack. 'They made us strip the bodies. We had to undress them and we were given pliers to extract any gold teeth. The Kapo threatened that if I dared keep one of the teeth, I would be accompanying the body into the afterlife.'

By the beginning of December, no fewer than 125 prisoners were dying every day. Schoschana Rabinovici was in a barrack next door to Maria's. 'Morning after morning the women carried the night's dead out of the blockhouses and laid them down next to the wall. From there they were taken away on wagons beyond the fence. Since the crematoria were no longer sufficient, they began burning the dead on a pyre. It was not far from the Jewish women's camp, and we could see it on the other side of the fence. First wood was piled up, and then corpses on top, then wood again, and so on. Once the pile had reached a height of about 16 feet, the Germans poured fuel on it and set it on fire. The burning pyre looked as if devils were dancing on it. As the wood burned, the corpses contracted, and suddenly the dead were moving; raising their hands and feet, bending over and sitting up.'

Political prisoner Władysław Boniński was assigned to the 'crematorium commando', the working party responsible for constructing the pyres: 'The fires were lit between four and five o'clock in the morning. About twenty of us worked on them and the preparation took the whole day. Nine hundred bodies were burnt at a time and they would burn for twenty to twenty-four hours.'

25

In Warhorse 1, while Fey and the others saw the glow from the pyres and smelled the burning bodies, they did not know the scale of the atrocities taking place a few hundred yards away. The high wall outside their barrack screened their view of the camp and they had no means of communicating with the other inmates. Their food, however, came from the camp kitchens, where the 'ordinary' prisoners worked. Two weeks after the group arrived at Stutthof, most of them, including Fey, caught dysentery: 'Nearly all of us had to take to our beds. After a few days I started to recover. But I was hardly up and about again when Gagi, who slept next to me, came down with a severely inflamed throat. When the camp commandant realized that most of us were too sick and weak to help ourselves, let alone each other, he suddenly became terribly concerned. That's how we came to discover the strangest of details regarding our situation.'

Finally Fey was to understand why they had been kept alive. It was Himmler, the Reichsführer SS, who had given the order that none of them should be allowed to die: 'We were, in other words, "hostages". Though for what purpose Himmler intended to use us, the commandant could not say.'

In a panic, Hoppe asked Dr Goerdeler, who was a GP, what medicines he needed and ordered blood tests for everyone in the group. Since their imprisonment was 'top secret', a trusted SS doctor was summoned to take the tests – one of the very same doctors who, on a daily basis, administered lethal injections to the sick and the elderly in the camp infirmary.

The results indicated that Gagi's sore throat was in fact scarlet fever. Fey had had the illness as a child and, as she was one of the few on her feet, it was decided that she should move into an isolation room with Gagi so that she could nurse her under Dr Goerdeler's supervision. It was coming up to Christmas and, confined to the sickroom, Fey made crib figures out of cardboard to take her mind off the boys.

On Christmas Day, after spending ten days alone with Gagi, Fey was allowed out on condition she disinfected her clothes and hands. Half of the group – including Alex – were still ill in bed, and she gathered with the others in the communal room in the barrack. Midway through the morning, Sergeant Foth appeared bearing a small Christmas tree and other festive gifts, which he distributed with his best seasonal wishes.

Foth had spent the previous evening on the parade ground in the main camp, where the guards had assembled the inmates. 'The Germans put up a beautiful Christmas tree,' Schoschana Rabinovici remembered. 'It was big and decorated with coloured candles. All the prisoners were called to roll call late in the evening. This roll call lasted for hours. Suddenly a young Pole was brought into the middle of the square. Only then did we realise that a set of gallows had been erected next to the festively decorated tree. After the SS officers had conversed for a long time and had abused the youth over and over again, he was hanged in front of our eyes. On the eve of that high Christian holiday the prisoners were made to view the hanging – as if the Germans wanted to let us know that the cruelty would not stop, despite the holiday. The young man had been condemned to death for the theft of bread.'

Fey was taking quinine, which she had packed in her suitcase at Brazzà, in the hope of warding off illness. But on Boxing Day, she developed a sore throat and a high temperature. A number of the others were also showing symptoms of serious illness and, once again, Commandant Hoppe appeared and ordered new blood tests. The results revealed that Fey, Mika and Jutta* Goerdeler had typhoid; Lotte and her daughter, Ännerle, had scarlet fever; and Mrs Goerdeler and her daughter, Benigna, had bacillary dysentery, a potentially dangerous, and highly contagious, form of the disease. 'In order to at least appear in control of the situation, Hoppe decided that a

---

* Carl Friedrich Goerdeler's niece.

sickroom should be organized for the seven of us,' Fey recalled. 'He ordered proper beds to be sent from the camp infirmary, rather than the wooden pallets we usually slept on. Crammed together in the isolation room, there was a danger we would swap these highly contagious diseases. After this "ingenious" order, Hoppe vanished. We didn't see him or Foth for several weeks; they were terrified of catching our diseases.'

It fell on Dr Goerdeler to care for the group. Fey was running a temperature and, equipped only with a rusty stethoscope and the medicine that Hoppe's guards left at the back door to the barrack, he attended her daily. 'He would give me injections to strengthen my heart against the constant changes in my temperature. He had a sort of chronic cold, so that when he leaned over me there was always a drop glistening on the end of his nose. Funny to recall that so vividly. Although I waited for the drop to fall, it never did.'

Fey remained seriously ill for three weeks, with a 40-degree temperature: 'The whole of that period passed in a blur. The Russians were getting closer, and they had started bombing the camp. I lay there, listening to the sounds of the sirens and bombs crashing around me, delirious, and too weak to move. For the first time, I felt that I might not make it. In my feverish state, I was racked by the thought of dying so far away from my family. I worried constantly about my sons, fearful for their future if I should perish. Having lost them to the SS, I was convinced that I, and only I, could get them back.'

The other women in the makeshift sickroom were also dangerously ill, and it was during this period that a letter arrived from the People's Court in Berlin to inform Lotte von Hofacker that her husband had been executed. As she and her daughter, Ännerle, were confined with scarlet fever, Eberhard, her sixteen-year-old son, had opened the letter. He went straight to Dr Goerdeler and begged to be allowed to break the news to his mother. But Goerdeler refused; both women were in a critical condition, and he feared that it would jeopardize their recovery.

For four days, Eberhard shouldered the traumatic knowledge of his father's death. It was the second blow in the space of only a few months. A serious boy, who seemed far older than his years, he was still struggling to come to terms with his father's part in the 20 July plot. Born in 1930, Eberhard had grown up under the Nazis. After joining the Hitler Youth at a young age, he had been inculcated with negative propaganda concerning the 'Enemy', and the idea that his father had plotted against Hitler had come as a terrible shock. Fey noticed his disquiet when she first met him: 'You could see that a part of him was suffering a lot. Yet at the same time he felt responsible for his mother and his sister. He was the "man" of the family now, he wanted to be strong.'

It was not until Lotte's condition showed signs of improvement that Dr Goerdeler relented. The risk of contagion was too great to allow Eberhard into the isolation room, but the doctor permitted him to write a letter to his mother. Ännerle's condition, however, remained critical. With all his authority, Goerdeler impressed on the boy that, as well as breaking the awful news, it was imperative to keep it from his sister.

On 10 January, three weeks after his father had been executed, Eberhard sat down to write the letter. He thought about how his mother would react and wanted to break the news gently. Yet at the same time he was terrified of losing his sister. At a loss to find words to stop Lotte from venting her grief and alerting Ännerle, who was in the bed beside her, at the top of the page he wrote 'Please read all the way through first!!!':

Dear Mummy

Today, unfortunately I have to prepare you for the serious and sad news that is contained in the enclosed letter. Therefore, darling Mummy, please don't be too shocked when I tell you that our dear, beloved father is no longer alive, as confirmed officially by the letter from the People's Court of Justice, which came last Saturday. It is a terrible blow for all of us, but particularly for you, and you can imagine how my heart almost stopped when I opened it, unaware of what it would contain. It hits us all the more now as we had, justifiably, built up our hopes so much recently, and I still can't understand how Our Lord would do something this terrible to us, but He must know why. I am so dreadfully sorry that I have to leave you on your own with this deep sorrow and bitter pain. But take some comfort in the thought of how we have borne up so resolutely in captivity.

Now I have a big favour to ask of you; for now, please keep this news to yourself. Please don't on any account tell Ännerle or Fey, or the others who are ill, especially old Mrs Goerdeler, and don't let it show. In Dr Goerdeler's view, as well as everyone else here, Ännerle, who has reached the critical phase of the scarlet fever, would not be able to cope with this news. Even if she could, it would only cause a serious setback . . . I know that you will have to make an enormous effort to pull yourself together – but you'll do it. Later, once she is better, you can tell her.

We must – and we will – pull through! We will overcome our fate, however hard it may be. So darling, farewell. All the very best.

Your Eberhard

Dr Goerdeler was equally concerned about Fey, and his sister-in-law, Anneliese, both of whom remained critical. Cäsar von Hofacker's execution had come late in the day; the relatives of others in the group had been executed immediately after the coup. Knowing that Fey believed her father was alive and that Anneliese was convinced that her husband, Ulrich, was safe, he feared that the news of Hofacker's execution might cause them to abandon hope. A doctor of long standing, he recognized that hope was key to a patient's survival. For this reason, he had also spoken to Alex.

Like everyone else in the group, Goerdeler was aware of Alex's close relationship with Fey. Knowing that she was in danger of dying, he thought it important that Alex should see her. Tactfully, in a display of sensitivity that belied his brusque manner, he gave him a pretext to enter the sickroom. On condition that he kept his distance from the patients, he assigned Alex the job of looking after the small stove.

Alex watched over Fey throughout her illness. Aside from Goerdeler, he was the only other person allowed in. His presence was a huge comfort to Fey: 'Alex would come in the morning, and again in the afternoon. I could hear him when he entered, rustling around with his armful of logs and stoking the little iron stove in the corner of the room. Both of us had a great longing to speak to one another, but we were not allowed to because of the risk of contagion. I was too weak to say much anyway. Then unexpectedly, one afternoon early in January, Alex came over to me and pressed a piece of paper into my hand. It was a poem he had composed for me, a very lovely poem.'

It was the first poem Alex had written for her, and the first time he had expressed the strength of his feelings:

> With longing, exquisite and tender, I greet you
> But only in dreams
> So let me dream.

It was not until Fey began to feel better that she understood its full meaning: 'I realized then that the poem was a play on an old German myth that whatever you dream in the twelve nights after Christmas will come true. I must have read that verse a thousand times.'

By the middle of January, Dr Goerdeler pronounced Fey well enough to leave the sickroom for short periods. Still weak, and suffering from dizzy spells, she was looked after by Alex, who made her cups of tea and ensured that she was as well fed as possible. Surrounded by the others, there was never an opportunity for them to talk alone and, as the days went by, they saw less and less of each other. Outside, it was bitterly cold, the temperature dropping as low as minus 25 degrees on some nights – so cold that the group took to spending most of the day in bed, fully dressed in their clothes.

Aside from Alex, and eighteen-year-old Otto Philipp, the men were too weak to chop the piles of wood the guards left in the yard outside and it became impossible to keep the small stoves going. Commandant Hoppe, still worried about their survival, assigned two Russian female prisoners to do the job instead, and it was then that they learned of the horrendous conditions in the rest of the camp. While the women did not speak German, Mika von Stauffenberg and Aunt Anni were able to speak to them in Russian. For the first time, Fey heard how the gas chambers were being used systematically in camps across Germany and in the occupied countries, and she was deeply shaken when she discovered the truth about Sergeant Foth.

The horrors taking place yards from the barrack preoccupied the group. Sensing that some sort of endgame was approaching, they wondered about their own fate. While they had no access to the radio, or to newspapers, it was clear that the war was going badly for the Germans. Russian planes flew over constantly, sometimes buzzing low over the rooftop of the bunkhouse. Soon, they began to hear the rumble of shells in the distance. Uncle Moppel, a veteran of the First World War, was able to calculate how far away the fighting was from the sound of the explosions. He warned them that the front line was getting closer; perhaps 20 or 30 miles away – no more. 'Our dread of the Russians dominated everything,' Fey recalled. 'Because of our associations with men who had served as high-ranking military commanders under the Nazis – men who had led the Wehrmacht's campaign in Russia – we were terrified of falling into Russian hands. The fact that our relatives had conspired to kill Hitler was immaterial. In all probability, we would be sent to a Gulag in Siberia.'

With the Russians closing in by the hour, the imperative was to escape. By the last week in January, however, escape from Stutthof – whether for the SS, the 60,000 camp inmates, or for the prisoners in Warhorse 1 – was looking ever more unlikely. The launch of the Soviet winter offensive had precipitated the biggest panic migration in history and the only route out – the narrow forest road that ran past the camp – was blocked by 450,000 German civilians, all of them fleeing for their lives.

26

The Soviet assault on East Prussia had begun in thick fog early on the morning of 13 January. Three armies – a force of nearly 1.7 million men – were deployed against 580,000 German troops, 80,000 of which were *Volkssturm* soldiers, a ragged army of young boys and old men. The temperature that morning was minus 10 degrees Celsius and a thin layer of frost enveloped the Soviet tanks, ensuring that they were well camouflaged in the snow-covered landscape. Slogans, painted by the crews, were emblazoned on the turrets: 'Forward into the Fascist Lair!' and 'Revenge and Death to the German Occupiers!'

'A blind feeling of hatred' was how one veteran described the attitude of Soviet troops as they entered Reich territory. After the Wehrmacht's crimes in Russia, it was the Germans' turn to suffer. More than 12 million Russian civilians had been killed by the Nazis following the invasion of the Soviet Union. A month before the attack, Hitler authorized German troops 'to strike such terror into the population that it loses all will to resist'. Now Red Army commanders had whipped up their troops to rape, pillage and murder without fear of punishment.

The propaganda of hate was intended to arouse Soviet soldiers to fight more fiercely; it was also necessary to counteract four years of war weariness. Major Lev Kopelev, a dissident writer, later arrested by Stalin for anti-Soviet behaviour, noted a conversation with his superior in the Political Administration of the 50th Army: 'Zabashtansky called me in for a heart-to-heart talk. "You can understand," he said, "we're all sick and tired of this war, and the front-line soldiers most of all. When we were fighting on our own soil, everything was simple: we were fighting for our homes, to drive the enemy away. But now we're on their soil, and the soldier who's been under fire for four years now, and has been wounded – and knows that his wife and kids are hungry back home – he's got to go on fighting, on and on! Forward, always forward! . . . So what's needed now? First, for the soldier to go on hating, so he'll want his revenge. And second, for the soldier to have a personal interest in going on fighting, to know why he should climb out of that trench and face that machine gun once again. So now, with this order, everything is clear: he'll get to Germany; and there everything is his – goods, women, do what you want! Hammer away! So their grandchildren and great-grandchildren will remember and be afraid!" '

To begin with, the Russians encountered fierce German resistance and progress was slow. After the first few days, however, defences started to crumble and the Red Army moved at speed across the frozen ground. The landscape of East Prussia was mainly flat and forested and the approaching thunder of artillery created terrible fear in the isolated towns and villages. Etched into the minds of people living there were images of the atrocities committed at Nemmersdorf in the north-east of the province. The Red Army had briefly occupied the town in October 1944 and, after the Wehrmacht recaptured it, Goebbels sent propaganda units to film the 'gruesome Bolshevik crimes'. There were reports and images of mutilated dead bodies, of naked women nailed to barn doors, and babies with their 'heads bashed in'. Dozens of women and young girls had been raped many times over by Red Army soldiers before they were murdered.

Panic at the thought of suffering the same fate as the residents of Nemmersdorf spread like a contagion, compounded by the fact that there were no plans for the evacuation of the civilian population. Claiming that the Wehrmacht would 'smash any enemy attack', Nazi authorities considered any talk of evacuation treason. They exhorted East Prussians to defend their province to the last, and threatened punishment to anyone caught fleeing, while simultaneously making preparations for their own departure. The consequence was that the greater part of the civilian population was not evacuated from the towns until the force of the explosions from the Soviet artillery began to shatter the windowpanes in their houses.

By then, they were trapped in towns without water, gas or electricity, waiting for transport that the Nazis promised, but never came. All motorized vehicles had been requisitioned by the retreating Wehrmacht, and the trains had stopped running. Even by East Prussian standards, it was a bitterly cold January, and the prospect of days and nights out in the open, trying to make headway on icy roads, was frightening. Some chose suicide, taking capsules of cyanide readily available in town pharmacies. Others fled to the forests, digging foxholes in the snow, where they hoped to remain undetected by the Russian troops. Most, however, elected to flee by road. Total confusion reigned. 'Panic grips the people as the cry goes up: "The Russians are close," ' one woman recalled. 'Then a man comes by on horseback, shouting in a loud voice: "Save yourselves, you who can. The Russians will be here in half an hour." We're overcome by a paralysing fear.'

In the last ten days of January, some 2 million East Prussians fled into the unknown. The forced induction of all men into the Volkssturm meant that the majority of those taking flight were women, children and the elderly. Mothers had to harness horses and load up the family's belongings, together with food and other provisions necessary to survive the coming days in the open. Seizing whatever transport was available – hay carts, wagons, even prams – they set off along the roads out of their towns and villages. Hurriedly fabricated awnings, made from strips of carpet, covered the possessions they had managed to pile on to the wagons. 'It was sad and touching to an extreme degree to see the sorry farm carts, out of which the muffled heads of children peeped in curiosity,' one woman noted. 'The pots and pans tied to them clattered loudly. Often a sheep or a cow followed behind.'

In the snow and ice, progress was painfully slow. Columns kept halting because carts were overloaded and axles broke. On icy surfaces, undernourished horses found it hard to work, and in places the drifts were so deep that the animals had to be uncoupled from the wagons while the women dug the snow from under the wheels. Some carts were drawn by oxen, whose unshod hooves, worn raw by the roads, left trails of blood in the snow.

The flight of the 'trekkers', as they were called, meant that medieval towns founded by the Teutonic Knights in the thirteenth century, whose shields bore a black cross similar to the swastika, were depopulated within days, sometimes even hours. Advancing from the south and from the east, Soviet troops found themselves entering ghost towns where the only signs of the former inhabitants were the packs of dogs roaming the streets and messages pinned to the doors of the houses. They had been left for menfolk fighting at the front in the hope they would return. 'Dear Papa!' one read. 'We must escape to Alt-P★ by cart. From there on to the Reich by ship.'

Rampaging through the abandoned towns, Soviet troops wreaked havoc. Leonid Rabichev, a signals lieutenant with the 31st Army, described the sacking of Goldap in the eastern part of the region: 'The entire contents of shops were thrown out on to the sidewalks through the broken shop fronts. Thousands of pairs of shoes, plates and radio sets, all sorts of household and pharmacy goods and food were all mixed up. From apartment windows, clothes, pillows, quilts, paintings, gramophones and musical instruments were hurled on to the street. The roadways were blocked with all this stuff.' A few hours later, in the nearby Rominten Forest, the troops stormed through Göring's hunting lodge, formerly owned by the kaiser, destroying valuable pictures and furniture. With black paint, one soldier scrawled '*khuy*', the Russian for 'prick', across a nude of Aphrodite by Rubens. Envy, as well as revenge, prompted the mindless destruction: 'German villages looked like heaven compared with ours,' one Russian officer noted. 'Everything was cultivated. There were so many beautiful buildings. They had so much more than we did.' The loathing for anything German was so visceral that, as another wrote, 'Even the trees were enemy.'

The wrecking continued in town after town. Private Efraim Genkin witnessed the stripping of Gumbinnen, 20 miles to the north of Goldap. 'Germans abandoned everything and our people, like a huge crowd of Huns, invaded the houses,' he wrote home to his family. 'Everything is on fire, and down from pillows and feather-beds is flying about. Everyone, starting with a soldier and ending with a colonel, is pulling away loot. Beautifully furnished apartments and luxurious houses were smashed in a few hours and turned into dumps

★ Alt-Pillau, a suburb of Pillau, now Baltiysk, on the Baltic Coast.

where torn curtains are covered in jam that is pouring from broken jars . . . this town has been crucified.' Three days later, after leaving Gumbinnen, he wrote: 'Soldiers have turned into avid beasts. In the fields lie hundreds of shot cattle, on the road pigs and chickens with their heads chopped off. Houses have been looted and are on fire. What cannot be taken away is being broken and destroyed. The Germans are right to be running away from us like from a plague.'

Moving at speed through the flat landscape, the Soviet troops quickly caught up with the trekkers. The driving wind and the snow deadened all sound; muffled against the cold, with scarves wrapped around their heads, the columns of refugees often did not hear or see the frost-camouflaged tanks until they were upon them. Sometimes, the tanks simply ploughed on, their tracks crushing all in their path. If the troops stopped, it was to rape young girls and women. Leonid Rabichev described the scene outside Goldap: 'The roads were filled with old people, women and children, large families moving slowly on carts, on vehicles or on foot towards the west. Our tank troops, infantry, artillery, signals, caught up with them and cleared the way for themselves by pushing their horses and carts and belongings into the ditches on either side of the road. Then thousands of them forced the old women and children aside. Forgetting their honour and duty and forgetting about the retreating German units, they pounced on the women and girls. Women, mothers and their daughters, lie to the right and the left of the highway and in front of each one stands a laughing gang of men with their trousers down. Those already covered in blood and losing consciousness are dragged to the side. Children trying to help them have been shot. There is laughter and roaring and jeering, screams and moans. And the soldiers' commanders – majors and lieutenant colonels – are standing there on the highway. Some are laughing, but some are also conducting the event so that all their soldiers without exception could take part. This is not an initiation rite, and it has nothing to do with revenge against the accursed occupiers, this is just hellish diabolical group sex.'

Further along the road, Rabichev came across another column of trekkers. This one had been mowed down by Soviet tanks: 'As far as the eye can see, there are corpses of women, old people and children, among piles of clothing and overturned carts.' Later that day, after he was ordered to find a billet for his platoon for the night, he recorded other atrocities: 'I took my platoon to a hamlet two kilometres from the highway. In all the rooms are corpses of children, old people and women who have been raped and shot. We are so tired that we don't pay attention to them. We are so tired that we lie down among the corpses and fall asleep.'

Rabichev's platoon reached Goldap on 20 January – a week after the launch of the offensive. By then, tens of thousands of East Prussians had been killed or captured; but hundreds of thousands were still on the roads, streaming westwards. For upwards of half a million trekkers it was too late. On 24 January, advance units of the Red Army reached Elbing, closing the escape route to the west and trapping the refugees in a pocket of land along the Baltic Coast. Compressed alongside them were the last remaining forces of the German Army, fighting with their backs to the sea.

The pocket – about 40 miles long and 12 miles wide – reached up to the banks of the Frisches Haff, a huge lagoon formed from the narrow spit of land that jutted into the Baltic Sea a few miles east of Stutthof.

Only two means of flight – both extremely perilous – were left for the half a million trekkers. One way was to escape by ship from Pillau, the harbour at the entrance to the lagoon. The alternative was to cross the frozen lagoon to the Nehrung, the narrow spit of land opposite. From there, they could get to the port of Danzig, where they hoped to be evacuated by sea to the west.

To reach Pillau meant having to skirt the Soviet troops outside Königsberg. With time running out, over 450,000 trekkers opted to risk the 6-mile journey across the ice.

The ditches along the roads leading to the banks of the Frisches Haff bore witness to their tragedy. Soviet air attacks, exhaustion and the extreme cold had taken their toll, and horses and people lay dead or dying beside all sorts of household items: parcels of linen, pots and pans, pictures and valuable pieces of antique furniture – things people had jettisoned to lighten their load or to free up space in their carts for those travelling on foot.

Now, stranded on the banks of the lagoon, the trekkers had to wait their turn to cross the ice. A constant barrage of artillery rained down and Soviet planes raked the columns with machine-gun fire. Looking across the lagoon, the leaden sky merged with the grey expanse of ice, making it impossible to see the spit of land the families were trying to reach. The one blessing was that a foot of snow fell on 24 January and the approach roads were impassable, even for the Red Army's tanks.

That night, the endless columns began to cross the Frisches Haff at the risk of their lives. While the ice on the lagoon was 18 inches thick, Soviet shells had blown great holes in it, forcing the Wehrmacht to map out the route with trees and branches. For many, the hazardous journey ended in tragedy. In some cases, wagons and entire families tipped into the ice. Gertrud Dannowski made the crossing after fleeing from a small village some 15 miles inland: 'Bullets and pieces of ice ricocheted off the tin roof of our cart . . . It was every man for himself in a desperate attempt to get off the ice as quickly as possible. Dawn broke over a horrific scene: body upon body, man and horse alike. Often enough, only the drawbars of the carts protruded out of the ice.'

'The ice was breaking and in some places we had to drag ourselves through painfully cold water, 25 centimetres deep,' remembered one trekker, who crossed the lagoon on foot. 'We continually tried the surface with sticks . . . We often slipped and thought we were already lost. With our clothes wet through, movement was difficult. But blind terror drove us on, in spite of the shivering cold.'

Others on foot, already exhausted after the arduous trek from their towns and villages, were grateful for a lift. Lore Ehrich and her two young children were offered space on a farmer's cart: 'During the very first half-hour the colt, which was tied to the side of the cart, broke both legs and had to be left behind. A short time afterwards one of the two strong horses pulling the cart fell into a hole in the ice. With great difficulty, it was liberated with an axe. The farmer was shaking from head to foot because he was afraid that this animal might also break its legs, for one horse alone would not have been able to do the hard work of pulling the cart. We were compelled to cross at long intervals from the other carts, and also to remain for hours at the same spot. Anyone who tried to overtake the others was greeted with the most violent words.'

While thousands died, hundreds of thousands of trekkers survived the perilous journey across the ice. When they reached the other side, just one road led off the thin spit of land to Danzig, where they hoped to be evacuated to the Reich. No wider than the width of two carts, a mile after it joined the mainland it passed directly in front of Stutthof – less than 10 yards from the main gates to the camp.

Here, between two right-angled bends, the road narrowed. After 24 January, with 450,000 trekkers fleeing along it, it did not take long for the road to become gridlocked.

27

At 5 a.m. on the morning of 25 January, the alarm sounded throughout the camp.

Fey opened her eyes and listened out for approaching aircraft.
Above the wail of the siren, she could hear the thud of shells in the
near distance; but as the minutes passed and no planes flew over, it
was clear this was not an air-raid warning. Instead, from the direction of the camp, came the sounds of great commotion: revving
engines, screeched orders, packs of dogs barking and snarling. It
could only mean one thing: the Russians were very near.

The other women were awake too. Steeling themselves against the
cold, they got out of bed and crowded around the window. It was
still dark and it was snowing heavily. White, strobing lights flickered
across the sky to the south, but it was impossible to tell what was
going on from the angle from which they were looking. Through the
curtain of snow, backlit by the perimeter lights, all they could see
was the high wall that blocked their view of the camp.

'We stood there, shivering with cold and fear,' Fey recalled. 'We
were convinced the SS would simply abandon us to the Russians and
escape themselves.'

On the other side of the wall, the lights were on in all the barracks.
Usually this was the quiet hour, before the camp stirred, but the
entire workforce was on the move, heading towards the parade
ground. The siren was still going and the snow blurred the lines of
men and women – some 25,000 in total – snaking around the perimeter fence and back along the narrow roads to the barrack. Kapos,
wielding sticks, and groups of SS, each with an Alsatian on a short
leash, stood at intervals of twenty paces, harrying the lines along.
The temperature was minus 10 degrees Celsius and a strong wind,
backing in gusts, was blowing off the sea.

A fleet of motorcycles stood parked up by the main gates, ready to escort the columns of prisoners. With the Russians at Elbing, 30 miles from Stutthof, the commandant was preparing to evacuate the camp. Over the preceding days, the guards had worked around the clock to destroy incriminating records; now, the order from Berlin was to get the prisoners out before the Russians arrived.

At 6 a.m., Commandant Hoppe addressed the assembled inmates over the PA system. 'The icy wind cut through our bones,' political prisoner Meta Vannas recalled, 'but we were full of hope. The thunder of artillery coming from the east was getting louder and louder. We were expecting the Red Army to liberate us at any moment . . . The commandant called out the German prisoners and promised them freedom if they agreed to defend the Fatherland from the Bolshevik hordes. The criminals declared their support. A few German Communists managed to hide among this group and get out of the camp. Then we were given our orders.'

The remaining prisoners, and a further 20,000 from Stutthof's satellite camps, were to march to Lauenberg in Pomerania, some 75 miles to the west. Forty-one columns of 1,000–1,500 prisoners would leave the camp at 25-minute intervals. The distance was to be covered in seven days. Rations, consisting of half a loaf of bread, half a packet of margarine and a piece of cheese, would be allocated to each prisoner. They were to be escorted by SS guards, riding motorcycles and armed with machine guns and revolvers. Any prisoner caught falling behind would be shot.

No sooner had the first two columns marched out of the camp than the commandant's evacuation plan began to go awry. On the road outside, the queue of refugees and carts stretched back more than 10 miles to Kahlberg on the banks of the Nehrung, where the trekkers had crossed the ice. 'Oh this awful Nehrung Road! This was destined to be the most shocking part of our flight,' one trekker recalled. 'In addition to being mushy with snow and churned up by mud, there was one hole after another, each one half as big as a room . . . There were many halts and everything was chaotic. A third of the carts had been left behind on the ice; a further third broke down here. If anyone in front of us had a broken wheel, it was hours before we could go further . . . Progressing in this way, it took us a whole day to do one or two miles.'

Now, with the snow falling, and the wind blowing it into drifts, the 10-mile-long queue had ground to a halt. The scene at the entrance to the camp was horrific. People and horses were dying by the side of the road; frightened children ran up and down, looking for mothers from whom they had become separated; women, young and old, shovelled snow, trying to free a wheel, or to clear the drifts from the road. With the Russians on their heels, the trekkers were desperate to get moving and fights broke out as people tried to push their way through.

Thick forest bordered the road on either side. In the confined space, the Stutthof guards had no means of forcing a gap between the lines of trekkers to allow the columns of prisoners to proceed. By nightfall, the snow lay 3 feet deep. Of the forty-one columns of 1,000–1,500 prisoners, only seven had left the camp.

It was three o'clock in the morning when the eighth column, made up of 820 men, got under way. It had stopped snowing and the lines of refugees were moving again. Thirteen-year-old Schoschana Rabinovici and her mother, Raja, were due to leave in the next column, comprising 1,300 women, most of whom were Jewish. They had been woken by Sergeant Foth, who had come into their barracks and ordered them to undress. Prior to the march, their clothes needed to be disinfected and he told them to wash while they waited for their things to be returned. Minutes later, the guards ambushed the women in the shower room, herding them into the yard outside. 'Snow, frost, ice, rattling cold – none of these words can sum up what I experienced on the night of 25th–26th January 1945, as I stood naked in the open air,' Schoschana recalled.

> I found myself in the middle of a ball of women who were trying to warm one another by rubbing their naked bodies against each other. The cold enveloped us, but the worst cold came from beneath us. We were standing on snow and ice, our feet were bare and we couldn't stand still because the cold burned the soles of our feet. So we hopped from one leg to the other, often stepping on each other's feet in the crush . . .

Sometimes, I was pushed aside by the women who stood outside the circle and who were trying to get in. We shoved and were shoved – constant shoving and being shoved. Raja stayed beside me the whole time, fighting for a space for us both in the tangle of bodies, and rubbing my back with her cold wet hands, urging me to keep moving.

But I didn't want to go on. You can't imagine this cold. It seemed to me that the cold was not only on my skin; that it wasn't only my legs that had lost all sensation, so that I didn't care if anyone trod on them; that not only my hands were so frozen that I couldn't move them any more – I was cold, deep down inside . . . I was trying to stand next to women who were taller than me, so that at least from above I would be somewhat shielded from the cold air.

The cold made us want to urinate the whole time and even I couldn't hold back. The women would let themselves go, all over their own and their neighbours' legs whilst they were grouped closely together. It didn't bother anyone. On the contrary, for a brief moment, one blessed moment, the urine warmed our feet.

The hours went by; I couldn't count them. Again and again, Raja said this was probably our final ordeal, for we had heard that the front was no longer far away. She comforted me: 'It's good the wind off the sea is not so strong today; it's good it's not snowing tonight.'

No, it wasn't snowing that night; that night there was no wind. The air was frozen and so stiff it seemed you could cut it with a knife. It was minus 25 degrees centigrade (13 degrees below zero Fahrenheit). One woman crumpled to the ground and couldn't get up again. Another one collapsed. Hands stretched out to pull them back up, but it was too late; they could no longer be helped. Finished.

At first light the women's clothes arrived back from the disinfecting station. They were told to dress and given cups of weak tea.

Then a motorcycle escort appeared, followed by a black car containing Commandant Hoppe and some SS officers. 'We got the order to line up in rows of four and to begin moving in the direction of the main gates,' Schoschana recalled. 'Thus began the death march.'

★

Just two more columns left Stutthof that day. Soon after Schoschana's column marched out of the camp, it started snowing again.
Owing to the conditions on the road, the commandant abandoned
the evacuation of the remaining thirty columns – a total of some
36,000 prisoners.

With the Russians closing in and the weather getting worse by the
minute, his priority now was to evacuate the special prisoners in
Warhorse 1.

28.

The heavy snow meant it was not until four o'clock the following afternoon – 27 January – that Hoppe ordered Fey and the others to pack their bags and get ready to leave. More than forty-eight hours had passed since they had first heard the warning sirens, and they had spent an anxious time listening to the distant shellfire drawing closer, fearing that the SS had abandoned them to the Russians.

'You will leave in one hour!' Hoppe ordered. 'Anyone not ready will be left behind!'

Eight of the group, including Dr Goerdeler, who had finally succumbed to illness, were too weak to stand. Fey doubted whether they could survive a long journey: 'I was fearful for the weaker members . . . Onkel Moppel already had a high temperature and kept shivering uncontrollably. We were convinced he had caught typhoid. Clemens von Stauffenberg's hands and feet were swollen, and he had great difficulty breathing, and Lotte and Ännerle still hadn't recovered from scarlet fever.'

The stronger ones helped the others to pack and gathered blankets for the journey. Then Hoppe marched them out into a raging blizzard. Those too frail to walk were loaded into two makeshift ambulances; the rest of the group were left to stagger in the dark to the railway station at the entrance to the camp – the very same 'Woodland Camp' station at which the trains carrying tens of thousands of 'ordinary' prisoners had arrived the summer before.

'There, an old third-class carriage awaited us,' Fey recalled. 'It had a sliding door, which was jammed and would not close, and most of the windows were broken. The snow blew in in gusts and settled in great heaps on the hard wooden benches. The wind howled outside, and it was icy cold. I struggled to find a place beside healthy people, because I could no longer bear the company of the sick.'

'We had to brush the snow off the benches,' fifteen-year-old

Ännerle von Hofacker remembered. 'Two stoves gave off a little warmth, but it was all for nothing as there were no doors to the carriage. We lay down on the benches, covered in blankets and coats. But we were still freezing. It took an hour until everything was ready. We had to wait while another wagon was coupled to our carriage. Finally the commandant came to bid us farewell. Accompanying us were two SS guards – Fräulein Papke and Sergeant Kupfer.'

What none of the special prisoners realized was quite how privileged they were. With the road to Danzig clogged with trekkers, the SS had prioritized their evacuation over all other civilian and military traffic. After 24 January, when the Red Army severed the last main rail link to the Reich, the tiny branch line from Stutthof to Danzig was the only land route open to the west. The order to evacuate the special prisoners had in fact come through on 25 January, but the snow had prevented the train from leaving, and it had been waiting at the station ever since.

The train set off at a crawl, the icy wind blowing in through the open door. After a few hundred yards, the line, no more than a tram track, merged with the road to Danzig and continued parallel to it. Gas lamps lit the way at intervals, casting pools of green-white light. Dimly, through the swirling snow, Fey and the others could see the trekkers. They were only 10 yards or so away from the train, but the snow deadened and hushed everything. As if frozen, the unending line of carts, animals and people stood soundlessly, unmoving – a sinister pointer to some calamity ahead. Seated between Alex and Eberhard von Hofacker, Fey felt sick with fear: 'Aside from the air raids, we had been completely cut off from the war in our barrack at Stutthof. Now we were in the middle of it, journeying into the unknown. Would the Russians catch up with us? Were they behind us, or ahead of us? Seeing the unending lines of refugees I was convinced this was the end for us all.'

Ten minutes after the train left Stutthof, it came to a halt. Snow blocked the line ahead and the SS came into the carriage, calling for 'volunteers' to help in the almost impossible task of clearing it away. Alex was one of them. He returned two hours later, soaked and frozen to the core. Grimly, he reported that the carriage behind theirs was an open cattle wagon, full of Hungarians and German soldiers accused of spying by the SS. Some of the prisoners had already frozen to death, and the guards had simply tossed their bodies on to the tracks.

Still the train did not move. It was stranded in open country on the outskirts of Steegen, where the line veered away from the Danzig road. To avoid the queues, trekkers travelling on foot or horseback had opted to follow the tram track and streams of people went past – shadowy figures Fey was unable to see in the pitch dark. It was only when dawn broke that she was confronted with the scene around her: 'Silent and grim, they swarmed doggedly over the railway line, groping their way westward. Some wore tattered uniforms and greatcoats, but most were just wrapped in woollen clothing, salvaged at the last moment. Many, too weak to go on, had collapsed and lay dead or dying beside the corpses of mules and horses. The sight of these poor people moved us terribly. There we were complaining about our own conditions. We were certainly in no paradise, but it was nothing compared to their situation. I thought of an old Italian proverb: "One must always turn round and look back. For the person who complains about only having figs to eat will discover another eating the discarded skins." It might seem banal, but confronted with that terrible reality, I realized at that moment that this proverb contained a profound truth.'

Watching the kaleidoscope of horror passing before her eyes, two images would stay with Fey. The first was of Fräulein Papke, swathed in her fur-trimmed SS greatcoat, coolly eating a sandwich from the 'picnic' she had brought with her, while craning to see the carnage outside. The second was the sight of a small boy, who lay unmoving in the snow: 'Sergeant Kupfer picked him up. At first I thought he must be dead, but after a vigorous massage the boy regained consciousness and was given some food. Shortly afterward he was handed down to the care of a group of retreating soldiers. This incident had a profound effect on me and once again sent me into a fit of despair and depression thinking of the fate of my own children. I was completely silent for hours afterwards.'

Midday came, and they were still at Steegen. At a loss, Kupfer, who was in charge of the transport, sent a radio message to Stutthof and at two in the afternoon a party of prisoners was dispatched from the camp to clear the line ahead. Someone had hung coats and blankets around the door in an attempt to block out the freezing air but, as Fey described, the wind blew in through every crack in the carriage: 'Listless and silent, we sat huddled and shivering for hour after freezing hour, concentrating only on warmth and survival. Relieving oneself meant going out into the storm, where within seconds one's hands became so stiff and numb that it was impossible to undo the necessary buttons. After many hours had passed, the few able-bodied men still left were once more ordered out to try and help the prisoners shift the snow. Finally, the train jerked forward.'

They reached the mouth of the Vistula at seven o'clock that evening. It was just 10 miles from Stutthof and they had been on the train for over twenty-four hours. There was no sign of the ferry that was supposed to take them across. Along the bank of the river, tens of thousands of refugees were camped in the fields, the line of carts stretching as far as the eye could see. It had finally stopped snowing and it was a clear night with a brilliant full moon. The flat, open country bordering the Gulf of Danzig offered no cover and, looking across at the scene, Fey feared they were a sitting target for Russian bombers.

For five tense hours, they waited for the ferry. When it finally arrived, the ferryman refused to load their train. He told Sergeant Kupfer that he was only authorized to ship troops and refugees, not concentration-camp prisoners. Ännerle von Hofacker witnessed the row that ensued: 'Kupfer had a go at the ferryman. "These are not prisoners," he said. "They are relatives of members of the SS and as such take precedence, even over troops." Against his will, the ferryman obeyed, full of resentment. When he came to load our carriages, he loaded them with such force that they were hanging over the buffers of the ferry, almost tipping over, and only by a whisker avoided falling into the water.'

It was two o'clock in the morning when the ferry docked on the other side of the river, but their journey, as Fey described, was not

over: 'After several more hours, we arrived half-dead in Danzig, having covered 30 kilometres in thirty-seven hours. There, the guards
ordered us roughly out of the carriage, telling us that all trains had
been commandeered by troops or refugee transports, and we would
have to continue by road. Of course, they refused to tell us where we
were going.'

Outside the station, the group joined a line of male prisoners waiting to board a fleet of trucks. To their horror, they discovered that
these were the prisoners who had been in the open wagons behind
them since Stutthof. The fact that they were being transported
with men whom the SS had treated like animals filled Fey with fore-
boding: 'It indicated a change in our status. I was convinced that
wherever we were being taken, it would be worse than our barrack
at Stutthof.'

Two hours later, the trucks stopped on a remote country road.
High up on a hill, Fey could see a set of gates. The site was enclosed
by a tall barbed-wire fence and a medieval *cheval de frise* – a barrel-
shaped structure, covered with projecting spikes. 'The drive ahead
was blocked by snow, so we were ordered off the truck. In our weak-
ened state it was simply impossible to half climb, half swim through
the deep drifts toward the gates. One by one we collapsed from
exhaustion on the way up. Realizing that we would never reach the
top, SS men were sent down to help. Roughly and with brute
strength, they dragged us to the top, as if they were hauling up tobog-
gans. I thought we would never make it, especially Clemens and
Onkel Moppel. From something one of the guards said, I had the
impression they thought we belonged to the SS. But I was past caring. All that mattered was that we were still alive. From there we
were directed to a filthy barrack.'

The columns of prisoners who set off from Stutthof in the days before
Fey and the others left the camp were still on the road. The march to
Lauenburg was supposed to take seven days. In fact, it would be
another week before the survivors of the 'Death March' arrived at
their destination. An estimated 4,500 died – most of them from the
segregated columns of Jewish prisoners. Once the Nazi authorities

finally recognized that the Danzig road was the last route of flight to the Reich, troops and civilians were given priority and Jews were banned from using it. Forced to take back roads, often no more than tracks, thousands died from the cold, or were executed by the SS for falling behind the columns.

A further 5,000 prisoners – all Jewish women – left the camp at the end of January. With the Danzig road closed to Jews, Hoppe ordered them to march east to the port of Pillau on the Baltic Coast. From there, the SS intended to evacuate them to the Reich by ship. On 30 January, after the ships failed to materialize, in one of the last mass atrocities of the war, 3,000 were lined up on the iced-over sea outside Pillau and shot.

29.

'In the camp. 08.45 hrs. A mass of SS approach us, grab our luggage with compassion and drag us up the hill to the barracks. They believe us to be members of the SS. We are done for and exhausted. Tante Anni crashed out with a fever, a suspected lung inflammation.'

This was Gagi von Stauffenberg's diary entry – hurriedly scribbled at the end of the harrowing journey from Stutthof. After hauling the group up the hill, the SS carried them through the gates to the camp and across a courtyard to a barrack. A squadron of troops bound for the front had just vacated it, and it was full of their rubbish. Owing to the cold, the windows had been closed all night. No one had opened them and the room reeked of the men's sweat. 'Our misery was complete, our courage spent,' Fey wrote.

Located 5 miles south of Danzig, Matzkau – as the camp was called – was a correctional prison for SS troops. With a capacity for 1,600 prisoners, its purpose was to 're-educate' soldiers charged with bringing the SS into disrepute. Their offences included insubordination, military disobedience, drunkenness, corruption and homosexuality. The punishment regime was severe; there was a shoot-to-kill policy for escapees; there were whipping blocks, where the prisoners were beaten over a trestle table; and execution squads for those condemned to death.

Homosexuals were a targeted group in Nazi Germany. Himmler, on becoming head of the SS, estimated the number to be 7–10 per cent of German men: 'If this remains the case, it means our Volk will be destroyed by this plague . . . a people of good race which has too few children has a sure ticket for disgrace.' Vowing to eliminate 'this plague', he instructed the Gestapo to compile lists of gay men, and 100,000 were arrested. Of these, some 50,000 were imprisoned. At Matzkau, following an interview with the camp doctor, prisoners judged incapable of renouncing their homosexuality were selected for castration.

The Sippenhäftlinge slept throughout their first day at Matzkau. Late in the evening, they were woken by the camp doctor. After examining them individually, he announced that new beds with feather mattresses would be brought for them, and a detachment of prisoners sent over to clean the barrack. Uncle Moppel and Aunt Anni, both seriously ill, were to be transferred to the camp infirmary, where they would be under his personal care. None of the group had eaten since leaving Stutthof, and the doctor said they would be given a hot meal. 'We waited in vain,' Fey remembered. 'Later we learned that the inmates who had been told to bring it had devoured it on the way. At ten o'clock a second meal was prepared and actually arrived. We were amazed by the luxury of it. There were tasty potatoes, green vegetables, and small pieces of sausage!'

The next morning, breakfast was of the same standard. For the first time in weeks, they were given fresh fruit and honey with their toast. The good food, and the doctor's evident concern, indicated that the SS intended to keep them alive. But they could not be sure and remained on edge. A few days after they arrived, Fey was unnerved by a visit to the shower room: 'In the hard, cold light we were accompanied across the eerie, ugly camp to a special barrack at the far end. There we were ushered into an enormous room and told to strip naked. I suddenly realized that it bore a frightening resemblance to the gas rooms we had heard about at Stutthof. For a moment my heart stopped beating, but the SS left the door open, and when the guard turned on the taps, boiling water poured out.'

The days went by, waiting for the SS to make their next move. Men and women were segregated in the barrack, and Fräulein Papke, the SS guard in charge, patrolled the building, ensuring there was no contact between them. Fey found her an unpleasant character: 'A nasty, arrogant woman, with a thin, pointed face and beady dark eyes, she missed nothing and was constantly enforcing petty regulations. We were convinced she knew what was in store for us, but of course she refused to say.' There was little to do, and Fey spent her time watching the SS guards drilling the prisoners in the yard outside. 'The sergeant in charge took particular pleasure in making them drag themselves along the cold ground on their elbows. This evidently went into the making of a good SS man.'

A squad of SS prisoners undergoing correction came in and out of the barrack daily, cleaning the rooms and bringing the group their meals. Towards the end of the first week, one of the prisoners revealed a piece of information that shook them to the core. The morning they arrived at Matzkau, both Fey and Gagi had over-heard the inmates referring to them as 'members of the SS'. They assumed this was a misunderstanding or that the men had simply jumped to this conclusion. But the prisoner confided that the camp authorities had warned the other inmates about the 'special' group of new arrivals. They were 'members of the SS' and their names were 'top secret'. If any of the inmates discovered their true identities, they would be shot.

In the circumstances, the knowledge that they were now categor-ized as SS caused acute anxiety. The front was at Marienburg, 30 miles away. While they were further from the Russians than they had been at Stutthof, as Fey recognized, 30 miles was hardly a safe distance: 'Every day we would crouch down on the floor of the bar-rack, deafened by the thunderous air battles overhead, fearful from one minute to the next that a bomb would crash down on us. But this paled in comparison to our fear of the Russians. If the Red Army overran the camp, as "members of the SS", we would be summarily executed. Our new status was common knowledge among the inmates and someone was bound to betray us. Whatever we said, the Russians would not believe us.'

Desperate to be moved, the group worried incessantly. While they were grateful for the plentiful food, which continued to arrive, the luxurious meals were proof that the SS had a hidden agenda. Evi-dently, they were being 'fattened up' for a reason. 'As the days passed and our health improved, we spent much time speculating about our fate,' Fey recalled. 'The general opinion was that Himmler was keeping us alive for his own ends, perhaps in order to use us as bar-gaining counters in the last hours of the Reich. But we had no idea for what purpose or for how long we would remain of value. We did not believe that Hitler, who had vowed to eliminate the families of the plotters, even knew of our continued existence. This, we concluded, explained why we were forbidden to call each other by our surnames and both the guards and the camp inmates were told they would be shot if they revealed our identities.'

Fey was acutely conscious of the bitter irony in their situation. Their survival depended on Himmler's survival. If he were to be killed or the Allies refused to countenance any attempt on his part to use 'hostages' to save his own skin, the group would cease to have any currency. They would lose their protection and, as 'members of the SS', be subject to dire recrimination.

Confronted with the precariousness of her position, Fey thought about Corrado and Roberto constantly. 'If they were still alive, I could only hope that their situation was better than mine. Better not to think about it. Don't think about it, I kept telling myself. I was terribly afraid for my own fate but got desperate at the least thought of what could happen to the children.'

'February 5. No news still of our transport from here. Tante Anni now gripped by typhus, can't be saved,' Gagi wrote in her diary.

A week had passed since they first arrived at Matzkau, during which Baroness Anni von Lerchenfeld had been slipping in and out of consciousness. The following afternoon – 6 February – she died. In her last days her thoughts had been with her daughter Nina, Claus von Stauffenberg's widow, who had just given birth to their last child.

While Fey had gone out of her way to avoid Aunt Anni, whose loquaciousness irritated her, she, like the others, was profoundly affected. 'It was our first death. We had become so closely bound together that it seemed to herald the end for everyone. Until that point we had overcome all odds. Now we felt defeated. Some of us poured out our anger against the SS, who told us that she was to be buried in an unmarked grave in Danzig. We knew of a Stauffenberg family estate nearby, and we wanted her to be buried there.'

That evening, they placed Aunt Anni's body in a black coffin, decorated with a sprig of pine leaves, which the SS allowed them to pick from the trees around the perimeter fence. Fey was aghast when the camp commandant had the temerity to send his condolences: 'What a lying hypocrite, I thought. Much later we found out that, in spite of the rapid advance of the Russian Army, the SS had in fact buried Anni on the estate. What illogical behaviour. On the one hand, the gas chambers, and on the other, this act. It would have been so easy, so in character, for them not to have bothered.'

Another two days went by, until, halfway through the morning of 8 February, Fräulein Papke came rushing into the barrack.

'Get ready! You leave today!' she shouted.

As Fey and the other women gathered their things, Papke strode around the room, issuing further orders. 'Take away what you can. Pull the hooks out of the closets, the screws and nails from the walls, anything that might be useful. Leave nothing behind!' Stopping in front of Fey, looking directly at her, she snapped, 'You might as well get used to stealing!'

Fey felt a surge of hope. 'Such an order, coming from Papke, who was normally so strict in enforcing useless rules and so careful of her dignity, made me feel that the collapse of the "Thousand-Year-Reich" was but a hair's breadth away. We did as she ordered, ripping out everything from the barrack that might prove useful.'

30

Fey stood in the courtyard watching the SS move between the barrack and the lorry as they loaded the things she and the others had 'stolen' at Fräulein Papke's instigation. It was ten o'clock on the morning of 8 February and they were due to leave within the hour. Seeing the mounds of junk piled up by the entrance, among them sections of flooring, metal coat racks and an old iron stove, she wondered how and in what circumstances they would prove 'useful'. Worryingly, Papke had again refused to divulge their destination.

It was a cold, blue day and the sun glinted on the snow. Despite her relief to be on the move at last, Fey's mood was low. A few minutes before, she had bid a silent farewell to Uncle Moppel, who was unconscious. He had spotted fever, a virulent form of typhoid, which she knew was usually fatal. Unfailingly courteous and kind, the former cavalry officer had become a father figure to her and she doubted she would ever see him again. His family were still with him in the camp infirmary as she left, and she could tell from their faces they were prepared for the worst.

It took the SS several hours to load up. Finally, at midday, the truck carrying the prisoners of kin pulled out of the gates to the camp. Crammed in the back with their luggage, the group exchanged few words. So soon after Aunt Anni's death, they were all feeling the wrench of leaving Uncle Moppel.

Ten minutes later, they drew up at a small train halt in the valley below Matzkau. A single cattle car, which was to be their transport for the journey, was waiting in a siding. It was then that Papke told them that they were going to Danzig, where they would be 'evacuated to the Reich'.

Papke had not said how they would be evacuated. 'Our fear of a ship is enormous,' Gagi noted in her diary as the train set off. The recent sinking of the *Wilhelm Gustloff* – the worst maritime disaster in history – had been widely covered in the German press and they had been told of the tragedy. The *Gustloff*, Germany's largest cruise liner, had sailed from Gotenhafen, the port outside Danzig, on 30 January. It was the first large ship to reach the city following the launch of Operation Hannibal – the name given by the German Navy to the mass evacuation of civilians from the Baltic Coast. Danzig had become the destination for hundreds of thousands of refugees desperate to escape from the Russians. In the space of three weeks, 400,000 had descended on the city, swelling its population to almost a million. They included the first wave of trekkers, recently arrived after crossing the ice on the Frisches Haff. Stranded on the quayside at Gotenhafen or living in camps hastily erected by the authorities, their best chance of escape was by boat.

The *Gustloff* was designed to carry 2,000, but when the ship docked 6,600–9,000 had scrambled on board. Soon after leaving the port, it was stalked by a Soviet submarine. Some 20 miles out to sea, the submarine fired three torpedoes into the ship's stern. Within forty minutes, the *Gustloff* sank, bow down. Between 5,300 and 7,400 died – far exceeding the toll of 1,500 lives lost on the *Titanic*. The victims included an estimated 5,000 children. Many died as a result of direct hits from the torpedoes or by drowning in the onrushing water; others were crushed to death in the initial stampede for the lifeboats. But the majority succumbed to exposure in the freezing water as terrified passengers, leaping from the decks, capsized the crowded lifeboats, tipping people into the icy Baltic.

The cattle car left the halt at four o'clock in the afternoon, only to arrive at Danzig at one o'clock the next morning – normally a journey of less than an hour. Refugees blocked the railway lines on the approaches to the city, and there were endless stops, waiting for the lines to clear. Throughout the journey, Fey was alarmed by the shouts outside and the constant pounding on the walls of the wagon as the refugees demanded a place on board: 'Papke and Kupfer had bolted the doors and were standing by, ready to shoot anyone who broke in. Whenever we stopped, people were using objects to batter the sides of the wagon. Listening to these blows of despair was awful; but I was also terrified of what would happen if the wagon was overrun and the guards started shooting. In the cramped space, with bullets flying around, any one of us could be killed.'

When they finally reached Danzig, the station was crammed with hundreds more refugees, most of them crashed out asleep on the floor. A blackout was in force and it was pitch dark. Picking their way through the bodies on the concourse, Papke and Kupfer directed the group to a bridge. It was a gantry-type structure, built of metal, high over the tracks. Crossing over, Fey could see the silhouettes of the cranes in the nearby harbour. The air was damp and smelled of the sea, making her shudder. It reminded her of Stutthof.

Soldiers, armed with machine guns, guarded the platform on the other side. As the group approached, they made way for them to pass. The platform was eerily empty; solitary SS men paced up and down, and spots of red and green light bobbed in the darkness as the station guards, carrying lamps, moved soundlessly about. A goods train was drawn up, waiting to depart. A wagon had been reserved for the group and the SS directed them to the front of the train. Walking the length of the platform, past the long line of closed wagons, Fey sensed that they were packed with people. Thin trails of smoke drifted from the high windows and she could hear voices coming from inside.

Soon after they boarded, the train jolted forward, only to stop a few minutes later in the marshalling yard behind the station. It remained there for the rest of the night. There were no benches in the wagon and, while it was more spacious than the cattle car, the windows, which ran round the carriage at head height, had no glass in them and it was freezing.

Endeavouring to make the best of the situation, the men set up the stove, ripped from the wall of their barrack at Matzkau, and lit the paraffin lamps they had also 'stolen'. Fey helped the other women unpack the luggage: 'The nails and screws we had brought with us turned out to be very useful for attaching all manner of things to the wooden sides of the car. Food, clothes and shoes hung precariously above our heads. Every crack and opening in the boards was stuffed with our pathetic bits and pieces. We could all lie down at the same time, which was at least something. But there was not enough room to turn over, which meant we had to sleep in a fixed position.'

The next day, the train did not move. 'Hanging around the platform. Second night in the wagon,' Gagi noted in her diary. 'We're lying together like herrings.'

'Unchanged,' she wrote the day after. 'Third night in the wagon.'

The guards allowed them off the train for short periods. But they were only permitted to walk the length of the carriage as the wagons behind were filled with prisoners whom they were forbidden to meet. There was no water on the train and the toilet consisted of a huge wooden tub, positioned next to the brakeman's cabin. For drinking water, they had to gather snow from the side of the tracks and boil it on the stove. Snow was also used for washing – a basic strip wash, standing outside on the running board of the carriage. Papke and Kupfer took it in turns to go off and find food. With the city under virtual siege and crammed with vast numbers of refugees, there was little available, and they lived off tins of canned fish, bread and cheese, and a few potatoes and cabbages, which they used to make soup.

The marshalling yard, filled with rolling stock and situated close to the docks, was an important target for the Allies. US and British bombers pounded the zone day and night. 'The whine of bombs and the roar of fighter planes became as familiar as breathing,' Fey recalled. 'None of us, not even Papke and Kupfer, had any idea why we could not move on. We assumed it was because the tracks had been destroyed in the raids, or simply that all lines were already taken up with troop trains.'

Sensing the tension in the group, Papke and Kupfer suggested a walk in the nearby docks. It was a beautiful morning and the first time, after four months of imprisonment, that Fey was able to experience the bustle of ordinary people on the 'outside': 'They too were suffering from the pressures of total war, but they were at least free. The sun was breaking through the pale, misty northern sky and the sense of freedom as I wandered along, watching the energetic life of the docks, was intoxicating. So far we had been saved; there was so much that life had to offer. Yet this feeling was immediately destroyed when I thought about my two little boys. Where were they? Were they sick, maybe? Were they asking after me? I still had no answer to these questions after four months of separation. I vowed to myself then that I was going to stop dwelling on the unbearable. *I had to imagine their salvation.* All at once, buoyed by the beautiful day, I felt renewed in my determination to survive and to set out at the first opportunity to rescue my boys.'

Later that afternoon, the train finally left the marshalling yard. Imprisoned in the wagon again, Fey soon found her nerves beginning to fray: 'Papke and Kupfer jumped inside, pulling the doors shut against the bright sunshine. As the wagon gained speed it began to swing wildly from side to side. Our belongings, so carefully stashed away, rained down on our heads. This, along with the feeling of suffocation and the constant air attacks, practically drove me out of my senses. I was sure we would be hit sooner or later.'

The train was travelling in a south-westerly direction towards Neustettin, which was just 12 miles from the front. Through the slats in the side of the wagon, they could see hundreds of refugees, trudging along beside the track, still streaming towards Danzig. Now, travelling against the tide of refugees, they were seeing their faces, not their backs. The sight of their misery close up was heart-rending and it was then that Lotte decided to break the news she had withheld from her daughter since leaving Stutthof. In the tight confines of the goods wagon, she drew Ännerle close and told her that her father was dead. Lotte chose this moment because, confronted as they were with so much suffering, she thought it would help Ännerle put her own grief in perspective.

A few feet away from them, Fey still clung to the hope her father was alive: no one had yet confirmed his execution.

After another night in the wagon, the train stopped at Lauenburg, 50 miles to the north-west of Danzig. Papke told the group that it was a brief halt and they would soon continue on. But an hour and a half later she ordered them off the train.

Soldiers directed them to an abandoned building close to the station, which had once been a lunatic asylum. There they remained for eleven long days.

★

Papke and Kupfer allocated the group three rooms: one for the men, one for the women, and a communal room, where the stove, carried from the train, was installed. The weather was still bitterly cold and the stove was the only source of heat in the asylum. Due to the blustery wind outside, it smoked constantly, filling the room with clouds of choking fumes. 'After some adjustment of the pipe, the heat comes back,' Gagi noted two days after they arrived. 'In the meantime constant running up and down the passage to keep warm.'

Fräulein Papke sat in a corner of the room glued to the radio that she now kept permanently by her side. Even discounting the propaganda that coloured the Nazi war reports, the news for the Germans was grim. The Russians had crossed the Oder and were just 35 miles from Berlin. Fey relished Papke's discomfort as reports of Soviet reprisals against SS troops were broadcast: 'We heard that in Bromberg, a town 100 miles to the south of us, the Russians had executed all the SS officials they could lay their hands on. That sent shivers down Fräulein Papke's spine. Pinched and pale, she took on the brittle expression of someone in a controlled but ever-growing panic. Her sharp voice no longer resonated along the corridors. On the contrary, she became quite obsequious.'

Fey, however, recognized that Papke's fate could be her fate too. If the Russians caught up with the group, as 'members of the SS', they would also be executed. Knowing that her life depended on the survival of the Nazi regime caused her acute torment. Since her childhood in Rome, when her father had first crossed the regime, she had longed for Hitler's downfall. Instinctively, listening to the radio broadcasts, her heart leaped at every indication this moment was at last approaching. Yet the grim logic of her situation – regardless of any plan Himmler might have for the group – was that the immediate priority was to escape from the Russians and only the SS had access to the necessary means of transport. Part of her, therefore, was willing the Nazis to hold out for longer.

As the fear of being 'snapped up' by the Russians once again preoccupied the group, they found themselves listening to the news reports with the same avid attention as Fräulein Papke. While the front line was a hundred miles to the south of Lauenburg, the Red

Army had advanced a staggering 130 miles to the west. As Fey recognized, they risked being caught in a pocket of land just as the trekkers had been in East Prussia. 'We heard that the Russians were nearing Stettin. If they captured the city, it would close off our line of escape. From the radio reports, it seemed the Wehrmacht was defending a narrow corridor of land between Stettin and Stargard. But for how long? I was beside myself with impatience to get away, to stop wasting time. Berlin was being bombed every night, and it was obvious we would have to move quickly if we were not to be surrounded by the Russians.'

Every morning, Papke told the group that 'departure was a possibility' and that they must be ready to leave at a moment's notice. But to their frustration – and for no apparent reason – the move was constantly postponed.

The terse entries in Gagi's diary point to the demoralizing uncertainty of those days:

Departure still always <u>a possibility</u>.

Departure still uncertain.

Rumour of a departure tomorrow morning.

As always, our departure is shifted to the following day.

On 17 February, five days after they arrived at Lauenburg, Kupfer let slip that a train was waiting for them at the station. In an embarrassed manner, he told the group that it was in fact the very same train that had brought them from Matzkau and that it had been waiting in a siding ever since. Cryptically, he added that the train was not authorized to leave because the 'living inventory was missing'. Then – to their alarm – he revealed that *they* were the 'living inventory'. Until he received orders from SS headquarters, neither they nor the train could proceed.

The implication was clear. Himmler had not yet authorized their departure. Two days of speculation followed as the group tried to fathom the reason for the delay. Had Himmler abandoned them? Were they no longer of value to him? In an attempt to second-guess his motives, they listened out for his name on the radio. A few weeks earlier, Hitler had appointed him commander of the war on the Eastern Front and it cropped up frequently in the catalogue of defeats. Their one hope was that the delay was due to the fact that they were simply low on Himmler's list of priorities.

This hope was reinforced when, on 19 February, Uncle Moppel appeared, escorted by two SS guards. Everyone was thrilled to see him – Fey particularly. 'He was thin and very weak, but miraculously alive. What a tough constitution he had! When he saw us all, tears came to his eyes. We were as happy as if we had heard that we were to be liberated, so strong were the ties between us.'

Extraordinarily, from Matzkau, the SS had initially taken Uncle Moppel back to Stutthof. The area was still in the hands of the Wehrmacht and the Russians had not yet liberated the camp. As soon as his escorts discovered that the prisoners of kin were no longer there, they had turned round immediately. With tens of thousands of trekkers still on the roads, the journey, both ways, had been horrendous. The error pointed to administrative chaos: at SS headquarters, wires had obviously been crossed. At the same time, the lengths to which the SS had gone to reunite Uncle Moppel with the group indicated their importance. At the very top of the organization, they were still part of some sort of agenda. They had not been abandoned.

At last, on 23 February, Papke announced they really were leaving. While she refused to answer questions about their destination, she allowed the men to remove panes of glass from the asylum so they could be used to cover the gaping windows in the wagon. Clemens von Stauffenberg was too weak to stand and, without a bed to sleep on, Dr Goerdeler doubted he would survive the journey. Once the bed was in the carriage, there was not enough room for them all to lie down, which meant having to take it in turns to sleep.

They set off punctually at nine o'clock in the morning. Papke allowed Fey to sit on the running board, providing she stayed within sight: 'It was a fine day and we rolled along with the doors open. I sat perched on the steps, gazing out at the passing countryside, fighting off unsettling thoughts about my children. On the curves, I could see that the train was extraordinarily long and seemed to be carrying everything: prisoners, troops, refugees, and even cattle, which I could hear mooing at the far end. We took advantage of the frequent stops for obvious reasons. But because the train would always start again without warning, I was terrified of being left behind or having to jump into a wagon filled with strange people. The idea of using these opportunities to escape did not occur to me, nor, I think, to anyone. The thought of being alone in that frozen countryside, without papers, money, or food, was enough to put one off the idea immediately.'

Alex also occupied her thoughts. Since leaving the Hindenburg Baude on 30 November, the two of them had never been alone. The strain of constantly having to conceal her feelings in front of the others had worn her down. At the start of the journey from Matzkau, she and Alex had continued to speak to each other in Italian – as they had done at Stutthof. But in the close confines of the carriage, it was always within earshot of the others, some of whom found their private conversations irritating. Now, their sole from of communication was through notes and lines of poetry, which they wrote down on scraps of paper and passed to each other when they could.

In the coming days, however, so focused were they on surviving the journey, even these were abandoned.

The train was now heading west, parallel to the front. The region – the western part of Pomerania – had been badly bombed and the wreckage was everywhere – derailed trains, burning vehicles and the rubble of countless buildings. The raids were still in progress and, as they drew closer to the front, it seemed to Fey that an angel was watching over them: 'Time after time, we would leave a town just before it was occupied, or a station just before it was blown up. But the train continued on its way untouched. I began to think it was predestined that I would get Corradino and Robertino back.'

Then, early on the morning of 25 February, they came to a halt outside Stargard. This was the most dangerous stretch of their journey. The front was just 2 miles to the south and the Russians were trying to trap the Wehrmacht in a pocket by taking the corridor between Stargard and Stettin.

Outside, soldiers were running up and down the length of the train, shouting, 'Counter-attack in progress! All passengers take cover!' Papke and Kupfer bolted the doors and ordered the group to lie down. Seconds later, the firing began. They were only yards from an anti-tank gun; as they lay piled on top of each other in the confined space, the noise and the vibration from the force of the explosions was terrifying. The attack lasted all day. In the breaks between the firing, they could see lines of infantry pushing forward from trenches dug into the flat ground. Most distressing of all was the long cattle train, crammed with women and children, which had pulled up alongside them. The wagons were open and they could hear the cries and screams of frightened, frozen children.

Cowering on the floor of their carriage, they expected the Russians to fire back at the anti-tank position at any moment. Miraculously, this did not happen and, after twelve awful hours, the train started moving again.

Papke and Kupfer kept the doors closed. Fey lay awake listening to the constant banging as refugees pounded the sides of the wagon, desperate for a place on board. Her impression was of complete break-up and collapse.

The Allies were bombing the line ahead and the train soon came to a halt again. The incident that followed, as Fey recounted, had a dramatic bearing on the group's situation:

A Wehrmacht officer knocked on the door and yelled up impatiently: 'Open up immediately! Some more people must be put in this wagon.'

Papke answered, 'Impossible. I have orders to let no one inside!'

'That is idiotic,' shouted back the officer. 'There are women and children out here half-frozen to death. They must find shelter!'

'We are travelling with the Sippenhäftlinge under the special protection of the Reichsführer SS Heinrich Himmler,' barked back Papke.

'Oh, my God, that idiot!' exclaimed the officer angrily. 'I've had it up to here with that pig!'

The officer's insolence and Papke's startled silence made the group laugh; yet more than anything else, they were laughing with relief.

As 'members of the SS', the threat of summary execution had dogged them since Matzkau but, in one sentence, Papke had let slip that their status had changed. Himmler – for whatever reason – had ruled that they were once again 'prisoners of kin'.

For the next two days, the train moved from siding to siding. Forty miles to the south, the Americans were bombing Berlin. It was the biggest attack in months, involving 1,207 bombers and 726 fighter escorts. One woman described the chaotic scene in Potsdam, a suburb of the city, as civilians and troops vied to escape: 'Heavy tanks rolled down the streets next to sedate old trams, rural wagons and landaus. In long columns, this grey mass of soldiers, refugees and natives pushed each other urgently through the streets; ragged figures beside elegant Potsdam ladies; lice-infested country people next to flashy officers; filthy barefoot children next to shiny prams; grey, old and tired women beside dolled-up girls, horses, dogs, cows, sheep, and cats. On and on they swarmed, squeezing through the gridlocked tanks on the bridge . . . Ladies at the top of Potsdam society competed with poor women for bits of coal falling from a lorry and men of every class and type stooped unashamedly to pick up old cigarette butts . . . What a terrifying change in the space of a year! No, you couldn't conceal it anymore; no people look like this when they are within grasp of victory.'

When – on 27 February – the prisoners of kin arrived at Rüdnitz on the outskirts of Berlin, the ruins of the town were still smoking. Once again, they were unable to go on because the Americans had blown up the line ahead. By this stage, Clemens von Stauffenberg's health was of grave concern. His breathing was laboured and, with his condition weakening by the hour, the others feared he might die. Dr Goerdeler gave him two days at most and even Kupfer, muttering that after Anni von Lerchenfeld's demise one death was quite enough, felt he had to do something.

Fey was astounded by the swift response from SS headquarters in Berlin: 'Kupfer phoned through to them – a miracle in itself given the pounding the city had taken. They must have been alarmed, because a doctor was immediately sent to examine Clemens.' The doctor's verdict was that he should be transferred to Sachsenhausen, a nearby concentration camp, where there was a hospital. Elisabeth pleaded to be allowed to accompany her husband. If he was going to die she wanted to be near him. Eventually, the doctor agreed and, towards seven in the evening, an SS squad arrived to take the couple away. 'Poor Clemens, barely conscious, was lifted out on a stretcher, with Elisabeth following,' Fey wrote. 'She had to leave her three children behind and had no idea if she would ever see them again. None of us said a word as they left. There was nothing to say.'

So bleak was the parting for Gagi, writing her diary later that evening, she could hardly bring herself to mention it: 'Papa goes with Mama to the hospital in Sachsenhausen in an ambulance. Difficult farewell. Will we see each other again?'

Nothing was moving on the railway. With the air raids continuing, the lines ahead were destroyed as quickly as they were repaired and the Sippenhäftlinge remained at Rüdnitz for several days.

It was not until 2 March that they set off again – heading west, away from Berlin. At six o'clock the next morning, Papke told them to gather their things. After ten days on the train, they were an hour away from their destination: Buchenwald.

31

Jedem das Seine. 'To each what he deserves'. These were the words engraved in large wrought-iron letters on the gate at the entrance to Buchenwald. Dawn was breaking, a grey, damp day. Kupfer and Papke had disappeared and Fey tried to catch the exchange between the officer in charge and an unseen guard on the other side of the gate. The unmistakable, nauseating stench from the crematoria clung to the air, catching in the back of her throat and her nostrils. Through the latticed gate she could see hundreds of prisoners milling around, the thick black and white stripes of their uniforms standing out in the murky light. Double rows of barbed-wire fencing, some 12 feet high, enclosed the huge compound. Instinctively, she glanced up, counting the watchtowers around the perimeter. There were twenty-two in total. A terrible fear seized her. Why here? Was this a temporary move? Or was this the end?

The gate did not open; instead, after a long wait, Fey and the others were marched away from the main entrance, across a vast square. At the far end, smoke billowed from a huge factory complex, ringed by more watchtowers. It was the first time Fey had seen a concentration camp at close quarters: 'New SS guards led us at a brisk pace through the immense camp, which was a small city with tarmac streets. There was a nucleus of maybe 200 barracks surrounded by barbed wire. Beyond these I caught a glimpse of yet more barracks where we were told thousands of prisoners lived and worked. Further behind were buildings of all sizes used as kitchens, storerooms, factories, crematoria and, as I later learned, execution rooms and a hospital for medical experiments. Everywhere you looked, human skeletons marched in columns. They were no more than skin and bone and the blank look in their eyes was horrifying. Pus oozed from the weals on their faces – presumably the marks of beatings from the camp guards . . . I could not believe what I was seeing and I was gripped by the same feeling of helpless fury that I felt when I thought about what the SS had done to my children.'

Ten minutes later, the group arrived at a crescent-shaped line of barracks – the accommodation blocks for the SS. Here, the guards turned down a narrow road strewn with rubble from the bombed-out buildings on either side. At the end of the road, they came up against a high, red-brick wall with a door set into it. The door opened on knocking and, following a discussion between the SS and the guard manning it, they found themselves in a courtyard in front of a long, low building.

After the dreadful sights she had just witnessed, Fey was stunned by the scene in front of her: 'A crowd of strangers, dressed in shabby, yet evidently once elegant clothes, spilled out of the barrack towards us. Suddenly there were cries of delight as people fell into each other's arms. It emerged that these strangers were also relatives of people involved in the bomb plot.'

Incredibly, Uncle Moppel's children were there. All three had been transported to Buchenwald from a nearby prison: Ines, aged twenty-four; Alexandra, twenty-two; their brother Clemens, fifteen years of age. Annelise Goerdeler* also found two more of her children and her daughter, Irma, was reunited with her husband.

Still reeling from the walk through the camp, the sea of happy faces reduced Fey to tears: 'I knew we were safe. Our fate was not the fate of those poor wretches outside. Yet while others in the group had found their children, mine were not there and, in the midst of all this joy, I was flooded with despair.'

The prisoners remained in the courtyard for some time, exchanging greetings and swapping news. Fey felt alone and excluded: 'Everyone seemed to know someone and I felt too crushed to interrupt their conversations. Then I suddenly heard the name Maria von Hammerstein. Although I had not really known her myself, she had grown up at court with my mother and was one of her greatest friends. So I went up to say hello. Straight away, she began speaking about my father's execution. She didn't realize of course that no one

---

* Carl Friedrich Goerdeler's wife.

had confirmed his death and I still clung to the hope that he was alive. Choking back my rising sobs, I stiffly pretended to be well acquainted with the facts as she described his last days in great detail. Maria recounted how he had been tried at the People's Court by Roland Freisler, the worst and most fanatical of the Nazi judges. During the cross-examination, my father so impressed the audience of Nazi party guests that stories leaked out about what went on. It was said that no one knew who was the accused and who the accuser. At the thought of my father so honourably defending himself, I could no longer control my emotions. Muttering some excuse, I rushed away to be alone with my grief.'

It was then that Fey understood why, in the few letters she had received from her, her mother had omitted to tell her that her father had been executed: 'Knowing that I was alone and imprisoned far away from her, she had wanted to shield me from the truth. I thought about how lonely she must feel now that the very essence of her life had been taken away . . . Those first days at Buchenwald were dominated by this thought of her suffering, and also my own pain. In this shared suffering we were close. It dissolved the physical distance between us.'

For the first time since Stutthof, Fey and the others were sharing rooms in twos and threes, rather than living communally. The rooms were warm and comfortable; each had a table, a wardrobe, a wash-stand and a stove, and the bunk beds had proper mattresses. The food was adequate, and they had flour to make their own bread. From time to time, the SS even brought them treats – beer, cocoa and real coffee.

Completely screened from the rest of the camp by a copse of trees, the barrack was named 'Sonderbau★ 15'. The location of the building was top secret, its isolated position deliberate. Housing some forty prisoners, it had been built for men and women whose faces Himmler decreed must never be seen. In addition to relatives of 20 July plotters, they included prominent individuals who had opposed Hitler – some of them from within the heart of the regime.

★ Literally, 'special construction'.

Fritz Thyssen, the former head of Germany's largest steel conglomerate, was the most well known of the Prominenten, as the SS
referred to them. In the early 1930s, his admiration for Hitler led him
to donate 1 million Reichsmarks to the Nazi Party and to support
Hitler's election as Reich chancellor. Adhering to the Nazis' racist
policies, he dismissed Jewish employees from his factories. He also
welcomed the suppression of left-wing political parties and trade
unions. The breaking point for Thyssen, however, came with
Kristallnacht on 9 November 1938, when Hitler carried out a violent
pogrom against the Jews. After resigning from the government, he
became an outspoken critic of the Nazis' warmongering policies and
in September 1939, while on holiday in Switzerland, he sent Göring a
telegram protesting against the invasion of Poland. In reply, Göring
offered to guarantee Thyssen's safety if he returned to Germany.
When he refused, his fortune and property were confiscated and a
warrant was issued for his arrest. A year later, the SS caught up with
him in Vichy France, and he was transported back to Berlin. From
there, he was taken to Sachsenhausen concentration camp.

Besides Thyssen, the inmates of Sonderbau 15 included relatives
of high-ranking Wehrmacht generals, among them Gertrude Halder, the wife of General Franz Halder, chief of the Army High
Command from 1938 until 1942. Ulrich von Hassell and his circle of
conspirators had plotted with the general to overthrow Hitler in the
first years of the war. Halder, a 'weak man with shattered nerves', as
Hassell described him, had let them down. While, in the spring of
1940, the general had carried a pistol in his pocket, intending to shoot
Hitler at one of their regular meetings, he could not bring himself to
carry it through. Earning Hassell's contempt, Halder, a 'caddy for
Hitler', had continued in command, lending his support to the massacre of entire villages during the invasion of Russia. After falling
out with Hitler over the conduct of the war in the autumn of 1942, he
had retired. Though Halder had not taken part in the 20 July plot, he
and his wife had been arrested after the Gestapo discovered his links
to the Hassell group and his involvement in earlier attempts to assassinate the Führer.

Other Prominenten were hidden around the camp. Some 50 yards from Sonderbau 15, Léon Blum, prime minister of France from 1936 to 1937, was secreted with his wife in a bunker beneath the Falkenhof (Falconry). A Gothic-style building, commissioned by Himmler for the enjoyment of the SS, it housed eagles, falcons and other birds of prey. 'I was in the hands of the Nazis because I was more than just a French politician – I was a social democrat and a Jew,' Blum wrote. 'The very reasons that made me such a detestable opponent also made me a precious hostage – as I was not only valuable for exchange purposes to the French State and all its allies, but also to the cause of socialism and international democracy.'

Despite the danger Blum faced as a Jew and a Socialist leader, he had not fled when the Germans occupied France in June 1940. Arrested and tried by the Vichy government, he and his wife were transferred to Buchenwald in April 1943. In his memoirs, he wrote about their time there: 'There are no words to describe the feelings of loneliness during our two years at Buchenwald. We saw no one except for the 25–30 SS men who guarded us. They were always fidgeting with the sub-machine guns slung over shoulders, and they kept their dogs on tight leashes in the tiny side passage between the barbed-wire fence and the Falkenhof . . . In reality, this Falkenhof was not a prison, but a tomb. We were completely shut off from the outside world. Some of my friends, who had arrived at Buchenwald before us and had been there for more than 18 months, had no idea we were there.'

Prominenten were also kept in cells beneath the SS accommodation block – among them the German theologian Dietrich Bonhoeffer. A Lutheran pastor and a vocal opponent of Hitler's persecution of the Jews, in the mid 1930s he had called for Christians to resist the Nazis: the Church should not simply 'bandage the victims under the wheel, but jam the spoke in the wheel itself'. With this objective, Bonhoeffer set up an underground network dedicated to preserving Christian values and practices. After war broke out, he joined the Abwehr (German military intelligence). Using his position as cover and exploiting his ecumenical contacts abroad, he served as a courier for the German Resistance, visiting Norway, Sweden and Switzerland in a bid to secure peace terms with the Allies. He was also involved in operations run by anti-Nazis within the Abwehr to help German Jews escape to Switzerland.

Bonhoeffer had arrived at Buchenwald with three other prisoners: Squadron Leader Hugh Falconer, a British SOE operative arrested in Tunisia; Vatican spy Josef Müller; and Major Ludwig Gehre. Müller had used Pope Pius XII as an intermediary to deliver peace proposals, drawn up by Hassell's circle, to US and British intelligence. Gehre, another Abwehr officer, had been privy to Henning von Tresckow's plan to assassinate Hitler in March 1943. The four men joined other 'special prisoners' in the cells beneath the SS barracks: Vassily Kokorin, a nephew of Vyacheslav Molotov, the Soviet minister for foreign affairs; General Falkenhausen, a former military governor of Nazi-occupied Belgium; Hermann Pünder, one of the founders of the CDU, the German Christian Democratic Party; and Captain Sigismund Payne Best, a British spy who, in November 1939, had been famously kidnapped by the Gestapo at Venlo, a town on Germany's border with the Netherlands. Himmler regarded Payne Best's capture as a major coup. The victim of a sting operation run by Gestapo agents posing as anti-Nazis, Payne Best, who was working for 'Section Z', a new branch of the British Secret Intelligence Service, had been arrested while trying to foment a coup against Hitler.

It was just a stone's throw from Sonderbau 15 to the Falkenhof and the cells where Payne Best and the others were held. Yet the strict regime of secrecy meant that the different groups were unaware of the others' existence.

For the forty prisoners in Sonderbau 15, however, it was obvious that Himmler was assembling his Prominenten. The Sippenhäftlinge were the first of the new arrivals; by the end of the second week in March, after movement orders were flashed from SS headquarters in Berlin to concentration camps across Germany, the number of prisoners in the barrack had risen to over sixty. A disparate collection, the newcomers included Isa Vermehren, a famous actress and cabaret artist; Countess von Plettenberg, a member of a Catholic resistance network; relatives of German POWs who had joined the National Committee for a Free Germany – a Soviet-run organization dedicated to overthrowing the Nazi regime – and numerous Wehrmacht officers found guilty of conspiring to murder Hitler.

1 Innsbruck, 1939

The Wiesenhof orphanage

3 The villa at Brazzà

4 A view of Brazzà showing the castle and the farm

5 Robert Foster, Air Officer
Commanding, Desert Air Force

6 Nonino at Brazzà

7 Ulrich von Hassell with Hitler and
Mussolini in Venice, 1934

8 Ulrich von Hassell with
Mussolini in Rome, 1936

9 Fey, aged sixteen, with her father

10 The Hassell family, *c.* 1936:
(*from left to right*) Wolf Ulli, Hans Dieter,
Ulrich, Almuth, Fey and Ilse

11 SS chief Heinrich Himmler with Hassell (*to his right*) on National Police Day, Villa Glori, 1937. Arturo Bocchini, Italian chief of police, and Reinhard Heydrich, chief of the Gestapo, are standing to the left of Himmler.

12 General Ludwig Beck

13 Major General Henning von Tresckow

14 Fey in 1942

15 Fey and Detalmo celebrate their wedding at
Ebenhausen, January 1940

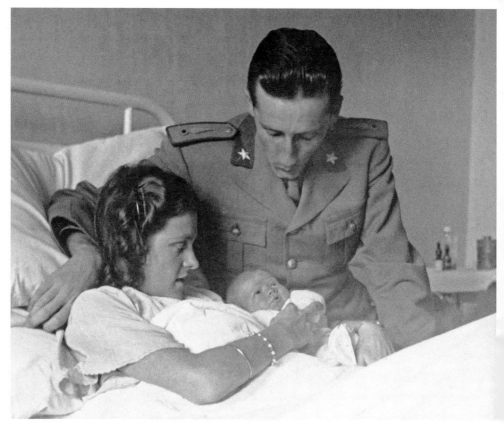

16 Fey and Detalmo with Corrado, November 1940

17 Nonino and the farmhands at Brazzà harness Mirko for an outing. Fey and Detalmo are seated in the trap.

18 Ulrich von Hassell with his grandsons, Corrado and Roberto, at Ebenhausen, June 1943

19 Fey with her mother, Ilse, and Detalmo at Ebenhausen, June 1943

20 Detalmo and Corrado in the garden at Brazzà. The photograph was taken shortly before Detalmo was posted to the POW camp at Mortara.

21 The Campo Imperatore Hotel, where Mussolini was imprisoned before being rescued by the SS on 12 September 1943

22 Cora di Brazzà Slocomb, *c.* 1890

23 Lieutenant Hans Kretschmann with Corrado at Brazzà, 1942

24 Corrado with the
airmen at Brazzà, 1943

25 The 'Thirteen Martyrs of
Feletto Umberto',
Premariacco, 29 May 1944

26 The wreckage of the map room at Hitler's headquarters in East Prussia, 20 July 1944

27 Ulrich von Hassell's trial, September 1944

28 Claus von Stauffenberg

29 Captain Sigismund Payne Best

30 Bomb damage in Munich

31 Litta von Stauffenberg

32 Alex von Stauffenberg

33 The liberation of Buchenwald, April 1945

34 The Hotel Pragser Wildsee

35 The view from one of the hotel rooms

36 'We are searching for these children!' One of the posters circulated by Fey and Detalmo in the summer of 1945.

Wir suchen diese Kinder!

Personalien der Kinder

1. Corrado Pirzio-Biroli
4½ Jahre alt
geb. 25. November 1940
in Udine, Italien
Haare: blond
Augen: blau
Gesichtsfarbe: blaß
Sprache: Deutsch, einige
italienische Worte
Rufnamen: Corradino,
Corradinchen
Kleidungsstücke: Marine-
blauer Mantel mit Kapuze,
gemacht aus einem alten
Militärmantel

2. Roberto Pirzio-Biroli
3½ Jahre alt
geb. 25. Januar 1942
in Udine, Italien
Haare: blond
Augen: blau
Gesichtsfarbe: lebhafte
Farben
Sprache: Deutsch
Rufnamen: Robertino,
Robertinchen
Kleidungsstücke: Marine-
blauer Mantel mit Kapuze,
gemacht aus einem alten
Militärmantel

Die betreffenden Kinder wurden ihrer Mutter, **Frau Fey Pirzio-Biroli**,
geb. v. Hassell am 29. oder 30. September 1944 von zwei Frauen der
N. S. V.-Organisation, aus einem Hotel in Innsbruck heraus, weggenommen.

Es ist anzunehmen, daß die Kinder in ein N. S. V.-Kinderheim gebracht wurden. Einzelnachrichten haben
ergeben, daß dafür auch solche Kinderheime im hiesigen Gebiet in Frage kommen könnten. Es ist jedoch
wahrscheinlich, daß besagte Kinder einen anderen Namen (deutschen) erhielten.

Personal solcher Kinderheime oder Personen, welche die oben abgebildeten Kinder in solchen Heimen
gesehen haben oder irgendwelche näheren Angaben machen können, werden gebeten, Auskunft zu
erteilen an das

Italienische Rote Kreuz
Sede di Bad Harzburg
Bad Harzburg, Rudolf-Huch-Straße 17

ŁAWA OSKARŻONYCH. STOJĄ OD LEWEJ: F. RACH, F. PETERS, A. PAULITZ, E. FOTH, T. MEYER.

37 Ewald Foth (*second from the right*) at the Stutthof trials in Gdańsk, January 1947

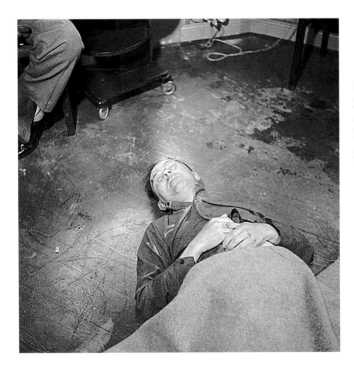

38 Himmler's corpse, photographed by a British Army official, minutes after his death from cyanide poisoning

Gathered in the communal room in the barrack, the group deliberated their position, using information supplied by the new arrivals. Evidently, SS headquarters had arranged things very precisely; behind the movements of the prisoners was the intention to pull the Prominenten together, where they were easily available, at any given time, to take part in some far-reaching future plan. But what plan? Himmler's security service still worked according to the same methods: complete arbitrariness in all decisions; no explanations given; the greatest secrecy.

As the days passed, waiting for Himmler to make his next move, the anxiety engendered by the uncertainty of their situation was overtaken by the fearfulness of the misery outside. The high wall that enclosed Sonderbau 15 hid the camp from view, but they could hear people being moved forcibly by the guards and shots being fired. 'We knew exactly what went on there,' Fey recalled. 'The SS employed Russian female prisoners to deliver our coal rations, and through them we learned of the horrific conditions in the rest of the camp.'

There were no gas chambers at Buchenwald; technically, it was a work camp, not an extermination camp. Nevertheless, 56,000 prisoners perished there. Hunger, illness, inhuman living and working conditions, executions, lethal injections and medical experiments – the causes were many. In the first three months of 1945 alone, 13,000 deaths were registered.

That winter, while thousands of Jews arrived at the camp after long, brutal marches from concentration camps in Poland, they were in a minority. Prior to the Soviet advances, the practice at Buchenwald had been to send Jews on for gassing at extermination camps such as Auschwitz and Dachau. Of approximately 80,000 prisoners held at the camp in March 1945, the majority were 'politicals' – men the SS had rounded up and arrested throughout Germany and the Nazi-occupied countries. Encompassing some thirty nationalities, they included military deserters, resistance fighters, priests, writers, actors, Gypsies, Communists, monarchists and so-called 'work-shy' individuals – people classed by the regime as 'asocial' because they could not, or would not, find gainful employment.

The prisoners lived in a compound, roughly 300 yards from Sonderbau 15. It contained over a hundred accommodation blocks and the living conditions were horrendous; many of the barracks were bare, lacking benches or beds, and the inmates slept on the floor without mattresses or blankets. One block housed 850 children. All boys, they were mostly Jewish and a high percentage were orphans. Many had been transported from Auschwitz, where they had seen their parents murdered before their eyes. The youngest 'partisan' – as the SS referred to the children – was three years old.

The work regime was harsh. Inmates, including children as young as seven, worked a fourteen-hour day in the nearby quarry or in the armaments factories located at the southern end of the camp. Their day began with a roll call on the much-feared parade ground, a show-place for public executions and punishments. The crematorium stood in one corner and corpses were used to taunt the prisoners. Frequently, the duty officer would call out over the loudspeaker to the professional criminals operating the ovens: 'Let's have the birds in the crematorium take a peek outside!' Then the attendants would grab the bodies and hold them up to the windows.

Blocks 46 and 50 operated as clinical stations where eminent Nazi physicians and scientists used prisoners to test new drugs and medical techniques. The SS forcibly selected the guinea pigs – usually Communists, Gypsies and homosexuals. In one experiment, 800 'patients' were inoculated with an anti-typhus vaccine and then inoculated with the virus itself. The vaccine failed and 700 out of the 800 died of typhus. Trials to 'cure' homosexuality were carried out, which involved planting a synthetically produced hormone in the groin to induce a change in sex drive. And there were other experiments. To test the effectiveness of a balm for wounds from incendiary bombs, 'very severe' white-phosphorus burns were inflicted on inmates. One SS surgeon used a specially constructed apparatus to cut sections out of the livers of live subjects, who without exception died from these experiments. Another drug trial aimed at determining the fatal dose of a type of alkaloid poison. According to the testimony of one inmate, four Russian POWs were administered the poison, and when it proved not to be fatal they were 'strangled in the crematorium' and subsequently 'dissected'. Challenged at a post-war trial about the nature of the medical experiments at Buchenwald, the doctor's defence was that he was 'a legally appointed executioner'.

Between Block 46 and the infirmary stood the 'Special Building'. Under this nondescript name the camp brothel was chastely concealed. From 1942, Himmler encouraged the use of prostitutes in the camps. 'Women in brothels must be provided for hard-working prisoners,' he wrote to Gruppenführer Oswald Pohl, the head administrator. Driven by the need to increase productivity, brothels were introduced to supplement the existing reward scheme. Hard graft earned the prisoners smaller workloads, extra food and monetary bonuses, and Himmler was of the view that prostitutes would provide a further incentive. Beginning with the Austrian camp at Mauthausen in 1942, the SS opened ten brothels, the biggest of which was at Auschwitz. Jews, however, were banned, owing to the Nuremberg Laws of 1935, which forbade sexual relations between Jews and Aryans.

Eighteen young girls were transferred to Buchenwald from Ravensbrück when the brothel opened in the summer of 1943. Prior to starting work, they were sent to the camp hospital, where they were given calcium injections, disinfection baths, better food and a stint under a sunlamp. Some were forcibly sterilized.

Visits, overseen by the SS, were carefully regulated. Open from 7 to 10 p.m. every evening, the building closed at times of water or electricity shortages, during air raids and when Hitler's speeches were broadcast on the radio. To prevent the spread of sexually transmitted diseases, the men were given disinfectant ointments before and after each visit, and the women were regularly tested for gonorrhoea and syphilis.

South of the main camp was the huge compound containing the SS accommodation blocks. Here, 50 yards from Sonderbau 15, the SS lived in lavish barracks, with grocery stores, hospitals and cinemas. They even had their own zoo, where bears and monkeys were kept. The luxury of their situation was made the more grotesque by the continual stream of prisoners who passed beneath the windows of their quarters on their way to work in the camp's quarries and factories.

★

'I was never flogged or beaten, no one shaved my head, no one tat-tooed a number on me, I never had to do any hard labour, all we had to do was sit around in our block from morning until night,' Isa Ver-mehren, one of the special prisoners in Sonderbau 15, wrote.

Yet, chillingly, Isa articulated the 'inner, psychological hell' she experienced: 'Fear and anxiety filled one's mind to the exclusion of all else; fear of the cold and of hunger; fear of punishment and pain; fear of being despised, betrayed; anxiety about the hopelessness of one's situation, about one's own and the other people's distress; anx-iety about the evil within and around one; anxiety about one's physical and spiritual death.'

Aged twenty-eight when she was imprisoned at Buchenwald, Isa was a well-known actress and cabaret artist. Famous for singing songs that parodied the Nazis, she performed in underground clubs all over Germany until, in 1938, a search for faith, prompted by her loathing of Nazism, led her to join the Order of the Sacred Heart as a novice nun.

Before she arrived at Buchenwald, unlike the other prisoners in Sonderbau 15, Isa had witnessed the horror of a concentration camp at close quarters. Arrested in 1943, after her brother fled to England and joined the BBC, she had been imprisoned at Ravensbrück. While she had received privileged treatment during the ten months she spent there, the window of her cell overlooked the parade ground at the camp. 'What I became aware of on a daily basis,' she wrote, 'was a drama, which wasn't being played out by human beings. It took a long time until what I saw found an ingress into my heart, so deter-mined was I to block out what was going on outside.'

At the end of the war, she would recount some of the scenes she witnessed to a war-crimes investigator from the British Army: 'There was a special cell quite near to mine in which the beatings were given and I heard both the noise and screams of the women being punished. I knew that executions took place. The execution site was behind a wall near the crematorium and was about 5 metres from my cell. I could hear the footsteps of people walking there and also the shots. Shootings took place in the evenings after ten o'clock and that was the hour one became nervous. I heard about sixty executions, and as far as I could gather they were usually Polish or Russian women.'

Isa's experiences at Ravensbrück did not cause her to lose her faith: 'Man's inhumanity to man was a reflection of what Jesus Christ had had to endure and he never abandoned us,' she said. But they caused her to question whether she could ever be a true Christian. As a religious person, confronted by the conditions at Ravensbrück – and then at Buchenwald – she knew her fear and anxiety constituted weakness: she was meant to trust in God. And she was supposed to be selfless, to put herself in the shoes of the other person before thinking of herself. Instead, so horrific were the conditions in the rest of the camp, she found herself turning away from the suffering around her to focus on her own survival. In examining her conscience, this selfishness represented the death of her soul. In the battle to survive, she had become a dead person, without spiritual concerns. It was what she meant when she wrote about the 'evil within one'.

The crises of conscience Isa experienced were common to the other prisoners in Sonderbau 15, the majority of whom were devout Catholics and Protestants. 'Guilt at our privileged position weighed on us all,' Fey remembered, 'but as a group we did not talk about it. It was too painful, too private. There was little talk of anything except the most immediate future. It is surprising how little one communicated with other people. I think everyone simply withdrew into themselves.'

As a week went by, and then another, waiting to hear what the future had in store, Fey did, however, confide in Alex. While they were never alone, their attraction to each other was an open secret and the others kept their distance, so they could talk privately.

Sitting quietly together in the communal room, they spoke for hours. Still grieving for her father and bitterly disappointed not to have found her children at Buchenwald, Fey was comforted by Alex's presence; with him she could admit to feelings that she could not confide to anyone else – namely her envy of others in the group who had been reunited with their children. Sometimes the two of them played bridge with Markwart and Otto Philipp or worked together on a German translation of Dante's *La Vita Nuova*. Alex chose the text; whether because Dante's love for Beatrice mirrored his feelings for Fey, she did not say. But the choice was apposite; the piece explored the medieval concept of courtly love – a highly formal, often unrequited love.

In the rare moments when Fey was not with Alex, she gave lessons to a ten-year-old boy. A new arrival, he had been arrested with his mother – Frau Schroeder, the wife of an evangelical pastor – and his brother and sister, aged four and seven. Their imprisonment was in retaliation for the weekly service the pastor held on Moscow Radio. A German POW, he belonged to the National Committee for a Free Germany, an anti-Nazi, pro-Communist organization operating from the Soviet Union.

In the absence of news of Corrado and Roberto, Fey was drawn to the boy: 'I began the lessons as much for my own sake as for his. As I taught him elementary mathematics and languages, I often wondered about my own children. Was it better for them to stay with their mother and thus witness horrific scenes in camps like this little boy, or were they better off in a children's home? Though it was, of course, pure speculation, it kept me from dwelling on much worse things that could have happened to Corradino and Robertino.'

The tension in the barrack increased with every day that went by. The Americans were getting closer and, as the Russian women reported, the prisoners in the main camp feared that Himmler would order the liquidation of all inmates before they arrived.

'The days without news were agonising,' Ännerle remembered. 'We had absolutely no idea of how things were going to turn out.'

Then, out of the blue, on the morning of 14 March, an SS official arrived from Berlin.

32

The official's name was Sergeant Lenz and he worked at the Reich Main Security Office – Himmler's headquarters. Tall, with a slim frame and a long, pale face, his obsequiousness immediately made Fey suspicious: 'He was one of the classic oily types, all good manners and kindness. Smiling graciously, he said that he was at our disposal and asked if we had any complaints or questions. Of course, we women all started clamouring for news of our children.'

Unabashed, Lenz replied that the children were being brought up and 'trained' by the Gestapo. They were in good spirits and were being well looked after, he assured them. To support this claim, he produced three letters, which he handed to Lotte von Hofacker with a flourish. They were from her youngest children – Christa, Alfred and Goldi, aged twelve, nine and six. Reading the letters, Lotte was amazed to see that they did indeed seem to be 'very happy'. Lenz went on to confirm that, along with Irma Goerdeler's two boys – the younger a sixteen-month-old baby – and Mika von Stauffenberg's six-year-old son and five-year-old daughter, Lotte's children were at Bad Sachsa, an SS orphanage about 80 miles from Buchenwald.

He had little news, however, of Corrado and Roberto. They were not with the other children, but in a smaller home, he told Fey, and he said he would return the next day with more precise information: 'He promised me a thousand things, even information on the children's health and exact whereabouts. Though I knew in my heart that he would tell only lies and more lies, I desperately wanted to believe him.'

Emboldened by Lenz's cooperative manner, the group flooded him with further questions. Why were they being held at Buchenwald? What was the point of their captivity when their relatives had now been executed and the cases closed?

Lenz replied that it was entirely possible that they would be released in ten days. 'But nothing is certain,' he added.

Before he left, he distributed a large number of letters, which the SS had kept from the group for many weeks. There was just one for Fey – a graphic letter from a friend in Dresden describing the terror of the recent British bombing raids. Coming on top of the absence of news of the boys, it was a double blow. She had not heard from her mother since leaving Brazzà and had assumed this was because the SS had withheld her letters. Yet it seemed she had not written at all.

There was, of course, no word from Detalmo. Though Fey recognized the impossibility of contact with him, a part of her held on to the hope that, somehow, he would find an ingenious way of getting a message through. Fourteen months had passed since she had last seen him. His most recent message – delivered by a partisan courier – had been to tell her that he was not coming home and that he had decided to stay in Rome. That was in August and it was now mid March. More than ever, with the children perhaps irretrievably lost, she needed to hear from him. Was he still in Rome? Did he know that she and the boys had been arrested? It was possible that the note she sent via the Red Cross had failed to get through. But then neighbours at Brazzà had also sent him messages, using the partisan network. His silence was bitterly disappointing and reinforced the feelings of abandonment she had felt for a long time.

Fey spent the next twenty-four hours anxiously waiting for Lenz to return with the information he promised about the boys. As she feared, he had none. He did not even bother to lie; flatly, he told her that he had been unable to establish their whereabouts. Either his superiors at SS headquarters had their reasons for not wanting to divulge this information or the boys were lost. Summoning her courage, she asked him what her chances were of being reunited with them: 'He simply shrugged his shoulders and said that if they were alive, they would have new names. He doubted I would ever find them. Until that moment, I had refused to consider the worst – that they were dead, or permanently lost. But the fact that the other children were all in one place and mine had disappeared removed any hope I had of seeing them again. The thought of permanent separation from my children brought me to the edge of madness.'

Just when Fey thought she had reached her lowest ebb, something occurred that caused her to shut down entirely. Matter-of-factly, she recorded the extraordinary event that took place on the morning of 16 March, the day after the second visit from Lenz: 'A Storch, a two-seater airplane used by the Luftwaffe for reconnaissance and training, circled low over our barrack. It was Litta von Stauffenberg, Alex's wife.'

Litta, one of the most highly decorated female pilots in the Luftwaffe, had been looking for Alex for almost two months. Officially, she was still in charge of the Experimental Centre for Special Flight Equipment, where she instructed pilots in the use of optical night-landing equipment that she had pioneered. She was also continuing her work as a test pilot, developing target-hitting devices for Stukas, which necessitated diving vertically from a great height. Yet her energy was entirely directed towards finding Alex. 'She was adamant that she could only take on and bear the burden of her war duties if she was able to see and speak to her husband once a month,' Nina von Stauffenberg, Claus's widow, recalled.

After Stutthof, Litta had lost all trace of Alex. Until then, as the recipient of the Iron Cross and the Gold Front Flying Clasp for Bombers, she was able to keep track of his movements using her high-level contacts within the Nazi regime. But, as rumours of her own opposition to the regime circulated, her access to this classified information was withdrawn.

Undeterred – and at great risk from Allied aircraft – she flew all over northern Germany, trying to pick up Alex's trail. Starting at Stutthof, where she landed at the end of January, she followed every lead, however tenuous. Rather than the fighter jets she normally flew, she chose the unarmed Storch. The small single-engine plane was perfect for short-distance landing and take-off and, with a cruising speed at low altitudes of 80 miles an hour, she was able to fly just above tree level – out of the line of vision of enemy pilots. Her search, necessitating many flying hours, had been fruitless. But then, in mid March, she received a tip-off from a Gestapo official at Lauenburg. He told her that Alex and the others had spent several weeks in the town, imprisoned in a converted lunatic asylum, and that they had recently been moved south of Berlin. He doubted, however, that they had managed to get through the Russian lines. They had probably been captured and were 'unlikely to have survived'.

On the off-chance, Litta decided to try Buchenwald – the nearest concentration camp south of the capital. Before leaving, she packed the Storch with supplies – rabbit meat, fruit, vegetables and clothes for Alex, with little notes hidden inside.

It was a three-hour flight from Würzburg, where she was temporarily based. If Alex was at Buchenwald, the biggest challenge she faced was to find the barrack where he was imprisoned. She knew he would recognize her plane. Early in January, she had visited him at Stutthof. Fey had not known of the visit, as it had taken place around the time she had been dangerously ill.

From the air, the rows and rows of barracks at Buchenwald all looked the same. Flying low over the rooftops, Litta circled the camp several times, searching for a signal from her husband. It was not long before she spotted a knot of people, waving furiously from the courtyard of a barrack; in the building behind, others were signalling from the windows with handkerchiefs and bed sheets. Touching down in a field, as close as she could get to the isolated barrack, she handed her papers to the guards. With her Iron Cross pinned firmly to the lapel of her flying jacket, her credentials were impeccable and the guards escorted her to Sonderbau 15. A few minutes later, the gate in the wall opened, and Alex was brought out. 'It was very secret and rather miraculous,' Mika von Stauffenberg, Alex's sister-in-law, recalled.

The guards retreated, leaving the couple alone in the narrow, rubble-strewn road. They spoke for forty-five minutes. There is no record of their conversation but, as Gagi and Ännerle noted in their diaries, Litta brought news of the children at Bad Sachsa, and of Elisabeth and Clemens von Stauffenberg, who were still at Sachsenhausen concentration camp. Determined to help Alex's family where she could, Litta had flown to both places, taking food parcels and warm clothes. She had also visited Nina von Stauffenberg, who was imprisoned near Frankfurt. In January, six months after Claus had been executed, Nina had given birth to their fifth child: 'Litta looked after us all. She thought of everything and used her rank and charm to obtain whatever she could. While I was pregnant, she found a Gestapo official who got hold of a pregnancy support belt, and she brought me fruit and vegetables, and cod liver oil . . . She was in a difficult position, playing a dangerous double game: on the one hand, a "friend" of the Gestapo, on the other, the provider for the prisoners of kin.'

After the meeting with Alex, Litta walked back to her plane. She cut a dashing figure as she strode across the field; tall, slim, blonde, with high cheekbones and a striking profile, she wore a Luftwaffe uniform beneath her brown leather flying jacket and long leather boots. Taking off from the field, she flew low over the barrack, circling three times. It was her way of saying goodbye.

Litta knew she was in constant danger of being shot down by the Americans, who now dominated the air space over western Germany. Nonetheless, between 17 March and 1 April, she made eight further trips to Buchenwald. While her war work meant that some of the visits could only be flypasts, on three occasions she was able to land and speak to Alex.

To the Sippenhäftlinge – and particularly Gagi – she was the 'Flying Angel'. On 30 March, after hearing that the Russians were about to liberate Sachsenhausen, Litta, oblivious to the risk from Soviet aircraft, flew to the camp to rescue Elisabeth and Clemens von Stauffenberg. After persuading the guards to release the couple, she took Clemens to a military hospital before returning Elisabeth to Gagi at Buchenwald. As Gagi later acknowledged, if Litta had not undertaken the daring rescue, her parents would probably have died.

In thinking of everything and everyone, Litta was also secretly preparing for the liberation of Buchenwald. In the hope that the group would be released once the Americans arrived, she bribed some locals to lend her a house within walking distance of the camp. Filling it with food, blankets and other essential supplies, she turned it into a refuge, which they could use when the moment came.

'Flight was her element and she was a pilot of rare skill and courage,' Fey wrote of Litta. But this was all she wrote. She did not recount how she felt when Alex left the barrack to meet his wife, out of view on the other side of the gate. At the very least, given her estrangement from Detalmo, she must have felt terribly alone. She also had to face the looks and whispered speculation from others in the group to whom her affair with Alex, however platonic, was an open secret.'

Yet while Fey chose to keep her feelings to herself – or possibly, coming so soon after the terrible news from Lenz, she felt so low that she was unable to express them – around the time of Litta's third visit, she did something quite extraordinary. Desperate to find some excuse to escape her situation in the barrack, she claimed to have 'very bad toothache' and asked the SS to take her to the dentist. 'As I was escorted on foot through the camp, I revisited this immense city of barracks with renewed disbelief and disgust,' she wrote. 'At one point a large lorry drove past, filled to the brim with naked corpses. Nobody seemed to notice. The guards told me 200–300 prisoners were dying every day from typhoid and starvation.

'On my way back from the dentist, I witnessed a second grotesque scene. Columns of inmates were returning from work and we had to stop and wait while they passed by. The prisoners were dressed in the usual camp overalls – shapeless uniforms with wide black and white stripes. They had sunken cheeks – or worse, no cheeks at all – and their heads were shaved. Marching in rows of four, some were so weak they could hardly stand. The SS struck the ones that couldn't keep up with the butts of their rifles. Leading this column was an SS band, playing one cheerful march after another. At the end of the stretch, the "musicians" moved to one side and these poor wretches had to march up and down in front of them, keeping time to the music, as if on parade. It was one of the most sadistic sights I have ever seen.'

The prospect of release, to which Lenz had so tantalizingly alluded, had come to nothing. Almost three weeks had gone by since he had told the group there was a possibility they would be freed 'within ten days'. 'We waited and waited,' Ännerle recalled, 'but of course nothing happened.'

Fey had at least been buoyed by a letter from her mother. 'You seem to have had no news of us, although I have been writing once a fortnight,' Ilse wrote. Aside from communicating news of Hans

Dieter, Fey's brother, who had been arrested after the 20 July plot and imprisoned in a castle in the eastern part of Germany, she had said very little; evidently, she knew the SS would read the letter. But at least Fey knew her mother was safe.

The air-raid alarm sounded every day and, on the evening of 31 March, a US bomb missed Sonderbau 15 by a whisker. 'It made the barrack shake, and doors and windows were blown out,' Gagi reported. 'There were shards of glass all over our room. But the shock of the near miss was worse than the damage.'

At 8 a.m. the next morning – Easter Sunday – everyone gathered in the passage to sing the Te Deum and Bach's '*Lobet den Herrn*' ('The Lord be Praised'). Midway through the morning, they began to hear the rumble of artillery. The US Army was at Eisenach, just 50 miles from the camp. In a state of high excitement, they gathered around the radio. It seemed it would only be a matter of days before they were liberated. With the Russians to the east, German forces were virtually encircled. This time, it looked impossible for the SS to snatch them away.

At lunchtime, when the female Russian prisoners brought over their food, they said the guards were packing up and preparing to flee. The women also reported that Communist prisoners were stockpiling weapons, stolen from the camp armoury, in preparation for a showdown with the SS.

It was clear the guards were tense; as the sound of the shelling grew louder, the group noticed a change in the behaviour of the two female supervisors in Sonderbau 15. They had identical blonde perms and their names were Fräulein Knocke and Fräulein Rafforth. Grotesque in their SS uniforms, their modus operandi was to march up and down the passage in their jackboots, shouting loudly. Now, both women were showing signs of hysteria. 'Fräulein Knocke had already divested herself of her uniform in spirit,' Isa Vermehren observed. 'She did everything in her power to gain our sympathy. She tried to give herself an intellectual air, using many, often incorrect, foreign expressions. She underwent a visible transformation: her patronising superiority, the mask adopted by all SS, gave way to an ever-increasing nervousness, which degenerated into intense anxiety.'

Fräulein Rafforth – 'the fattest, most lascivious, most vulgar person I've ever seen running around in a skirt', as Isa described her – reacted very differently. A woman whose life revolved around her many SS lovers, she became obsessed with the impact the Americans' arrival would have on her sex life. 'With absolutely no regard for the tension growing in the barrack, she sat with her lardy arse on a stool, which groaned under her weight. "It's not nice being without a man at night," she growled over and over again.'

Two SS lieutenants by the names of Ditmann and Sippach guarded the Prominenten in the cells under the SS barracks. Sippach, a disarmingly 'pleasant-looking young fellow', as one prisoner remarked, was notorious for having participated in executions at the camp. He boasted that he 'enjoyed shooting and hanging' and claimed to have killed scores of Russian POWs, for which he had been rewarded with 'schnapps and cigarettes'. More frightened of reprisals from the Russian prisoners than he was of the Americans, as Captain Payne Best, the British spy captured at Venlo, recorded, Sippach was preparing to flee the camp at the first opportunity: 'He told me himself that they would tear him limb from limb if they ever got hold of him. He had been attacked before and had a nasty scar on his throat which he said had been caused when a Russian prisoner went for him with a knife.'

Ditmann, by contrast, intended to stay and fight to the last. A brutal man in his early fifties, he started threatening the prisoners as the Americans closed in. 'I shall still have my pistol with one shot for you and one for me,' he told Payne Best. 'You will never leave this place alive.'

On 2 April – Easter Monday – the Russian women disclosed a new development. At dawn that morning, a gang of prisoners, mostly criminals with long sentences, had reported to the gate for a secret assignment with the SS. Their orders were to dig a trench 10 to 15 yards long and 6 feet wide, and they were to work in shifts until it was finished. The fear in the camp was that this was a liquidation detail and that the SS were constructing a mass grave for the bodies of prisoners they intended to execute.

In his cell under the SS barracks, Payne Best was pessimistic. 'This has been a hell of a month,' he wrote in his diary. 'Doubt much whether shall ever get home. Probably shall be liquidated by a pistol bullet if our troops get too near. Only real hope is if our troops land here from the air. The Germans say we intend to destroy them and see no reason to spare those of us who are in their power.'

On the morning of 3 April, the Americans reached Erfurt, just 13 miles from Buchenwald. Later that day, the SS doubled the guard in Sonderbau 15, and in the cells where Payne Best and the others were held.

None of the prisoners anticipated what actually happened.

At midday on 3 April, Fey was in her room when she heard a commotion outside: 'I could hear the SS storming along the passage, shouting: "Pack up! You can only take a small bag, the rest stays behind! We're leaving in an hour!" *How?* This was my first reaction. From the constant roar of shellfire and the streams of American fighter planes overhead, it was obvious the camp was surrounded.'

Along the passage, Isa was in the communal room with the others when the troops burst in: 'Pure rage came from the Stauffenbergs, a shaking of the head from Thyssen, a sigh of confusion from Frau Schroeder – from everyone, however, determined resistance. Fräulein Gisevius buzzed around with excitement, flying rather than walking through the rooms. The whole barrack took on the appearance of a startled hen coop.'

Everyone rushed to pack, protesting that an hour was not long enough. The order to take only what they could carry caused consternation and most of the group, including Fey, rebelled against it: 'The things we had carried with us for over 1,500 kilometres were precious. They were not just things, they represented all we had left of ourselves: photographs of our families, clothes we'd worn in happier times, and all sorts of objects of sentimental value . . . I still had some of the children's things – items that been left behind the day they were taken from me at Innsbruck: toys, pairs of odd socks, their little vests and a drawing book of Corrado's.'

Few things were discarded and the mound of luggage was ready and waiting in the hall by one o'clock. Isa was amazed at the sheer

volume of it: 'From the heavy, opulent suitcases of the Thyssen family, around twelve in total, to the Stauffenbergs' enormous pile of
luggage, it included countless bits of hand baggage, shapeless ruck-
sacks and bundles and even crates, chests and boxes . . . Gisela [von
Plettenberg] and I were the only sensible ones; we carefully packed
the most indispensable stuff in a small bag, the less important things
in a large suitcase and what we could do without in a cardboard box.
This we decided we would jettison if the SS insisted, and the large
suitcase after that. Whatever the cost, we were determined to hold on
to our small bags and my accordion.'

One hour extended to three. The SS told them the delay was due
to the fact that no transport was available. Nerves began to fray as
they waited, the camp siren sounding constantly. Isa was irritated by
the way the others fretted over their luggage: 'First of all they took
everything outside and heaped it up along the wall by the gate. Then
it began to rain, so they brought everything back in. Then they
thought it would be a while before departure, and they began to
unpack, move things around and then pack again.'

The afternoon came and went and there was no sign of their 'imminent departure'. Food was brought over to the barrack, and there was
more unpacking as everyone searched for plates and cutlery.

At eight o'clock, Fey gathered with the others in the communal
room to listen to the evening bulletin. 'We were all hoping against
hope that the Americans would reach the camp before the SS could
whisk us away. The news report was not encouraging. It seemed the
German Army was holding out near Erfurt. Then, an hour later,
Fräulein Knocke came in, ashen-faced. It was all over, she said.
According to the BBC news, which she had been listening to in the
SS barracks, the Americans were no more than 10 miles from the
camp. Stopping only for a minute, she rushed off to the guardroom.
She was so agitated, she did not bother to close the door and someone
saw her burning her SS documents and stripping the insignia from
her uniform. Apparently, she had procured false papers and was preparing to escape. We went to bed around 10 o'clock. All of us were
in high spirits, believing the Americans would liberate the camp the
next day.'

Two long blasts from a whistle woke them shortly before midnight. Isa was the first to stagger along the passageway: 'SS men were piling into the hall, their weapons drawn. Outside, from the entrance to the barrack, all the way to the gate, there were more guards with machine guns, standing at two-metre intervals. One by one, our names were called out and we had to step forward and present ourselves to the transport organiser. The darting spotlight of a pocket torch lit our way to the vehicles.'

Three grey army buses, with blacked-out windows, waited on the road behind the wall: one for the prisoners of kin, one for the Prominenten from the cells beneath the SS barracks, and a separate one for the former French prime minister, Léon Blum, and his wife.

SS Lieutenant Bader was in charge of the transport. His hostile attitude and his Aryan features alarmed Fey: 'Tall, bronzed, lantern-jawed, he was one of the cold, blue-eyed types. He screamed at us to stop complaining and to gather everything and get moving at once. A rumour went round that he belonged to a "Liquidation Commando". The two female guards who had been in charge of us throughout our imprisonment at Buchenwald were nowhere to be seen. Bader's gang of tough-acting SS pushed us roughly on to the bus, shouting aggressively: "Get in. You've all got to get in. Don't imagine you deserve any better." There was really not room for half our number, so we were all squeezed together in the most contorted positions, around and on top of the baggage.'

33

The convoy of buses, the windows sinisterly blacked out, drove through the night and did not stop until the next morning. 'It was a hell of a journey,' one prisoner recalled; 'there was no light, we had nothing to eat or drink . . . literally, we could none of us move an inch for our legs were embedded in luggage and our arms pinned to our sides.'

By this stage, everyone knew that Lieutenant Bader, the officer in charge of the transport, was an executioner. One of the guards had confirmed the rumour to Captain Payne Best: 'This man Bader was a member of the chief Gestapo execution gang and passed his life in travelling from one concentration camp to another, like a pest officer engaged in the extermination of rats. We all realised that the fact that such a man had been chosen to guard us did not presage anything particularly good.'

Soon after dawn, the convoy pulled over to the side of the road. Seated in the front of the bus, Fey could see they had come to a halt halfway down a long sloping hill. 'By then we were all in urgent need of relief, so we asked the guards if we could get off for a few minutes. They refused. It was obvious, given the right excuse, they were ready to dispense with us altogether. "Who do you think you are?" snapped Bader. "You'd better be careful: we could treat you differently if we wanted to." Maria von Hammerstein raised her voice from the back. "If you do not let me off this bus this very minute, I will make a lake right here on the spot! That will not be pleasant for anybody!" When the guards tried to ignore her, Maria forged a path through the luggage, thrusting herself against the sergeant at the door. He hesitated, obviously not accustomed to such behaviour. Then, with a shrug, he gave in. Thanks to Maria's insistence, we were allowed off one at a time, the armed guards watching over us as we relieved ourselves by the side of the road.'

A short while later, a black Gestapo Mercedes pulled up behind the parked buses. Two Gestapo officers got out and, after conferring briefly with Bader, they ordered the SS guards to fetch Josef Müller, Franz Liedig★ and Ludwig Gehre. The three men, Abwehr agents who had worked closely with Admiral Canaris to overthrow Hitler, were travelling with Payne Best: 'The pile of luggage was pulled down and, after a difficult search, their bags were found and after a curt goodbye and "see you later", the three men got out . . . we were all certain that our friends had gone to their death, and that we had seen them for the last time. But life goes on and soon we were pretending high spirits to disguise our real feelings.

'Someone recognised a village through which we passed,' Payne Best continued. 'After discussion, the conclusion was reached that we were on our way to Flossenbürg. Not so good this, for the Flossenbürg concentration camp was primarily used for the extermination of unwanted prisoners.'

Among the prisoners in Payne Best's bus was Dr Rascher, a former member of Himmler's personal staff. Until his arrest for fraud in the spring of 1944, Rascher had planned and supervised the construction of gas chambers at concentration camps in Germany and Poland. He had also persuaded Himmler to allow prisoners to be used as guinea pigs in medical experiments. Based at Dachau, Rascher had conducted his own medical research, experimenting with Polygal, a substance made from beet and apple pectin that was supposed to aid blood clotting. His experiments aimed to determine whether it could be used to reduce bleeding from gunshot wounds sustained during combat. To test its efficacy, prisoners were given a Polygal tablet and shot through the neck or chest.

Rascher's inclusion in the transport unnerved the other prisoners. His presence undermined the theory that Himmler intended to spare their lives in order to use them as hostages. Rascher's SS career had ended when, in an attempt to ingratiate himself further with Himmler, he falsely claimed to have found a means of extending child-bearing age. Citing his wife as an example, he sent the Reichsführer photographs

---

★ A naval officer associated with the Abwehr circle of conspirators.

of their three children, 'born', he said, when she was 'over the age of 48'. Himmler's preoccupation with increasing the German birth rate led him to use the photographs for propaganda purposes, and he felt personally betrayed when it was discovered that the couple had either purchased or kidnapped the children. It seemed unlikely that he intended to spare the life of a man who had publicly humiliated him and who he had declared his sworn enemy.

Around noon, Bader brought the convoy to a halt at the entrance to Flossenbürg camp. He ordered the guards to lock all the vehicles, leaving the prisoners to wait inside. A long delay followed while he and his men spoke to the camp officials in the administration block, a forbidding building, which those on board could see through the gates. 'When they came out,' Payne Best recalled, 'one of them, who was more friendly than the others, said, "You will have to go farther, they can't take you here. Too full." We weren't at all sorry at this news, and Rascher became quite optimistic and told us with the authority of a concentration-camp expert that obviously there was no present intention to liquidate us, for Flossenbürg was never so crowded that it could not accommodate a few more corpses.'

The convoy drove on. Straight away, Fey noticed a change in the guards' behaviour. 'They were nervous and irritable. We had landed them with a burden (as one of them put it). Evidently, Lieutenant Bader had left Buchenwald with orders to take us to Flossenbürg and it was obvious that he had no idea what to do with us. Apparently, he had been given vague instructions to continue southwards until he found some place to deposit us. He was in a terrible mood, made worse by the fact that he and his men had not been given any money for food or other expenses. When Alex suggested that he would be "delighted" to put us all up at his family's castle at Jettingen, which was not that far away, the guards became even more furious. But at least it made us laugh.'

At dusk, they reached Regensburg, an imposing medieval town on the banks of the Danube. It had started to drizzle and Bader directed the convoy through the darkening cobbled streets, stopping every now and then in front of a building. Inching through the narrow arches that marked the different quarters of the town, they passed through squares lined with Gothic mansions and churches with paired towers. After a while, the buildings took on a familiarity, and it was clear that Bader did not know where he was going. One of the guards said that if they could not find somewhere to stop for the night here, they had no idea what they would do.

At last they pulled up outside the *Landesgefängnis* (state prison). A huge white building, dating from the sixteenth century, it was the only place large enough to accommodate the sixty prisoners. Bader and his men ordered them out of the buses and herded them through the entrance into a spacious hall, and up a steep iron staircase. At the top, prodding them in the back with their guns, they marched them along a corridor and shoved them, four or five at a time, into small, dirty cells.

Fey was sharing a cell with the Hofackers: 'As they began locking the doors, Major Dietrich Schatz, a young officer who joined us at Buchenwald, lost his temper and shouted, "You've no right to lock us up like criminals!" There was then a good hour of heated discussion, following which Lieutenant Bader called in the prison director, an authoritative-looking man with a large bald head and pince-nez glasses. The director explained in a serious tone that the prison rules were that cell doors were to be kept locked at all times. "There can be no exceptions. I regret that, regardless of your status, these rules must be followed!" With that Schatz (still complaining loudly) and the rest of us were pushed back into our dirty little cubicles, with the iron doors bolted firmly behind.'

On one side of the building, the prisoners' cells overlooked the train station. While the Allies had largely spared the historic centre of Regensburg, the station was a target. 'Really I have never seen such a mess in my life,' Captain Payne Best wrote. 'Engines and coaches lying on their backs with their legs in their air, burnt-out coaches in long rows, and railways sticking up in great hoops like pieces of wire.' At around ten o'clock, the air-raid alarm sounded and SOE agent Falconer watched as the bombs dropped: 'The target was the railway marshalling yard and, as this was only separated from the prison by a wall, and our cell window looked straight down on it, we had a splendid view of some very good precision bombing. Our interest cooled considerably, however, when a large lump of metal whizzed in through the window, breaking the glass and clanging against the opposite wall.'

Hammering on the cell door, Falconer demanded to be let out. When it opened, he ran past the guard and slipped the bolts on the other cell doors. Collectively, the prisoners then refused to leave the corridor. 'The warders, having been told to treat us politely, simply did not know what to do with us,' Payne Best recalled. 'I heard one old warder say to another, "You try and get them back into the cells. They don't seem to know that they must obey orders." Every now and then one of the warders would shout: "Everybody go to his cell", but this only resulted in laughter and loud cheers. Then one of them had the bright idea of putting food in the cells and after a while most of us were locked up. But then the air-raid alarm went off again and we were all marched down to a shelter in the basement, where the fun started again.'

The next morning, the helpless warders left the cell doors open: 'For the first time in the history of Regensburg prison!' Fey noted. It was also the first time the different groups from Buchenwald had had the chance to meet properly; the atmosphere, as Payne Best described, was more akin to a party than a morning in prison.

Bader's orders were to remain at Regensburg until nightfall; the danger of strafing from enemy aircraft was too great to risk moving the prisoners during daylight hours. Himmler's strict rules of secrecy meant that the individual groups were not meant to know who the others were, let alone come into contact. To Bader's irritation, the air-raid siren sounded throughout the afternoon, and he had to sit with them in the shelter beneath the prison while they continued their party.

Just before dusk, anxious to get moving, he ordered the prisoners to get ready to leave. A few minutes later, they assembled by the waiting buses. The guards instructed them to sit in the same seats as before, and Fey took her place at the front. 'The confusion among the SS was even greater than previously. We still seemed to have no precise destination. Someone said that we were being taken to Dachau concentration camp. But someone else had heard that Bader had already phoned through to Dachau and was told the place was full. Alarmingly, as we left Regensburg, we realized we were heading east.'

It started to rain and, as the night wore on, it rained harder and harder. The road seemed to be quite dead and for hours they passed no one. The fields on either side were pitted with bomb craters, and the verges littered with the skeletons of burnt-out vehicles. The buses were powered by wood and gas and the combination of lurching and stopping, due to the erratic supply of fuel to the engine, made sleep impossible. Periodically, those seated at the front passed on their location to the person behind, and it was then relayed, as in a game of Chinese whispers, to the passengers unable to see through the blacked-out windows. Isa was seated at the back of the bus: 'This nocturnal journey wore down our nerves. Not only was our mood affected by the constant starting and stopping and limping along of the engine, we were tormented by the uncertainty and secrecy of this move under the cover of darkness. It worried us that we were heading toward the Czech border, far away from the Western Front and deeper and deeper into the very recesses of the Bavarian Forest.'

Yet, as dawn came, their mood lifted. It was a beautiful spring day and the trees were in bud and the daffodils in bloom. Following the course of the Danube, they passed through landscape largely untouched by the war. 'It was a delightful drive through lovely rolling country, past quiet farmhouses and fields with every now and then a stretch of dark pines,' Payne Best recalled. Crossing the Danube at Deggendorf, they drove up into the Bavarian hills: 'It was the sort of trip that, in more settled times, tourists pay money to enjoy,' Hugh Falconer noted wryly.

Around eleven o'clock, they stopped outside an inn at Schönberg, a village of tall, pastel-coloured houses in the middle of the forest. Bader got out and went inside to talk to the innkeeper. Some minutes later, he reappeared. Their accommodation was not yet ready and they would have to wait. A crowd of villagers had gathered around the buses. Mostly old women, dressed in peasant clothes, they stared stonily up at the prisoners. Bader had told the innkeeper that he was transporting SS families and word had quickly spread. 'The upshot,'

Ännerle remembered, 'was that the inhabitants didn't want to have anything to do with us.' Later, Fey learned that the village had suffered terribly at the hands of the local People's Court, one of hundreds set up by the Nazis: 'There were no professional judges; whichever local Nazi happened to be around had the power to arrest anyone on the spot. When someone was denounced there was no attempt to weigh the evidence. Justice was administered swiftly, often by firing squad. It was enough to have spoken out against the war or to be related to soldiers who had deserted or even surrendered. Most people lived in fear of the authorities and tried to keep out of sight.'

An order, issued by SS headquarters, had gone out to clear two schools in the village to accommodate the newcomers, further arousing the indignation of the inhabitants. The schools were being used as hospitals for troops and, throughout the morning, sick and wounded soldiers limped past the convoy on their way to look for beds in the next village. As Fey described, the long wait, facing the mutely hostile crowd, was discomforting; further, none of the prisoners had had anything to eat since leaving Regensburg: 'Bader told us that no arrangements had been, or could be, made for feeding us. This village of 700 inhabitants already housed 1,300 refugees and when the mayor heard that another sixty-odd had been wished on him, he refused to draw on his reserves. The Gestapo had brought them and the Gestapo must feed them. Bader said there was nothing he could do as he had no more fuel to go in search of food, so we would have to do without.'

After several hours, Bader disappeared again and Ännerle and some of the others were able to speak to the villagers: 'We lost no time in explaining the situation and secretly giving them our names, for example Stauffenberg, Goerdeler and Lindemann.* The result was amazing! All the inhabitants were on our side and wanted to help us. They said they would bring us food.'

The schools – a boys' school and a girls' school, situated side by side in the village square – were cleared by seven o'clock in the evening.

---

* Probably a relative of Wehrmacht officer General Fritz Lindemann, one of the 20 July plotters.

There were four large rooms for the sixty prisoners. As there were many more men than women, for the first time since their imprisonment, the Sippenhäftlinge slept in the same room. 'Some funny scenes took place in those overcrowded rooms, with men and women sleeping together,' Fey recalled. 'For instance, the guards had arranged for a small basin to be placed in the centre of our big room for washing. We agreed that when the women were washing the men would stand in the corridor, and vice versa. This seemed to be working perfectly except that, when it was our turn to wash, the elderly Fritz Thyssen asked if we would mind if he stayed on, since he was a slow dresser and still had to shave. He assured us he would look the other way when we women were naked. What we had not noticed was the angle of Thyssen's shaving mirror. It kept us in his full view at all times. When we half laughingly accused him of being a dirty old man, he replied that he had already seen many women "in the costume of Eve" and that old men should be allowed such "small pleasures". As if this was not enough, he crept round to each woman's bed in the evenings, paying old-fashioned compliments.'

The villagers kept their promise and delivered large quantities of food to the kitchen where the SS cooks prepared the prisoners' meals. After a few days, however, it emerged that the cooks were keeping all the food for themselves and a means had to be found to smuggle supplies in. 'Stiller,★ with most of the SS escort, disappeared soon after our arrival, leaving only a Sergeant and two men to guard us,' Hugh Falconer recalled. 'The advantage of this situation was that, with only two guards (one on duty and one off), the Gestapo could only watch one side of the house at a time. As we had windows on all four sides, we were able to open them and talk to any passer-by who was prepared to stop and chat. Quite a number of people were too nervous to do this, but one who came every morning to enquire how we were getting along was the mayor of the village.'

Once the mayor realized that provisions were not getting through, he organized a party of villagers to deliver the food at night. For fifteen-year-old Ännerle, they were 'midnight feasts': 'When the sun

★ SS Lieutenant Edgar Stiller.

set over Schönberg we started living it up! Every evening when the guard left us and it became dark, some of us would go to the window with a long rope to await the delivery of the things that were being smuggled to us. Our relationship with the baker was particularly close. Every evening he would attach a bucket to the end of the rope, filled with bread, butter, apples, sweets and chocolate. Often, we'd send the empty bucket back down two or three times and he would fill it up again!' One delivery alone consisted of twenty loaves of bread, two pounds of butter, two long sausages, two packets of tobacco, two packets of cigarettes, two enormous bags of biscuits and sweets, and a bucket of marmalade.

It was Isa's job to smuggle supplies to the Blums, who had been assigned a flat on the floor above. To maintain the secrecy order, Bader had erected a door on the landing outside, which he kept permanently locked. 'The door was an absurd addition,' she wrote. 'One could get to the Blums' flat from the window of our room by climbing up the gutter on to another roof. There was also a light well, which ran between our room and theirs, and this provided an alternative means of delivery.'

Yet, however much the group mocked Bader for his nonsensical observation of the rules, he remained a figure of terror. A few days after they arrived, they watched from a window as Bader and his guards hustled Pastor Dietrich Bonhoeffer into a black Gestapo car. Later, they learned that Bonhoeffer was taken to Flossenbürg, where he was hanged the next day along with Admiral Canaris and other Abwehr men who had plotted against Hitler.

The stay at Schönberg lasted for two weeks. For Fey, it brought back her time with Alex at the Hindenburg Baude. However shaken she had been by Litta's visits, she and Alex were as close as ever and they slept side by side in the large room they shared with the others. For the first time in months, they were able to escape into the countryside. 'The weather was improving and, with a great deal of insistence, we persuaded Bader to let us out for a walk every day. Two guards accompanied us. We were, of course, forbidden to talk to the local people or to say our surnames. This was completely ridiculous as they knew exactly who we were! The pleasure of being able to wander around freely after being cooped up for so many long, cold months is hard to describe. It was an exhilarating feeling. Spring had come. The catkins were out and the fields were carpeted with flowers. The horrors of the war seemed to fade into the background.'

But, as Fey admitted, she was unable to enjoy the walks with Alex: 'The children were the greater pull and I had lost them. I knew that all my worrying over them would do no good and only make me miserable in front of Alex. But I simply couldn't help myself. Realizing that there was nothing to be done only made me more upset. Alex did his best to comfort and reassure me, yet I sensed he was also troubled. While nothing had happened physically between us, I knew he felt guilty about Litta. But we didn't talk about it and, as the days went by, the combination of my unhappiness and his preoccupation clouded the way we were with each other.'

Litta had not seen Alex before he left Buchenwald. After her visit on Easter Sunday, bad weather had prevented her from returning the next day as she had hoped. 'Weather very windy. Litta didn't come unfortunately,' Gagi noted in her diary. 'She says she can only fly when the weather is good.'

The weather did not improve for several days and it was not until Thursday 5 April that Litta set off from Weimar, where she was now based, flying a two-seater aerobatic monoplane. It was a ten-minute flight to Buchenwald, but the Americans now controlled the skies over her route and it was extremely risky to fly in daylight. Staying low, rarely climbing above 100 feet, she hugged the trees, arriving without incident.

Usually, when circling over the camp, she could see people waving from Sonderbau 15, but this time there was no sign of movement. Dropping low over the barrack, she saw that the compound was empty. A few hundred yards away, piles of bodies were stacked against the wall of the crematorium. Even from the air, she could smell the 'thick and hanging' odour that clung to the camp. Not knowing whether Alex was among the dead – finally executed like his brothers – or whether he had been transported on again, she landed at a nearby airfield.

Frantic with worry, she put in an urgent call to the administration office at Buchenwald. She was told that the prisoners of kin had been moved, but the official would not say where. Hubertus von Papen-Köningen, a friend and fellow pilot, was with her and he remembered her taking the news very badly: 'she was in shock and needed to lie down'. A committed anti-Nazi, having lost two brothers on the Eastern Front, he volunteered to call the camp again. Bluffing his way through the conversation, Papen-Köningen claimed he was acting on secret orders from Berlin that had been signed by Himmler himself. The bluff worked. He found out that Alex had been transferred to Straubing – a small town just south of Regensburg – on 3 April.

The next day Litta obtained an official flight order for 'a special operation, important to the war effort' – a remarkable feat given that this unspecified operation was to fly to Straubing to visit the brother of the man who had so nearly assassinated Hitler. Straubing turned out to be a false steer; but after flying on to Regensburg, Litta was again able to use her rank and charm to extract her husband's whereabouts from a Gestapo official. He told her that, less than forty-eight hours before, Alex had been moved from the state prison, and was on his way to Schönberg. Then he gave her a permit to visit him.

The morning of 8 April was bright and clear, and Litta was in the air by seven. It was less than 50 miles to Schönberg. Following the course of the Straubing–Passau railway line, she was able to fly just 30 feet above the ground. As she passed through a small village, a wounded serviceman was standing at the door of his house. Intrigued by the sight of the unusually low-flying plane, he watched its progress.

Seconds later, an American fighter jet 'thundered past'. Lieutenant Thomas A. Norbourne of the US Air Force 15th Squadron reconnaissance unit, then tasked with sweeping railway lines for trains, was also following the Straubing–Passau line. Mistaking Litta's unarmed plane for a Focke-Wulf fighter and reluctant to miss such an unexpected opportunity, he fired 'two salvos of about five to eight shots'. A retired railway foreman saw the encounter. He watched as Litta's plane veered to the left and then spun into a field. There was no sound of an explosion, and no smoke. The railwayman grabbed his bicycle and pedalled over to the site, joined en route by a French POW who was working nearby.

The two men were the first to arrive on the scene. To their great surprise, they saw an elegant woman in her early forties sitting in the pilot's seat. From her composure, they did not consider her condition to be critical. 'She just said please help me,' the railwayman reported. After freeing her from the wreckage, they laid her on the ground. One of her legs seemed to be broken, and her other foot appeared 'unnaturally twisted'.

Shortly after, the local military took over the site and a Luftwaffe doctor arrived to treat Litta. She was taken by ambulance to a hospital at a nearby airfield where, a few hours later, she died. The cause of death on the certificate issued by the medical superintendent was a fracture at the base of her skull.

Mysteriously, a substantial amount of cash and expensive items of jewellery were found among her belongings. In speculating about her death, her sister, Jutta, thought the flight to Schönberg in the two-seater plane was a 'bold attempt' to rescue Alex, one that Litta had 'long since planned and was long overdue'. That she had intended to fly them both across the lines to the Allies in the hope of beginning a new life in the West was evident in the 'disproportionately large' sums of money found among her possessions.

The news of Litta's death did not reach Alex until four days later. Fey was with him at Schönberg when he heard: 'The SS called him out of our room to give him the tragic news. When he came back in, he was as white as chalk. Everything that remained of his past life had been rubbed out. First, his two brothers executed by firing squad; then his house and treasured library destroyed in a bombing raid; now, his wife killed. In the circumstances, his self-control was incredible. All of us were profoundly shocked and tried to console him. How painful it must have been for him to be surrounded by people at such a moment. But you could see that he didn't want to be alone. After a while, he asked Elisabeth and me to sit with him, saying he wanted people near him who understood. I tried my best to comfort him, but there was little anyone could do.'

★

Rumours of an impending German surrender dominated the last days at Schönberg. In the east, Vienna and Karlsruhe had fallen to the Russians, and in the west, the Americans had taken Cologne. Chaotic lines of retreating soldiers began to stream through the remote village, passing directly beneath the windows of the school. While the group was willing the war to end, the men were, after all, fellow Germans and, as Isa described, the scenes were distressing: 'Masses of disorderly soldiers in filthy, shredded uniforms made their way along the road. Exhausted horses pulled heavy carts with ripped tarpaulins; battered trucks rattled over the market square, piled high with incredible luggage; next to machine guns and gas masks were mattresses and bedheads; next to petrol canisters and crates of ammunition were washing baskets and birdcages.

'More upsetting still,' Isa continued, 'was the contrasting attitude of Lieutenant Bader. He was suffused with an unshakeable belief in his own omnipotence. He strode through the present as if it was the same as the past, unable to grasp the reality of the collapse taking place around him.'

Seeing the defeated army, Ännerle worried about her younger siblings at Bad Sachsa: 'The anxiety over the little ones increased. Where were they? Were they still alive? There had been much fighting in the Harz mountains and we were worried that something had happened to them.' Gagi recognized that, without Litta, they were unlikely to find out: 'Now, no more news to be had with regard to the children in Bad Sachsa,' she wrote the night she heard that Litta had been killed.

On 15 April, the SS took the prisoners on the floor below away. This was Payne Best's group – the men who had been imprisoned below the SS barracks at Buchenwald. Fey learned from Lieutenant Bader that they had been taken to Flossenbürg, where Pastor Bonhoeffer and other conspirators in the July plot had been executed: 'Their removal was depressing. We assumed this was the last we would see of them and we all sensed that it would be our turn next. Amidst all the chaos, it seemed doubtful that we were still considered worth looking after by somebody back in Berlin. The most likely scenario was that we would go to Flossenbürg too.'

The familiar order came the next day. 'Pack your bags! Be ready to leave in an hour!' This time, the departure was prompt. As the group filed into the waiting buses, they were amazed to see that, in spite of the strong SS presence, most of the village had turned out to say goodbye. Standing in the doorways of their houses or leaning out of windows, they looked on in silence. Ännerle was touched by the courage of the dentist's wife, who came over on the pretext she was owed money for unpaid bills and gave them food for the journey.

By the time they left Schönberg it was dark. The one consolation was that they were heading away from Flossenbürg. Driving through the night, they arrived at Landshut, near Munich, at dawn. A few hours before, the town had been pounded by American bombers and almost every building was on fire. Gagi jotted down her impressions in her diary: 'Everywhere we look there are columns of disbanded troops and refugees on the road . . . Constant sirens – much stopping and crawling in dim light. The sky red from the fires.'

Fey could hardly believe her eyes when they reached Munich. Her mother's house at Ebenhausen was just a few miles south and she knew the city well. Driving through the ruined streets, she was flooded with memories of childhood shopping expeditions with her parents, and visits to cafés for coffee and cakes, which had been a special treat. 'As we approached the city centre, it seemed that many buildings were still standing. But as we got closer, I saw that there was nothing behind the walls. The houses were hollow, as in a stage set. There was a profound silence and I did not see any people or cars; the only vehicle in sight was the twisted hulk of a burnt-out tram. It was awful to see and I had a big lump in my throat.'

Leaving the city, she felt torn: 'I was barely 15 miles from Mutti and Almuth. I could walk to Ebenhausen. But I didn't have the courage. The time in captivity had made me passive and frightened. I didn't want to be alone under any circumstances. But more than anything else, I could not bear the thought of leaving Alex.'

A few miles outside Munich, the bus turned off the main road. 'Dachau 7 km' was written on the signpost.

34

It was coming up to noon when the bus pulled up at a side entrance to the camp. The double-fronted gate, 12 feet high and made of solid oak, was shut. Straight away, Bader jumped down and disappeared. As he left, he instructed the SS guards to lock the prisoners in; on no account were they to leave the bus until he returned.

The day was warm and close and clouds of dust, churned up by passing military vehicles, came in through the open windows. Two high walls ran along the road on either side; the huge bronze eagle that towered above the gate heightened the feeling of being hemmed in. Its talons clutched a swastika and its wings were spread, the wing-span stretching almost the entire width of the gate.

The name 'Dachau' resonated horribly with all the prisoners waiting in the locked bus. Built in 1933, it was the oldest and most notorious of the Nazi concentration camps. Himmler, then chief of police in Munich, officially named it 'the first concentration camp for political prisoners'. During the first year, some 5,000 men, primarily German Communists, Social Democrats and trade unionists, had been imprisoned. Later, in 1938 after Kristallnacht, more than 10,000 Jewish men had been interned there. Fey remembered her father speaking of friends and colleagues – both Jews and political opponents of the Nazis – who had 'disappeared' from Dachau. Others in the group also knew of people who had vanished.

Fey described the fear that overtook them all: 'With the sun beating down, it was hot and suffocating. As the minutes and then the hours rolled by, everyone became more and more anxious. Some of us were so frightened we simply had to relieve ourselves on the spot.'

Shortly before three o'clock – almost three hours after the bus pulled up at the gate – Bader appeared with another SS officer. They ordered the group to repack their bags, jettisoning all but essentials, then disappeared again, only to return some minutes later to countermand the order. This charade continued for the next few hours, infuriating Isa: 'Both men came to see us three or four times during the afternoon constantly bringing new orders. Just as we were about to obey these orders, they would leave, remarking that they only wanted to see whether we would comply and that they would be back soon. When they returned they issued new orders, which they again revoked. They admitted that they were facing difficulties in arranging things, but the manner in which they told us, laughing patronisingly at us, was so shameless, one wanted to hit them, and it was an effort to control oneself.'

It was another two or three hours before they were finally ordered off the bus and marched through the gate, where they were told to wait in front of a large brick building. 'Behind it, an entire town of houses, barracks and streets stretched out almost as far as the eye could see,' Fey remembered; 'although it was only mid-April, the early-evening sun beat down relentlessly.'

They had been there for an hour when an SS official arrived and ordered the male prisoners to line up against the wall of the building. After inspecting the men, he shouted at them to follow him 'at the double'. Recruits were needed for the Volkssturm – Himmler's last-ditch army of boys and old men – and they were to join a local brigade. Looking on with the other women, Fey was horrified: 'Some of us started to cry openly as the men were marched off. For all we knew, the Volkssturm idea was just an excuse for the SS to take the men away and murder them inside the camp.'

The SS left the women outside the building for another three hours. It was dark when – some ten hours after they had arrived – SS Lieutenant Colonel Eduard Weiter, the camp commandant, appeared. Full of apologies, he announced that there was no intention to separate the men from the women and it had all been an unfortunate 'misunderstanding'. In his mid forties, immaculately turned out in his SS uniform, Weiter had run the camp since 1943. Tens of thousands of men and women had died during his tenure.* And yet here

---

* The final death toll at Dachau remains unknown. At the American military tribunal held at the camp in November 1945, the prosecution stated that 161,939 prisoners

he was, apologizing. He was very sorry that they had been kept waiting for so long but Dachau was very crowded and it had really been
most difficult to find suitable accommodation for such distinguished
guests. He had done his best but, even so, the quarters to which they
were about to be conducted were far inferior to those they deserved
and he hoped they would forgive their shortcomings. Then, after
clicking his heels and bowing to the women, he added that they
would find their menfolk waiting for them in the barrack.

Fey and the others clambered back on to the bus. Situated outside
the main camp, the barrack was a short drive away along the Avenue
of the SS, the majestic four-lane approach road to Dachau. The darkness prevented the women from seeing the flowers or the splendid
villas that lined the avenue. But, ten days later, when the Americans
arrived to liberate the camp, a lieutenant colonel in the 42nd Division
of the US 7th Army would drive along this same road. 'One could
imagine from the impressive massiveness of the grey Administration
Buildings and Barracks, the fine lawns, great walls and black iron-
grilled gates, that you were approaching a wealthy girls' finishing
school in the suburbs of one of our great cities,' he wrote. 'All was so
neat, so orderly, so beautiful.'

The commandant's 'welcome' speech was one he had made many
times in the preceding days. Finally, after months of manoeuvring,
involving large detachments of SS guards and perilous journeys in
the face of the Allies' advancing armies, Himmler had pulled his
Prominenten back to one place. With Europe in the last throes of
war, Weiter was now the custodian of 137 men, women and children
whom the Reichsführer SS intended to use as bargaining counters in
negotiations that he hoped to set in train with the Western Allies.

The bus carrying the Sippenhäftlinge was the last to arrive at
Dachau. Between 8 and 17 April – the day they arrived – over forty
special prisoners had been transported from Flossenbürg, Sachsenhausen and other concentration camps around Germany. They were

---

had been processed through Dachau between 1940 and 1945 and that over 25,000 of
them had died. An official report estimated that 14,700 of these deaths occurred in
the first four months of 1945.

secreted, out of view from Dachau's 35,000 inmates, in closely guarded buildings within the main camp.

The new arrivals joined other prominent individuals, many of whom had been there for months. One barrack housed members of the Wittelsbach family, whose dynasty had produced two Holy Roman Emperors and reigned as Kings of Bavaria until 1918. Another held Prince Xavier of Bourbon, the pretender to the Spanish throne. Arrested in France when the Gestapo discovered his links to resistance leaders, he had spent eighteen months in solitary confinement in the Starvation Bunker at Dachau and weighed under 6 stone. Prince Leopold of Prussia, a cousin of Germany's last kaiser, had been equally harshly treated. Born into one of Europe's wealthiest families, he was arrested after the servants at his castle informed the Gestapo that he was homosexual. Arriving at Dachau in September 1944, the prince had been assigned the job of cleaning the camp latrines and had nearly died from diphtheria. On his recovery, Commandant Weiter had transferred him to the camp brothel, where he had worked as a batman and errand boy for the prostitutes.

Acting on orders from the Reich Main Security Office in Berlin, Weiter had closed the brothel at the beginning of April to make space for the new arrivals. A remarkable collection of courageous individuals, many were celebrities in their own countries, famous for resisting the Nazis. From all over Europe, they included clergymen, resistance leaders, high-ranking military figures, former government ministers, journalists, senior civil servants and scientists. Among the most well known were Monsignor Gabriel Piguet, Bishop of Clermont-Ferrand, arrested in Vichy France for harbouring Jews and anti-Nazi priests; Alexandros Papagos, the commander-in-chief of the Greek Army; Italian partisan leader General Sante Garibaldi, grandson of the famous politician and nationalist; Georg Elser, the German factory worker who had almost succeeded in killing Hitler and other leading Nazis in Munich before the war; Martin Niemöller, a Lutheran pastor who had resisted the Nazification of German Protestant churches; Nikolaus von Kallay, a former Hungarian prime minister; Léon Blum, the ex-prime minister of France; and Kurt von Schuschnigg, chancellor of Austria at the time of the Anschluss.

There was also a sizeable British contingent. With the exception of Captain Payne Best, the British spy arrested in the Venlo incident, the fourteen men were prisoners of war. Two bore the name Churchill: Lieutenant Colonel Jack Churchill, captured leading the Commandos in Yugoslavia; and SOE officer Peter Churchill, who, early on in the war, had led four clandestine missions to France, for which he was awarded the DSO and the Croix de Guerre. Himmler erroneously believed the two officers were related to Winston Churchill. Three of the British POWs had survived the massacre that followed the 'Great Escape' from Stalag Luft III* in March 1944 – men who had taken part in the breakout and whose lives for some mysterious reason the SS had spared. They were Wing Commander 'Wings' Day and Flight Lieutenants Sydney Dowse and 'Jimmy' James. On the night of 23 September 1944 all three had succeeded in tunnelling their way out of Sachsenhausen concentration camp, where they were taken after Stalag Luft III, but had been recaptured the next day.

There were Polish, Hungarian and Russian prisoners of war too, among them several Russian generals captured on the Eastern Front, and Vassily Kokorin, the nephew of Stalin's foreign minister, Vyacheslav Molotov.

Exactly what conditions Himmler intended to extract from the Allies in exchange for these 137 prisoners it is impossible to determine. Few records relating to the Prominenten survived the war. Yet fragments of information remain, making it possible at least to speculate about Himmler's intentions after 17 April – the day the Sippenhäftlinge arrived at Dachau.

Numerous sources – US intelligence cables, top-secret British government telegrams, intercepted German signals traffic and conversations the prisoners themselves had with their SS guards – indicate that, initially, Himmler planned to use the Prominenten to barter for

---

* Seventy-six men succeeded in escaping from the camp on 25 March 1944. Seventy-three were recaptured, most of them within a few days. Of these, fifty were executed on the personal orders of Adolf Hitler.

his own life; possibly, even, his intention was also to use them as a human shield. For this plan to be viable, with the Americans closing in on Dachau, it was imperative that he retained control over them until the last moment. Himmler's immediate priority, therefore, was to move the prisoners to a secure location, out of reach from the Allies.

The obvious place was the Austrian Alps.

By 17 April, it was clear that Germany's war was over. In Berlin, 360 miles to the north of Dachau, Hitler had not left his bunker under the Reichstag for three months. The day before, a Soviet force of 2.5 million troops, 6,150 tanks and some 42,000 pieces of artillery and mortars had begun its assault on the capital, attacking from the south and east. To the west, city after city had fallen to the British and American armies. Berlin was all but encircled.

Already, agents working for the OSS,* the US intelligence agency, were reporting that senior Nazis were fleeing to hideouts in the Alps. That week, Fred Mayer, attached to Operation Greenup, a three-man mission parachuted into Nazi-occupied Austria in February, sent a coded message from Innsbruck to the OSS station at Bari in Italy:

TWO SPECIAL TRAINS WITH OPERATIONS STAFF OF HIGHEST REICH LEADERSHIP LEFT BERLIN APRIL 14. MEMBERS NOW IN OFF LIMITS AREA IMSTERBERG. 18 MEMBERS OF THE MINISTRY OF INTERIOR IN HOTEL POST. UNDER SEC OF STATE VON BURGSDORF IN GARMISCH PARTENKIRCHEN.

A few days later, Mayer sent a second cable reporting that Himmler was in the area:

HIMMLER ARRIVED WITH STAFF NIGHT OF 17 IN IGLS NEAR INNS-BRUCK IN HOTEL GRUENWALDER HOF. THREE SS DIVISIONS EXPECTED

* Office of Strategic Services.

BUT SO FAR ONLY ONE REGIMENT OF LEIBSTANDARTE* PRESENT OF
WHICH COMPANY A IS ROUNDING UP ALL POLITICALS POSSIBLY
DANGEROUS. SOURCE KRIPO.†

The Grünwalderhof, located in a remote valley close to the Brenner Pass, belonged to the aristocratic Thurn und Taxis family. That Himmler had earmarked the luxury hotel as a hideout for himself, and possibly the Prominenten, is corroborated by a series of Gestapo radio messages intercepted by Lothar Rohde, one of the prisoners at Dachau.

Rohde, a brilliant young electrical engineer, had been arrested by the SS for listening to enemy radio stations. Brutally interrogated and threatened with execution, he was granted a reprieve after he claimed that he was close to discovering a means of sabotaging the ignition systems of Allied planes, using a special radio beam. Hearing of his research, Hitler had intervened to save the engineer's life in the hope that the 'magic ray' would end hostile air attacks on Germany. The Führer also ordered that Rohde be given special facilities to develop his weapon at Dachau. Imprisoned with other Prominenten in the *Kommandaturarrest* – the building reserved for prisoners under the jurisdiction of Commandant Weiter – Rohde was allocated his own room, filled with the latest radio equipment.

His 'research' offered the perfect cover. Since he was expected to spend his day with headphones on, he could listen to whatever he liked without fear of being caught by the SS. Abandoning his work, he used the equipment to tune into BBC broadcasts and to listen to the conversations between Gestapo and Wehrmacht units in the vicinity and between the squadron leaders of British and American planes as they flew over the camp.

On the morning of 17 April, Rohde intercepted a series of Gestapo radio signals indicating that he and the other Prominenten were about to be moved to the Alpenfestung (Southern Redoubt) – Hitler's

---

* The first SS Panzer division, *Leibstandarte SS Adolf Hitler*, an elite unit initially responsible for guarding the Führer.
† *Kriminal Polizei*, the police department in charge of criminal investigations in the Third Reich.

so-called Alpine fortress. Captain Payne Best was imprisoned in the Kommandaturarrest building with Rohde: 'Hour after hour, Rohde brought us news that we were going to Switzerland to be handed over to the International Red Cross, that we were to be moved to a chateau on Lake Constance, and finally that we were being taken across the Brenner to Italy.' The Grünwalderhof, where Himmler would arrive that evening, was just 2 miles from the Brenner Pass; further, while the Gestapo did not mention the Reichsführer SS specifically, Rohde's eavesdropping revealed that the Prominenten were 'hostages whose lives could be bartered for those of Nazi leaders'.

A last-minute change of plan for reasons that are not clear meant that none of the prisoners was in fact moved that day. Payne Best was told by one of the SS guards that they were to remain at Dachau until 'other accommodation' was found. But the fact that Himmler's intention was to move them possibly explains why the Sippenhäftlinge were kept waiting for so long outside the camp.

Whatever the reason behind the change of plan, a message sent by OSS agent Mayer to Allied military headquarters soon after he reported that the SS chief was staying at the Grünwalderhof ruled out its future use as a secret hideout. To enable the US Air Force to bomb the hotel, Mayer, based on information supplied by a Wehrmacht deserter, wired details of its location. Unusually, given that the hotel was situated in a remote mountain valley, an air-raid shelter had been specially built nearby:

GRUENWALDER HOF IS APPROX 3 KMS FROM IGLS ON ROAD TO PATSCH . . . THE HOTEL CONSTRUCTED AIR RAID SHELTER IN ROCKS ON EAST SIDE OF ROAD TO PATSCH APPROXIMATELY TEN METRES ABOVE HOTEL. ENTRANCE DIRECTLY FROM ROAD. PROPRIETOR NAME ARNOLD.

By the time Allied military HQ received Mayer's message – at 14:00 hours on 18 April – Himmler had left.

For over a month, the Reichsführer SS had been constantly on the move, rarely staying in one place for more than a night. As the Third

Reich collapsed around him, he had devoted his energy to securing his own personal situation. Behind Hitler's back, in a bid to open up negotiations with the Allies, he had attended a series of secret meetings with representatives from the World Jewish Congress and the Red Cross.

In orchestrating the meetings, Himmler had one objective: to change the way the Allies perceived him. Recognizing that the revulsion to the genocide associated most directly with his name would prevent the Allies from accepting him as a plausible negotiator, his strategy was to establish his credibility. He aimed to convince them that, potentially, he was a humanitarian and conciliatory negotiating partner whose primary concern was to ameliorate the suffering of the Jews and other prisoners in the concentration camps.

Incredibly, given that he had overseen the murder of more than 6 million Jews and many millions of non-Jews in a systematic programme of ethnic and political cleansing, he believed that a few gestures of goodwill would be sufficient. To this end, in mid March, using his personal physician Felix Kersten as an intermediary, he informed the Swedish Foreign Ministry that concentration camps would not be blown up as the Allies advanced. Further, he promised, executions in the camps would stop and inmates would be handed over, rather than be evacuated. Simultaneously, he arranged a meeting with Count Bernadotte, the head of the Swedish Red Cross, to negotiate the release of 10,000 Jewish prisoners.

The shamelessness of the letter Himmler sent Kersten to inform him that 2,700 Jewish men, women and children had been transported to Switzerland is breath-taking: 'This accomplishment is in line with the policy I and my co-workers had been pursuing for years, until the war, and which the unreasonable attitude it brought in its wake made it impossible to continue. You must surely know that in the years 1936, 1937, 1938, 1939, and 1940, I founded an organisation, in conjunction with Jewish-American societies, which did excellent work of its kind. The transportation of Jews to Switzerland is a continuation of this work which, in spite of great difficulties, I carried out deliberately in the past.'

Himmler met Count Bernadotte for a second time at the

beginning of April. A week later, Sir Victor Mallet, the British Ambassador to Sweden, sent a top-secret telegram to the Foreign Office in London, summarizing the conversation:

COUNT BERNADOTTE TODAY GAVE ME IN STRICT CONFIDENCE SOME ACCOUNT OF HIS INTERVIEW WITH HIMMLER IN BERLIN LAST WEEK WHICH LASTED FOR FOUR HOURS:

CONTRARY TO WHEN BERNADOTTE SAW HIM 3 WEEKS AGO HIMMLER THIS TIME ADMITTED THAT ALL WAS UP. BERNADOTTE SUGGESTED THAT THE PROPER COURSE WAS IMMEDIATE SURRENDER WHICH WOULD SAVE INNUMERABLE LIVES. HIMMLER REPLIED THAT HE WOULD FAVOUR THIS COURSE BUT THAT HITLER REFUSED TO HEAR OF IT AND HE FELT HIMSELF BOUND BY HIS OATH OF LOYALTY TO HITLER. BERNADOTTE SUGGESTED THAT HIS LOYALTY TO THE GERMAN PEOPLE WAS MORE IMPORTANT BUT HIMMLER ANSWERED THAT HE OWED EVERYTHING TO THE FÜHRER AND COULD NOT DESERT HIM AT THE END. HIMMLER DID NOT APPEAR AT ALL FLUS-TERED BUT GAVE THE IMPRESSION OF BEING COMPLETELY SANE AND RETAINING HIS ENERGY AND ORGANISING ABILITY. HE EVEN HAD TIME TO INTEREST HIMSELF IN A BOOK OF RUNIC INSCRIP-TIONS WHICH HAVE APPARENTLY ALWAYS BEEN A HOBBY OF HIS. HIMMLER REMARKED THAT HE KNEW HE WAS NO. 1 ON OUR LIST OF WAR CRIMINALS. BERNADOTTE TOLD HIM THAT IT WAS ONLY NAT-URAL THAT HE SHOULD BE CONSIDERED A WAR CRIMINAL BECAUSE HE WAS HEAD OF THE GESTAPO WHOSE APPALLING CRUELTIES HAD BEEN PROVED. I ASKED BERNADOTTE WHETHER HIMMLER GAVE THE IMPRESSION OF BEING A SADIST AND BERNADOTTE TOLD ME TO HIS SURPRISE HE DID NOT. HIMMLER HIMSELF TOLD HIM THAT HE KNEW THAT OUTSIDE GERMANY HE WAS CONSIDERED BRUTAL BUT IN FACT HE DISLIKED CRUELTY AND AN ENTIRELY FALSE PICTURE OF HIS CHARACTER HAD BEEN BUILT UP ABROAD . . .

The senior civil servant at the Foreign Office in receipt of the telegram scrawled a note at the bottom of it: 'I think this is poor stuff and that Bernadotte has been fooled.'

Ten days after his second meeting with Bernadotte, Himmler met

Norbert Masur — Sweden's representative to the World Jewish Congress — at Kersten's farm about 50 miles north of Berlin. It was the night of 20 April — Hitler's birthday — and Himmler arrived at two o'clock in the morning having come straight from the muted celebrations in the Führer's bunker, located beneath the garden of the Reich Chancellery. According to Masur, a German Jew forced to flee Germany before the war, 'Himmler was elegantly dressed, in a beautifully cut uniform, wearing all his medals and the insignia of his rank. He looked well-kempt, and appeared fresh and wide awake despite the lateness of the hour. He was outwardly calm and controlled.'

It was the first time Himmler had met a Jew on equal terms. Almost immediately he launched into an apologia for the Holocaust, which lasted forty-five minutes. He told Masur that the emigration policy he had devised in the late 1930s, which 'could have been very advantageous to the Jews', had been sabotaged by other nations who would not receive them. 'Then the war,' he continued, 'brought us in contact with the proletarianised Jewish masses of the Eastern countries, thereby creating new problems. We could not suffer such an enemy in our rear. The Jewish masses were infected with terrible epidemics; in particular, spotted typhus raged. I myself have lost thousands of my best SS men through these epidemics. Moreover, the Jews helped the partisans.'

To Masur's question, 'How could the Jews help the partisans when the Germans had concentrated them all in large ghettos?' Himmler replied: 'They conveyed intelligence to the partisans. Moreover, they shot at our troops in the ghetto. In order to put a stop to the epidemics, we were forced to burn the bodies of incalculable numbers of people who had been destroyed by disease. We were therefore forced to build crematoria, and on this account they are knotting a noose for us.' He then complained bitterly of the 'false' atrocity propaganda that the Allies were making out of conditions at Belsen and Buchenwald, which had just been liberated by the Americans. 'Nobody has had so much mud slung at him in the last ten years as I have. Even in Germany any man can say about me what he pleases. Newspapers abroad have started a campaign against me which is no encouragement to me to continue handing over the camps.'

Masur asked Himmler for the following assurances: that no more Jews would be killed and that the remaining Jews should be kept in the camps and under no circumstances evacuated. Himmler replied that he had already given these orders. On condition that their conversation remain absolutely secret, he agreed to the release of more prisoners and repeated his pledge not to evacuate the camps – a promise that, unsurprisingly, he would not honour.

The meeting ended at four-thirty in the morning and Himmler drove straight to Hohenlychen, an SS sanatorium, 30 miles further north, where he had agreed to have breakfast with Count Bernadotte. He repeated the assurances he had made to Masur and, in addition, offered to release 'women of all nationalities' from Ravensbrück.

Three days later – on 23 April – certain that he had done enough to convince the Allies that he was a credible negotiating partner, Himmler arranged a fourth meeting with Bernadotte, which was scheduled to take place at the Swedish Consulate in Lübeck at 23:00 hours. A severe air raid meant the two men were forced to take shelter in the consulate cellar and it was only at midnight – and by candlelight – that the meeting began.

Within hours, the conversation would be flashed in a series of top-secret reports to London, Moscow and Washington. The US Ambassador to Sweden summarized its content in a telegram to the US State Department:

(1) COUNT BERNADOTTE MET HIMMLER AT LÜBECK AT 1 O'CLOCK [SIC] THE MORNING OF APRIL 24, AT HIMMLER'S REQUEST.

(2) HIMMLER SAID THAT HITLER WAS SO ILL HE MIGHT ALREADY BE DEAD AND COULD NOT LIVE MORE THAN TWO DAYS (GENERAL SCHELLENBERG, HIMMLER'S CONFIDENTIAL STAFF OFFICER, SAID HITLER WAS SUFFERING FROM A BRAIN HAEMORRHAGE, AND THAT HE, HIMMLER, WAS THEREFORE IN A POSITION OF FULL AUTHORITY).

(3) HIMMLER ASKED THE SWEDISH GOVERNMENT TO ARRANGE FOR HIM TO MEET EISENHOWER IN ORDER TO ARRANGE TO CAPITULATE ON THE WHOLE WESTERN FRONT (INCLUDING HOLLAND).

BERNADOTTE ASKED IF NORWAY AND DENMARK WERE INCLUDED
IN THE CAPITULATION. HIMMLER AGREED TO ORDER HIS TROOPS
IN NORWAY AND DENMARK TO SURRENDER TO AMERICAN,
BRITISH OR SWEDISH TROOPS.*

(4) HIMMLER SAID HE HOPED TO BE ABLE TO CONTINUE THE FIGHT
ON THE EASTERN FRONT AND STIPULATED THAT HIS OFFER WAS
FOR THE WESTERN ALLIES ONLY.

Himmler did not doubt that the Allies would accept his offer. After the meeting with Bernadotte, he drove back to the SS sanatorium at Hohenlychen, where he saw Hitler's architect Albert Speer and told him about his approach to Eisenhower. 'Himmler was still moving in a fantasy world,' Speer wrote in his memoirs. ' "Europe cannot manage without me in the future either," he said. "It will go on needing me as Minister of Police. After I've spent an hour with Eisenhower, he'll appreciate that fact. They'll soon realise that they're dependent on me – or they'll have a hopeless chaos on their hands." '

Not once in his many conversations with Bernadotte did Himmler mention the Prominenten. Nor do they crop up in the SS and Wehrmacht signal traffic intercepted by decoders at Bletchley Park or in communications between the Reichsführer and other high-ranking Nazi leaders, also intercepted.

It seems that Himmler's 137 special prisoners were a secret known only to himself and to the guards he entrusted with their safekeeping – a card he was keeping up his sleeve to play only when negotiations with Eisenhower began.

* According to a report submitted to Winston Churchill, Bernadotte told Himmler that he would not relay his offer to the Americans unless he agreed to this condition.

35

At Dachau, while Himmler carried on with his craven efforts to rebuild his reputation, Commandant Weiter ensured the Prominenten were 'comfortable' – and this in the midst of a camp where hundreds were dying daily from typhoid and where, in the preceding years under Weiter's command, thousands had died from illness or been murdered by the SS.

A large number of the male Prominenten were housed in the brothel. Of the same configuration as those at other concentration camps, it consisted of a large waiting hall off which were rows of rooms where the prostitutes had serviced their clients. Dusty tinsel and withered paper garlands, intended to brighten up the 'recreation salon', still hung from the ceiling and extra beds had been brought in for the prisoners. The different nationalities divided up the rooms, preferring each other's company. Much to the British POWs' amazement, so affronted were the Catholic bishops at being housed in a brothel, they insisted on 'ridding the building of all vestige of sin'. As Payne Best wrote, 'every nook and cranny was thoroughly scrubbed and purified with Holy Water' and 'one room sanctified for use as a chapel where Mass was celebrated daily'.

Opposite the brothel was the Kommandaturarrest. It held the group that had been moved from Schönberg a few days before the Sippenhäftlinge left; among them, the Thyssens, the Blums, General Falkenhausen, the Schuschniggs and Captain Payne Best. Initially, the accommodation struck Payne Best as luxurious; the rooms were spacious and light with smart parquet floors, and in the shared bathrooms there was hot water and lavatories that flushed. There was even a garden outside with deckchairs for sunbathing. Soon after he arrived, however, he learned from the gardener that the building had been used for executions. A former clown arrested by the Gestapo for cracking a joke at Goebbels' expense, he had been assigned the task of tidying the garden for the Prominenten by Weiter. When Payne Best met him, he was busy making a new flower bed beneath a wall: 'He pointed out thousands of pit marks on the wall and described to me how prisoners had been brought in through a narrow doorway, ordered to turn their faces to the wall, and had then been shot in the back of the neck. He said that digging up the beds he had removed a hundredweight of pistol bullets.'

Himmler had not kept his promise to halt executions and it was at this point that Payne Best learned that Georg Elser, a socialist who had almost succeeded in his attempt to assassinate Hitler in November 1939, had been executed in the garden that afternoon. The time bomb Elser planted at a rally, held in a beer hall in Munich to celebrate the anniversary of the 1923 Munich Putsch, had killed eight people and injured sixty-two others. The bomb had exploded on time, but Hitler and other high-ranking Nazis had escaped after leaving early. For Payne Best, the news of Elser's execution was ominous; he had been arrested at Venlo the day after the bomb attack and falsely accused of having engineered the assassination attempt on behalf of the British government.

Uncertain of their fate and oblivious to Himmler's manoeuvrings, the threat of execution preoccupied the prisoners. 'Sudden death was the order of the day; at any moment an order might come for some or all of us to be gassed, shot or hanged,' Payne Best recalled. General Delestraint was the second prisoner in the KA* building to be executed. A personal friend of Charles de Gaulle and a prominent figure in the French Resistance, Delestraint had commanded the *Armée Sècrete*, the 150,000-strong paramilitary unit that de Gaulle hoped would form the nucleus of a future French Army. One morning, an SS officer came in and picked the general out. He was then escorted through the camp to the crematorium, where he was summarily shot.

No one was sorry when, a few days later, another prisoner was executed. This was Dr Rascher, the former director of medical experiments at Dachau. Yet for Hugh Falconer, who was sharing a cell with the doctor, his execution was both unpleasant and traumatic.

* Kommandaturarrest.

Rascher, as Falconer described in his memoirs, was convinced he would be killed at Dachau – either to prevent his medical research becoming known to the Allies or because Himmler wanted to avenge the false claims he had made regarding women's ability to bear children at a late age. From the moment he arrived, he sat in the corner of the cell, facing the wall with his back to the door – 'a position from which he refused to budge'. Falconer was in the cell when the inevitable moment came:

At about half past twelve the midday meal arrived. In these cells there was a hatch about fifteen inches square in the door, which could be opened from the outside and through which food was passed. When our turn came I went to collect the bowls for Rascher who was still terrified of showing his face. As soon as I arrived, instead of passing the food, the SS man stooped down so that he could see my face. When he recognised me, he shouted:

'Not you, the other one.'

'That's all right,' I said, 'give it to me. The other one's not feeling very well.'

'No,' insisted the guard, 'you must each fetch your own.'

I had no alternative but to step aside and, with the greatest reluctance, Rascher went up to the door, approaching it from the side and trying to hide his face. As Rascher came up to the door, the guard fired two shots from his Luger into his stomach and the hatch was slammed shut.

The impact of the heavy bullets fired at so short a range threw Rascher several feet back across the cell and he lay spread-eagled on the floor. There was plainly nothing I could do for him . . . one of the bullets must have hit his spine for he never regained consciousness and died quite quickly. I think my diagnosis was probably correct for I spent some time searching the cell but I could only find one spent bullet.

I quite expected the guard to return with my lunch – for which I felt little desire – or, more probably, to liquidate the only witness to a cold-blooded murder but I was left undisturbed with the rather messy corpse until late in the afternoon.

With the exception of Himmler's enemy, Rascher, it was the arbitrariness of the executions that unnerved the prisoners; there appeared
to be no logic behind the SS electing to kill one man over another.
In this nerve-racking environment, they clung to the hope that the
Americans would rescue them.

Kurt Schuschnigg, imprisoned in the KA building, kept a diary
during this time. 'The Americans advance along the Danube and the
River Lech,' he wrote on 18 April. 'Occasionally we hear the artillery. The air attacks on Munich and its surroundings increase daily.
All of us are virtually sick with excitement. It can't be long now.
It can't be long. If only they don't evacuate the camp at the last
moment . . .'

But on 20 April he learned that the SS had evacuated a number
of the Prominenten the previous night. 'The wildest rumours
circulate . . . Nobody can tell us what is going to be done with those
of us who remain in Dachau. It is said that we, too, will be evacuated.
One rumour says that the International Red Cross is going to take
over the entire camp. That, of course, would be ideal, but I have
learned my lesson about rejoicing too soon and I refuse to believe it.'

His next entry – on 22 April – consisted of just three words. 'We
are waiting.'

Payne Best, who had been moved from the KA building to the
brothel, was also on tenterhooks. Rohde, via his radio equipment,
had made contact with men who were prepared to take a message
across the lines to the American forces on the Danube, and Payne Best
had heard that one of them had 'almost certainly succeeded in getting
through'.

The next morning – 24 April – air activity over the camp increased
and Payne Best reported seeing a number of US planes apparently
engaged on reconnaissance. 'We all got highly excited hoping for a
speedy delivery,' he wrote in his diary.

These hopes would be dashed.

Some 430 miles to the north of the camp, Himmler had arrived back
at Hohenlychen at 4.30 a.m. after his final meeting with Count
Bernadotte. At twelve-thirty, his adjutant, General Schellenberg,

found him still in bed. He looked 'the picture of misery and said that he felt ill'.

From 17 to 24 April, shuttling between Berlin and the north of Germany, Himmler's uncertainty as to whether the count would agree to convey his offer of surrender to Eisenhower meant that he had left the majority of the Prominenten at Dachau. Only a handful of the prisoners had been moved on to the Alps. Confident now that Eisenhower would negotiate, at some point that morning he gave orders for the remaining prisoners to be moved to a secure location in the Tyrol. There, high in the mountains, they would be 'safe' until the negotiations with Eisenhower could begin.

Payne Best and the other prisoners spent that morning crowded around the windows of the brothel, watching the US planes flying over the camp. Then, shortly before midday, an SS guard came in to warn them they would be leaving at five o'clock that afternoon. Incredulous and despairing, they began to gather their things. But at around three-thirty, their hopes were raised again. 'Just as we had finished packing,' Payne Best wrote, 'we saw about half a dozen US fighter planes dancing over the camp and obviously firing on some ground target. Garibaldi, who knew the layout of the camp, said that they were firing at the transport park, and a little later we got word that five buses, which were ready to take us on our journey, had been shot up and that we should not move that day. We were to be ready at five o'clock on the next day. Our hopes rose to fever point and I really began to believe that Rohde's man had been able to get a message through and that steps were now being taken to prevent our removal.

'When the next afternoon came,' Payne Best continued, 'we all clustered round the window from which the transport park could be seen, waiting for our friends the fighter planes. Time went on, three, four and five o'clock. We were told to take our luggage out to the trucks . . . at last, there was a renewed sound of low-flying planes and of firing. Back into our building and to the window. Six or ten planes diving at the transport park and apparently firing with their guns as well as machine guns . . . Three of five buses set on fire and thirteen casualties was what we heard. No move apparently that day either, and we all did a sort of dance, jigging from one foot to the other.'

An hour later, however, Payne Best's group left Dachau. Three buses had been destroyed but the SS had brought in three lorries from Munich to replace them.

On the other side of the perimeter fence, many hundreds of yards from the camp, the Sippenhäftlinge were not privy to Rohde's intelligence. Nor, in that last week of April, did they know that the other Prominenten were being moved. Imprisoned in the SS hospital, a large, elegant villa on the Avenue of the SS, they were sharing a wing with the wives of men who had rounded up and overseen the detention of countless thousands of inmates at concentration camps like Dachau.

Refugees now, the women were using the hospital as a staging post on their way south to escape from the Allies. Isa was astounded by the way they responded to their situation: 'Around 10 to 15 wives of senior SS leaders from Oranienburg and other concentration camps sat there with innumerable children and mountains of luggage – "Ah, this is only hand luggage. You know, our large stuff has all been lost. I had so much real coffee among those things and all the lovely silver. You know, my husband, the Obergruppenführer etc. etc." Eager to prove themselves clever and resourceful wives to their SS husbands, they busied themselves with last-minute preparations for a comfortable continuation of their journey. They genuinely believed they could avoid the horror of retribution or whatever else fate had in store for them. They all said they would be meeting their husbands the following day – "At the latest" – and claimed to be certain that such and such a piece of luggage would turn up. But when you asked them where they thought they were heading, this was greeted with a brazen shrug of the shoulders: "Ah, somewhere" and "We'll get through all right" and "They won't do anything to women and children, after all we can't help it." '

Streams of SS personnel and their families passed through the hospital complex, seeking refuge. One morning, Isa and Fey spotted Fräulein Rafforth, the warder from Buchenwald. She was on the run after fleeing from the camp shortly before the Americans arrived. 'Rafforth was in cracking form and as vulgar as ever, and fatter still than she was at Buchenwald,' Isa wrote. 'She told us how Fräulein Knocke had gone over to the Western Front under cover of darkness. She had stayed behind with other SS personnel from Sonderbau 15, and she regaled us with stories of "delightful" days in the empty barrack, with no work to do and filled with nothing other than eating and sleeping. Her description of what they managed to fit into those few days, in terms of the amount of alcohol, chocolate and cigarettes they had consumed, was quite staggering. It was all stuff they had raided from the SS canteen.'

Fey described how Rafforth also told them about the evacuation of Buchenwald as the American tanks approached. 'Just before the end, about a thousand prisoners had been packed into twenty cattle wagons, with food and provisions for three or four days. But the journey from Buchenwald had taken two weeks, and the wagons arrived at Dachau filled with the dead and dying. I was horrified to hear that so many innocent people, like these poor prisoners, were still dying uselessly. What was the point of this monstrous sadism? Everything was on the brink of collapse.'

Security was lax at the hospital and Fey and the others were allowed to move about freely. 'In order to get away from the SS families, we spent most of our time in the hospital garden, which was spacious and beautifully tended. Our guards only appeared sporadically and were so visibly engrossed in their own concerns, we had little contact with them.'

All the guards were listening to Allied radio stations, which were reporting the capture of one German city after another. In Berlin, the Russians had reached the outskirts of the city and were shelling government buildings in Leipziger Strasse and along Unter den Linden. German radio countered that, in the coming days, the capital now faced 'its hardest test' and blamed the fact that the Russians had 'penetrated so deeply' on 'German traitors' who had guided the Red Army in: 'Many have been unmasked and given short shrift, each on discovery being hanged from a lamppost or suitable doorway.'

While the Prominenten over in the main camp believed they were within days of being liberated by the Americans, the Sippenhäftlinge were under no such illusion. In the space of five months the SS had moved them seven times; from the Hindenburg Baude to Stutthof; then to Matzkau, Buchenwald, Lauenburg, Regensburg, Schönberg and Dachau. Always, the moves came at the eleventh hour. It seemed inconceivable that, with Germany collapsing all around them, the SS would spring them from the camp; but time after time it had happened before and they did not doubt that it would happen again.

Uppermost in Fey's mind were two concerns. The first was that, in the unlikely event they were still at Dachau when the Americans arrived, they would be lumped in with the SS families. Daily, German radio was reporting the shooting of captured SS troops by Allied soldiers who, enraged by the atrocities they had discovered, had not stopped to ask questions. Her second concern – and the most immediate – was that they risked being killed by an American bomb.

Day and night, the air-raid sirens wailed. The Americans were dropping hundreds of tons of explosives on Munich, which was just 10 miles to the south of Dachau. Such was the ferocity of the assault, the sensation, Fey wrote, was like being on a ship in a very rough sea.

At night, when the siren sounded, the guards tried to move the group to a shelter in the nearby SS training school. To begin with, many of them did not want to go. 'The training school was a far more likely target than the hospital, which had an International Red Cross symbol painted on its roof,' Fey recalled. 'Whenever the guards came to get us, we hid under the beds or in cupboards. We continued to play this cat and mouse game until they gave up trying and simply took those of us willing to go. I could not be bothered to get up, get dressed, and move to another place where there was at least an equal chance of being obliterated.'

On 24 April, the night the US fighter planes attacked the SS transport park, Fey ignored the air-raid warning as usual. 'Everyone left hurriedly for the shelter, even the stalwart Maria von Hammerstein, who usually stayed behind with me. Suddenly, the bombing began and I found myself alone in the middle of that pounding, shaking building. Perhaps it was the solitude, perhaps the noise and the flashing, but I panicked, convinced that the next second would be my last. I jumped out of bed, grabbed my clothes, and dressed in about ten seconds. Still pulling up my trousers and with shoes unlaced, I ran outside as fast as I could. At the entrance to the building, I was almost blown off my feet. The courtyard was filled with an eerie orange light from the phosphorous flares the bombers used to illuminate the target. I dashed toward the training school, scared out of my wits. Finally, to my relief, I plunged in through the open doors. Stopping in the hall to regain my composure, I went downstairs to sit with the others. One of the guards smiled cynically. I just looked at the floor, trying to stop shaking.'

Fey – as she admitted – was completely exhausted, her nerves shattered. 'There was no doubt the war was coming to an end, but the destruction, the chaos, the senseless loss of yet more lives, made me even more fearful for my children. Germany had become one big bombing target; cities were in flames, and even the countryside was ripped up and overrun by British and American tanks . . . All I could think about was where, in all this, were Corradino and Robertino? I felt so helpless and trapped I could hardly stand it.'

And still it wasn't over. At nine o'clock on the morning of 26 April – forty-eight hours before the Americans liberated the camp – the order came to pack.

The inevitable delay followed, and it was almost dusk when the Sippenhäftlinge left the hospital – this time on foot.

Thirty-seven in number, they were led by the guards back along the Avenue of the SS, past the grand villas with their immaculately kept lawns, to the entrance of the main camp. Due to the bomb damage on the perimeter road, they were told they would have to walk through the camp to the railway station, where a fleet of buses waited to transport them south. The guards refused to disclose their destination – 'It's a journey into the blue,' one taunted.

It was a thirty-minute walk to the station, past rows and rows of seemingly empty barracks. Enclosed by barbed-wire fences, with scrubby compounds in front, later Fey learned they were full of sick and dying prisoners – some 42,500 in total – who were too weak to be evacuated from the camp.

Himmler had not kept his promise to halt the evacuations from concentration camps. At Dachau, they had been in progress for three days. Some 5,000 prisoners had left by train on 24 and 25 April; 7,000 more were due to leave on foot that evening. Destined for the Tyrol, one of the last remaining territories of the Reich still controlled by the Nazis, they were to be deployed in armaments factories that had been built in bunkers under the Alps.

As the Sippenhäftlinge approached the parade ground, they caught up with the inmates who were leaving that evening. Fey was almost knocked off her feet in the crush: 'There were thousands and thousands of them. The whole camp seemed to be on the march, streaming from all corners to the parade ground . . . Shoulder-to-shoulder, they moved slowly towards the exit in complete silence.'

Bludgeoning their way through the prisoners, the guards led the Sippenhäftlinge to another floodlit parade ground, which had been ringed off. Frenetic activity ruled in this open space: SS men of every rank ran back and forth; motorcycles arrived and left; lorries moved at speed. US fighter planes buzzed low over the camp, watching the proceedings. The SS carried on blithely, safe in the knowledge that the presence of thousands of prisoners prevented the planes from shooting.

Three trucks stood parked in a corner of the square. As the Sippenhäftlinge waited to board, a low murmur rippled through the inmates, massed on the other side of the troops. Kurt Schuschnigg, together with his wife and daughter, was being escorted from the K A building. The camp held a large number of Austrians – both Jews, and non-Jews imprisoned for resisting the Nazis. Some recognized their former chancellor. 'Our departure was dramatic,' Schuschnigg wrote. 'A narrow aisle was kept open by the guards, through which we were to go. Suddenly, as we passed, a worn-out hand stretched out from the mass. Here someone called, there a familiar face smiled tiredly. At first only a few, then more and more, hundreds, thousands even . . . Hands were raised in salute – some of them in the Hitler salute by force of habit, others with the closed fist . . . It was perhaps the most impressive moment of all these years.'

The last to arrive at Dachau and the last to leave, the Sippenhäftlinge were being transported with two other groups of special prisoners: the 'Seydlitz group' – relatives of Wehrmacht soldiers now fighting for the Red Army on the Eastern Front; and the politicians, Kurt Schuschnigg and Léon Blum. After boarding the trucks, they waited for several hours. Their convoy could not leave until the columns of inmates, passing through a nearby gate to begin the forced march to the Alps, left the camp. 'The sight of the evacuation,' Léon Blum wrote in his memoirs, 'is the most appalling thing that I can ever remember . . . The prisoners were pushed along the roads with blows from rubber truncheons and the ones who couldn't go any further were shot on the spot.' Fey also had a view of the entrance: 'Thin and worn out, column after column passed in front of us. They were not carrying any clothes or belongings with them; instead there were one or two overloaded carts, which groups of prisoners, their backs bent double, were trying to push. Some were too weak to walk any distance, and I could see several of them on their hands and knees. The guards would go over and shout at them, poking them with their rifles. If they couldn't get up, they were shot through the back of the neck. As I watched, helpless, from the truck, it was all I could do not to be sick. What was the murdering SS intending to do with these poor, stumbling people? How they could be capable of such cruelty was incomprehensible. After hours of this agony, our trucks moved forward. On the road outside, we passed by these columns terrified and with hearts full of pity for these poor people.'*

Skirting Munich, the convoy of trucks headed south towards Austria. The drivers drove fast, anxious to reach their destination before daylight. 'The fact that we were being driven at such high speed heightened our frayed nerves,' Isa wrote. 'We felt the pull of leaving the Western Front further and further behind. To resign oneself to the evident senselessness of this journey was an act of real courage and we had to exercise a great deal of self-control in order not to drag

* Of the 7,000 prisoners who left Dachau that night, over 1,000 died on the march to the Alps. In what was to be the last week of the war, SS guards shot those unable to maintain a steady pace. Others died from physical exhaustion or starvation.

each other down into the vortex of despair and frustration we were all feeling.'

They crossed into Austria over the Scharnitz Pass and, by dawn, they were in a deep valley, flanked by snow-capped mountains, the summits tinged pink from the first streaks of sunlight. The convoy made two short stops in the hours that followed. At the first, the trucks drew up alongside a bread van, which the SS had miraculously coordinated to meet them on an isolated stretch of road. The tarpaulins on the trucks had not been properly fastened and the prisoners were able to help themselves to as much bread as they liked from the open-backed van. The second stop was unscheduled. US fighter planes were patrolling the valley, and the drivers were forced to turn off the road, down a forest track, to shelter under trees to avoid being attacked.

Shortly before ten o'clock, the convoy drew up outside Reichenau, an SS-run labour camp on the outskirts of Innsbruck. The guards ordered the prisoners out of the trucks. Behind a barbed-wire fence, in the courtyard in front of a block of low, wooden huts, they could see scores of men sitting in deckchairs and milling about, chatting in groups. These were the Prominenten transferred from Dachau on 20 and 25 April.

Some of their faces were familiar to the Sippenhäftlinge from Schönberg, where they had been imprisoned together in the two village schools. Isa described their delight at seeing each other again: 'We fell into each other's arms in a wave of genuine sympathy and shared suffering. At that moment, it felt as if our entire war had come to a happy end.' Fey was equally overcome: 'It was like a surprise birthday party filled with long-lost friends! Immediately, we all began chatting, exchanging stories of what had happened. People mingled freely, moving from one group to the next, calling each other by their names (something they had previously been forbidden to do). There were about 130 prisoners there of all nationalities. It really was a remarkable sight. There were bishops in magnificent red robes, royal princes, dressed in striped prison uniforms, and Italian partisan leaders, strutting about like peacocks. With conversations going on in every European language imaginable, the place was a true Tower of Babel!'

The prisoners outnumbered the SS by five to one and the guards left them alone, retreating to a barrack in the middle of the camp. The weather was gloriously sunny and the mountain landscape spectacular. In this heady atmosphere, chairs were drawn up, cups of tea made and cigarettes handed around. Isa was particularly happy as, in the melee, she met Flight Lieutenant Sydney Dowse. A veteran of four attempted breakouts, including the infamous Great Escape from Stalag Luft III, Dowse had been imprisoned at Sachsenhausen in a cell near her parents.* She had not heard from them since their arrest in the winter of 1943, and it was a great comfort to hear what Dowse had to tell her: 'My mother, so he told me, spent the greater part of her daily walk allowance under his window, and the conversations with her had been the single most longingly awaited moments of his day. In turn, he would always find time during his walks to throw something up to the window of my parents' cell – a flower, a few cigarettes or a few biscuits. At Christmas, they had traced greetings for each other in the snow.'

The different encounters were an emotional experience for all the prisoners. For Payne Best, though, imprisoned since 1939, his conversations with the British POWs were uncomfortable. 'It was the first time in nearly five and a half years that I had been able to talk freely to men of my own nationality, men too, who by virtue of their indomitable courage and refusal to accept defeat, were the heroes of all their fellow prisoners. They were all extraordinarily nice and kind to me but in my heart I felt very much ashamed that, whilst they had broken out of prison time and time again, I had done nothing but sit in my cell leading the well-fed life of a prize poodle.'

Confronted with so many prisoners, each with their own grapevine, Fey hoped for information relating to the boys. 'During that afternoon I eagerly sought out people who I thought could tell me about children still being held by the SS. But no one knew anything, only that some were being held in SS "institutes" or had had their names changed and may have been given over for adoption. Though

---

* Like Isa, Kurt and Petra Vermehren were arrested after their son, Dr Erich Vermehren, joined the BBC to broadcast anti-Nazi propaganda.

anxious for information, I finally dropped the subject when I saw I
was getting nowhere. The fact was that no one really wanted to be
bothered with problems that were not immediate, about which nothing could be done. Death and destruction were everywhere, and the
main thing was to survive and get free. I must admit that, in the
circumstances, even I was able to set my worry about the children
aside – at least temporarily.'

Most of the prisoners thought that it was all over, that they might
be held at Reichenau for another day or two and then released. Payne
Best, however, was sceptical. 'There was one thing I did not like at
all, and that was that I had seen Lieutenant Bader and a considerable
number of his SS men in the camp. If it was the intention to permit
our liberation, why had Bader and his men, whose function was the
liquidation of unwanted prisoners, been sent with us?'

While Fey did not imagine that they were about to be killed, she
shared Payne Best's scepticism for different reasons: 'It was clear that
we were hostages not prisoners. From the outset the SS had gone to
extraordinary lengths to keep us alive. Why, after carting us from
camp to camp, would they suddenly let us go?'

At Supreme Headquarters in Rheinsberg, where Himmler was that
day – 27 April – he was still waiting for a reply from the Western
Allies.

His offer to meet General Eisenhower to arrange the capitulation
of German forces on the Western Front had been flashed to President
Truman and Winston Churchill on 25 April.

That afternoon, Churchill's War Cabinet met in Whitehall. As the
minutes of the meeting reveal, Churchill suspected that Himmler's
reluctance to surrender on the Eastern Front was a move to drive a
wedge between Britain, the US and the Soviet Union: 'The Prime
Minister said that this important development must clearly be communicated to Marshal Stalin without delay. He thought that we should
at the same time make it clear that, so far as His Majesty's Government
were concerned, there could be no question of anything less than
unconditional surrender simultaneously to the three Major Powers.
Himmler should be told that German soldiers should everywhere

surrender themselves, either as individuals or in units, to the Allied troops or representatives on the spot; and until this happens the Allies' attack upon them in all theatres would be pursued with the utmost vigour.

'There was no occasion,' the summary of the meeting continued, 'for Himmler to meet General Eisenhower, as he had suggested: indeed, it would be inappropriate that such a proposal for a general surrender should be discussed with the military Commander in the field.'

The moment Himmler's offer was brought to their attention, both Truman and Churchill dismissed it out of hand. Yet for reasons that are not clear – possibly because of their disdain for the man they regarded as the second-most brutal war criminal after Hitler – by the morning of 27 April, neither the US president nor the British prime minister had yet replied to Himmler.

Still confident, however, that Eisenhower would negotiate, that afternoon Himmler issued orders for the Prominenten to be moved to a hotel in the Tyrol.

At Reichenau, at around three o'clock, Payne Best noticed a change in the guards' behaviour. Emerging from the barrack, where they had been closeted for most of the day, they now stood, conferring in groups, at the entrance to the camp. From their conspiratorial stance and the way they kept turning to look over their shoulders at the prisoners, Payne Best sensed something was afoot.

Seeing Stiller, one of the SS officers, on his own, he went over to him. He was on reasonable terms with the young lieutenant, who he judged to be more malleable than the other guards. 'Button-holing him, I managed to get from him an admission that we were moving again that night to the Italian Tyrol. He said that he was taking us to a hotel where we would await the arrival of our troops, and that his orders were to see that our liberation should be effected in an orderly manner. He was, as always, very friendly and polite.'

Lieutenant Stiller was less polite when he spoke to Isa Vermehren. 'His orders,' she wrote, 'were to take us away, to hide us, to bring us to where the enemy wouldn't find us.'

These orders were to change overnight.

*

As the SS loaded the prisoners on to the convoy of buses waiting outside the camp, Count Bernadotte was with General Schellenberg, Himmler's adjutant, who had flown to Sweden to discuss the contents of the telegram that had arrived from President Truman rejecting Himmler's offer:

A GERMAN OFFER OF SURRENDER WILL ONLY BE ACCEPTED ON CONDITION THAT IT IS COMPLETE ON ALL FRONTS AS REGARDS GREAT BRITAIN, THE SOVIET UNION AS WELL AS USA. WHEN THESE CONDITIONS HAVE BEEN FULFILLED, THE GERMAN FORCES MUST IMMEDIATELY ON ALL FRONTS LAY DOWN THEIR ARMS TO THE LOCAL ALLIED COMMANDERS. SHOULD RESISTANCE CONTINUE ANYWHERE, THE ALLIED ATTACKS WILL BE RUTHLESSLY CARRIED ON UNTIL COMPLETE VICTORY HAS BEEN GAINED.

Schellenberg, the bearer of this bad news, was terrified of relaying it to Himmler. He waited until midnight before telephoning his headquarters: 'I was only able to speak to [Rudolf] Brandt [chief of Himmler's personal staff], who asked very excitedly what the results were. I said that they had been negative, but the Count wanted to meet Himmler in Lübeck to discuss the question of the German armies in the Scandinavian area. This proposal was sharply rejected; I was to report to Himmler alone.

'I realised that my position with Himmler would now be so difficult that I should have to face the fact that I might be liquidated,' Schellenberg continued. 'I therefore arranged for an astrologer from Hamburg to accompany me. Himmler knew this man personally, and thought very highly of him. He could never resist having his horoscope read, and I felt that this would soften his reaction to the disappointment.'

In the event, when Schellenberg met him the following morning, Himmler already knew that Truman had turned down his offer. Recognizing that the approach had been made behind Hitler's back, the Allies – in the hope of fracturing the relationship between the Führer and his SS chief – had leaked it to Reuters, the international news agency. By dawn on the morning of 28 April, it was dominating newspaper headlines and radio bulletins around the world.

Exactly when Himmler learned that Truman had rejected his offer – whether Brandt told him or whether he was listening to the radio in the dead of that night – it is impossible to know. Nor is there a first-hand account of his reaction to the news. But for the Prominenten, the consequences were catastrophic. Now that there was no opportunity to use them as bargaining chips in possible negotiations with General Eisenhower, their lives were worthless.

At some point between midnight and nine o'clock on the morning of 28 April, Himmler ordered Lieutenant Bader to liquidate all 137 of the prisoners.

Yet Schellenberg's delay, principally to save his own skin, had given them a stay of execution. Had Himmler learned of Truman's decision while they were still at Reichenau, they probably would have been killed then and there. As it was, by the time he heard, they had already left the camp and were on their way to the hotel in the Tyrol.

36

The convoy of seven buses, carrying 137 prisoners and fifty SS and Gestapo guards, had left Innsbruck just after sunset. The mountains were silhouetted against the darkening sky as they drove up through the Wipp Valley to the Brenner Pass. The road, an old carriageway built in the eighteenth century, climbed steeply. Leaving the spring landscape of the Inn Valley behind, they could feel the temperature drop as the buses crawled round the sharp bends, climbing higher and higher towards the snow line.

Unwitting of the true purpose of the journey, Fey stared blankly out of the window. She had come full circle; it was six months since she had left Innsbruck without the children. The memory of that day, which she had tried so hard to shut out of her mind, was made the more vivid by the passing landscape. Looking across the valley, seeing the mountains she had seen from the train on the journey east, reminded her of how she had felt then.

Hundreds of Italians lined the route, slowing the convoy's progress. Deported to Germany after the Nazis occupied Italy in 1943, they had walked from concentration camps and labour camps that had been liberated by the Allies and were following the mountain road home. Some were pushing carts; others were driving a few cattle, pigs or donkeys. 'We didn't need to feel sorry for them,' SOE officer Peter Churchill noted grimly. 'They were going in the right direction.'

It took three hours, grinding up the old carriage road, to reach the Brenner Pass, which marked the border between Austria and Italy. Here, at the frontier post, the drivers stopped the buses to allow the engines to cool, and the SS got off and disappeared into the ruins of a concrete blockhouse.

There was a full moon and the prisoners could make out tides of rubble and the gaping shell of a bombed-out chapel. All the mountain passes through the Alps were being bombed by the Allies to prevent any large-scale movements of troops and munitions to the Southern Redoubt and, as Falconer described, the prisoners' overriding fear was that they would be killed by a British or American bomb. 'We all got out and stood around . . . We could hear the almost incessant bursting of bombs and rattle of machine guns and shellfire coming from the southern side of the pass. Germans moving north told us that traffic was under constant attack from bombers and low-flying aircraft.'

Though it was the dead of night and the snow thick on the ground, the oncoming traffic was heavy. On the other side of the Alps, in a line stretching across the north of Italy from Genoa to Trieste, the Wehrmacht was fighting a rear-guard action against the Allies. Within four days, the German Army in Italy would surrender and, already, soldiers were fleeing across the Brenner to avoid being taken prisoner. 'Germans in Italy who could raise a car and the necessary petrol were trying desperately to get back to Germany with the intention of submerging into the civilian population,' Falconer wrote. 'There were lots of superior-looking staff cars, usually filled with five or six very young officers.'

After a few hours, the SS reappeared and the convoy set off again. 'The main preoccupation for us all,' Fey recalled, 'was where were we going? Did the SS even know where we were going? We could see the motorcycle outrider at the head of the convoy. We watched him weaving through the traffic; sometimes he disappeared, accelerating ahead to reconnoitre. Then he would return, stopping the convoy at a crossroads or a turning, where Bader and his sidekick, Lieutenant Stiller, would join him. Much shrugging of shoulders and shaking of heads followed.' Isa's verdict was that the SS had no idea of their destination and were making it up as they went along. British POW 'Jimmy' James thought Bader's indecision was due to the fact that he 'had lost touch with his headquarters'.

But Bader knew exactly where he was taking them. The numerous discussions with the motorcycle outrider were due to the difficulty in pinpointing the hotel's remote location.

'His orders were to take us away, to hide us, to bring us to where the enemy wouldn't find us,' Isa was told by Lieutenant Stiller before leaving Reichenau. If ever a place fitted these requirements, it was the Hotel Pragser Wildsee – Bader's destination. Situated deep in the Pustertal (Puster Valley), it stood at the end of a 5-mile no-through road overlooking a small lake. Mountains walled the hotel in on all sides, the sheer rock rising from the lake to the summits – a Cretaceous fortress of sharp points, broken crests and jagged angles.

A perfect hiding place, the Hotel Pragser Wildsee was also the perfect site for a mass execution. Earmarked until the previous evening as a hideout where the Prominenten were to be held while Himmler negotiated with General Eisenhower, now the 180-room hotel was to be Bader's killing ground.

As the convoy left the Brenner Pass, turning on to the SS 49 – the main road, running in an easterly direction through the Pustertal – the prisoners, still unaware of Bader's orders, continued to speculate about their destination. Fey was sitting next to Uncle Moppel: 'He was convinced that the SS were taking us to Bolzano, a provincial capital in South Tyrol where the Nazis were apparently preparing to make a last stand. It seemed a bitter irony if, having survived for so long, we should be killed in the last battle of the war.'

The British POWs were also convinced that Hitler's famous Alpine Redoubt was the most likely destination and, as the convoy progressed along the valley, Falconer was relieved that the Wehrmacht's defences were unmanned: 'As soon as we entered the Pustertal, we could see that it had been prepared to withstand a siege. There were tank traps across the valley; pillboxes had been built at strategic points and the mouths of each of the side valleys were similarly defended. But there was no sign of any garrison, SS or otherwise, manning these defences.'

Then, on an open stretch of road between Monguelfo-Tesido and Villabassa, the convoy came to a stop. Turning off to the right, the buses pulled up in a lay-by. On one side, fields, dotted with pretty chalet-style farmhouses, sloped up to conifer woods; on the other, the forest came down to the road and was separated only by a railway track. Some 1,200 feet above, the peaks of the mountains edged the valley.

Bader ordered the SS to form a security cordon around the convoy, and the guards, armed with machine guns, drifted down the road and took up positions at intervals of about 10 yards. Then Bader and Stiller got out.

Fey could see them from where she was sitting: 'I couldn't hear what they were saying, but they seemed to be arguing. At a certain point, they must have reached a decision since Bader suddenly turned and walked off, leaving Stiller with us.'

The convoy had pulled up just short of a busy crossroads. The signpost pointing in one direction – 'Pragser Wildsee 8 km' – was of no significance to Fey and the other 136 prisoners. But the reason for the stop – and the argument between Bader and Stiller – was that the Hotel Pragser Wildsee was full. The day before, despite the fact that Franz Hofer, the Nazi Gauleiter of the Tyrol and Vorarlberg, had assigned the building to Bader's unit, three Wehrmacht generals and their staff had occupied it and the hotel was now overrun with soldiers.

It was another stroke of luck for the Prominenten. Just as Schellenberg's failure to communicate the content of President Truman's telegram to Himmler before the move from Reichenau had brought a stay of execution, so the Wehrmacht's occupation of the Hotel Pragser Wildsee prevented Lieutenant Bader from transporting the prisoners to the place where he intended to kill them.

Without that destination, Bader was about to lose control.

No sooner had he set off to contact SS headquarters than two of the prisoners demanded to be let off the bus immediately. They were Colonel von Bonin, a Wehrmacht officer arrested for ordering his troops to retreat during the Soviet winter offensive, and Wilhelm Flügge, a German aerospace engineer considered 'politically unreliable'. Fey was not aware at the time but, as she later described, the two men now had wind of Bader's plans to liquidate the group: 'During the journey over the mountains, Bonin and Flügge, who were sitting at the front behind two SS Sergeants, overheard a conversation between them. Assuming the prisoners were asleep, after a quick glance round, they began discussing the plans to execute us. In fact, Bonin and Flügge were only feigning sleep, and so heard these words:

"When are they going to be executed?" Although neither of the two could make out the rest of the conversation, they had heard enough to realise that something had to be done urgently.'

The spire of a church rose from the village of Villabassa, which was about a mile away from the crossroads. Bader was walking in that direction and, waiting until he had rounded a bend in the road, Bonin and Flügge followed him. To their surprise, neither Stiller nor the other guards stopped them. Other prisoners, recognizing that the SS seemed indifferent, were stepping cautiously from the buses. As Bonin and Flügge walked past, they quickly relayed the conversation they had overheard. They also told the men to keep it to themselves for fear of spreading panic.

Their concern meant that Fey, together with other women and children, would spend the greater part of the next thirty-six hours waiting in the lay-by, all of them unaware their lives were hanging in the balance.

In Bader's absence, the male prisoners were able to scatter. Some, including British POW Jack Churchill, opted to save themselves and disappeared. But the majority selflessly elected to stay in order to protect the vulnerable members of the group. In the search to find a fast means of rescue or escape, five men quickly emerged as leaders. They were Italian partisan Sante Garibaldi; British POW 'Wings' Day; General Georg Thomas, implicated in Operation Valkyrie; and Colonel Bonin and Payne Best.

A number of significant, though separate, initiatives were set in train that morning.

The first was a rescue plan, devised by Garibaldi and 'Wings' Day. Exploiting Bader's absence, they struck out in the opposite direction to Flügge and Bonin. The convoy had stopped near a level crossing and, by chance, they discovered that the crossing keeper was a sergeant in the South Tyrol Resistance; further, in the forest, a few hundred yards from where the buses were parked, there was a force of 1,000 partisans who could attack the convoy immediately and liberate the prisoners if called upon to do so.

But after the attack, would there be any prisoners left alive to liberate? With the SS guards ringed around the exposed convoy, and the large numbers of women, children and elderly in the group, 'Wings' Day and Garibaldi decided that an immediate daylight attack was too risky. Instead, they agreed that the ambush would take place the following night, once they had had the chance to work out how they could overpower the SS and give maximum protection to the prisoners when the partisans made their move.

While 'Wings' Day and Garibaldi were working out the details of the ambush in the crossing keeper's hut, Payne Best, who was with the convoy, was pursuing a different tack. Sensing that some of the guards seemed nervous and on edge, he decided to sound them out. 'I was by this time on pretty good terms with quite a number of our guards, including some of Bader's men who had been with us at Schönberg, and although they would have shot us if ordered to, they did not seem at all keen to begin – one or two to whom I talked seemed to think that it would not be a bad idea to make a start by shooting Stiller and Bader.' Payne Best also spoke to Stiller himself: 'He was quite obviously scared and inclined to favour our survival in the hope that we might put in a good word for him if he were cap-tured by our troops. He was senior in rank to Bader* and had thirty of his own men to Bader's twenty.'

By the murderous standards of the SS, the two units were of a very different calibre. Bader's squad, formed of fanatical Nazis, had been set up as a liquidation unit from the beginning, whereas Stiller's men were mostly ex-Wehrmacht soldiers, drafted into the SS after recov-ering from wounds. Payne Best had consulted a number in Stiller's unit and was of the view that none of them had 'the slightest wish to be involved in mass murder'. If Stiller himself could be bribed, he thought it would be possible to persuade the men to help the prison-ers escape.

After speaking to the guards, Payne Best sought out industrialist Fritz Thyssen and Hjalmar Schacht, previously Hitler's minister of economics. Both men were travelling in the Sippenhäftlinge's bus and, taking them aside, Payne Best persuaded the two to put up

---

* Stiller was a first lieutenant, Bader a second lieutenant.

100,000 Swiss francs as a reward for Stiller if he agreed to direct the convoy to the Swiss frontier and help the prisoners over the border. But Thyssen and Schacht were too frightened to put the offer to Stiller themselves, and Payne Best thought it too dangerous to approach the SS lieutenant with a proposal based on anonymous guarantors.

Into this tense situation, with the rain pouring down, came Anton Ducia. The convoy, now stationary for some hours and parked as it was by the side of the road, had drawn the attention of passing locals. 'Slowly, the first peasants approached,' Schuschnigg remembered. 'They kept a certain distance as the rather unfriendly SS guards did not encourage them to come nearer. But secretly they waved to us. Here and there a light of recognition went over their faces. Soon they knew what was going on.'

Schuschnigg was a well-known figure in this part of the Tyrol, which until the end of the First World War had belonged to Austria. Someone had recognized him and alerted Ducia. Ducia immediately left his office in the centre of Villabassa and walked the mile or so out to the convoy.

'A youngish alert-looking man', as British POW 'Jimmy' James described him, Ducia introduced himself to Lieutenant Stiller as the official billeting officer for the region, with the authority of Franz Hofer, the Nazi Gauleiter. What he did not tell him, however, was that he also happened to be the regional commander of the South Tyrol Resistance Movement. Producing his Nazi identity papers, he offered to arrange accommodation in Villabassa for the SS troops and the prisoners. While Stiller cautiously accepted him as an ally, Ducia was obliged to make two more journeys on foot to the village and back before Stiller agreed to a general move to Villabassa.

Trudging to and fro between the convoy and the village, Ducia was able to relay a message to Payne Best. He told him that he had managed to contact the US Army by clandestine radio and that he had asked them to mount an air rescue.

Meanwhile, Bonin, after walking into Villabassa, had gone to the post office, where he had tried to call General von Vietinghoff, an old friend and Wehrmacht contemporary. Vietinghoff was the Supreme

Commander of the German Army in Italy and his headquarters at Bolzano were close by. Bonin's idea was to ask the general to send a company of infantry to protect the prisoners from the SS. Unable to get through to him, Bonin spoke to General Roettiger, the chief of staff, whom he also knew. Roettiger agreed in principle but said he would have to clear it with Vietinghoff, who was not at headquarters. He promised to ask him as soon as he returned.

By the end of that day, the Prominenten were no closer to being rescued: Bonin had been unable to get through to his friend; Thyssen and Schacht lacked the courage to bribe Stiller; and the partisan ambush was not scheduled to take place until the following evening. Ducia's radio message to the US Army remained their best hope; but there was no airfield nearby and the chances of the Americans diverting much-needed ground troops to rescue prisoners, more than half of whom were German, were remote.

Conversely, Bader, in executing his order to liquidate the prisoners, was confronted with an impossible scenario. While most of the women and children remained on the buses, the others had drifted into Villabassa and were now scattered in bars and restaurants around the village. Logistically, until he could assemble them in one place, he had no means of killing them, other than picking them off one by one – an option he ruled out. At this late stage in the war, with so many witnesses, he risked compromising himself. Via informants, Bader had also learned of the coming partisan attack. The layout of the medieval village, with its web of back streets and narrow alleyways running off the main square, made it awkward to defend and – against a rumoured partisan force of over a thousand – it was obvious that his detachment of fifty SS would be overrun.

In these circumstances, early that evening, Bader opted to round up the POWs and the younger Wehrmacht officers. But, in a place that had altered little since the fifteenth century, even this was not straightforward. One of the few coaching stations in the Puster Valley, Villabassa had been an important commercial centre and its hub – the Piazza Santa Trinità – was lined with mansions that had formerly belonged to wealthy merchants. With their pretty pastel-coloured facades and gabled roofs, the advent of the tourist industry meant they were now hotels. The small rooms and the multiple entrances, some giving on to courtyards behind, made them unsuitable prisons.

The one secure building was the town hall, which overlooked the piazza. Formerly a customs house, the ground-floor windows were barred. After posting sentries throughout the building, Bader set up a makeshift headquarters in front of it – the SS supply trucks, grouped together in the centre of the square, incongruous in the picturesque setting.

It was clear to the military prisoners that Bader was purposely rounding up 'the troublemakers'. As 'Jimmy' James recalled, when word circulated that the SS intended to billet them in the town hall, 'Wings' Day considered bringing the partisan attack forward. 'An attack by the Partisans who could certainly have overpowered the SS by weight of numbers alone, perhaps with minimum loss of life, was preferable to sitting around waiting to be massacred by the Bader gang.' The German officers, favouring Bonin's plan, overruled this idea, creating tension in the group. Understandably, POWs captured by the Wehrmacht mistrusted the Germans, and found the idea of being involved in a call for help to their captors distasteful. 'We wanted the satisfaction of freeing ourselves without German help,' James wrote.

Fabian von Schlabrendorff, the Wehrmacht officer who in March 1943 had planted a bomb on Hitler's plane (the bomb subsequently failing to detonate), and had later been imprisoned with Ulrich von Hassell, was among the men the SS corralled towards the old customs house. 'We had to wait in the pouring rain before we were finally quartered in the town hall, where we slept on the stone floor. More than ever that night we had the feeling that the SS would find an opportunity to liquidate us and then try to make good their own escape. And so, before lying down to sleep we arranged to have several of us take turns standing guard through the night. It was not that we, unarmed as we were, could have done much against the heavily armed SS, but we did not want to be caught unawares and slaughtered in our sleep.'

British SOE officer Hugh Falconer worried about the unusually generous amount of straw they were allocated: 'We discussed how well the straw would burn and how effective such a fire would be if it happened to occur in the middle of the night when we were safely locked in. We were on the first floor of the building and it was a long drop to the ground. We decided to post a watch to give the alarm if necessary.'

Lying awake, not daring to sleep, all the men were conscious of their perilous situation. It was not clear who was planning to shoot whom. Would the SS shoot the prisoners? Would the soldiers shoot the SS – if and when they arrived? Or would the partisans shoot the SS and the soldiers and anyone else caught in the crossfire?

Some 50 yards away, in a back street behind the town hall, Payne Best was at the Hotel Bachmann, where he had been billeted with General Thomas and a number of other prisoners. He spent the evening drinking in the kitchen with the two SS guards. In the hope of extracting information, Payne Best plied them with alcohol and, by midnight, both men were 'glassy-eyed'. One was Sergeant Fritz, Bader's quartermaster. 'Fritz was by turns lachrymose and truculent, talking about his wife and innocent children or about how he would never be taken prisoner alive,' Payne Best recalled. 'He told me how his wife and children had no idea that he had killed hundreds, no thousands of people, and that war was a terrible thing, but that it was all the fault of the Jews and plutocrats in England and America. The Führer was a good man and only wanted peace, and so did the common people everywhere, but the Jews were a pest which destroyed everything in their path . . . Then he pulled a paper out of his pocket and said: "Here is the order for your execution; you won't be alive after tomorrow." '

Fritz told Payne Best that Bader was proposing to take the prisoners to a hotel in the mountains, where they would be shot. Afterwards, the hotel would be set on fire. In the brightly lit kitchen, in front of the proprietress, who was busy washing pots and pans, the SS officer drunkenly explained his objections to Bader's plan: ' "I don't like it at all. I know what shooting people with machine guns is like, half of them are not properly dead – the bullets are too small and you can't aim properly – so a lot of people won't be dead when the place is set on fire.

' "Herr Best, you are my friend," he continued. "I will tell you what we will do. I will give you a sign before they start shooting and you come and stand near me so that I can give you a shot in the back of the head . . . that is the best way to die – you won't know anything about it – I am a dead shot – never miss." '

Pulling out a gun, the sergeant went on to explain the technique: ' "You mustn't touch them with the pistol for then they may flinch and your shot go astray. No, you have to aim very carefully as the bullet must take a certain line to kill a man instantly and you must do it quickly. I can do it without looking almost . . . Just turn around and I will show you." '

Payne Best tried to persuade him that it would be foolish to shoot anyone at this late stage in the war, and that Fritz himself would be a prisoner in a few days. 'This started him off again saying that no one would ever take him prisoner, and that all SS men would fight to the last, and his glassy-eyed friend revived sufficiently to start muttering, "Shoot them all down – bum, bum, bum – bump them all off is best," and with a sweep of his arm knocked bottle and glasses from the table.'

Extricating himself, Payne Best returned to his room. At 3 a.m., he was woken by General Thomas. A message had finally come through from General Vietinghoff, and a Wehrmacht officer and a company of infantry were on their way.

Vietinghoff, it transpired, had also alerted General Karl Wolff – the Supreme Commander of all SS forces in Italy – to the presence of '160 prominent hostages in the Bolzano area'. Wolff in turn then sent a secret message to Field Marshal Alexander – Supreme Allied Commander, Mediterranean Forces – calling for his help in rescuing the prisoners.

This extraordinary gesture is explained by the fact that, later that day, Wolff would sign a document at the Royal Palace at Caserta – the Allied headquarters near Naples – formalizing the surrender of German forces in Italy, ending the Italian campaign.

The surrender – the culmination of negotiations with US intelligence chief Allen Dulles – was to come into effect three days later, on 2 May.

The hostages, however, were still not out of danger.

In fact, when General Thomas had woken Payne Best, Vietinghoff's officer had already arrived in Villabassa.

His name was Major Wichard von Alvensleben and he was related to Polizeiführer Ludolf von Alvensleben, the notorious SS chief in Udine.

The major's orders from General Vietinghoff were unclear. All he was told was that there was an SS 'convoy of Prominenten' in Villabassa and he was to see what the 'trouble' was and 'if necessary find food and shelter for them'. With negotiations at Caserta at a sensitive stage, Vietinghoff, still fearful of rogue elements within the SS, had purposely kept his orders vague. But he knew he could trust Alvensleben, whose loathing of the SS was compounded by shame. His cousin's involvement in atrocities in the Crimea and then as Polizeiführer in Udine had brought his family, otherwise anti-Nazi, into disrepute. 'Let's not talk about him,' the major would say if asked. 'As you can imagine, he is the black sheep of the family. I only hope that he doesn't make it through to the end of the war.'

It was late in the evening when Alvensleben arrived. Leaving his company outside Villabassa, he set off alone on foot to investigate. Walking through the empty streets, he could see no sign of the convoy or the Prominenten who, at this late hour, were under guard in the town hall, and in numerous hotels and inns. But as he approached the Piazza Santa Trinità, he saw the SS, grouped in the centre.

The sight of the fifty-strong detachment unnerved him. He only had fifteen men with him; moreover, he had no authority to take military action if Bader refused to surrender the prisoners.

Nonetheless, as dawn broke over Villabassa, he moved his company into position, facing the SS on the edge of the square.

A few hours later, under pressure from the villagers, who were demanding that the prisoners be fed, Bader had no choice but to release them from their overnight billets. 'Jimmy' James described the scene that confronted him as he emerged from the town hall:

> Across the square the SS men were grouped uncertainly around their vehicles, Bader standing in front exuding hatred and defiance. Facing them was a Wehrmacht unit of about fifteen men commanded by a young Lieutenant. The SS were having a heated discussion among themselves and were obviously unwilling to surrender to a Wehrmacht unit whose commander, von Alvensleben, seemed uncertain of taking any definite action . . .
>
> I could see Bonin, very much in command of the situation, standing beside the Wehrmacht platoon. He now told Alvensleben that he would accept full responsibility for the actions of his unit, and that he should get on with the job of disarming the SS. Orders were barked out by the company Sergeant and two heavy machine guns were mounted quickly and trained on the SS. Colonel von Bonin strode across the square to Bader, and told him that the SS must throw down their arms. If they refused, he warned, the machine guns would open up on them. There was a moment's hesitation, then they dropped their weapons . . .
>
> Bader was soon pleading for petrol so that he could drive off with his men. Not only was this refused but Bonin could barely be restrained from shooting all the SS men on the spot.

37

At the crossroads outside Villabassa, Fey was still on the bus, waiting with the other women and children: 'We were anxious for news of the others. I was particularly worried about Alex, who I knew had been imprisoned in the town hall with the military prisoners. Suddenly, not long after dawn, we saw a man running towards us from the direction of Villabassa. Shouting and waving his arms to draw our attention, he was one of the Hungarian prisoners of war and, as he came closer, we were relieved to see the happy expression on his face. Incredibly, he told us that Lieutenant Bader and his squad had gone. We crowded out of the bus and rushed into the village in great excitement. There, at the Hotel Bachmann, we found the others celebrating. For the first time, we ordered drinks like ordinary people!'

To ensure that Bader did not cause any further trouble, General Vietinghoff had ordered him to return to the Wehrmacht's headquarters at Bolzano. But, as Fey described, the celebrations did not last long: 'Von Alvensleben stood up to address us. He said he and his soldiers would remain with us, but as protectors rather than warders. These were General Vietinghoff's orders. The war was not yet officially over and the General was worried that other SS units, acting on Himmler's orders, might make a last determined attempt to carry out the order to liquidate us.'

There were reports, too, of fighting between the different factions of partisans – Communists, pro-Austrians and Italian nationalists – and there was a danger the prisoners might be caught in the crossfire. In the circumstances, believing the Hotel Pragser Wildsee to be the safest place for them, Vietinghoff ordered the Wehrmacht generals to move out. The next day, the prisoners piled into the buses to make the 4-mile journey to the hotel which – but for Alvensleben's courage – was to have been the scene of their execution.

It was snowing heavily and they had to walk the last mile as the single-track road on the approach to the hotel was impassable. The owner, Emma Heiss-Hellenstainer, was waiting at the entrance. 'They were all so happy to have their lives back, thankful for every kind word, for any small attention. My hand was squeezed and kissed over and over again,' she wrote in her diary. After entering their names in the hotel's guestbook, she allocated them rooms and a porter showed them upstairs.

Built in the style of a chalet, with decorated wooden balconies running along the length of each of its four storeys, the 180-room hotel was an impressive building. Some 5,000 feet above sea level, before the war it had been a retreat for European royalty who had come to enjoy the spectacular scenery. The hotel was usually closed during the winter and, with no heating, its well-appointed rooms and spacious salons, decorated with all manner of taxidermy – badgers, stags, kites and eagles – were freezing. But, as 'Jimmy' James wrote, 'After my years of viewing barbed wire, guard towers and cell walls, it seemed like a wonderful dream.' Fey was also enchanted with the hotel. 'I had a lovely room all to myself for the first time in what felt like a lifetime. The view over the turquoise lake, ringed by snow-covered mountains, was so beautiful that I could hardly tear myself away from the window.'

There was plenty of food, brought by villagers and local farmers, and a rota was set up for cooking and kitchen duties. The men were sent out to gather wood to heat the fires in the rooms and, directed by Frau Emma, each of the prisoners was asked to make a list of the things they required. Many had only the clothes they stood in; they needed shoes, coats, underwear, shirts, trousers, stockings, razors, hairbrushes, socks and toothbrushes. There was also a box for complaints and suggestions, and the times of the four daily Masses, held in the small chapel on the shore of the lake, were posted on a blackboard.

Hugh Falconer, a wireless expert, found an old radio and made it work. That evening, gathered in the dining room, the group listened to the BBC. They cheered and clapped when it was reported that

Hitler had sacked Himmler for his 'treachery' and that an elite squad, composed of the Führer's personal bodyguards, had been ordered to track him down and kill him.

Outside, Alvensleben's troops formed a protective chain around the hotel. They were mostly out of sight in the woods behind and at the sides of the building, and the group was hardly conscious of their presence. As they settled in for their first night, Peter Churchill described their relief. 'In this glorious setting, under the protection of Alvensleben's unit, we felt that our freedom had almost begun.'

Yet Himmler, having fled Berlin to escape Hitler's assassins, was still determined to kill his former hostages.

The next morning – 1 May – General Vietinghoff alerted Major Alvensleben to the presence of a large number of SS in the area. Later that day, a message went out from his headquarters asking Himmler's office to clarify the purpose of their mission.

Extraordinarily, code-breakers at Bletchley Park, who intercepted the communication, picked up this unease at Vietinghoff's headquarters. That evening – marked 'Top Secret Ultra' – the decoded message was included in a file for Winston Churchill, containing the most important intercepts of the day.

The time and date that it had been sent were stamped on the copy the prime minister saw: '2.15 p.m. 1.5.1945' – twenty-three hours after Hitler committed suicide in his bunker beneath the Reich Chancellery in Berlin, and ten hours before the German surrender in Italy was due to come into effect:

TO REICHSFUEHRER SS HEINRICH HIMMLER FROM A.O.K. 19[*]

IN THE GAU-TIROL-VORARLBERG LARGE NON FIGHTING GROUPS OF THE WAFFEN SS, SD AND GESTAPO ARE STAYING IN THE VALLEYS. DETACHMENT COMMANDOS DO NOT COMPLY WITH ORDERS TO JOIN IN THE FIGHTING AS THEY ALL ALLEGE THAT THEY HAVE A SPECIAL

---

[*] Armeeoberkommando 19, a unit of the German High Command.

TASK FOR THE REICHSFUEHRER SS. REQUEST ORDER FROM THE
REICHSFUEHRER SS TO A.O.K.19

If Himmler's office replied to the message, it was not intercepted at
Bletchley. But more than fifteen years later, Josef Hanser, a priest in
the village of Sillian in East Tyrol, shed light on the 'special task' the
Reichsführer had assigned to the SS. At some point on '1 or 2 May',
he received a visit from Hans Philipp, the Gestapo chief in the dis-
trict. In great distress, Philipp asked the priest to hear his confession.
Showing him a copy of the Reichsführer's orders, he said his mission
was to recapture the hostages – either at Villabassa or the Hotel Pragser Wildsee – and transport them to Klagenfurt, where they were to
be executed. The priest managed to talk him out of committing mass
murder but later recounted that the Gestapo chief 'left in a spin'.
Some hours later, fearing he would be forced to carry out the order
anyway, Philipp took his own life with a lethal dose of the sedative
Veronal.

The war in Italy ended at midnight on 2 May. His was one of
the first of many suicides among SS and Gestapo officers in the
coming days.

At last, unannounced – at six-fifteen on the morning of 4 May – a
company of US troops reached the Hotel Pragser Wildsee. Jeeps and
light tanks came roaring up the drive, Italian partisans clinging to
every handle-hold. Straight away, the troops rushed to disarm the
German guards.

'Jimmy' James was returning with a group of prisoners from an
early Mass in the chapel by the lake: 'As we approached, we saw a line
of vehicles parked on the road in front of the hotel and there were
soldiers, unmistakably American soldiers. It seemed unbelievable . . .
In no time, the Americans were sharing their rations of chocolate and
cigarettes with us, a mobile laundry had been set up on the lawn, and
nets were erected for handball and other games. Our rations were
supplemented by such mouth-watering and long-forgotten items as
waffles and syrups, eggs and bacon, while they apologised for having
only front-line rations!'

The Germans in the group, horrified that Alvensleben and his men – their true saviours – were now prisoners of war, were less ecstatic: 'Our soldiers had to pile their weapons in a heap. Then they were placed under arrest. A shocking picture,' Gagi von Stauffenberg noted in her diary.

Seeing the men as they waited to be taken away, Isa felt desperately sorry for them: 'The majority of the German soldiers sat somewhere quietly in the sun, their legs stretched out in front of them, with expressions of tired sadness on their faces. It had nothing to do with them or their want of courage that the war was lost. Their strength was spent. Spent and wasted was the blood and life of countless comrades too, every one of them, sold and toyed with by a clique of unscrupulous scoundrels.'

The efficiency of the US troops – and the resources available to them – astounded the group. Almost immediately, GI uniforms were handed out to the Allied prisoners of war and a strict delousing and bathing regime imposed. Using a pump to draw water from the lake, and an oil-fired tank to heat it, rows of showers were erected on the lawn in front of the hotel. Soap and fresh towels were handed out to everyone – the soldiers bathing at 2 p.m., the men in the group at 3 p.m. and the women at 4 p.m. That same evening, the troops set up a cinema in the dining room showing the film *America*.

'The American troops make a deep impression on us,' Kurt Schuschnigg wrote in his diary after the screening. 'They do what they can for us; they are helpful, sympathetic, understanding, unobtrusive – in short, they are human. So this is America. This is the un-soldierly, utterly mechanised and decadent nation of which we read in the Nazi papers. Well, it is easy to understand now why they have won the war. There is only one flaw: the Press Reporters.'

With the US troops came hordes of camera crews and newsmen, eager to question the celebrity prisoners. They clamoured for interviews with Léon Blum, Prince Xavier of Bourbon and Schuschnigg himself. 'I cannot begin to express our feelings,' he wrote. 'Who can describe Freedom? . . . What can we tell them? Plans? Why we don't know; we have not yet thought about plans.'

★

For Fey, the days at the Pragser Wildsee were 'intensely romantic . . . an earthly paradise'. Freedom meant she was able to spend every minute of the day with Alex. Finally, after months of being surrounded by others, they were alone.

Despite her moral qualms, she could not find the strength of will to stop herself from being completely turned by him. 'I found an inner peace with Alex such as I'd never found before,' she wrote. 'I couldn't bear the thought of a future without him. I wanted to start a new life with him.'

When, in the still of one night, Alex asked Fey to leave Detalmo and marry him, she said yes.

38

On the afternoon of 9 May, Brigadier General Leonard Gerow, commander-in-chief of the US 15th Army, arrived at the hotel to address the group. He was under orders from the Allied High Command to take them to Naples and they were to get ready to leave.

The next morning, punctually at nine o'clock, a long line of vehicles pulled out of the large courtyard in front of the hotel.

Fey was in an open-top jeep with Alex, Payne Best and the Schuschniggs. The comfort and style in which they were travelling could not have been more different than their experience of SS transports. Leading the convoy was a light tank, followed by army personnel vehicles, with numerous spares in case of breakdown. Then came an ambulance, military buses for the older people, further light tanks and a rear-guard of more jeeps. A US fighter plane flew overhead; for 'their protection', the American officers said.

The convoy followed the course of the River Adige down through the mountains, past Lake Garda. The four-hour drive to Verona, from where the US Air Force would fly the group south, was dusty, the road littered with abandoned German vehicles. 'Everywhere we met with destroyed bridges and there were thousands of refugees,' Fey recalled. 'It was my first sight of Italy since leaving Brazzà and it was heart-breaking to see how, amidst the beautiful landscape, war had ravaged the country and its people.'

Arriving in Verona, the group was put up in a luxury hotel, where they were treated to a three-course dinner of asparagus, roast chicken and ice cream. The next morning, after 'an enormous breakfast', they were driven to an airfield outside the city. There, as Peter Churchill described, 'We beheld something like fifty shining transport planes capable of holding thirty passengers each in comfort. There was no squeezing or stinginess about the number set aside for the political prisoners; at least six were used for the purposes of flying us to Naples.'

For most of the non-military members of the group, it was their first flight and, on the approach to Florence, the pilots obligingly descended to 5,000 feet so they had a view of the city. Some 250 miles further on, they descended again, flying low over Monte Cassino – of interest to the prisoners of war. Circling two or three times above the ruins of the abbey, they could see the battlefield which, between January and May 1944, had claimed 115,000 Allied soldiers – dead, wounded or missing.

At Naples, scores of film crews and news reporters were waiting when the planes landed after the two-and-a-half-hour flight. Here – for the Germans in the group – the celebrity treatment ended. Separated from other nationalities, they were escorted by American soldiers, armed with machine guns, to a hangar behind the airfield. 'We were not even allowed to say goodbye to the others, people I liked so much and with whom I had shared so many experiences,' Fey wrote. 'They were going home. We, on the other hand, as people of a defeated nation, were once again prisoners. We hung around that airport for hours, waiting for someone to tell us what was going on.'

None of the Germans had passports and, without papers, the Allies had no means of telling who they were. Before being repatriated to Germany, they had to be vetted to allay concerns that they were war criminals. After a long wait in the hangar, an American official appeared and announced that they were being taken to Capri, where there was a US Army clearing station run by the Counter Intelligence Corps (CIC).

A British ship ferried them across to the island. As soon as they disembarked, soldiers separated the men from the women and took them to a nearby POW camp. 'It was awful seeing Alex and the others being led away,' Fey remembered; 'the guards said we were to be kept apart until the interrogation process was over. The rest of us were taken to Anacapri at the southern end of the island where we were put up, under armed guard, in a small hotel. The Americans warned us that it was forbidden to leave the hotel until they had finished interrogating and identifying us.'

Anacapri, situated high on the side of Monte Solaro, was a

beautiful spot with splendid views over the Mediterranean. The Hotel Paradiso, however, did not live up to its name. A modest building, with a white stucco front, it was located in a narrow back street. The rooms were small and it was unusually hot for May, the temperature over 36 degrees. Sleeping four to a room, the heat was stifling.

A week went by, and nothing happened. Incarcerated in the hotel, with access only to a tiny garden, Isa recorded that 'after a very short time the mood became unbearable . . . in an attempt to give each other space, we kept treading on each other's toes . . . No one told us anything and it felt as if the "American machine" was taking forever to set itself in motion.'

Recognizing their distress at being held captive, the soldiers finally allowed the women to leave the hotel. None of them had summer clothes, and the Red Cross equipped them with swimsuits, straw hats and sandals so they could go to the beach. While they were allowed to roam freely around the island, the men were not granted the same privileges and it bothered and depressed them all.

To their relief, after ten days, they began to be questioned. CIC officers responsible for investigating war criminals conducted the interrogations. The sessions were long and onerous. The officers needed to know exactly who they were freeing and who they should detain. Once the group's stories had been checked and cross-checked, detectives from Scotland Yard's Special Investigation Bureau took over. The women were asked to supply details of the SS and Gestapo men who had guarded them in the camps – their names and rank, a physical description (including height, build, eye colour and any distinguishing marks or facial features) and specific incidences of brutality.

After the sessions, in the few hours of daylight that remained, Fey and the others went for long walks on Monte Solaro, with its spectacular views of Vesuvius and Naples. It felt strange and unnatural to be in such a beautiful place, untouched by the war, when their families at home might be starving. It seemed that they had swapped one prison for another and everyone longed to go home. For the mothers in the group who knew their children were waiting at the SS orphanage at Bad Sachsa, Isa noted, it was a disquieting time: 'Every moment spent in this magical garden was a guilty one – they could not escape the thought of their little ones anxiously expecting their return.'

Throughout this difficult period, Fey was engaged in a very private struggle. No longer living in the moment of her time with Alex at the Pragser Wildsee, her conscience plagued her and she realized the impossibility of her promise to leave Detalmo.

Her father was also constantly in her thoughts. The officers conducting the interrogations at the Allied clearing station admired his courage and wanted to know all about him: his life, his character, his motives in opposing Hitler. Comforted by the opportunity to honour her father's memory, Fey spoke about his sense of duty, his faith and his strict moral code. As she did so, she knew it was her duty to stay with Detalmo; to leave him would be to abrogate the values her father had taught her and which he had given his life to uphold.

And she thought about the children. Since her conversation with Sergeant Lenz at Buchenwald, while she had clung to the hope that the boys would be found, a part of her recognized that, sooner or later, she would have to face up to the fact that they were irretrievably lost or dead. But, not long after arriving at the hotel, representatives from the International Red Cross came to see her, giving her renewed hope. Slowly, they said, families were being reunited and there was every chance the children would be located. Vatican Radio had even broadcast a list of missing children, which included Corrado and Roberto. If, by a miracle, the boys were found, Fey knew that should she marry Alex she risked losing them again; under Italian law, the children would remain with their father.

Yet, after 18 May, when Fey and the others were finally allowed to leave their hotel, she could have sent a telegram to Detalmo to tell him she was safe and well and in Capri. But she did not. She wanted to see Alex one last time to explain her decision and to say goodbye to him.

A week went by and there was no sign that the Americans would allow him to leave the camp where he was detained. Still Fey postponed contacting her husband. After the long sessions at the clearing station she spent most of that time on her own – swimming off the beach at the foot of Monte Solaro or walking through the country-side. 'The beauty of the island made me feel even bleaker,' she wrote. 'When I thought about Detalmo and the future, it was with dread.'

It was now eighteen months since she had seen her husband and almost a year since she had heard from him. Their last contact – the message he had sent via a courier to tell her that he was staying in Rome – had rankled throughout her time in the camps. She could not help feeling that if he had come home, rather than abandoning her and the children, things might have turned out differently. Had he been with the partisans in the mountains, he might have come up with his own rescue plan after her father's execution. Notwithstanding these feelings of resentment – and her feelings for Alex – could any marriage survive such a gulf of separation and experience? Would Detalmo ever understand what she had been through in a way that would not leave her feeling permanently alone?

On 25 May, having given up hope that Alex would be allowed out of the prisoner-of-war camp, Fey went to the post office in Anacapri. The residue of admiration she had for her husband meant that it did not occur to her that his silence was because he had not come through the war; she had no doubt that his political career was flourishing and that he was living at his family's palazzo in Rome.

It was to this address that she sent her telegram, which consisted of just nine words:

AT ALLIED CLEARING STATION CAPRI. PLEASE COME. AFFECT[IONATELY] FEY.

Detalmo answered almost immediately. He would come and fetch her the following day.

That next morning, the Americans finally allowed Alex to leave the prisoner-of-war camp. He went straight to the Hotel Paradiso, but it was too late. Fey had already left to meet Detalmo from the ferry.

She went on foot, taking the flight of steps that coiled around the side of Monte Solaro, linking Anacapri with Marina Grande, the main port on the island.

The steps – 921 in number – ran down through steep terraces, planted with vines and olive trees. It was a beautiful clear day and she could see across to the mainland. The sea was an intense, turquoise blue and small boats, their wakes no more than thin trails, pulled in and out of the harbour below.

Arriving in Marina Grande, she went to a café overlooking the port to wait for the ferry.

'The setting was idyllic,' she remembered. 'The café was in a small square lined with ancient houses of all different colours – pale blue and yellow and a deep Pompeiian red. I sat there, watching the comings and goings in the port; the fishermen mending their nets, the women selling every conceivable type of fruit and vegetable, attractively arranged in front of them on the market stalls. I should have been happy. The war was over and I was free. After all this time, I was about to see Detalmo. But I was utterly miserable.'

Fey was waiting on the quayside when the ferry docked and Detalmo stepped off the small boat: 'We were so overwhelmed, we didn't know where to start. We couldn't find any words. Too much had happened.'

Then came a heart-stopping moment.

Disappointed not to see Corrado and Roberto waiting with her on the quayside, Detalmo asked Fey to go and fetch them. 'He had thought that the boys were still with me and I had to tell him about Innsbruck' was all she wrote.

Fey's brief account of those first days with Detalmo is matter-of-fact. She did not describe what they talked about nor did she express what it felt like to see him again after the long months of separation. Instead, all her emotion was caught up with parting from Alex, and from the people with whom she had experienced so much:

> Rather than leave right away, Detalmo thought it would be better to stay in Capri another day or two so that we could get used to each other again before going back to Rome. He arranged for us to move into a bigger, more comfortable hotel. He also wanted to meet the people I had been imprisoned with and he organized a big dinner for our last night.

The dinner took place at a nearby restaurant and we all sat round a long table. There were about twenty of us, including Alex. I had not been able to speak to him alone, but I sensed he knew it was all over and that I had decided to go back to Rome to try and rebuild my shattered family.

The food was delicious and the wine flowed freely. Detalmo was rather upset because some of the guests did not seem to have much appetite. Still having the 'prison mentality', they had been afraid of not getting enough to eat and had also eaten dinner at the hotel. There were lots of jokes and speeches, but all the time I had a knot in my stomach. I did not want to go home. I was not only leaving Alex, I was leaving friends with whom I had endured and suffered so much. Only they could truly understand the thoughts and feelings I knew would always haunt me. Nothing binds people closer to each other than common suffering in dark times and I had come to love them as much as those I had loved and cared for deeply for years.

The next morning, Otto Philipp, who had helped me with my luggage in the moves from camp to camp, arrived to help for the last time. He came down with us to the harbour, where Detalmo had booked the ferry to take us to the mainland. Alex did not come. But I was holding in my hand the last poem he had written for me. One verse began: *You are mine, I shout it to the winds* . . .

As the boat pulled away from the quay, I felt my heart breaking into a thousand pieces. Poor Detalmo tried to console me but I just sobbed and sobbed.

PART SIX

39

Detalmo had not received any of the letters Fey wrote during her captivity or the telegrams friends at Brazzà had sent via the Red Cross, telling him that she and the boys had been arrested.

At the time of their arrest – September 1944 – Detalmo was in Rome, where he was working as political secretary to Sergio Fenoaltea, a senior minister in Italy's first democratic government in twenty years. At this stage in the war, Italy remained divided. Mussolini's puppet regime – de facto the Germans – controlled the north of the country, and the Allies – in conjunction with Prime Minister Bonomi's new government – the south. Detalmo's job, which involved liaising with the Allies and working on political strategy with his colleagues in the Partito d'Azione, meant that he was a prominent figure. But the Red Cross, inundated with tens of thousands of requests from Italians anxious for news of relatives in the Nazi-occupied north, had failed to pass on the telegrams and it had been five months before he learned that the Gestapo had taken Fey and the children.

That autumn, the German Army's entrenched position along the Gustav Line, a series of heavily fortified defences stretching across central Italy, made it almost impossible for partisan couriers to carry messages between the north and south. It was only after the Allies launched their winter offensive in January 1945 that the situation changed and it was not until February that Detalmo received the note from Nonino, sent via an underground courier, telling him that Fey had been arrested and that she and the boys had been deported to Innsbruck. It explains why, when Detalmo arrived at Capri, he expected to see the boys: he assumed that they had remained with Fey throughout her imprisonment.

★

On the night he and Fey arrived back in Rome from Capri, thrilled to be able to tell his mother-in-law that she was home, Detalmo sat down to write to Ilse. It was the first letter he had written since her husband's execution the previous September:

29 May 1945

My dear Mutti

It is very difficult to write to you, and I don't know how to begin. I'm sure you can imagine my thoughts and feelings. September 1944 was very painful for me, I thought of you every moment. Later, in February, I found out about Fey's deportation five months earlier. This made it all the worse. I withdrew from every activity, feeling that the world had collapsed around me. I realised that there wouldn't be much interest in life without Fey, and I awaited my own sentence.

Fey has been spared. I got her back in good health, and she encloses her own letter for you. You will see her distressing news about the boys. I thought it best for her to tell you the details.

Now I hope to find the two little ones. If this happens, the balance will have closed with the loss of a father-in-law, a friend who can never be replaced.

My thoughts are not too clear. They shift from Christian patience to anarchic rebellion. I am not prepared to accept what has happened to us. If I still feel like fighting and working for a better world, it is only out of loyalty to the sacrifice of those who have shown us the way. Father has been a great example for us, and we are still under his shadow. It is as if an enduring monument has been raised inside our hearts.

Fey has been wonderful. There must have been some of your spirit in her; otherwise she could not have pulled through the prisons and the camps. I feel like marrying Fey anew. I would marry her ten times if I had ten lives.

Dear Mutti, until we hear from you, very much love,
Detalmo.

Despite his touching faith in Fey's ability to 'pull through', in the weeks after she arrived back in Rome, unsurprisingly, she came close to suffering a complete breakdown. With her children still missing, and with her love for Alex having subsumed her relationship with her husband, it seemed all the meaning in her life lay in the past: in her childhood in Rome; in the early years of her marriage; in the war years at Brazzà with the children; and in the close bonds she had formed with the other prisoners in the camps. 'I was twenty-five years old and I felt my life was over,' she wrote.

Finding it extremely difficult to engage in everyday tasks, she barely ate or slept. She suffered from panic attacks and could not relax. Her mind was a constant spiral of thoughts, often flipping back to traumatic events, which she felt Detalmo, however supportive and sympathetic, could never understand: 'It was not his fault; he had not been behind those walls.'

Her sense of isolation was reinforced by the world he moved in. His job in government meant he was expected to attend a constant round of official dinners, receptions and cocktail parties hosted in palazzi belonging to the 'Via Veneto set'. During his time in the Resistance, Detalmo had witnessed the collaboration between the Nazis and some of Rome's oldest aristocratic families at close hand and Fey was shocked to hear how they had behaved after the Allies liberated the city. 'Detalmo described how, within the space of two days, American officers had replaced Germans on the Via Veneto cocktail circuit. There had been farewell dinners in the best houses for the German commander Field Marshal Kesselring. A few days later, there had been welcome dinners in these same houses for the head of the Allied forces, General Mark W. Clark.'

Revisiting this world, so familiar from her childhood, Fey felt completely alienated: 'Every landmark, every street corner, brought back memories: of my growing up at the embassy, of my friends from school, of the balls and parties, of my father. But it felt wrong. Nothing seemed to have changed. There was no sign of the horror and destruction that had ravaged the rest of Europe. The Via Veneto people lived just like they had before, taking pleasure from frivolous and meaningless things, as if there had never been a Stalingrad, a Dunkirk or a Buchenwald. Understandably, Detalmo wanted me to accompany him to these receptions. He thought it would help me overcome memories of my imprisonment and keep my mind from dwelling on the fate of the boys. But I did not want to talk to people, especially people I did not know and to whom I had to pretend that nothing had happened, so I often found excuses to stay at home.'

Fey's struggle to readjust to normal life was unexceptional. Across Europe, millions were mourning the loss of loved ones and endeavouring – or failing – to rebuild relationships with husbands and wives after years of separation. Millions more – prisoners who had managed to survive the Nazi death camps without the privileged treatment meted out to Fey and the other Prominenten, and members of the armed forces, who had fought in any number of air, sea or land battles – had endured far worse. With such a commonality of experience, this *was* normal life. As a consequence, in country after country, there was no institutional response to this collective emotional crisis. People had to find their own coping mechanisms.

For Fey, recovery lay in finding a way to vocalize her experiences – and her emotions – to Detalmo. First, however, she bought herself a fan to help her overcome her anxiety attacks. 'It was amazing how this small gesture helped restore my confidence,' she wrote. 'In crowded situations or on the rare occasions that I went to one of Detalmo's receptions, as soon as I felt a wave of panic coming on, I used the fan: it was cooling and it gave me something to do with my hands.'

Recognizing that she found it almost impossible to talk to Detalmo about her experiences, Fey decided to write a memoir about her captivity and her time alone at Brazzà. In writing a frank account – including her relationship with Alex, and her feelings of resentment towards Detalmo for abandoning her and the children – she hoped he would understand and they could begin to rebuild their marriage.

And yet, as Fey acknowledged, however separate she felt from her husband, the loss of the children bound them together. They had a shared understanding in the pain of their loss and a joint purpose in searching for the boys. Very quickly, this was heightened by fury and frustration.

In Anacapri, they had begun planning their search; Germany and

Austria were the obvious places to start. But on their return to Rome, they discovered that the regulations imposed by the Allied Military Government prevented them from setting out to find the boys.

'For eight months I had longed for the moment when I could begin the search for the children but I remained as helpless and trapped as I had been in the camps,' Fey wrote.

Due to Italy's status as a co-belligerent, all travel for Italian nationals was forbidden; to go any distance beyond 10 kilometres required a permit from the Allied authorities. Using his government connections, Detalmo tried pulling every string, but it was impossible. 'In response to our pleas to be allowed to go to Germany to search for the children,' Fey recalled, 'one official after another repeated that doing so was strictly forbidden. We tried every conceivable means to get a travel pass, but in every office we met with the same response: "Can you imagine what would happen if we let everybody in Europe go out and search for their missing families?" I could understand their reasoning. I had seen the chaos in the former Reich – the destruction of towns and cities, the endless columns of refugees. But Detalmo just got furious, saying bitterly that of the "everybody" the officials talked about, many were long dead.'

Upwards of 19 million Europeans had been killed in the war and tens of millions more were dispersed across the continent. In the summer of 1945, in the area encompassing the former German Reich, there were over 25 million 'displaced persons' – the term used by the Allies to categorize refugees and those who were homeless. Of these, a large number were children.

During the war, more than at any other time in history, children had suffered on an unprecedented scale. They had been murdered, kidnapped, starved and abused. In the concentration camps alone, as many as 1.5 million children had been killed, about 1 million of them Jewish. Another 50,000 children from Nazi-occupied Europe, especially Poland, Yugoslavia, Czechoslovakia and the Netherlands, were estimated to have been 'Germanized' in the Nazi period – i.e. taken from their families, stripped of their identity and indoctrinated in so-called *Heimschulen* (boarding schools), institutions of the

Nationalsozialistische Volkswohlfahrt (NSV)★ or in orphanages run by the *Lebensborn* society.†

Whether through bombings, military service, evacuation, deportation, forced labour, ethnic cleansing or murder, huge numbers of children had been separated from their families. The Red Cross estimated that, in Europe alone, 13 million had lost parents. In the final days of the war, the dire needs of those found among the ruins of towns and cities, trekking westward on crowded roads or housed in refugee camps all over Europe, became abundantly clear. In the Soviet zone of occupation there were no fewer than 1.17 million unaccompanied children, the majority of whom were German.

As early as 1943, the Allies realized that displaced people would pose a grave problem when the war ended, and in an effort to avoid a crisis they created UNRRA‡ to care for and repatriate those who had been displaced. But when the time came, facing a series of daunting challenges – the need to feed and house the vast numbers of refugees, and to punish those guilty of war crimes – it was beyond the Allies' capabilities to identify and reunite all unaccompanied children with their families.

Tragically, retribution played a part in dealing with these unsupervised children. In setting up the Child Search arm of UNRRA, one of the guiding principles was that efforts to locate those missing, of which there were hundreds of thousands, would exclude 'enemy' children. Instead, the agency's limited resources were allocated to prioritizing the identification of 'Germanized' and 'Allied' children (those belonging to nations on the winning side), and the small percentage of Jewish children who had survived the concentration camps.

In seeking to reunite them with their families, the agency's officials faced an almost impossible task. Many families could not be re-established because both parents were dead; fathers had died in the

---

★ The state organization for the people's welfare.
† Established by the SS in 1935 to inculcate children of those deemed to be 'racially pure and healthy' with Nazi ideology.
‡ The United Nations Relief and Rehabilitation Administration.

fighting, were missing or were prisoners of war; mothers had died in Allied bombing raids, starved or simply disappeared into the East as forced labour. The concentration camps had also claimed many parents, leaving their children orphaned. Children arriving in the refugee camps were frequently unidentifiable. Although some had name tags around their necks or names sewn into their clothing, most did not. Those accompanying them occasionally had some information, but often nothing was known beyond the point of origin of their train, bus or boat. Further, a name tag did not necessarily confirm a child's identity. As one official wrote, 'From experience we have learned that children from these transports are often labelled with the wrong names.' The fact that 'the child's name is inscribed in her dress', he added, 'is absolutely not definitive, since in many cases it has become clear that children – especially ones sent on by the NSV – are very often wearing other children's clothing.'

In June 1945, for unsupervised German children, no effective system to locate, support and reunite them with their families was in place. While the Allied authorities did their best to offer them some sort of temporary stability by feeding and housing them in refugee camps, as 'enemy children' it was up to their relatives to find them. The majority had fled from the rapidly advancing Soviet Army; but there were hundreds of thousands of others who had been unable to escape, either because they were too young or too sick to travel or because they had been wounded. Some remained in children's homes in areas that no longer belonged to Germany; others, found by the roadside after their mothers had died on the treks from the east, had been rounded up by Soviet troops and sent to orphanages in Russia. Yet more were held by foster families reluctant to give them up.

As Fey and Detalmo were all too aware, while Corrado and Roberto were technically both 'Allied' and 'Germanized' children in that they were of Italian nationality and had been kidnapped by the Nazis, the SS had given them false *German* identities. Inevitably, the Allies would categorize them as *enemy* children. UNRRA officials were scouring the very camps where the boys could be, looking for Jewish, 'Germanized' and 'Allied' children, but their brief was to leave German children *in situ*. And because UNRRA records were confidential, parents looking for missing 'enemy' children could not access them. There was an outside chance that Corrado, who had a grasp of English, might tell the officials his real name. But after the trauma of what had happened to him, would he remember his name or his few words of English? Fey clung to the hope that he would, yet in her heart she knew this was a fantasy. A four-year-old boy could hardly be expected to have the presence of mind to speak to UNRRA officials.

Fey and Detalmo remained in Rome throughout that June. 'The frustration of that period was unbearable,' she wrote. 'Helpless in the face of visions of the children uncared for, perhaps even starving, we kicked our heels, wasting time and effort in the continuous importuning of bureaucrats. They remained inflexible.'

To help overcome her frustration, Fey spent most of that period sending out posters and pamphlets with details of the children. They went to any organization or individual she and Detalmo could think of: to every bishop and archbishop in Germany and Austria; to the Italian, German and International Red Cross; to the British, French and American secret services; to the Italian ambassadors in Washington and Warsaw; to Vatican Radio and to countless other addresses.

The notices – the size of a sheet of A4 or an advertising poster which could be pinned to a wall – were printed in five different languages: German, English, French, Russian and Italian. Beside a large photograph of Corrado and Roberto was a huge caption: 'We are searching for these children!' Beneath it was a physical description of the boys, followed by other information that Fey and Detalmo thought would help to identify them:

CORRADO PIRZIO-BIROLI, aged 4½
Italian citizen, Roman Catholic, born in Udine (Italy), Nov 25 1940
Colour of hair: light blond
Colour of eyes: light blue
Complexion: fair, pale
Language spoken: German (owing to detention in Germany), Italian
Nicknames used: Corradino, Corradinchen

Words he should remember: Nonino (a butler), Mila (a cook), Mirko
(a horse), Oberleutnant Kretschmann (a German officer)
Clothes: small dark blue coat with cowl made of navy cloth

ROBERTO PIRZIO-BIROLI, aged 3½
Italian citizen, Roman Catholic, born in Udine (Italy), Jan 25 1942
Colour of hair: light blond
Colour of eyes: light blue
Complexion: fair and rosy
Language spoken: German (owing to detention in Germany)
Nicknames used: Robertino, Robertinchen
Words he should remember: None
Clothes: small dark blue coat with cowl made of navy cloth

It pained Fey to have to list Lieutenant Kretschmann, who had been
responsible for the children's arrest in the first place, among the names
Corrado might recognize. But the bond formed between her son and
the German officer while he was stationed at Brazzà meant she had
no choice but to mention him.

With every poster Fey sent out, she included a document entitled
'Suggestions for the Search'. It pointed to her despair and to her ex-
asperation with the Church and Allied authorities. Doubting their
ability to think laterally – or to even focus on the search for Corrado
and Roberto – by sheer force of will, she sought to attract their attention and to do their thinking for them:

1. On 29 Sept 1944 at Innsbruck the children were seized by
   Gestapo agent Tiefenbrunner and handed over to two SS women
   working for the NSV (Nationalsozialistische Volkswohlfahrt).
   This suggests that the children were interned in one of the NSV
   institutes, of which there are many in Germany.
2. There are indications that the children were interned under false
   German names to prevent their parents from tracing them.
3. It must be presumed that, after 29 Sept, the two children
   were initially held at an institute in Innsbruck. It is therefore
   from Innsbruck that investigations should begin. <u>Although it</u>

is advisable, in order to save time, to search in every other
place nearby.

4. It must be remembered that
   a) the enclosed picture is a year out of date
   b) the children may now have short hair
   c) they may have forgotten both their name and mother-language
   (Italian)
   d) the small one will have no memory of home, while the eldest
   should react intelligently to the words reported in the enclosed
   notice, and to easy Italian phrases
   e) THE SEARCH FOR THESE CHILDREN IS URGENT. THE MORE
   TIME PASSES, ANY RESEMBLANCE THEY BEAR TO THE ENCLOSED
   PHOTOGRAPH WILL GO AND THE CHILDREN WILL BE LOST.

By the end of June, Fey had sent out over 300 of these notices: 'It
was like throwing pebbles into the sea. All the international organizations were bombarded with so many requests that we knew it
would be months or even years before anyone looked into the case of
the Pirzio-Biroli children. All we were left with was the sinking feeling that, with every week that passed, the chances of finding the boys
diminished. They were lost, perhaps in the east, perhaps without a
name. We could not relax, nor could we do anything.'

June 1945 was exceptionally hot in Rome and, with their efforts leading nowhere, Fey longed to return to Brazzà: 'Anything was better
than pointlessly beating our heads against the stone wall of official-
dom, and I felt that if I was there, where it had all begun, somehow I
would be nearer the children.'

But Brazzà was in the hands of the Desert Air Force under its commanding officer, Robert Foster, and, as an official Allied headquarters, it
was out of bounds. Moreover, the ban preventing Italians travelling
any distance beyond 10 kilometres still applied; without a permit,
Fey and Detalmo had no means of getting there.

Then, in mid July, Detalmo learned that an English acquaintance
of his, Charles Meadhurst, was in Rome on a brief visit. Meadhurst,
formerly the air attaché at the British Embassy in Rome, was now

Air Officer Commanding-in-Chief RAF Mediterranean and Middle East. Detalmo managed to get through to his suite at the Grand Hotel and invited him over for drinks. Clearly shocked by the story of Hassell's execution and the loss of the children, Meadhurst offered to ring his friend Foster to see if he could organize the necessary permissions and arrange transport for them to return to Brazzà. Using a military phone, he managed to get through straight away, astounding Fey and Detalmo, who had been trying to contact Nonino for weeks.

To Fey's joy, they left the next morning from a military airfield outside Rome. 'We boarded a funny-looking DAF plane that seemed primitive inside and rather cold when we climbed above the clouds. But we arrived on schedule to find a British staff car waiting at Treviso airfield. Driving through the familiar countryside toward Brazzà, my spirits rose. Finally, I was really going home.'

As they turned into the courtyard in front of the house, Nonino, Bovolenta and the three maids ran up to greet them. With its sad echoes of the day Fey had left Brazzà with the children, the reunion was emotional. Yet the house, despite having been occupied by troops for so long, still looked strikingly beautiful and Fey was thrilled to hear that the contadini families had not been persecuted by the Germans and that the estate was in good shape.

Robert Foster, Air Officer Commanding, Desert Air Force, was also there to greet them. After all that he had heard from Nonino, he was relieved to see that the couple had come through the war. 'But the children, of course, were still missing,' he later wrote, 'and I could see that this beautiful young woman was in a most unhappy state.'

To Foster's discomfort, he had to tell Fey and Detalmo that the house was full and that he was unable to release any rooms for their use. Nonino had a spare bedroom and they moved into his house overlooking the old *barchesse* – the Venetian barns at the entrance to the villa. 'No sooner had we begun to unpack than an airman arrived with an invitation for drinks that evening with the officers,' Fey remembered. 'It was rather disconcerting to be guests in our own house! But the twenty or so officers we met were all very courteous and charming.'

★

Those first weeks at Brazzà were a healing time for Fey. Every day, she and Detalmo would join the officers for an early-morning ride: 'The British had captured some fine thoroughbreds from an Austrian regiment and about ten were stabled in one of our barns, alongside Roberto's beloved little carriage horse, Mirko. Those long rides in the morning, through the park and out over the hills, did more than anything else to ease my troubled mind. The officers often organised "paper chases" and "point-to-point" races and it was exhilarating to gallop along the tracks behind Brazzà and then stop somewhere for an impromptu picnic.'

Fey had finished writing her memoir and she gave it to Detalmo to read. As she had hoped, they were able to talk about their relationship, and her time in the camps. He understood about Alex, and he also understood how abandoned she had felt when he had stayed in Rome after the city was liberated by the Allies. Detalmo recognized that his decision had been wrong and admitted that his failure to protect her and the children would haunt him for the rest of his life.

As the weeks passed with no news of the boys, they had to begin the hard journey of reconciling themselves to the possibility that they might never be found. Fey's mother was their one hope. Living in Germany, she could at least set out to look for the children. But did she know that the boys were missing? As soon as they arrived back in Rome, Fey and Detalmo had written to her, but almost a month had gone by and she had not replied. The few telephones in operation had been commandeered by the military authorities. As Fey acknowledged, she was not even sure her mother was alive.

40

Entering her sixtieth year, Ilse had survived the war, though at great personal cost. She was living at Ebenhausen at the home she had shared with Ulrich. 'He never disappointed me,' she would later write to Fey; 'his luminous character, his spirituality, his big heart, his courage, always there, were my daily delight. I pray that his death will show the world that there is a better Germany, that there were men who were willing to sacrifice their lives to free the world from evil.'

Born in 1885, Ilse had grown up at the court of the last kaiser, the daughter of one of his most trusted advisers. In the years before the First World War, her father, Grand Admiral von Tirpitz, had transformed the German Imperial Navy into a world-class force, capable of challenging the British Royal Navy. Ilse's teenage years had been spent in close proximity to the German royal family. A favourite of the kaiser, her pet name was 'My Little Destroyer' because of her strong character and her capacity to break men's hearts.

In May 1945, Ilse's modest household was a far cry from the splendid surroundings of the kaiser's court. Like so many others, it consisted entirely of women: her 85-year-old widowed mother, her unmarried sister, and Fey's sister, Almuth. Neither of her sons had returned home. Hans Dieter had been imprisoned after the bomb plot before escaping ahead of the Russians to the French occupation zone. His elder brother, Wolf Ulli, had last been heard of somewhere behind the Russian lines. Yet it was Fey and her only grandchildren she worried about the most.

Ilse had not received the letters Fey and Detalmo had sent from Rome. But, incredibly, she had received the note that Fey dropped from the train the day she left Innsbruck. Hurriedly scrawled on a scrap of paper, and addressed to Ilse at Ebenhausen, it was to tell her mother that she was being transported east and that the SS had seized the children. This was the only information Ilse had and, with the chaos in Germany, she had no means of knowing whether her grandchildren had been found or whether indeed Fey had survived the camps.

A devoted grandmother, she had been with her daughter when both boys were born. The thought that they might still be missing made her frantic. Yet with one in four Germans searching for missing relatives, it was impossible to find out. The American Military Government in Munich was besieged by requests from people seeking information about their families and Ilse knew it was pointless to make the journey into the city. Besides, she had no means of getting there. Public transport was not working; the Gestapo had seized her husband's car, and it was a 30-mile walk there and back.

Then, almost a month after the end of the war, Dr Johannes Neuhäusler, the former Canon of Munich and one of Himmler's Prominenten, sent news of Fey. She was well and in Rome with Detalmo. But he confirmed that the children were still missing. It was thought that they had been taken to an SS-run orphanage somewhere in Germany, where they had been given new names.

'I realised that Fey and Detalmo would never get a permit to search for Corrado and Roberto,' Ilse later explained; 'I was their only hope. But where to start? Two small boys, whose names I didn't know, among the millions of missing people scattered throughout the ex-Reich? SS and Gestapo officials who might have known about missing children had disappeared. The Allied authorities were refusing to help search for lost "enemy" children. Besides, I could not move except on foot. It upset me terribly but it seemed pointless to walk the length of Germany when the boys could be anywhere – Austria, Poland, Czechoslovakia or even further east.'

Early in June, her situation changed. While clearing the wreckage of Munich – removing tons of rubble and searching through abandoned buildings – the authorities found a dark blue BMW. They were able to identify it as the one confiscated from Ulrich von Hassell after his arrest in July 1944. Now, at least, Ilse had a car.

First, however, she needed to secure the necessary petrol coupons and travel permits.

Her quest led her to the American military headquarters in Munich, one of the few buildings left standing in the city. Formerly the national procurement office for the *Sturmabteilung*, a paramilitary wing of the Nazi Party, the six-storey block was pitted with bullet holes. Ilse did not hold out much hope. There were queues of people inside, clamouring for permits and petrol coupons so that they too could go in search of missing relatives, and she did not think the Americans would give her an interview. 'Yet I had no choice. I adjusted my black veil and walked in with as much dignity as possible.'

To her surprise, after she had told her story to the soldier at the front desk, he immediately arranged for her to see Colonel Charles Keegan, the headquarters commander and military governor of Bavaria: 'Keegan was a gentle middle-aged man, obviously shocked and distressed by what he had found in Germany. But his interest and sympathy were genuine. He wrote out a note requesting that the American authorities assist me. I could have hugged him! Nothing, I felt, nothing could stop me now!'

Ilse spent most of that night sitting up with Almuth planning where to begin their search. With so many Germans looking for missing relatives, and with no help from the authorities, a rumour mill was in operation and there were reports that many children taken by the Gestapo had been put in children's homes in the mountains in the south of Bavaria.

The mountains were only a two-hour drive from Ebenhausen and, for want of a better lead, they decided to start there.

The roads were clear, except for the occasional military convoy, and they reached the orphanage in Rottach, a small village on the shore of Lake Tegernsee, by mid morning. 'I was so naïve,' Ilse recalled; 'I thought there would be records and people willing to help us. Instead, when we arrived at the children's home there was just one directress, looking ragged and depressed.'

As soon as she began to tell her about the boys, the woman interrupted her impatiently. 'To her we were just another two people who had come to the door looking for lost children. Her indifference upset me: "No, the children you are looking for are not here. Nor in any of the homes nearby. I have visited them all by bicycle and identified all the children." That was it. She made no effort to soften the blow.'

Overwhelmed by the enormity of their task, Almuth and Ilse returned to Ebenhausen. A few days later, they received another message from Canon Neuhäusler, urging them to go to Bad Sachsa. The Stauffenberg and Goerdeler children had been found at an SS-run orphanage in the town and there was a chance that Corrado and Roberto were also there. But he said they must hurry: Bad Sachsa lay in the new Russian occupation zone and would soon be out of bounds.

Situated on the old border with Czechoslovakia, the town was 350 miles from Ebenhausen and, before they could set off, they needed a new travel permit from the Americans. After a long wait to see Colonel Keegan, they were told that he was unable to issue a permit; the Americans had no jurisdiction over the Russian zone. But he thought the pass that he had given Ilse previously would get her as far as the frontier, and he advised her to try her luck anyway. Like Canon Neuhäusler, he insisted on the need to move quickly. In the confusion of the changeover, he thought she still had a chance.

To Ilse's frustration, the car broke down on the way back from Munich: 'It was maddening. I just wanted to get going straight away. Instead I had to wait two days while it was repaired.'

Had Fey been in touch with her mother, she could have told her that the dangerous journey she was about to embark on was futile. She knew the boys were not at Bad Sachsa. Sergeant Lenz had told her at Buchenwald.

It was a full day's drive to Bad Sachsa. In the last weeks of the war the Americans had advanced well into the Soviet occupation zone, negotiated with Stalin the previous October. Now that the agreement had been ratified, they were withdrawing and the roads were jammed with US Army trucks, filled with soldiers and equipment. With them came thousands of refugees, anxious not to be caught in the Russian sector. During the frequent stops, Ilse spoke to a number of them and they told her that Soviet troops were already preventing people from leaving the zone and many were trapped.

The drive took longer than Ilse and Almuth expected and they stopped for the night at Göttingen. All the hotels were full and they had to sleep in the car. Göttingen was on the edge of the British zone, and the next morning, still hoping for a permit to go on to Bad Sachsa, they queued outside the British military headquarters. Ilse was told that the Russians had entered the town three days earlier and that access was now impossible. 'I was totally exasperated but I knew we could not stop at that point. I was convinced the children were in the orphanage at Bad Sachsa. So I insisted. I begged and pleaded, and in the end the officer in charge gave in. He didn't think the pass would be of any use but, as he said, "No harm in trying, Madame."

'As we approached the zone,' Ilse continued, 'we drove slowly forward more or less feeling our way from one village to the next. When we reached the last village before Bad Sachsa, refugees told us that a checkpoint had been set up to mark the beginning of the Russian zone. We crawled nervously up to the wooden barrier. Bad Sachsa was three kilometres behind it.'

A British sergeant manned the barrier. Terrified of being trapped and not allowed back, Ilse did her best to persuade him to release one of his men to accompany her into the zone. But the sergeant was immovable. 'He could not leave his post or release his men. He tried to persuade me to give up and turn back. When I refused, he advised me to leave all my papers, money and jewellery behind and go forward on foot, carrying only the photographs of the children. Then he said, "The Russians have no respect for British or American documents nor do they have any respect for women, particularly young women. Therefore, for heaven's sake, leave your daughter behind and go alone."'

Ilse set out along the empty road, making a careful note of particular landmarks in case the Russians came and she had to flee across the fields back to the British zone. Arriving in Bad Sachsa in the early afternoon, she found the town completely dead. Not sure of the location of the orphanage, she went in search of the town hall. This was deserted too – or so she thought – but just as she was leaving she caught sight of a man sitting alone in an office on the ground floor. It turned out that he was the mayor and, amazed at her courage in venturing into the town, he immediately offered to drive her to the orphanage. Looking at his watch, he said they would have to be quick. They could only get there, he explained, when the Russians were changing guard.

The orphanage was in a commanding position at the top of a small hill. When they arrived, they found just two people there: the director, a large blonde woman of about fifty; and a small boy, aged around five, sitting on the porch, eating a plate of strawberries. Ilse showed her the pictures of Corrado and Robert. Studying them carefully, the woman assured her they had never been there: 'After all the difficulty in getting to Bad Sachsa and such high hopes, it was a terrible let-down and I was very upset. I asked who the solitary child was, and she said he was one of Carl Goerdeler's grandchildren. I offered to take him back with me, but she refused. She was under strict orders to release children to relatives only. I felt so sorry for that poor little soul.'

The mayor drove Ilse back to the frontier: 'Both of us were weeping; I, myself, from fatigue and disappointment, the mayor from general misery. Almuth was waiting at the barrier in a frantic state. She had seen two Russian guards walking toward the village. We drove back to Ebenhausen, totally disheartened. What next? What on earth were we going to do?'

In the absence of any other leads, Ilse and Almuth decided to go to Innsbruck, where the children had been seized.

It was a long shot, but Almuth remembered the names of the two SS officials she and her brother had dealt with when they had tried to visit Fey at the Gestapo prison in Adamgasse. If only the officials could be traced, this might yield something.

First, Ilse had to get another travel permit from Colonel Keegan. 'I had started to think of him as an old friend. He was charming and gracious as always but he threw cold water on the plan. "I'm afraid I just can't help you this time, Mrs von Hassell. As of yesterday, Innsbruck is in French hands. If you still think it worth it, you will have to deal with the new French administration to obtain a permit." '

Ilse asked Keegan if he could at least try to find out whether the two SS officials were still in Innsbruck. 'Though he was pessimistic, he rang up an American agent in the town. The answer was negative. The agent didn't have "the foggiest idea" as Keegan put it. The agent said that all SS had escaped from the city. "Tell the lady that it is hopeless for her to think she can accomplish anything here. If she rushes around on a wild goose chase she'll never find the children. A special committee will be set up for that sort of thing. It has to be done systematically.'

As Munich was in the US occupation zone, the French did not have an office in the city. At a loss as to how to obtain a permit, Ilse hurried to the Displaced Persons Bureau. The different occupation zones were only just being enforced and her one hope was that the officials at the bureau did not know that the French now controlled the area round Innsbruck: 'I found a young, innocent-looking American sergeant running things. I was in luck! Immediately and without any fuss he wrote out an official permit for us to travel to Innsbruck. It was only valid for a day but it seemed like solid gold to me. Thanking him profoundly, at which he seemed rather amazed, I dashed down the stairs and out to the car, shouting to Almuth, "I've got it, I've got it!"'

Innsbruck was 75 miles from Ebenhausen and they left at dawn the next morning. Crossing into Austria over the Scharnitz Pass, they took the same route as the SS convoy that had transported Fey and the other Prominenten from Dachau to Reichenau two months before.

Arriving in the city, they went straight to the Archbishop's Palace overlooking the Gestapo's old headquarters. Ilse hoped someone there might know about missing children but, when they knocked at the main door, a servant came out and said, 'Their Honours are still asleep and cannot be disturbed.'

Ilse was furious: 'Can you imagine that! There was the whole of Europe on its knees and Their Honours were sleeping!'

Next, they went to the main police station, hoping to obtain information about the SS officials whose names Almuth remembered.

Again, they met with indifference. The police commander simply shrugged his shoulders and said that most SS and Gestapo officials were in hiding under false names and with false papers.

By then it was almost twelve o'clock; over half the day granted by the precious travel permit had already gone. Despairing, and running out of time, they decided to split up. Ilse would try the prison where Fey had been detained and Almuth the Albergerhof; according to one of the two SS officials, Fey and the boys had stayed at the hotel on their first night in Innsbruck.

Ilse was able to see the prison governor straight away. Nazi-appointed personnel had not been purged and he had been in charge nine months earlier when Fey had been at Adamgasse 1. While he remembered her well, he had no information about the children: they had been the responsibility of the SS, over whom he had no jurisdiction. He was, however, sympathetic and urged Ilse to enquire at the *Jugendamt* – the Youth Assistance Office. It was possible one of the clerks would know the names of local SS women who had run the various orphanages in the area.

This office was located at the town hall, a gloomy baroque building. Inside, Ilse found a maze of offices and corridors: 'I rushed from one office to the other, asking for the Jugendamt. I was told to go to Room 140, but the whole place was in such chaos that nobody could tell me where it was. It was already past two o'clock and the permit was due to expire in less than three hours. Finally, I found the room, only to be told, "Sorry, Madame, displaced children are not the responsibility of this office. There is a special office for this. You have to go . . . etc. etc." '

At her wits' end, Ilse told the clerk that she simply had no time to find yet another office and pleaded with him to make a few calls on her behalf. Seeing her distress, he picked up the phone and started calling people he thought might know where children seized by the Gestapo had been taken. The conversations, as Ilse described, were awkward. 'Since no one would admit to being directly involved, he had to be extremely diplomatic. Finally, after about five calls, he got through to a certain Fräulein Schlieger, who, somebody said, had had something to do with the transport of children whose parents had been arrested by the Gestapo. At first, she disclaimed any knowledge. Then, little by little, the clerk managed to extract the names of four "institutes" where the Gestapo often sent children, all fairly close to Innsbruck.'

To passers-by, Ilse must have presented an extraordinary sight on leaving the town hall. Wearing a widow's veil and clad in traditional mourning dress, she ran through the centre of the city back to the car.

Almuth was waiting for her; by a stroke of extraordinary luck, she had also found an important lead.

It had taken Almuth a while to locate the Albergerhof, which she had visited the previous October when she and her brother had tried to see Fey: 'I remembered more or less where it was. But I had trouble finding it. Innsbruck had changed so much with all the bombing. You can imagine how shocked I was when I found nothing but a pile of rubble and a half-standing wall where the hotel had been.'

She was about to give up and go back to the car when she saw a shabbily dressed man poking about in the ruins, looking for something to salvage. On the off-chance that he might know something about the place, Almuth went up to him.

Incredibly, the man explained that he had been the chauffeur and handyman at the hotel. She had barely launched into a description of Fey and her two boys, then aged two and three, when the man interrupted her, his expression pained. 'Of course. I remember the beautiful young lady and the two little boys very well. They were in Room 112,' he said.

He went on to tell her that he had been polishing the banister rail on the stairs outside the room when two SS women took the children away: 'One child was screaming wildly and had to be dragged down the stairs.'

Almuth asked him if there was anything else he could remember. He said that he had overheard the women arguing about where they were taking the boys. Struggling to recall the names of the orphanages, after a long pause, he remembered.

'Wiesenhof and Allgäu,' he said.

★

Both were on the list that Ilse had obtained from the Jugendamt.

Wiesenhof was the closest – just 7 miles from Innsbruck – and the clerk had said that the orphanage was for children aged between three and five.

Driving at speed, they went there first.

As they approached the orphanage, Ilse was too agitated to notice the forbidding surroundings – the dense pine forest that enclosed the four-storey building, with its sinister Gothic turret, and the sheer rock, rising from the plateau on which it stood: 'All I took in was a large white house.'

Frau Buri, the head nurse at the orphanage, showed them inside and Ilse produced the photographs she had of the children. 'A good-looking woman in her late thirties, she seemed very kind and examined each picture carefully. Then, as I was already thinking of the next place on the list, Frau Buri stopped at the third or fourth picture and exclaimed, "Why, these are the Vorhof brothers, Conrad and Robert. Yes of course they're here!" With that, Almuth let out a shriek that must have resounded through the whole valley and I burst into a rare fit of tears.'

Frau Buri took them to a large dormitory at the back of the building. Just a few years before, when the Wiesenhof had been a sanatorium run by the Anthroposophy Society, it had been used as a dining room. Senior Nazis, including Rudolf Hess and General Ohlendorf – the murderer of more than 90,000 Jews – had dined here.

Thirty children lay on the rows of beds, taking their afternoon nap. Corrado and Roberto were sleeping side by side. Tiptoeing up to the bed, Ilse had her first glimpse of her lost grandchildren: 'I could see their little blond heads sticking out from under the bedclothes. They looked like little angels. But we did not want to wake them, so we slipped out of the room to let them finish their sleep.'

While they were waiting in Frau Buri's office, Ilse plied her with questions. Were the boys well? Did they seem distressed? Had they been at the home for long? Watching Buri's face closely, looking for any indication that she was withholding information or lying, she was reassured by her reply. 'Frau Buri confessed that she had often wondered who the boys could be, since the SS always changed the smaller children's names and never gave any information about who they were or why they were being held. She showed me the register she had filled in the night the Gestapo brought the children in: "Vorhof brothers, Conrad and Robert. Mother arrested." She told us the children had been at the orphanage for seven months. To begin with "Conrad" was very shy and always cried when he was put to bed. Robert, on the other hand, seemed to adjust to the home with much less difficulty and after a while began to play happily with the other children. She said that the brothers hated being separated and that she and the staff had been particularly touched by the way Conrad looked after Robert, helping him dress in the morning.'

Ilse felt a surge of pride when Frau Buri told her that she had tried to persuade 'Conrad' to tell her his real name, but he had refused. Her one concern was that both boys had apparently arrived at the Wiesenhof 'just before or just after Christmas'. Ilse knew from the note Fey dropped from the train that the Gestapo had seized the boys at the end of September. The dates did not add up. Where had they been between October and December? Frau Buri did not know.

After they had been talking for an hour or so, they heard the children getting up. Frau Buri went to fetch the boys and within a few minutes the door opened and she pushed the two little figures through, tactfully closing the door behind her.

Ilse felt as if all the breath had left her: 'They stood there gazing curiously at us, not saying a word. They looked so beautiful in their white shirts and dark blue shorts. They were obviously excited and their little faces looked so trusting. I knelt down and, grasping Corrado's tiny shoulders, asked, "Don't you remember your grandmother?" Without hesitating, he put his arm around my neck and said, "Can we go home now?"'

Yet, to Ilse's dismay, she did not recognize Roberto. 'When I had last seen him, he was a small baby, and I realised that I could not be sure he really was Robertino. I tried speaking Italian, but he did not seem to know a word; he only prattled on in an Austrian dialect that I could barely understand. My heart was torn between wanting to rescue this beautiful little boy and worry for my other grandson if this was the wrong child.'

Sitting the boy on her lap, she showed him photographs of Fey and Brazzà, hoping for some sign of recognition: 'On seeing the photographs, Corrado's eyes lit up, and he immediately said, "That's Mama!", "That's Brazzà!", and so on. But the little one just sat there, mute and looking vacant or, when I prompted him, repeating exactly what Corrado had said.

'I asked Corrado if the boy was his brother, and he said yes and gave him a big hug. But could I be certain? Frau Buri could not explain what had happened to the children before they arrived at the home. What if the boys had initially been split up and Corrado was only later told that this was his brother?'

Then, suddenly, as Ilse was wondering what to do next, the boy pointed at a tiny white spot on one of the photographs and started bouncing up and down on her lap.

'Mirko!' he shouted. 'Mirko!'

'My God! My heart jumped!' Ilse later told Fey. 'He kept staring at that little white horse, a small fleck on the castle lawn, as if it were the only thing in the world. At last I was sure. The children had been found!'

With only an hour on the travel permit still to run, Ilse and Almuth left almost immediately, taking the boys with them. As they were leaving, Frau Buri told them they had been extremely lucky. All Nazi children's homes, including Wiesenhof, were to be closed within the next ten days. After that, unclaimed children were to be given over for adoption to local farmers. She had already arranged a home for Corrado and Roberto and they were due to move there the following week. Had this happened, she said, the children would probably have been 'lost forever'.

41

The breakdown in communications between Germany and Italy meant that it was to be another two months before Fey and Detalmo heard that the boys had been found.

On the morning of Tuesday 11 September 1945, exactly one year after the SS first arrested her at Brazzà, Fey was working in the rose garden next to the chapel when Nonino appeared with a telegram. She assumed it was from Detalmo; he was in Rome and had already sent three or four cables. Absent-mindedly, Fey opened the envelope, still talking to Nonino: 'At first I could not understand the message. Then I stopped talking and reread it word by word. I could not believe it. It was over! The children had been found!'

As soon as Ilse arrived back at Ebenhausen with the children, she had written to a friend in Switzerland asking him to send word to Detalmo. It had taken eight weeks for the letter to reach him in Rome. Detalmo's telegram to Fey read:

CHILDREN FOUND THEY ARE WITH YOUR MOTHER STOP HAD CON-
FIRMATION CALLING COLONEL WILLE ZURICH STOP WILLE RECEIVED
LETTER FROM YOUR MOTHER WITH THE NEWS STOP THEY ARE IN
EXCELLENT HEALTH STOP TRIED TO TELEPHONE YOU BUT IN VAIN
DUE TO BAD WEATHER HOPE TO HAVE PERMITS FOR GERMANY
WITHIN A FEW DAYS LOVE DETALMO

The permits Detalmo hoped for did not materialize. He tried every-thing, but everywhere he met with the standard response: 'Italian citizens are not yet allowed to travel to Germany.'

A long month passed. Then Prime Minister Ferruccio Parri, whose private secretary Detalmo was at the time, asked him to arrange a reception at the Grand Hotel to honour General Mark Clark. In June

1944 Clark's 5th Army had liberated Rome and he was now commander-in-chief of US occupational forces in Austria.

Hundreds of officers and politicians attended the reception. At the
end of his tether, having tried everything, Detalmo waited for a
chance to speak to the general. The moment came when he saw Clark
break away from a group of reporters. Rushing over to him, he
offered him a whisky. Then he told him about his father-in-law and
the missing boys, and asked for his help. In one stroke, the impenetrable wall of bureaucracy gave way. Visibly moved, Clark turned to
an aide and instructed him to provide Detalmo with a jeep and a pass
to 'travel to Germany on special business'. He also asked the officer to
contact Ilse at Ebenhausen to let her know that Detalmo would be
coming to collect the children.

The jeep and the invaluable permit were delivered to Detalmo's
palazzo in Via Panama the next morning. Using the generous petrol
coupons provided, he drove through the night to Brazzà. Unable to
get through to Fey, when he suddenly appeared on the drive she was
bowled over: 'There he was with a US Army jeep, in US uniform
and boots, and with his Italian cavalry officer's cap on! Finally, we
were really going to see the boys!'

Wing Commander Colin Falconer, Foster's successor, immediately offered them three rooms on the ground floor of the villa and
they spent the day putting them in order. They also called on the
parish priest to ask him to arrange a special Mass in the tenth-century
chapel at Brazzà to be held on their return. The chapel was dedicated
to St Leonardo,* the patron saint of prisoners, and it seemed fitting
to hold a service of thanksgiving to celebrate the children's safe
homecoming. After the Mass, there was to be a big party, which Fey
planned with Bovolenta: 'We asked everyone to come – friends,
neighbours and all the contadini. There was to be food and wine for
all, and music and dancing. We wanted to bring everybody together
on that day so that we could lay to rest our sufferings and private

* One of the most venerated saints of the late Middle Ages, Leonard of Noblac
was thought to be a sixth-century Frankish nobleman and the godson of Clovis I,
founder of the Merovingian dynasty. According to legend, prisoners who invoked
St Leonard from their cells saw their chains break before their eyes.

tragedies. Detalmo said it would mark the end of the past and the beginning of a better life for all of us.'

Promptly, at six o'clock the next morning, they left for Ebenhausen. The jeep was packed with supplies – sacks of flour and sugar, enormous hams, huge rounds of cheese, salamis, fruit and several hundred eggs – things Fey knew her mother would appreciate, given the shortage of food in Germany.

It was already autumn and the trees were turning, the gold and copper colours brilliant against the snow-capped mountains. Fey and Detalmo barely exchanged a word on the journey. 'We were so intent on getting to Ebenhausen, we just stared straight ahead, praying there would be no hold-ups. We had no difficulty at the frontier. The permit worked wonders, and soldiers waved us through the checkpoints as if we were very important people.'

After driving without pause for almost ten hours, at four o'clock in the afternoon, they dropped down over the brow of the hill behind Ebenhausen and Fey saw the familiar spire of the church ahead. 'As we came closer and closer to the house, I felt sick with excitement.'

Ilse had heard their car coming up the gravel drive and was standing on the doorstep. Dressed in black, she looked much thinner than Fey remembered: 'It had been so long and so much had happened that, for a moment, it did not seem real. I jumped down from the jeep and rushed up to hug her. Choking with emotion, I managed to say "Poor Mutti" and her eyes filled with tears. But that was all. Her grief over my father's death was locked inside her. She could not or did not want to express it, even to me.'

Corrado and Roberto were out on a walk with Almuth and an agonizing wait followed, which to Fey, after all the months of waiting, seemed the longest wait of all. 'We sat down to tea as if it were the most normal thing in the world. As we were talking, Detalmo and I could not stop staring at the door, wondering just what we would find after one year. We talked about how we should react when Corradino and Robertino walked in. Should we hug them or should we hold back and be more formal? In the end, we decided to do the latter to see how the boys themselves responded.

'After a while we heard some footsteps and the door flew open. In walked Almuth with the children. They stood there in front of us and there was complete silence. I was trying terribly hard not to cry. Then, bending gently over Corrado, Almuth whispered, "Do you recognize that person?" He blushed and said immediately, "Yes, it's Mama." Pointing at Detalmo, Almuth asked him, "And do you know that man there?" Staring wide-eyed at Detalmo, Corrado hesitated for a moment. Then he said excitedly, "Yes, it's Papa! From the photograph!"

'After a few speechless seconds, Corrado broke free from Almuth and rushed over to Detalmo, who was standing in a corner of the room. He grabbed hold of Detalmo's trousers and put his little feet on top of Detalmo's shoes, something he had always done when he was younger. Robertino trotted over to me, clambered up on my lap, and sat without saying a word. Holding him in my arms, he seemed the most precious thing in the world.'

Epilogue

Corrado was four years old, and Roberto three, when Ilse found them at the Wiesenhof. Being that much older than Roberto, Corrado retains some memories of their time there. Particular scenes stand out: of a nurse playing a violin to them during air raids; of berry-picking expeditions to the nearby woods, when he had to keep an eye on Roberto in case he picked poisonous ones; of being warned that if he cried too much, he would be fed to the wolves in the forest. He can remember swallowing some beads which they had been given to make necklaces, and a doctor telling him that he would have to cut out his stomach. And he remembers seeing a dead man, killed in a bombing raid, lying in the road in front of the orphanage. He can still see his body – half inside, half out of a drain.

After he came home, Corrado suffered from a recurring nightmare: that he and Roberto were with Fey in a concentration camp. They were lined up in front of a trench, about to be shot. Later, he suffered from shyness and was mistrustful of people, never believing what he was told. 'As a teenager, I had to work hard to overcome this paranoia,' he said. Unsurprisingly, the therapist he saw thought his mistrust stemmed from the moment when he was seized by the SS: 'My mother told me that we were only being taken for a walk. She promised me she would join us. But of course she didn't.'

Today, Corrado and Roberto – now in their late seventies – are still living at Brazzà. Both brothers had successful careers. Detalmo had joined the European Commission in 1966 and Corrado would take the same path. His work as an economics adviser took him to Africa, to Japan and to America where, for a time, he was chargé d'affaires at the EU mission in Washington. Then, in 1992, he was appointed EU Ambassador to Austria – the country where the SS had hidden him as a small boy. In what was to prove an extraordinary coincidence, in his last position as chief of staff to the EU Commissioner for Agriculture, Rural Development and Fisheries, he worked with Commissioner Franz Fischler, who had grown up on a farm just a few hundred yards from the Wiesenhof orphanage. Fischler's family knew the farmer who was due to adopt Corrado and Roberto had Ilse not arrived at the eleventh hour.

Since retiring, Corrado has published biographies of his great-uncle, the explorer Pietro di Brazzà, after whom Brazzaville in the Congo was named, and his great-grandfather, Admiral von Tirpitz. He is married to Cécile, a Belgian artist, and they have one son.

Roberto's love for horses resulted in his becoming one of Italy's most accomplished riders. In 1964, at the age of twenty-two, he was selected to represent his country at the Tokyo Olympics. He did not, however, take part, opting instead to complete his diploma in architecture. He became one of the leading figures in the reconstruction of Friuli after the earthquake that devastated the region in 1976, and is well known for his landscape design projects, most notably the garden at Schloss Sanssouci in Potsdam. He married a South African and they have four children.

Ilse lived at her home in Ebenhausen until her death in 1982 at the age of ninety-six.

Following the loss of her husband, she devoted the remaining decades of her life to his memory. As soon as the war ended she dug up the diaries he had hidden in the foxhole at the end of the garden. Only she knew the code words he had used and she spent many months tirelessly editing the diaries prior to their publication in 1946.

In the years that followed, Ilse never failed to revive and defend her husband's memory, extolling his fight for justice and decency and his primary allegiance to moral values over and above State and Nation. Her greatest pleasure, however – her 'joy', as she described it – was the month she spent every summer at Brazzà with Fey and her grandsons. 'Naturally,' Fey wrote, 'my mother was the central figure at the children's weddings.'

Alex von Stauffenberg was detained by US war-crime investigators until September 1945. Broken-hearted at losing Fey, he continued to send her letters and poems from the villa in Frankfurt am Main where he was imprisoned.

While there, he had difficulty in convincing the Americans that he found it impossible to sit at the same table as fellow prisoner and war criminal Field Marshal von Rundstedt. Tasked by Hitler in 1941 with the conquest of the Ukraine, Rundstedt had urged his senior commanders to commit atrocities against Jews and Communists. Following the 20 July plot, he had overseen the posthumous expulsion of Alex's brothers – Claus and Berthold – from the army.

After his release, Alex went to live with a group of friends at Überlingen, on the northern shore of Lake Constance. During this time, he learned that Fey had had another child – a daughter, named Vivian – removing all hope that she would leave Detalmo and marry him. Three years would pass before he was ready to face the outside world.

In 1948, he was reappointed Professor of Ancient History at Munich University – a position he had filled before the war. With Gerhard Ritter, he was tasked with writing the history of the German Resistance which was included in Ritter's biography of Carl Goerdeler. He was also a staunch campaigner against nuclear weapons.

He married for a second time in 1949 – to Marlene Hoffmann, a widow whom he had met while at Überlingen. Alex had no children of his own, but he developed a close bond with his stepdaughter, Gudula. 'He was a true father,' she remembers; 'a loving, caring, attentive, generous and reliable man.'

Alex continued to correspond with Fey and the two met up on several occasions, in both Italy and Germany. Their last meeting was in Rome in 1963. Nearing sixty, he had lost none of his allure. Fey found him as striking then as she had done at the Hindenburg Baude.

A few months later, to her 'immense sadness', she received a letter from Uncle Moppel, saying that Alex had died of lung cancer.

Isa Vermehren, Gagi von Stauffenberg and the other Sippenhäftlinge left Capri on 13 June – two weeks after Detalmo arrived to collect Fey. They were not flown home, but to a British-run Displaced

Persons Camp at Versailles. There, undergoing further questioning, they remained for three days. 'It is not a nice feeling being in this very unfriendly environment,' Gagi wrote in her diary. 'We have to eat in an English canteen and the race to our table feels like running the gauntlet. Mika Stauffenberg can't bear this palpable animosity and goes up to people to tell them that we are related to the July plotters. This raises no comment, but afterwards cigarettes, chocolate and fruit land on our table.'

Gagi was flown to Munich in mid June. On her way home to Baden-Württemberg, she joined an official tour of Dachau with Canon Neuhauser, who had also been imprisoned there. While Gagi herself had briefly seen the camp as she and the other Sippenhäftlinge were marched from the hospital wing the night they left Dachau, the true scale of Nazi atrocities here and in other camps was only just coming to light. 'The tour of the camp is gruesome,' she wrote later that day; 'I wanted to sink into the ground for shame.'

Clemens, Gagi's father, never recovered from his ill-treatment at the hands of the SS and he died in February 1949. His death was followed nine months later by that of his 55-year-old wife; her health had been similarly compromised by her experiences in the concentration camps.

Gagi remained unmarried. Thirty-five years after the end of the war, she returned to live on her parents' old estate at Jettingen. She decided to publish her war diary on the seventieth anniversary of her release from captivity. She died in 2018, just short of reaching the grand age of 104.

Isa Vermehren began her own book after her release and repatriation in June 1945. Entitled *Reise durch den letzten Akt* (*A Journey Through the Final Act*), it charted her experiences in the camps, and also her thoughts on the Nazi regime and its crimes.

After the war, she trained as a teacher, entering a convent in 1951. She later became a headmistress. An advocate of moral education, she campaigned for its introduction to the curriculum: 'A society without a consensus on moral values . . . of what is desired and demanded on a moral plane . . . is doomed.'

Following her retirement from teaching, she became a presenter on

Germany's second-longest-running television show, *Wort zum Sonntag*, a forum for discussing religious themes. She died in 2009 at the age of 101.

Together with the other Sippenhäftlinge, in the late 1940s and 50s, both Isa and Gagi struggled to acclimatize to post-war Germany, where there were mixed feelings about the July plotters. Among some sections of the population they were seen as *Landesverräter* (traitors) who had broken their oath to the Führer. In the wider community, the families of the conspirators often encountered limited understanding and support and were forced to rely on close friends and relatives who shared their political views.

The anomalies within a country that was both trying to rebuild and come to terms with itself meant that, for a number of years after the war, Claus von Stauffenberg's wife, Nina, was denied a widow's pension. Yet the widow of Ronald Freisler,* the barbaric judge presiding over the People's Court, responsible for brutally executing hundreds of enemies of the Nazi state, was given a generous allowance.

Hitler had vowed to wipe out the 'brood of vipers' that had plotted against him. He had sworn to extinguish the lines of the aristocratic Prussians he loathed. When Nina died in 2006, at the age of ninety-two, the announcement of her death carried the names of her four surviving children and their spouses and also the following information: 'twelve grandchildren and twenty great-grandchildren'. She had made a nonsense of Hitler's revenge.

Himmler slipped out of Flensburg, the headquarters of the German High Command in the north of Germany, on the night of Wednesday 9 May 1945. It was on this night, at 01:00 hours, that the total surrender of German armed forces on all fronts came into effect.

He left Flensburg to evade arrest, taking five loyal SS men with him: his private secretary, two adjutants, the chief of the Gestapo and the chief of his personal security. Travelling in four armoured vehicles, they had stripped the insignia from their uniforms, and were dressed in an array of civilian and military clothes. Himmler

---

* Freisler was killed by a direct hit on the court building by a US plane on 3 February 1945.

had shaved off his moustache; in his pocket he carried the papers of Heinrich Hitzinger, a sergeant in a Special Armoured Company, whose identity he had now assumed.

For the first two nights, the group camped in a forest outside Flensburg while they prepared for their journey south. They were heading for the Harz mountains, east of Göttingen. Here, according to Werner Grothmann, one of the adjutants, Himmler hoped to hide out before making his way to the Alps once the 'hue and cry had died down'.

Reaching Marne, north of the River Elbe, on the night of 15 May, they were forced to abandon their vehicles. The river was several miles wide at this point and they paid an unwitting fisherman 500 Reichsmarks to take them across in his boat. For the next three days, they tramped slowly south, joining the hundreds of thousands of refugees and German soldiers on the road. En route, they slept in the open or inside railway stations or in peasant farmsteads. They spent the night of 18 May on a farm outside Bremervörde where unsuspecting British forces were billeted in the house next door.

For two more days, the six men evaded capture. Then, on the morning of 21 May, Himmler and his two adjutants, Grothmann and Sturmbannführer Macher, were arrested at a checkpoint manned by Soviet POWS.

The soldiers handed the men over to a passing British Army patrol. A report, based on the later interrogation of Werner Grothmann, describes this moment:

> Himmler was wearing civilian clothing and had a black patch over one of his eyes, whilst Grothmann & Macher were dressed half in uniform (tunics & greatcoats without badge of any kind) and half in civilian clothing. In view of this disguise, they were not recognised by the Russians . . .
>
> They were driven to a camp at Seedorf near Bremervörde where their captors still failed to recognise them. Grothmann says this was not surprising, since Heinrich Himmler in civilian clothing and without his glasses appears as an ordinary type of middle-class German and was definitely difficult to identify.

At Seedorf camp, the duty officer's questions were routine. But there were irregularities in the men's papers and they were detained in the cells overnight. The following morning, they were transferred to another camp for further interrogation. Again, their disguise remained undiscovered. In the words of Grothmann, the British interrogating officers assumed they were 'German civilian refugees or deserters from the Wehrmacht'.

Later that day, the three men were transferred again. As before, they remained unrecognized. After spending another night in British Army cells, the next morning – almost forty-eight hours after their capture – they were moved once more. This time to Camp 031, a British-run POW camp near Lüneburg.

Captain Selvester of the Black Watch, formerly an officer in the Salford City Police Force, was the commandant at the camp. 'At that time, large numbers of German troops were endeavouring to make their way home, and were carrying in most cases documents issued by senior officers of their respective regiments. These troops were being stopped and placed in ordinary POW cages, but if there was any doubt as to their identity they were sent to my Camp for further interrogation . . . The drill was for such prisoners to be paraded outside my office, and then allowed to enter singly, when it was my duty to obtain from them their names, addresses, ages, and any documents carried.'

At around two o'clock on the afternoon of 23 May, Himmler joined a queue of some twenty prisoners waiting to be interviewed by Captain Selvester. A few hours later, a guard came into the office to inform the captain that three of the prisoners in the queue outside were causing trouble. Apparently, they were demanding to be seen immediately. From experience, Selvester recognized that this was highly unusual; most prisoners were anxious to avoid drawing attention to themselves. His suspicions aroused, he ordered the guard to bring the three men in.

'The first man to enter my office was small, ill-looking and shabbily dressed, but he was immediately followed by two other men, both of whom were tall and soldierly looking, one slim and one well-built. The well-built man walked with a limp. I sensed something unusual, and ordered one of my sergeants to place the two men in close custody, and not to allow anyone to speak to them without my authority. They were then removed from my office, whereupon the small man, who was wearing a black patch over his left eye, removed the patch and put on a pair of spectacles. His identity was at once obvious, and he said, "Heinrich Himmler" in a very quiet voice.'

Himmler's motives for choosing this moment to turn himself in are unclear but, later that evening, he was driven to a small house in Lüneburg – number 31a Uelzener Strasse.

'At 22.45 Himmler was brought in,' Major Norman Whittaker, Commanding Officer of Second Army Defence Company, HQ, recalled. 'He was wrapped in a blanket. No arrogance about him. He was a cringing figure who knew that the game was up. We took him into the front room and the doctor began his search.'

Colonel Michael Murphy, the chief of intelligence on General Montgomery's staff, was in charge of the interrogation. Believing Himmler to be a suicide risk, the colonel needed to determine whether he was carrying poison before beginning the interview.

Himmler was ordered to strip and to stand, naked, in the centre of the room. Starting with his feet, army doctor Captain Wells – formerly a country GP from Oxfordshire – searched his body. He examined his buttocks, his navel, his armpits, his ears. Then he ordered Himmler to open his mouth. Hidden inside, as Colonel Murphy later described, Wells 'saw a small black knob sticking out between a gap in the teeth on the right hand side lower jaw'. In an attempt to remove what was evidently a phial of poison, Wells put two fingers into Himmler's mouth and it was then that Himmler twisted his head to one side and bit down hard on the doctor's fingers. 'My God! It's in his mouth. He's done it,' Wells shouted.

Immediately, Colonel Murphy and a sergeant jumped on Himmler and, throwing him to the ground, turned him on his stomach to prevent him from swallowing. Simultaneously, Wells held him by the throat, attempting to force him to spit out the poison. 'The dramatic rapidity of death I anticipated but slightly,' he later wrote. 'There were a slowing series of stertorous breaths which may have continued for half a minute, and the pulse for another minute after that. The stench coming from Himmler's mouth was unmistakably that of hydrocyanic.'

'This evil thing breathed its last at 23.14 [hours],' Major Whittaker noted. 'We turned it on its back, put a blanket on it and came away.'

Himmler's body, wrapped in camouflage netting and bound with telephone wire, was taken to a secret location near Lüneburg on 26 May. He was buried without religious ceremony. Sergeant Major Austin, a dustman in civilian life, dug the grave. Just three other members of Second Army Defence Company were present. 'These four were the only people who knew the location,' it was recorded in the company's War Diary. 'Subsequently the Map Reference of the location was handed by O. C. Defence Coy to Col. G (I) [Intelligence], HQ, Second Army.'

The exact location of the grave remains classified.

With the exception of Sergeant Foth, the head of the Jewish Camp at Stutthof, little is known of the fate of the numerous SS personnel appointed to guard the Sippenhäftlinge on their journey through the camps. While Sergeant Kupfer was imprisoned for a short time after the war, surviving records contain no trace of Fräulein Papke, who, with Kupfer, was in charge of the Sippenhäftlinge from Stutthof to Buchenwald – or of Rafforth and Knocke, their female overseers at Buchenwald.

A Polish war crimes tribunal sentenced Foth to death in 1947. During the six Stutthof trials, which took place in Gdańsk between 1946 and 1953, a total of seventy-two SS officers and six female overseers were found guilty of war crimes. Of these, twenty-two were subsequently executed.

Fey did, however, see Hans Kretschmann, the young lieutenant who had denounced her to the Gestapo in the autumn of 1944.

His telephone call came, out of the blue, one hot afternoon in the summer of 1984. Forty years had passed since the war and after Detalmo's successful career as an EU diplomat, primarily working in Africa, they were living in semi-retirement, dividing their time between Rome and Brazzà.

Fey was in their apartment in the centre of Rome when the telephone rang. 'The caller spoke in German and asked for me. I knew immediately that it was Kretschmann. He spoke just as he did then, flatly and to the point. He was with his wife at the Grand Hotel, attending a European telecommunications conference. He had become a director of the German telephone authority. To my amazement, he asked if I could join them for a drink at the hotel that evening to meet his wife and talk about old times.'

Reluctantly, after Kretschmann pressed her, Fey accepted the invitation. 'Punctually at seven o'clock, already feeling deeply troubled, I arrived at the bar at the Grand Hotel. There he was, looking very different from how I imagined. He had become fat and seemed much smaller than I remembered.'

The conversation was awkward from the beginning. Kretschmann had a photograph of Corrado and Roberto in his wallet, which he showed Fey, curious to find out what had become of the boys. Responding politely to his questions, Fey was taken aback when he began to speak about the war. 'He talked fondly of the good times spent with us at Brazzà, of "how pleasant and peaceful it had been when his regiment was stationed there". His wife smiled; she must have heard the "happy" story many times before.'

Overwhelmed, after a short time, Fey made some excuse and left. As she was leaving, Kretschmann gave her his card and asked if he could visit her at Brazzà.

That night, she was unable to sleep. 'I felt used and violated by the encounter. Why had he wanted to see me? He was in part responsible for my imprisonment and for my separation from the children. I could only think that he was eager to cleanse himself of his past as a fanatical Nazi, and his callous behaviour in betraying me to the SS.'

Seeing him brought her worst memories of the war to the surface – memories that, with the help of a psychiatrist and by focusing on her family and the household at Brazzà, she had, for the most part, managed to process.

Some days later, still haunted by the meeting, Fey made the decision to write to Kretschmann. Her letter quickly dispensed with the usual courtesies.

'Dear Kretschmann,' she began:

I was glad to meet you after all these years, and to meet your charming wife.

I write today to tell you that, after thinking about it at length, I would prefer not to see you again, and this for the following reasons.

Before meeting you at the hotel, I found myself incomprehensively anxious. After meeting you and your wife and coming home this anxiousness has not left me, and for many nights now I have slept very badly, my mind filled with thoughts of the past.

It has all come back so vividly – all the things which I have tried to forget. So many men and women have been destroyed by the memory of their terrible past, and I do not want my memories to destroy me. Yet, in seeing you, all stood before me: the sudden communication of my father's cruel death; the brutal separation from my two small boys; all the harrowing scenes I saw in the concentration camps; the traumatic search with my husband for the children after I was lucky enough to be freed, believing they would never be found.

Of course such things are impossible to truly forget, but your presence made the sights, the thoughts, the feelings from those times, come back – things that I have worked hard to bury.

Please give this letter to your wife; she will understand.

I wish you all the best for your future.

Fey's letter was frank and resolute. But, as she would later write, she forgave Kretschmann. 'He was young, and had no education other than under the Nazis. To forgive is one of the most important feelings in life.'

In her private struggle to come to terms with her experiences, this was one of her central tenets.

Like so many others who had come through the concentration camps, she suffered from survivors' guilt – a feeling that was compounded by the knowledge that, in comparison to the victims of the Holocaust, her experience, as she wrote, had been 'mild'. Her affinity with their suffering, and her need to try and answer the unanswerable question why, led her to read many of the memoirs written by the survivors of the camps. Viktor Frankl's *Man's Search for Meaning*, an account of his imprisonment at Auschwitz and other camps, became a touchstone for Fey. Throughout her life she kept it close by, pinning quotes from his writings to the desk where she worked. 'My mother never complained about what had happened to her because she saw her suffering as an intrinsic part of her destiny which had to be taken as it came, without bitterness or vengeance,' Corrado said.

In 1948 a report published by the International Tracing Service stated that, in Europe, 42,000 parents were still searching for their children.

Fey's gratitude that she had been reunited with her lost boys remained with her until the day she died at Brazzà at the age of ninety-two.*

On the face of it, it seemed they had been found by pure chance. But Fey thought differently. Her father, whom she adored, had been watching over her. As she said in an interview years after the war, 'He found the boys.'

---

*Fey died on 12 February 2010 – almost four years after Detalmo, who died in March 2006 at the age of ninety-one.

Acknowledgements

I owe an immense debt of gratitude to Corrado Pirzio-Biroli, without whom the book could not have been written. Besides allowing me access to his mother's remarkable collection of papers at Brazzà, he collaborated on much of the research. Indefatigably, and with great patience, he answered every question and was always ready to suggest new routes of enquiry. With his abiding interest in the history of Brazzà, and as the author of a biography of his great-grandfather, Grand Admiral von Tirpitz, he has shared his knowledge and expertise. I feel tremendously privileged to have had the opportunity to work so closely with him and I shall always be grateful to him for his generosity and encouragement.

Warmest thanks too to his wife, Cécile Pirzio-Biroli, who took me to Mount Joanaz to see the village of Canebola, the site of Allied supply drops to the partisans during the war, and to Villabassa and the Hotel Lago di Braies (Pragser Wildsee) in South Tyrol, where the Sippenhäftlinge spent their final days before they were liberated by the Americans in May 1945.

I would also like to thank Roberto Pirzio-Biroli for his invaluable insights into his extraordinary family.

I owe a great debt too to the late David Forbes-Watt, Fey's son-in-law through his marriage to her daughter, Vivian. The co-author of *A Mother's War*, his archives contain a wealth of papers, including notes he made of conversations with Fey and others relating to her story. Following Vivian's death in 1995, David married Helen and I am hugely indebted to her for her tireless efforts in searching through her late husband's papers for material for this book, and for her kind permission to use extracts from his work. David and Helen visited Fey and Detalmo often. I am grateful too to Helen for the many enjoyable hours spent listening to her fond memories of Fey and life at Brazzà.

Other family archives yielded valuable material. Orsina Hercolani, the granddaughter of Santa Borghese Hercolani, very kindly devoted a day to showing me the correspondence, spanning many decades, between her grandmother and Fey. It was fascinating, too, to meet Mike Foster, Robert Foster's son, who gave me a copy of his father's unpublished memoir, an insightful account of his first meeting with Fey and Detalmo and the Desert Air Force's occupation at Brazzà.

Thanks also to Valerie Riedesel, the daughter of Ännerle von Hofacker, and to Dr Gudula Knerr-Stauffenberg, who shared her memories of her stepfather, Alex von Stauffenberg.

In taking on a subject with primary sources in so many different European languages, I have depended on the work and guidance of others. I should like to express my thanks to Angelica von Hase for sourcing documents in Germany and Poland, and for pointing me in the right direction during the research; to Lily Pollack, for her help and enthusiasm at the outset; to Lucy Lethbridge for her perceptive reading of a section of the manuscript; and to Dan Booth, Sarah Niccolini and my mother, Carol, for their translations of the Italian material. Luca Colautti and Pietro Feruglio in Friuli, and Heinz Blaumeiser in the Tyrol, were invaluable in finding primary sources relating to Brazzà, and to the orphanage at Wiesenhof. The material they provided, including unpublished memoirs, local newspaper cuttings, and oral recollections passed down through the generations, offered an insight into the way of life during the Nazi period that I would otherwise have missed, and I am extremely grateful for their contributions.

I should like to thank Venetia Butterfield and all at Viking, especially my editor Mary Mount for her encouragement and her wise suggestions. Thanks too to my literary agent, Georgina Capel, to Rosanna Forte for her work in sourcing illustrations, and to Sarah-Jane Forder, my wonderful copy-editor.

It has also been a great pleasure for me to work with Alexandra Campbell and I cannot thank her enough. Besides culling German, French and Italian letters, diaries and published works, she has been a brilliant sounding board throughout. I am truly grateful to her for her eye for detail and her perceptive comments.

Finally, thanks to my family, and to my friends, Sarah Cole, Dorothy Cory-Wright, Jasper McMahon, William Sieghart and Sara Tibbetts, for their forbearance, and for their love and support during the writing of the book.

Notes

There are many different sources for Fey's story: the diaries she kept over the course of her life and the letters she wrote to her family and friends as well as her own memoir, *A Mother's War*, published in 1990 by John Murray. She also wrote copious notes about her father's work in the German Resistance and about her own experiences in the concentration camps, which she updated continually in the years after the war. These papers, together with the varying drafts of the manuscripts for the Italian, German, French and English editions of her memoir, are held in the archives at Brazzà, as are those of the late David Forbes-Watt, Fey's son-in-law and the co-writer of *A Mother's War*. Throughout the research and writing of this book I have tried to look at all sources for each stage of the narrative. Inevitably there is a difference in tone between work meant for publication and edited several years after the events described, and private correspondence and contemporaneous notes, so, in all cases, I have made every attempt to get as close to Fey's voice and experience as I could and have often used several different primary sources for one scene.

Prologue

1 '"Monika calling"' Fritz Molden, *Exploding Star: A Young Austrian Against Hitler* (Weidenfeld & Nicolson, 1978), p. 201

'The day' Thomas Albrich and Arno Gisinger, *Im Bombenkrieg: Tirol und Vorarlberg 1943–1945* (Haymon-Verlag, 1992), pp. 277ff.

'The Allies' Joseph E. Persico, *Piercing the Reich: The Penetration of Nazi Germany by American Secret Agents During World War II* (Viking, 1979), p. 10

2 'With Hitler holding' ibid.

'In these circumstances' Jim Ring, *Storming the Eagle's Nest* (Faber & Faber, 2014), pp. 240–44

2 'Soon after'   Albrich and Gisinger, op. cit., pp. 307–10; Headquarters 450th Bombardment Group, S-2 Narrative Report, Mission Number 194, 16 December 1944, 450th Memorial Association, www.450thbg.com 'It is a black'   Roland Sila (ed.), *Von Zerstörung und Wiederaufbau: Das Tagebuch der Innsbruckerin Anna Mutschlechner 1944–1951* (StudienVerlag, 2003), p. 36

3 'Fräulein Kummer's'   ibid., pp. 36–9
'The raid marked a change of tactic'   Albrich and Gisinger, op. cit., pp. 307–10
' "Tyroleans, we know that you will not permit it" '   Gerald Schwab, *OSS Agents in Hitler's Heartland: Destination Innsbruck* (Praeger, 1996), p. 104

1

7 'One night that December'   testimony of Frau Buri, Head Nurse, Wiesenhof Orphanage, July 1945, private family archive
'Both boys were dressed'   ibid.
'The road itself'   Matthias Breit, Head of the Municipal Museum, Absam, conversation with author, January 2017

8 'Within the grounds'   *The Times of Israel*, 20 October 2012

9 'This was the outskirts'   Peter Steindl, former vice mayor of Absam, conversation with author, January 2017
'In the centre of the village'   Heinz Blaumeiser, social historian and former lecturer, Innsbruck University, conversation with author, January 2017
'In the pagan mythology'   ibid.
'In the half-light'   testimony of Frau Buri, op. cit.

2

10 'To the locals'   information supplied by local historians Heinz Blaumeiser and Peter Steindl, conversations with author, January 2017
'Formerly a hunting lodge'   ibid.

10 'But he ran out of money' Peter Steindl, conversation with author, January 2017

'In the decade that followed' ibid.

11 'On the night of 10 November alone' *Anschluss and Extermination: The Fate of the Austrian Jews* (H.E.A.R.T., 2009), www.HolocaustResearch Project.org

'Walther Eidlitz, the grandson' Walther Eidlitz, *Unknown India: A Pilgrimage into a Forgotten World* (Rider & Co., 1952), p. 8

'But his mother' information supplied by Heinz Blaumeiser, op. cit.

'Yet, as the manager' Rudolf Hauschka, *At the Dawn of a New Age: Memories of a Scientist* (SteinerBooks, 2007), p. 69

'Three years earlier' Peter Staudenmaier, 'Between Occultism and Fascism: Anthroposophy and the Politics of Race and Nation in Germany and Italy, 1900–1945' (Doctoral thesis, Cornell University, 2010), pp. 186–7

12 'Throughout the 1930s' Hauschka, op. cit., p. 69

'Without formally endorsing' Staudenmaier, op. cit., pp. 186–7

'To Heydrich and' ibid., p. 245

'While continuing' ibid., pp. 182, 380

'No action was' ibid., p. 196

' "Despite the fact" ' Hauschka, op. cit., p. 69

'It was the villagers" Heinz Blaumeiser, conversation with author, January 2017

13 'Across the valley' Matthias Breit, Head of the Municipal Museum, Absam, conversation with author, January 2017

'On 18 April' Leopold Dollonek, *Tiroler Tageszeitung*, 9 February 1949

' "Mystically inclined" ' speech to NSDAP Parteitag, 6 September 1938, cited in Staudenmaier, op. cit., p. 207

'According to their files' Dollonek, op. cit.

'His flight' Staudenmaier, op. cit., p. 384

14 ' "Hitler was evidently" ' Peter Padfield, *Hess, Hitler and Churchill: The Real Turning Point of the Second World War – A Secret History* (Icon Books, 2013), p. 231

'The following day' cited in Staudenmaier, op. cit., p. 392

'The result was' ibid., pp. 390ff.

' "Suddenly, police cars" ' Hauschka, op. cit., p. 70

14 'Soon after'   Heinz Blaumeiser, conversation with author, February 2017
'Within months'   Matthias Breit and Peter Steindl, conversations with author, January 2017

15 'After lying vacant'   information supplied by Heinz Blaumeiser
'The suggestion is'   Corrado Pirzio-Biroli, conversation with author, November 2017; Frau Buri, Head Nurse, Wiesenhof Orphanage, July 1945, private family archive
'The local families'   Peter Steindl, conversation with author, January 2017
'For the rest of their lives'   ibid.
' "No one ever" '   conversation with author, January 2017
'Some of their descendants'   Trude Egger, resident of the hamlet of Wiesenhof, conversation with Heinz Blaumeiser, October 2017

16 'A local woman'   ibid.
'In the weeks after'   testimony of Frau Buri, Head Nurse, Wiesenhof Orphanage, July 1945, private family archive
'Conrad, the four-year-old'   ibid.
'Their angelic looks'   ibid.

17 'One day'   ibid.
'She tried'   ibid.

3

21 ' "Secret. AHQ DAF" '   Desert Air Force Operations Record Books, Commands, 1 January 1945–31 May 1945, AIR 24/444, The National Archives
'Five days previously'   Robert Foster, unpublished memoir, undated, private family archive
'This was the fourth'   Desert Air Force Operations Record Books, op. cit.
'He himself'   conversation with Mike Foster, Robert Foster's son, September 2016

22 'At forty-seven, his career'   ibid.
'While the Allies'   obituary, Group Captain Westlake, *Daily Telegraph*, 26 January 2006
'The major difficulty'   'Operation "Bowler" ', AIR 23/1819, The National Archives

22 'The planes took off' ibid.

23 'So accurate were the pilots' obituary, Group Captain Westlake, op. cit.
'One was from' Air Marshal Guy Garrod to Sir Norman H. Bottomley, 6 May 1945, AIR 20/3216, The National Archives
'Foster peered' Mike Foster, conversation with author; notes of a conversation between David Forbes-Watt and Air Marshal C. L. Falconer, stationed with Foster at Brazzà (and subsequently Air Officer Commanding, DAF), undated, private family archive
'In the last days of the Italian campaign' Desert Air Force Operations Record Books, op. cit.
'Seeing the photographs' Corrado Pirzio-Biroli, conversation with author, November 2016

24 'Back in April' Robert Foster, op. cit.
'Seeing it all' ibid.

25 'Yet, as he walked' Forbes-Watt and Falconer, op. cit.
'As he passed' Robert Foster, op. cit.

26 'The only time' ibid.

27 'Following years of' Major 'Tommy' Macpherson (Colonel Sir Ronald Thomas Stewart Macpherson, CB, MC & Two Bars), Commander, SOE Coolant Mission, Situation Reports, May–June 1945, HS 6/852, The National Archives
'Already, Yugoslav' ibid.

4

28 ' "Total of unidentified" ' Sir Noel Charles to Foreign Office, 16 May 1945, cited by David Stafford in *Mission Accomplished: SOE and Italy 1943–1945* (Vintage, 2012), p. 331
'At Ziracco' Major 'Tommy' Macpherson, SOE Coolant Mission, Situation Reports, May 1945, HS 6/852, The National Archives
' "... a ditch" ' ibid.

29 ' "... perhaps the most" ' ibid.
'Garibaldi commanders' ibid.
' "*Zivio Stalin*" ' David Stafford, *Endgame 1945* (Little, Brown, 2007), p. 345
' "Citizens of Udine" ' Macpherson, op. cit.

30 ' "... witches' cauldron" '   Geoffrey Cox, *Race for Trieste* (William Kimber, 1977), p. 158

'Besides flying sorties'   ADV HQ DAF, Operations Record Book for Month of April/May 1945, Summary of Events, AIR 24/444, The National Archives

5

31 'One looked'   conversation between David Forbes-Watt and Air Marshal C. L. Falconer, stationed with Foster at Brazzà (and subsequently Air Officer Commanding, DAF), undated, private family archive

'Straight away'   ibid.

32 'Nicknamed'   Angelo D'Orsi, 'Vittorio Emanuele III', *Il Manifesto*, 19 December 2017

'Pushing it'   Forbes-Watt and Falconer, op. cit.

'One face'   ibid.

33 'Among the'   ibid.

34 'As Foster was leafing'   ibid.

6

35 'He came'   Detalmo Pirzio-Biroli, *Finestre e Finestrelle su Brazzà e Altrove* (Campanotto Rifili, 2005), pp. 78–9

'The family's name'   Corrado Pirzio-Biroli, conversation with author, November 2016

'Then, shaking'   conversation between David Forbes-Watt and Air Marshal C. L. Falconer, stationed with Foster at Brazzà (and subsequently Air Officer Commanding, DAF), undated, private family archive

36 'One night'   Corrado Pirzio-Biroli, conversation with author, November 2016

'*An American*'   Forbes-Watt and Falconer, op. cit.

'Then, quietly'   ibid.

36 'Crossing the garden'   ibid.

37 'To begin with'   David Forbes-Watt and Fey Pirzio-Biroli, manuscript notes, private family archive
'It was where'   ibid.

38 'Their first night'   ibid.
'Looking around'   Forbes-Watt and Falconer, op. cit.
'It was where'   Robert Foster, unpublished memoir, undated, private family archive

39 'Along the'   Private Papers of J. R. T. Hopper, Documents 6342, Imperial War Museum
'They came'   Forbes-Watt and Pirzio-Biroli, op. cit.
'Despite all'   Foster, op. cit.
'Where were'   ibid.
'Moreover'   ibid.

7

43 'At exactly'   *Il Messaggero*, 19 October 1937
'The ovation'   ibid.

44 '. . . "the totally destructive tyranny" '   speech by Himmler on taking up his appointment as Chief of the German Police, 18 June 1936, Prussian Interior Ministry, cited in Peter Longerich, *Heinrich Himmler* (Oxford University Press, 2012), p. 204
'That summer'   Longerich, op. cit., p. 242
'Taking his cue'   *Il Messaggero*, 19 October 1937

45 '. . . "a nation of murderers and pederasts" '   cited in Eugen Dollmann, *With Hitler and Mussolini: Memoirs of a Nazi Interpreter* (Skyhorse Publishing, 2017), p. 49
' "They are fanatical" '   Christopher Duggan, *Fascist Voices: An Intimate History of Mussolini's Italy* (Vintage, 2013), p. 282

46 '. . . "mould, mice and basements" '   *Il Messaggero*, 19 October 1937

47 'It was almost nine'   Ilse von Hassell, unpublished memoir, undated, private family archive

48 ' "I advised him" '   Dollmann, op. cit., p. 54
'An orchestra'   Ilse von Hassell, op. cit.

48 '. . . "his only method"' Duchess of Sermoneta, *Sparkle Distant Worlds* (Hutchinson, 1947), p. 134

49 '"his sharp, pale"' Carl J. Burckhardt, quoted in Eugen Dollmann, op. cit., p. 96

'"We Italians"' quoted in Ilse von Hassell, op. cit.

'"The Ambassador looked"' Dollmann, op. cit., p. 45

'. . . "politics, intrigue"' ibid., p. 97

'"We were just wondering"' Ilse von Hassell, op. cit.

'"When I insisted"' Ulrich von Hassell, *Römische Tagebücher und Briefe 1932–1938* (Herbig, 2004), p. 207

50 '. . . "interests lay principally"' quoted in Ilse von Hassell, op. cit.

'"Unpleasant and treacherous"' Galeazzo Ciano, *Diary 1937–1943* (Phoenix Press, 2002), p. 63

'. . . he was taught absolute' This was US intelligence chief Allen Dulles's assessment of Hassell's upbringing. See his introduction to *The Von Hassell Diaries 1938–1944* (Doubleday, 1947).

51 '"A German nobleman"' Gottfried von Nostitz, quoted by Richard Overy, introduction to *The Ulrich von Hassell Diaries* (Frontline Books, 2011), p. ix

'. . . "trenchant humour"' Hans Bernd Gisevius, ibid.

'Hitler, however' Dulles, op. cit., p. x

'By the autumn' Ilse von Hassell, op. cit.

'Earlier that year' ibid.

'Sometimes he used' Ulrich von Hassell, op. cit., pp. 19–20

53 'From a political' ibid., p. 194

54 '"There is no limit"' ibid.

'To Hassell's embarrassment' Ilse von Hassell, op. cit.

'"Göring will come"' Ulrich von Hassell, op. cit., p. 195

'"He found our car"' ibid.

'"His remarks"' ibid., p. 195

'"It's just a toy"' Ilse von Hassell, op. cit.

'"These were the thoughts"' Ulrich von Hassell, op. cit., p. 196

55 '"*Pour moi*"' Corrado Pirzio-Biroli, conversation with author, October 2018

56 '. . . "crude and brutish"' Ilse von Hassell, op. cit.

56 '. . . "full authority to scupper"'   ibid.

'. . . "block-building"'   ibid.

57 '. . . "dangerous adventure"'   ibid.

' "I took advantage"'   Galeazzo Ciano, op. cit., p. 19

'The professor'   Richard Beyler, 'Werner Heisenberg, German Physicist and Philosopher', *Encyclopaedia Britannica*, britannica.com

'During the meeting'   Ilse von Hassell, op. cit.

' "Politics and diplomacy"'   Ulrich von Hassell, op. cit., p. 209

58 'On the night of 9 November'   'The Night of Broken Glass', website of the United States Holocaust Memorial Museum

' "I am writing"'   *The Ulrich von Hassell Diaries* (Frontline Books, 2011), p. 9

' "Conversations with"'   ibid., p. 10

8

61 'He was working'   Peter Hoffmann, *The History of German Resistance 1933–1945* (McGill-Queen's University Press, 1988), p. 123

' "For several months"'   *The Ulrich von Hassell Diaries* (Frontline Books, 2011), p. 167

62 ' "He carefully closed"'   *The Von Hassell Diaries 1938–1944* (Doubleday, 1947), p. 256

' "For the time being"'   ibid.

' "When I started"'   ibid.

' "The memory"'   ibid., p. 258

63 ' "According to"'   ibid.

' "I get fed up"'   ibid., p. 290

'Every soldier'   Hoffmann, op. cit., p. 251

'Additionally'   Gregor Schöllgen, *A Conservative Against Hitler* (St Martin's Press, 1991), p. 116

' "Nothing is"'   Ulrich von Hassell's diary, 16 June and 20 September 1941, cited in Schöllgen, op. cit., p. 116

64 'To convince'   Schöllgen, op. cit., pp. 78–9

'Believing that Hitler's'   Andrew Roberts, *'The Holy Fox': A Biography of Lord Halifax* (Weidenfeld & Nicolson, 1991), p. 184

64 ' "Ridiculous stale" '   quoted in Schöllgen, op. cit., p. 84

65 'In their eyes'   ibid., p. 93

'At the beginning'   ibid., p. 86

' "I am sure" '   ibid.

'In January 1942'   ibid.

' "In Germany" '   Richard Lamb, *Churchill as War Leader* (Bloomsbury, 1991), p. 292

66 ' "If the generals" '   *The Von Hassell Diaries 1938–1944*, op. cit., p. 281

' . . . "some sort of" '   ibid., p. 286

' . . . "the whole building" '   ibid.

'Assassination, however'   Michael Baigent and Richard Leigh, *Secret Germany: Claus von Stauffenberg and the Mystical Crusade Against Hitler* (Jonathan Cape, 1994), p. 33

'He wore a'   Hoffmann, op. cit., p. 278

'When Hitler'   Baigent and Leigh, op. cit., p. 33

67 ' "In spite of" '   *The Ulrich von Hassell Diaries*, op. cit., p. 186

' "Hitler's prestige" '   *The Von Hassell Diaries 1938–1944*, op. cit., p. 286

'While Germany'   Baigent and Leigh, op. cit., p. 1

' "The last few weeks" '   *The Ulrich von Hassell Diaries*, op. cit., p. 185

' "For the first time" '   ibid.

' "Sad to say" '   ibid., p. 187

68 ' "They have undoubted" '   ibid., p. 194

'His family'   Michael Balfour, *Withstanding Hitler in Germany, 1933–1945* (Routledge, 1988), p. 124

69 ' "You, Tresckow" '   Offizierschule des Heeres, Tresckow monographie

' . . . "both duty and honour" '   Hoffmann, op. cit., p. 265

' . . . "ready to act" '   *The Ulrich von Hassell Diaries*, op. cit., p. 143

' . . . "the spark" '   Fabian von Schlabrendorff, *The Secret War Against Hitler* (Hodder & Stoughton, 1966), p. 227

'All two dozen'   Baigent and Leigh, op. cit., p. 23

' . . . "it was not seemly" '   ibid.

70 'As Schlabrendorff'   Fabian von Schlabrendorff, op. cit., p. 231

' "Dropping the idea" '   ibid.

' "With mounting tension" '   ibid., p. 236

71 ' . . . "a state of indescribable" '   ibid.

' "The reason" '   ibid., p. 237

72 'Here, Gersdorff' Baigent and Leigh, op. cit., p. 25
'As the acid' ibid.

10

85 'Yet, as one man' Umberto Paviotti, *Udine sotto l'occupazione Tedesca*, edited by Tiziano Sguazzero (Istituto Friulano per la Storia del Movimento di Liberazione, 2009), p. 5
'But then, on' Iris Origo, *War in Val D'Orcia: An Italian War Diary, 1943–1944* (Jonathan Cape, 1947), p. 61

86 'Twenty contadini' Corrado Pirzio-Biroli, conversation with author, November 2017

87 'The relationship' Sydel Silverman, *Three Bells of Civilization: The Life of an Italian Hill Town* (Columbia University Press, 1975), p. 61
'A wealthy heiress' Corrado Pirzio-Biroli, conversation with author, November 2017; Idanna Pucci, *The Trials of Maria Barbella* (Vintage, 1997), pp. 13–15

88 'Cora's progressive' Mariangela Toppazzini, 'Un Americana Innamorata Del Friuli', *Friuli Colinare*, undated
'Recognizing that' Corrado Pirzio-Biroli, conversation with author, November 2017

89 'In 1906' Corrado Pirzio-Biroli, conversation with author, November 2017

90 '"I arrived"' Paviotti, op. cit., p. 4
'"*Attention!*"' ibid., p. 6
'"*Orders to civilians!*"' ibid., p. 7

91 'Hitler had been' Rupert Colley, *Mussolini: History in an Hour* (William Collins, 2013), e-book
'It left him' ibid.
'Radioing for assistance' ibid.

92 'The Germans were' Paviotti, op. cit., pp. 11–12

93 '"I did not live"' Rosanna Boratto, quoted in *Una Disubbidienza Civile: Le Donne friulane di fronte all'8 Settembre 1943* (Udine, Comitato Resistenti, 2013), p. 46
'"Any Allied"' Paviotti, op. cit., p. 15

93   ' "Generally, people are" '   ibid., pp. 8–11
94   'Before fleeing'   ibid., p. 18

11

101 'For the population'   Vatican questionnaire, parish of Santa Margher-
     ita archives, 1939
     'The poverty'   Giorgio Botto, whose ancestors were tenant farmers
     at Brazzà, conversation with author, November 2017
102 ' "What is the percentage" '   Vatican questionnaire, op. cit.
107 ' "The time has come" '   Jane Scrivener, *Inside Rome With the Germans*
     (Holloway Press, 2007), p. 62

12

111 'Previously attached'   G. H. Bennett, *The Nazi, the Painter and the
     Forgotten Story of the SS Road* (Reaktion Books, 2012), p. 61
     ' "In the period" '   Operational Situation Report, USSR, No. 178,
     *Einsatzgruppen Reports: Selections from the Dispatches of the Nazi Death
     Squads' Campaign Against the Jews, July 1941–January 1943*, ed. Y. Arad,
     S. Krakowski and S. Spector (Holocaust Library, 1989), pp. 308–9
     'At the beginning'   Bennett, op. cit., p. 62
112 ' "Going past" '   Umberto Paviotti, *Udine sotto l'occupazione Tedesca*,
     ed. Tiziano Sguazzero (Istituto Friulano per la Storia del Movimento
     di Liberazione, 2009), p. 362
     ' "There are about" '   ibid., pp. 369–70
113 ' "The Germans are" '   Fey Pirzio-Biroli to Santa Hercolani, undated,
     private family archive
     'In Povoletto'   Paviotti, op. cit., p. 352
     ' "Mussolini" '   ibid., pp. 360–3
     ' "At four in" '   Fey Pirzio-Biroli to Santa Hercolani, 16–17 May
     1943, private family archive
114 ' "The storm" '   ibid.

114 ' "It's unimaginable" '   Paviotti, op. cit., p. 375

115 ' "Some weapons" '   ibid.

' "I was speechless" '   Walter Ceschia (ed.), *Dal Diario di Kitzmüller: Giorni di Caino 1943–1945* (Studio Effe, Udine, 1977), p. 21

117 ' "At about 8 o'clock" '   Vittorio Zanuttini, quoted in Ceschia, op. cit., pp. 44–5

' "At about half past nine" '   ibid.

' "The boys arrived" '   ibid.

118 ' "They were" '   ibid.

' "I heard" '   Paviotti, op. cit., p. 379

' "The seven crew" '   ibid., p. 377

119 ' "The Osoppo's work" '   Fey Pirzio-Biroli to Santa Hercolani, 26 May 1944, private family archive

120 ' "The word 'partigiani' " '   Paviotti, op. cit., p. 402

123 'Painted black'   Enrico Barbina, *The Modified Liberators*, B-24J 42-51778, Lt Solomon's aircrew, thesolomoncrew.com

'Codenamed Coolant'   David Stafford, *Mission Accomplished: SOE and Italy 1943–1945* (Vintage, 2012), pp. 133–43

'Jumping from'   Harry Hargreaves, 'The Sermon Mission to Friuli', *No. 1 Special Force and the Italian Resistance* (Federazione Italiana Associazioni Partigiane/Special Forces Club, 1990), vol. 2, p. 167

124 ' "Never remain" '   1 Special Force Reports from Missions, WO 204/7301, The National Archives

'Facing this'   Major Hedley Vincent's Mission Report, WO 106/3929, The National Archives

' "The execution" '   ibid.

125 'It was Vincent'   Stafford, op. cit., p. 137

'Typically'   ibid.

'As one SOE officer'   Patrick Martin Smith, unpublished memoir, Private Papers of Captain P. G. B. Martin-Smith, Documents 16757, Imperial War Museum

'The villagers'   Stafford, op. cit., p. 138

'. . . "with freefalling" '   Hargreaves, op. cit., p. 169

126 ' "One of my most" '   David Godwin, 'The British Mission to East Friuli', *No. 1 Special Force and the Italian Resistance*, op. cit., p. 177

126 'Throughout July'   1 Special Force Reports from Missions, WO 106/3929, WO 204/7301, HS 6/850, The National Archives

13

127 '. . . "in her isolation"'   *The Ulrich von Hassell Diaries* (Frontline Books, 2011), p. 238

'He refused to visit hospitals'   Michael Baigent and Richard Leigh, *Secret Germany: Claus von Stauffenberg and the Mystical Crusade Against Hitler* (Jonathan Cape, 1994), p. 34

'"It is tragic"'   ibid.

'As the country's military might'   ibid.

'. . . "desperately isolated attempts"'   *The Ulrich von Hassell Diaries*, op. cit., p. 191

128 '. . . "the only one"'   Ilse von Hassell, unpublished memoir, undated, private family archive

'Working late'   Baigent and Leigh, op. cit., p. 9

129 '"A man who doesn't"'   obituary, Ewald-Heinrich von Kleist, *Daily Telegraph*, 13 March 2013

130 '"Today, please"'   quoted in Eberhard Zeller, *The Flame of Freedom* (Oswald Wolff, 1967), p. 267

'At the end of 1943'   Ilse von Hassell, op. cit.

'At six in the'   Roger Manvell and Heinrich Fraenkel, *The July Plot* (The Bodley Head, 1964), p. 101

'Of the same type'   ibid.; Baigent and Leigh, op. cit., p. 43

131 'A gloomy, forbidding'   Baigent and Leigh, op. cit., p. 34

'The first gate'   Zeller, op. cit., p. 301

'The bunkers here'   ibid.

132 'With only fifteen minutes'   Baigent and Leigh, op. cit., p. 43

'. . . "busy with a wrapped parcel"'   ibid.

133 'Whereas the subterranean'   Zeller, op. cit., p. 303

'. . . "catch everything"'   quoted in Baigent and Leigh, op. cit., p. 44

134 '. . . "parade ground"'   ibid., p. 46

'"Colonel Count"'   quoted in Zeller, op. cit., p. 304

'"You heard"'   ibid.

14

135 ' "My comrades" '   Eberhard Zeller, *The Flame of Freedom* (Oswald Wolff, 1967), p. 341

136 'Hitler had escaped'   Roger Manvell and Heinrich Fraenkel, *The July Plot* (The Bodley Head, 1964), p. 119; Zeller, op. cit., p. 336
' "The door was" '   Zeller, op. cit., p. 336
'Guiding Mussolini'   Manvell and Fraenkel, op. cit., p. 120
' "When I reflect" '   ibid.

137 ' "Probably only" '   ibid., pp. 156–7
' "No military authority" '   Zeller, op. cit., p. 342
' "I shall crush" '   Eugen Dollmann, *With Hitler and Mussolini: Memoirs of a Nazi Interpreter* (Skyhorse Publishing, 2017), p. 323

138 'In the last week'   Umberto Paviotti, *Udine sotto l'occupazione Tedesca*, ed. Tiziano Sguazzero (Istituto Friulano per la Storia del Movimento di Liberazione, 2009), p. 426

139 ' "Udine is paved" '   Fey Pirzio-Biroli to Santa Hercolani, 29 July 1944, private family archive
'Shocked by the extent'   David Stafford, *Mission Accomplished: SOE and Italy 1943–1945* (Vintage, 2012), p. 139

140 'He knew that'   Corrado Pirzio-Biroli, conversation with author, October 2018

141 ' "My guests" '   Fey Pirzio-Biroli to Santa Hercolani, 30 August 1944, private family archive

15

142 ' "There goes someone" '   quoted in Roger Manvell and Heinrich Fraenkel, *The July Plot* (The Bodley Head, 1964), p. 173
' "His head" '   ibid.
'It was around'   Ilse von Hassell, unpublished memoir, undated, private family archive

143 'The sculptress'   Wolf Ulrich von Hassell, quoted in *The Ulrich von Hassell Diaries* (Frontline Books, 2011), p. 242

143 ' "My death is certain" '   ibid.

' "One method was" '   Fabian von Schlabrendorff, *The Secret War Against Hitler* (Hodder & Stoughton, 1966), pp. 311–14

144 ' "One night" '   ibid.

145 ' "A prison cell" '   Wolf Ulrich von Hassell, op. cit., p. 243

'He typed'   Ilse von Hassell, op. cit.

' "You can lead" '   Wolf Ulrich von Hassell, op. cit.

'. . . "facilitate mercy" '   Martin Bormann to Chef der Sicherheitspolizei und des SD, 2 September 1944, NS6/25, Bundesarchiv Berlin

146 'One of the German'   Gregor Schöllgen, *A Conservative Against Hitler* (St Martin's Press, 1991), p. 119

' "When he was addressed" '   Helmut Schmidt, *Was Ich Noch Sagen Wollte* (C. H. Beck, 2015), pp. 53–7

' "The whole trial" '   ibid.

' "He followed" '   ibid.

' "If a government" '   Joachim Mehlhausen (ed.), *Zeugen des Widerstands* (Mohr Siebeck, 1998), p. 64

' "My beloved" '   *The Ulrich von Hassell Diaries*, op. cit., p. 241

148 '. . . "hanged like animals" '   Marion Gräfin Dönhoff, *'Um der Ehre willen': Erinnerungen an die Freunde vom 20. Juli* (Siedler, 1994), pp. 10–12

'The widows'   ibid.

'The method of execution'   Michael Baigent and Richard Leigh, *Secret Germany: Claus von Stauffenberg and the Mystical Crusade Against Hitler* (Jonathan Cape, 1994), p. 63

' "Not a single" '   quoted in Baigent and Leigh, op. cit., p. 63

'The utter'   Manvell and Fraenkel, op. cit., p. 198

' "Imagine a room" '   ibid., pp. 198–9

16

154 'According to this'   Michael Baigent and Richard Leigh, *Secret Germany: Claus von Stauffenberg and the Mystical Crusade Against Hitler* (Jonathan Cape, 1994), p. 60

'The following weeks'   Robert Loeffel, '*Sippenhaft*, Terror and Fear in Nazi Germany', *Contemporary European History*, vol. 16, issue 1 (2007), p. 56

154 'More than 180' ibid.

156 'Saint Maria di Rosa' 'Spiritual Life', *Catholic Herald*, 9 December 2010

157 ' "I can't go" ' ibid.
'In founding the order' ibid.

17

159 'Along the ridge' Major Hedley Vincent's Mission Report, WO 106/3929, The National Archives; Umberto Paviotti, *Udine sotto l'occupazione Tedesca*, ed. Tiziano Sguazzero (Istituto Friulano per la Storia del Movimento di Liberazione, 2009), pp. 465–73

160 ' "Dearest Fey" ' Santa Hercolani to Fey Pirzio-Biroli, 16 September 1944, quoted in Fey von Hassell and David Forbes-Watt, *A Mother's War* (John Murray, 1990), p. 96

164 'The Nazis had even' Robert E. Conot, *Justice at Nuremberg* (Carroll & Graf, 1993), p. 300

18

167 ' "The blow which" ' Major Hedley Vincent's Mission Report, WO 106/3929, The National Archives
'Only by deploying' ibid.

169 'In recent months' ibid.
'. . . "certain reliable" ' ibid.
' "It seems possible" ' ibid.

170 'WE ARE AT CRAVERO' No. 1 Special Force: operation instructions, situation reports, intelligence reports by agents, partisan activities etc., WO 204/7295, The National Archives

171 'After the partisans' War Crimes Investigation conducted in the Nimis/Subit area by Section 77 Special Investigation Branch of the Corps of Military Police, Testimonies of the local priest, captured SS soldiers, and Allied prisoners of war, May–August 1945, WO 311/1267, The National Archives

19

176 'Upwards of'   Wilfried Beimrohr, ' "Gegnerbekämpfung": Die Staats-
polizeistelle Innsbruck der Gestapo', in Rolf Steininger and Sabine
Pitscheider (eds), *Tirol und Vorarlberg in der NS-Zeit* (Studien Verlag, 2002)
'Answering directly to Berlin'   ibid.

177 'The various departments'   Final Interrogation Report, Busch, Fried-
rich Heinrich, Assistant Gestapo Chief of Innsbruck, 15 September
1945, 307th Counter Intelligence Corps Detachment, RG263, Entry
ZZ-8, Box 34, National Archives and Records Administration, Wash-
ington DC
'But the bulk'   Beimrohr, op. cit.
' "There was no" '   Friedrich Busch, RG263, Entry ZZ-8, Box 34,
National Archives and Records Administration, Washington DC
'Aged forty-one'   Deputy Theater Judge Advocate Office, 7708 War
Crimes Group, United States Forces, 24 March 1947, Records of the
Central Intelligence Agency, RG263, Entry ZZ-18, Box 34
'In the summer'   ibid.
'Aged forty'   ibid.
'The majority were'   Beimrohr, op. cit.

178 'One of the chief interrogators'   Gerald Schwab, *OSS Agents in Hit-
ler's Heartland: Destination Innsbruck* (Praeger, 1996), p. 114
' "Don't be stupid" '   ibid.
'Trussing the prisoner'   ibid., p. 117

21

193 'A slim, stylish'   Robert Loeffel, *Family Punishment in Nazi Germany:
Sippenhaft, Terror and Myth* (Palgrave Macmillan, 2012), p. 145

194 'They included'   ibid., p. 128

195 'The Kuhns' son'   Peter Hoffmann, 'Major Joachim Kuhn: Explosives
Purveyor to Stauffenberg and Stalin's Prisoner', *German Studies Review*,
vol. 28, no. 3 (October 2005), pp. 519–46

22

198 ' "Mika" was'   Robert Loeffel, *Family Punishment in Nazi Germany: Sippenhaft, Terror and Myth* (Palgrave Macmillan, 2012), pp. 142–3

'Irma'   Irma Goerdeler, Statement to S.I.B., Royal Military Police, Capri, 6 June 1945, WO 328/6, The National Archives

199 'Walks, however'   Valerie Riedesel, Freifrau zu Eisenbach, *Geisterkinder: Fünf Geschwister in Himmlers Sippenhaft* (SCM Hänssler, 2017), p. 130

200 'The lack of logic'   ibid., p. 137

202 'As Professor'   Clare Mulley, *The Women Who Flew for Hitler: The True Story of Hitler's Valkyries* (Macmillan, 2017), p. 72

203 'They had met'   ibid., p. 19

'The work, testing'   ibid., pp. 115–18

23

215 ' "This man felt" '   Krzysztof Dunin-Wąsowicz, *Obóz koncentracyjny Stutthof* (Wydawnictwo Morskie, 1966), pp. 83ff.

24

216 ' "It was a gigantic" '   Trudi Birger with Jeffrey M. Green, *A Daughter's Gift of Love: A Holocaust Memoir* (The Jewish Publication Society, 1992), p. 21

'Surrounded by water'   *Stutthof*, Holocaust Education and Archive Research Team, www.HolocaustResearchProject.org

'The camp'   Marek Orski, 'The Extermination of the Stutthof Concentration Camp Prisoners Using the Poisonous Cyclone B Gas' (Oranienburg, 2008), pp. 1–2

'. . . thirty new barracks'   Holocaust Education and Archive Research Team, op. cit.

216 ' "There were so many" ' Gregori Semenjaka, quoted in Janina Grabowska, 'K. L. Stutthof: Ein historischer Abriss', in Hermann Kuhn (ed.), *Stutthof: Ein Konzentrationslager vor den Toren Danzigs* (Edition Temmen, 1995), p. 121

217 'Some 47,000 prisoners' Andrej Angrick and Peter Klein, *The 'Final Solution' in Riga: Exploitation and Annihilation, 1941–1944* (Berghahn Books, 2009), p. 417

' "They stretched" ' Kuhn, op. cit., p. 190

'The mass killings' Krzysztof Dunin-Wąsowicz, *Obóz koncentracyjny Stutthof* (Wydawnictwo Morskie, 1966), pp. 83ff.

'In the four months' Angrick and Klein, op. cit., p. 417

' "We reeked" ' Birger with Green, op. cit., p. 18

218 'When the trains' ibid., pp. 20–1

'On most transports' Holocaust Education and Archive Research Team, op. cit.

' "After they had" ' Schoschana Rabinovici, *Thanks to My Mother* (Puffin Books, 2000), pp. 190–1

'According to one' Angrick and Klein, op. cit., p. 426

219 ' "No one wanted to" ' Birger with Green, op. cit., pp. 17–19

' "We had to show" ' Maria Rolnikaite, quoted in Kuhn, op. cit., p. 142

220 ' "There was one" ' quoted in Orski, op. cit., p. 19

' "He looked" ' Birger with Green, op. cit., p. 18

' "The death sentences" ' Dunin-Wąsowicz, op. cit.

' "Once it happened" ' ibid.

'As SS officer' statement by Albert Petlikau, quoted in Angrick and Klein, op. cit., p. 423

' "Every day" ' Dunin-Wąsowicz, op. cit.

221 ' "I don't want" ' Birger with Green, op. cit., p. 144

'While camp' Orski, op. cit., pp. 2–3

'Former SS' testimony of Hans Rach during the Stutthof Trials in Gdańsk, 1947, AK-IPN SO Gd. Ref. 78

'Prisoners were expected' Gregori Semenjaka, quoted in Kuhn, op. cit., p. 121

'At night' Birger with Green, op. cit., p. 142

222 'Outlining this' 21 June 1944, NS 19/4014, Bl. 167–8, Bundesarchiv Berlin

222 ' "From experience" '   Rabinovici, op. cit., p. 195

'Every morning'   Orski, op. cit., p. 18

' "The toilets" '   Rabinovici, op. cit., p. 194

223 'They slept'   Gregori Semenjaka, quoted in Kuhn, op. cit., p. 122

' "The guards had" '   Erna Valk, quoted in Kuhn, op. cit., p. 149

'. . . "sucked on like" '   quoted in Angrick and Klein, op. cit., p. 424, from a statement by Zbroja, 28 March 1968, 407 AR 91/65, BD. 7, Bundesarchiv Ludwigsburg

'A number of women'   Rabinovici, op. cit., p. 198

' "There were several" '   Maria Rolnikaite, quoted in Kuhn, op. cit., p. 143

224 ' "This was harder" '   Birger with Green, op. cit., pp. 110–11

' "I would say" '   statement by Otto Knott, 24 September 1975, 407 AR 91/65, BD. 6, Bundesarchiv Ludwigsburg

' "The camp doctors" '   Maria Rolnikaite, quoted in Kuhn, op. cit., p. 143

' "They made us" '   ibid., p. 144

'So terrible were'   Angrick and Klein, op. cit., p. 426

225 ' "Morning after morning" '   Rabinovici, op. cit., pp. 200–1

' "The fires were lit" '   Orski, op. cit., pp. 5–6

25

227 ' "The Germans put" '   Schoschana Rabinovici, *Thanks to My Mother* (Puffin Books, 2000), p. 199

228 'As she and her'   Valerie Riedesel, Freifrau zu Eisenbach, *Geisterkinder: Fünf Geschwister in Himmlers Sippenhaft* (SCM Hänssler, 2017), pp. 173–7

229 ' "Please read all" '   ibid., p. 177

26

233 '. . . a force of'   Ian Kershaw, *The End: Germany 1944–45* (Penguin Books, 2003), pp. 168–9

'The temperature'   Antony Beevor, *Berlin: The Downfall 1945* (Penguin Books, 2003), p. 17

233 'Slogans, painted'   ibid.

' "A blind feeling" '   quoted in Ian Kershaw, op. cit., p. 180

'. . . "to strike such terror" '   quoted in Ulrich Merten, *Forgotten Voices: The Expulsion of the Germans from Eastern Europe after World War II* (Routledge, 2012), p. 3

' "Zabashtansky called" '   Major Lev Koplev, *No Jail for Thought* (Secker & Warburg, 1977), p. 52

234 'Etched into the'   Richard Bessel, *Germany 1945: From War to Peace* (Simon & Schuster, 2010), p. 71; Karl Potrek, German Displaced Persons Association, 1953

235 'Even by East Prussian'   Kershaw, op. cit., p. 177

' "Panic grips" '   ibid.

' "It was sad" '   Lore Ehrich, quoted in Theodor Schieder, *Documents on the Expulsion of the Germans from East-Central Europe* (Federal Administration for Expellees, Refugees and War Victims, 1960–1), pp. 135–6

'Columns kept'   Beevor, op. cit., p. 47

'Some carts'   ibid.

236 ' "Dear Papa!" '   ibid., p. 37

' "The entire contents" '   Antony Beevor, *The Second World War* (Weidenfeld & Nicolson, 2014), pp. 829–30

'With black paint'   ibid., p. 830

' "German villages" '   Lieutenant Gennady Klimenko, quoted in Max Hastings, *Armageddon: The Battle for Germany 1944–45* (Macmillan, 2004), p. 308

' "Even the trees" '   Beevor, *Berlin: The Downfall 1945*, op. cit., p. 33

' "Germans abandoned" '   Beevor, *The Second World War*, op. cit., p. 31

237 ' "The roads were" '   ibid., p. 827

' "As far as" '   ibid., pp. 827–8

238 ' "I took" '   ibid., p. 828

239 ' "Bullets and" '   'Paying with Life and Limb for the Crimes of Nazi Germany', *Der Spiegel*, 27 May 2011

' "The ice was" '   Merten, op. cit., p. 44

' "During the very" '   Schieder, op. cit., p. 140

27

242 ' "The icy wind" '   Meta Vannas, quoted in Hermann Kuhn (ed.), *Stutthof: Ein Konzentrationslager vor den Toren Danzigs* (Edition Temmen, 1995), p. 152

'Forty-one columns'   Andrej Angrick and Peter Klein, *The 'Final Solution' in Riga: Exploitation and Annihilation, 1941–1944* (Berghahn Books, 2009), p. 424

'Rations, consisting'   Meta Vannas, quoted in Kuhn, op. cit., p. 152

' "Oh this awful" '   Lore Ehrich, quoted in Theodor Schieder, *Documents on the Expulsion of the Germans from East-Central Europe* (Federal Administration for Expellees, Refugees and War Victims, 1960–1), p. 141

243 ' "Snow, frost" '   Schoschana Rabinovici, *Thanks to My Mother* (Puffin Books, 2000), pp. 202–5

244 ' "We got the order" '   ibid., p. 207

28

246 ' "We had to" '   Anna-Luise von Hofacker, 'Unsere Gefängniszeit', unpublished memoir, private family archive

249 ' "Kupfer had a go" '   ibid.

250 'An estimated 4,500'   Andrej Angrick and Peter Klein, *The 'Final Solution' in Riga: Exploitation and Annihilation, 1941–1944* (Berghahn Books, 2009), p. 426

251 'On 30 January'   ibid., p. 425

29

252 ' "In the camp" '   Marie-Gabriele Schenk Gräfin von Stauffenberg, *Aufzeichnungen aus unserer Sippenhaft 20. Juli 1944 bis 19. Juni 1945* (Haus der Geschichte Baden-Württemberg, Der neue Blick, 2015), p. 97

252 'The punishment regime' Stuart B. T. Emmett, *Strafvollzugslager der SS und Polizei: Himmler's Wartime Institutions for the Detention of Waffen-SS and Polizei Criminals* (Fonthill, 2017), pp. 170–1

'Himmler, on becoming' in a speech at Bad Tölz to SS Group Leaders, 18 February 1937

'"If this remains"' ibid.

'. . . "this plague"' ibid.

'Of these' 'Persecution of Homosexuals in the Third Reich', website of the United States Holocaust Memorial Museum

'At Matzkau' Emmett, op. cit., p. 152

255 '"February 5"' Marie-Gabriele Schenk Gräfin von Stauffenberg, op. cit., p. 98

30

257 '"Our fear of"' Marie-Gabriele Schenk Gräfin von Stauffenberg, *Aufzeichnungen aus unserer Sippenhaft 20. Juli 1944 bis 19. Juni 1945* (Haus der Geschichte Baden-Württemberg, Der neue Blick, 2015), p. 99

258 'It was the first' Ulrich Merten, *Forgotten Voices: The Expulsion of the Germans from Eastern Europe after World War II* (Routledge, 2012), p. 45

'In the space of' Antony Beevor, *Berlin: The Downfall 1945* (Penguin Books, 2003), p. 49

'The *Gustloff* was' ibid., p. 51

260 '"Hanging around"' Marie-Gabriele Schenk Gräfin von Stauffenberg, op. cit., pp. 99–100

262 '"After some adjustment"' ibid., p. 101

263 '"Departure still always"' ibid., p. 102

267 '"Heavy tanks"' Isa Vermehren, *Reise durch den letzten Akt: Ravensbrück, Buchenwald, Dachau. Eine Frau Berichtet* (Rowohlt Taschenbuch Verlag, 1979), p. 181

268 '"Papa goes"' Marie-Gabriele Schenk Gräfin von Stauffenberg, op. cit., p. 104

31

272 'In the early'   William L. Shirer, *The Rise and Fall of the Third Reich* (Pan Books, 1964), pp. 170–83

'After resigning from'   Fritz Thyssen, *I Paid Hitler* (Hodder & Stoughton, 1941), pp. 39–42

'While, in the spring'   Nigel Jones, *Countdown to Valkyrie: The July Plot to Assassinate Hitler* (Frontline Books, 2008), p. 92

'Though Halder'   Peter Hoffmann, *The History of the German Resistance 1933–1945* (McGill-Queen's University Press, 2001), pp. 513, 530

273 ' "I was in the" '   Léon Blum, quoted in Hans-Günter Richardi, *SS-Geiseln in der Alpenfestung* (Edition Raetia, 2015), p. 82

' "There are no" '   ibid., p. 83

'. . . "bandage the victims" '   Dietrich Bonhoeffer, speaking to a group of Berlin pastors on 'The Church and the Jewish Question', April 1933

274 'Bonhoeffer had'   see Hugh Mallory Falconer, *The Gestapo's Most Improbable Hostage* (Pen and Sword Aviation, 2018); Hoffmann, op. cit.; Captain S. Payne Best, *The Venlo Incident* (Frontline Books, 2009).

275 'There were no'   Psychological Warfare Division, Supreme Headquarters of the Allied Forces, *The Buchenwald Report*, translated and edited by David A. Hackett (Westview Press, 1995), p. 77

'Hunger, illness'   Valerie Riedesel, Freifrau zu Eisenbach, *Geisterkinder: Fünf Geschwister in Himmlers Sippenhaft* (SCM Hänssler, 2017), p. 206

'In the first three'   Clare Mulley, *The Women Who Flew for Hitler: The True Story of Hitler's Valkyries* (Macmillan, 2017), p. 298

'Of approximately 80,000'   *The Buchenwald Report*, op. cit., p. 138. At the last roll call at the camp, on 3 April 1945, there were 80,900 prisoners.

'Encompassing'   ibid., pp. 90ff.

276 'The prisoners lived'   ibid., pp. 45ff.

'. . . 850 children'   ibid., pp. 8, 89

' "Let's have the birds" '   ibid., pp. 68–7

'Blocks 46'   ibid., pp. 71–4

276 'In one experiment'   General George S. Patton, *War As I Knew It*
(Houghton Mifflin, 1947), p. 301

'Trials to "cure"'   *The Buchenwald Report*, op. cit., p. 79

'One SS surgeon'   ibid., p. 229

'Another drug'   Vivien Spitz, *Doctors from Hell: The Horrific Account of Nazi Experiments on Humans* (Sentient Publications, 2005), p. 210

277 'Challenged at'   ibid., p. 209

'Between Block 46'   *The Buchenwald Report*, op. cit., p. 73

'"Women in"'   'Concentration Camp Bordellos', *Der Spiegel*, 25 June 2009

'Eighteen young girls'   *The Buchenwald Report*, op. cit., p. 73

278 '"I was never"'   Matthias Wegner, *Ein weites Herz: Die zwei Leben der Isa Vermehren* (Ullstein, 2004), p. 172

'"Fear and anxiety"'   ibid.

'"What I became aware"'   ibid., p. 171

'"There was a special"'   Isa Vermehren, Allied Forces Headquarters (Central Mediterranean), Statements by Former Political Prisoners, Second World War, WO 328/41, The National Archives

279 '"Man's inhumanity"'   TV interview with Volker Kühn for *Zeugen des Jahrhunderts*, ZDF, 2001

280 '"The days without"'   Anna-Luise von Hofacker, 'Unsere Gefängniszeit', unpublished memoir, private family archive

32

281 'To support this'   Anna-Luise von Hofacker, 'Unsere Gefängniszeit', unpublished memoir, private family archive

'Reading the letters'   ibid.

'Lenz replied'   ibid.

283 'Officially'   see Clare Mulley, *The Women Who Flew for Hitler: The True Story of Hitler's Valkyries* (Macmillan, 2017), p. 295

'"She was adamant"'   Gerhard Bracke, *Melitta Gräfin Stauffenberg: Das Leben einer Fliegerin* (Ullstein, 1993), p. 207

'Rather than'   Mulley, op. cit., p. 300

284 'Before leaving'   ibid.

284 ' "It was very secret" '   ibid., p. 301

'"Litta looked" '   Bracke, op. cit., p. 207

285 'Litta knew'   Mulley, op. cit., p. 301

'. . . "Flying Angel" '   ibid.

286 'We waited'   Hofacker, op. cit.

287 ' "It made the barrack" '   Marie-Gabriele Schenk Gräfin von Stauffen-berg, *Aufzeichnungen aus unserer Sippenhaft 20. Juli 1944 bis 19. Juni 1945* (Haus der Geschichte Baden-Württemberg, Der neue Blick, 2015), p. 109

'. . . Fräulein Knocke'   Isa Vermehren, *Reise durch den letzten Akt: Ravensbrück, Buchenwald, Dachau. Eine Frau Berichtet* (Rowohlt Taschen-buch Verlag, 1979), pp. 193–7

288 ' "pleasant-looking" '   Captain S. Payne Best, *The Venlo Incident* (Front-line Books, 2009), e-book, p. 510

'He boasted'   Horst Hoepner and Hermann Pünder, Allied Forces Headquarters (Central Mediterranean), Statements by Former Politi-cal Prisoners, Second World War, WO 328/14 and WO 328/30, The National Archives

' "He told me" '   Payne Best, op. cit., p. 524

' "I shall still" '   ibid., p. 553

'At dawn'   Psychological Warfare Division, Supreme Headquarters of the Allied Forces, *The Buchenwald Report*, translated and edited by David A. Hackett (Westview Press, 1995), p. 326

' "This has been" '   Payne Best, op. cit., p. 555

289 ' "Pure rage" '   Vermehren, op. cit., p. 194

290 ' "From the heavy" '   ibid.

' "First of all" '   ibid.

291 ' "SS men" '   ibid., p. 200

33

292 ' "It was a hell" '   Captain S. Payne Best, *The Venlo Incident* (Frontline Books, 2009), e-book, p. 558

' "This man" '   ibid., p. 587

293 ' "The pile of" '   ibid., p. 561

' "Someone recognised" '   ibid., p. 560

293 'Based at Dachau'   John J. Michalczyk (ed.), *Medicine, Ethics and the Third Reich: Historical and Contemporary Issues* (Rowman & Littlefield, 1994), p. 95

294 ' "When they came" '   Payne Best, op. cit., p. 560

295 ' "Really I have" '   ibid., p. 573
' "The target" '   Hugh Mallory Falconer, *The Gestapo's Most Improbable Hostage* (Pen and Sword Aviation, 2018), p. 117

296 ' "The warders" '   Payne Best, op. cit., p. 572

297 ' "This nocturnal" '   Isa Vermehren, *Reise durch den letzten Akt: Ravensbrück, Buchenwald, Dachau. Eine Frau Berichtet* (Rowohlt Taschenbuch Verlag, 1979), p. 204
' "It was a" '   Payne Best, op. cit., p. 575
' "It was the" '   Falconer, op. cit., p. 121
' "The upshot" '   Anna-Luise von Hofacker, 'Unsere Gefängniszeit', unpublished memoir, private family archive

298 ' "We lost no time" '   ibid.

299 ' "Stiller, with most" '   Falconer, op. cit., p. 122
' "When the sun" '   Hofacker, op. cit.

300 ' "The door was" '   Vermehren, op. cit., p. 206

301 ' "Weather very windy" '   Marie-Gabriele Schenk Gräfin von Stauffenberg, *Aufzeichnungen aus unserer Sippenhaft 20. Juli 1944 bis 19. Juni 1945* (Haus der Geschichte Baden-Württemberg, Der neue Blick, 2015), p. 110
'Staying low'   Clare Mulley, *The Women Who Flew for Hitler: The True Story of Hitler's Valkyries* (Macmillan, 2017), p. 305
'A few hundred'   ibid.

302 '. . . "she was in" '   Gerhard Bracke, *Melitta Gräfin Stauffenberg: Das Leben einer Fliegerin* (Ullstein, 1993), p. 225
'. . . "a special operation" '   Mulley, op. cit., p. 309
'As she passed'   ibid., p. 311
'Lieutenant Thomas'   ibid.
'. . . "two salvos" '   ibid.
'A retired'   ibid.

303 'The two men'   ibid., p. 312
'Mysteriously'   Bracke, op. cit., p. 232

304 ' "Masses of" '   Vermehren, op. cit., p. 211
' "More upsetting" '   ibid.

304 ' "The anxiety over" '   Hofacker, op. cit.

' "Now, no more" '   Gräfin von Stauffenberg, op. cit., p. 116

305 ' "Everywhere we look" '   ibid.

34

306 '... "the first concentration" '   'Dachau', website of the United States Holocaust Memorial Museum

'Later, in 1938'   ibid.

307 ' "Both men" '   Isa Vermehren, *Reise durch den letzten Akt: Ravens-brück, Buchenwald, Dachau. Eine Frau Berichtet* (Rowohlt Taschenbuch Verlag, 1979), p. 214

308 'He was very'   Captain S. Payne Best, *The Venlo Incident* (Frontline Books, 2009), e-book, p. 600

' "One could imagine" '   Lt Col Walter J. (Mickey) Fellenz, Commanding Officer, 1st Battalion, 22nd Regiment in a report to the Commanding General of the 42nd Division of the US 7th Army, 6 May 1945

309 'Arriving at Dachau'   Payne Best, op. cit., p. 648

310 'There was also'   see Sydney Smith, *Wings Day* (Collins, 1968); B. A. 'Jimmy' James, *Moonless Night: The Second World War Escape Epic* (Leo Cooper, 2002); Payne Best, op. cit.; Peter Churchill, *The Spirit in the Cage* (Hodder & Stoughton, 1954)

311 'The day before'   Richard Bessel, *Germany 1945: From War to Peace* (Pocket Books, 2010), p. 104

'TWO SPECIAL TRAINS'   Gerald Schwab, *OSS Agents in Hitler's Heartland: Destination Innsbruck* (Praeger, 1996), p. 173

'HIMMLER ARRIVED'   ibid.

312 'Rohde, a brilliant'   Payne Best, op. cit., p. 611

'On the morning'   ibid., p. 627

313 ' "Hour after hour" '   Payne Best, op. cit., p. 627

'... "other accommodation" '   ibid., p. 628

'GRUENWALDER HOF'   Schwab, op. cit., p. 173

314 'Recognizing that'   Roger Manvell and Heinrich Fraenkel, *Heinrich Himmler: The Sinister Life of the Head of the SS and Gestapo* (Greenhill

Books, 2007), pp. 197–8; Peter Longerich, *Heinrich Himmler* (Oxford University Press, 2012), pp. 725–6

314 '"This accomplishment"' Herma Briffault (ed.), *The Memoirs of Doctor Felix Kersten* (Doubleday, 1947), p. 228

315 'COUNT BERNADOTTE' Himmler's Meeting with Count Bernadotte, Sir Victor Mallet to the Foreign Office, 13 April 1945, PREM 3/197/6, The National Archives
'The senior' ibid.

316 '"Himmler was"' Peter Witte and Stephen Tyas, *Himmler's Diary 1945: A Calendar of Events Leading to Suicide* (Fonthill Media, 2014), p. 143
'"Then the war"' ibid., p. 144
'To Masur's question' Norbert Masur, cited in Gerald Reitlinger, *The Final Solution* (Vallentine, Mitchell, 1953), p. 521
'"Nobody has had"' Briffault, op. cit., p. 288

317 'Masur asked' W. Schellenberg, *Memoirs* (André Deutsch, 1956), p. 444
'. . . scheduled to' Manvell and Fraenkel, op. cit., p. 233
'(1) COUNT' Herschel V. Johnson, US Ambassador to Sweden, to the US Department of State, 25 April 1945, cited in Witte and Tyas, op. cit., p. 157

318 '"Himmler was still"' Albert Speer, *Inside the Third Reich*, cited in Witte and Tyas, op. cit., p. 158

35

319 'Dusty tinsel' Sydney Smith, *Wings Day* (Collins, 1968), p. 217
'. . . "every nook"' Captain S. Payne Best, *The Venlo Incident* (Frontline Books, 2009), e-book, p. 637

320 '"He pointed out"' ibid., p. 615
'"Sudden death"' ibid., p. 546

321 '. . . "a position"' Hugh Mallory Falconer, *The Gestapo's Most Improbable Hostage* (Pen and Sword Aviation, 2018), p. 130
'"At about half past"' ibid., pp. 131–2

322 '"The Americans"' Kurt Schuschnigg, *Austrian Requiem* (Victor Gollancz, 1947), p. 237
'"The wildest"' ibid.

322 '"We are waiting"' ibid.

'"We all got"' Payne Best, op. cit., p. 644

323 '. . . "the picture of"' W. Schellenberg, *Memoirs* (André Deutsch, 1956), p. 445

'"Just as we"' Payne Best, op. cit., p. 646

324 '"Around 10 to 15"' Isa Vermehren, *Reise durch den letzten Akt: Ravens-brück, Buchenwald, Dachau. Eine Frau Berichtet* (Rowohlt Taschenbuch Verlag, 1979), p. 216

325 '"Rafforth was"' ibid., p. 198

'German radio' *The Times*, 24 April 1945

328 'Some 5,000 prisoners' Hans-Günter Richardi, *SS-Geiseln in der Alpenfestung* (Edition Raetia, 2015), p. 152

'"Our departure"' Schuschnigg, op. cit., p. 238

329 '"The sight of"' Léon Blum, *Le Dernier Mois* (Éditions Diderot, 1946), pp. 67–71

'"The fact that"' Vermehren, op. cit., p. 220

330 '"We fell into"' ibid., p. 222

331 '"My mother"' ibid., pp. 223–4

'"It was the"' Payne Best, op. cit., p. 658

332 '"There was one"' ibid., p. 663

'"The Prime Minister"' Meeting of the War Cabinet, 25 April 1945, PREM 3/197/6, The National Archives

333 'The moment' ibid.

'"Button-holing"' Payne Best, op. cit., p. 662

'"His orders"' Vermehren, op. cit., p. 227

334 'A GERMAN OFFER' Count Folke Bernadotte, *The Curtain Falls* (Alfred A. Knopf, 1945), pp. 61–2

'"I was only"' Schellenberg, op. cit., p. 452

36

336 '"We didn't need"' Peter Churchill, *The Spirit in the Cage* (Hodder & Stoughton, 1954), p. 211

337 '"We all got"' Hugh Mallory Falconer, *The Gestapo's Most Improbable Hostage* (Pen and Sword Aviation, 2018), p. 152

337 ' "Germans in" '   ibid., p. 153

'. . . "had lost" '   B. A. 'Jimmy' James, *Moonless Night: The Second World War Escape Epic* (Leo Cooper, 2002), p. 182

338 ' "As soon as" '   Falconer, op. cit., p. 152

339 'The day before'   Hans-Günter Richardi, *SS-Geiseln in der Alpenfestung* (Edition Raetia, 2015), p. 191

340 'The first was'   Sydney Smith, *Wings Day* (Collins, 1968), pp. 227–32

'But after the'   ibid., p. 228

341 ' "I was by this" '   Captain S. Payne Best, *The Venlo Incident* (Frontline Books, 2009), e-book, p. 667

342 ' "Slowly, the first" '   Kurt Schuschnigg, *Austrian Requiem* (Victor Gollancz, 1947), p. 240

' "A youngish" '   James, op. cit., p. 184

'While Stiller'   Smith, op. cit., p. 230

344 ' "An attack" '   James, op. cit., p. 186

' "We had to" '   Fabian von Schlabrendorff, *The Secret War Against Hitler* (Pitman Publishing Corporation, 1966), p. 334

345 ' "We discussed" '   Falconer, op. cit., p. 154

'It was not clear'   Schlabrendorff, op. cit., p. 333

' "Fritz was" '   Payne Best, op. cit., pp. 674–8

' "I don't like" '   ibid., p. 677

346 ' "You mustn't touch" '   ibid.

' "This started him" '   ibid., p. 675

'. . . "160 prominent" '   Richardi, op. cit., p. 216

347 '. . . "convoy of Prominenten" '   James, op. cit., p. 189n

' "Let's not talk" '   quoted in Fey von Hassell and David Forbes-Watt, *A Mother's War* (John Murray, 1990), p. 182

'Leaving his company'   James, op. cit., p. 189n

348 ' "Across the square" '   ibid., pp. 189–90

37

349 'In the circumstances'   Hans-Günter Richardi, *SS-Geiseln in der Alpenfestung* (Edition Raetia, 2015), p. 209

350 ' "They were all" '   ibid., p. 235

350 ' "After my years" '   B. A. 'Jimmy' James, *Moonless Night: The Second World War Escape Epic* (Leo Cooper, 2002), p. 191

'The men were'   Richardi, op. cit., pp. 230–3

351 ' "In this glorious" '   Peter Churchill, *The Spirit in the Cage* (Hodder & Stoughton, 1954), p. 221

'TO REICHSFUEHRER'   Government Code and Cipher School: Signals Intelligence passed to the Prime Minister, HW 1/3747, The National Archives

352 'But more than'   Richardi, op. cit., p. 238

'. . . "left in a spin" '   ibid.

' "As we approached" '   James, op. cit., p. 194

353 ' "Our soldiers" '   Marie-Gabriele Schenk Gräfin von Stauffenberg, *Aufzeichnungen aus unserer Sippenhaft 20. Juli 1944 bis 19. Juni 1945* (Haus der Geschichte Baden-Württemberg, Der neue Blick, 2015), p. 127

' "The majority" '   Isa Vermehren, *Reise durch den letzten Akt: Ravensbrück, Buchenwald, Dachau. Eine Frau Berichtet* (Rowohlt Taschenbuch Verlag, 1979), p. 240

'Almost immediately'   Richardi, op. cit., pp. 254–5

' "The American" '   Kurt Schuschnigg, *Austrian Requiem* (Victor Gollancz, 1947), pp. 241–2

' "I cannot" '   ibid.

38

355 'Leading the convoy'   Peter Churchill, *The Spirit in the Cage* (Hodder & Stoughton, 1954), p. 225

' "We beheld" '   ibid., p. 226

357 '. . . "after a very" '   Isa Vermehren, *Reise durch den letzten Akt: Ravensbrück, Buchenwald, Dachau. Eine Frau Berichtet* (Rowohlt Taschenbuch Verlag, 1979), p. 270

' "Every moment" '   ibid., p. 273

39

369 'In the summer' figures cited in Tara Zahra, 'Lost Children: Displacement, Family and Nation in Postwar Europe', *Journal of Modern History*, vol. 81, no. 1, European Childhood in the Twentieth Century (March 2009), p. 47

'In the concentration camps' 'Children during the Holocaust', website of the United States Holocaust Memorial Museum

'Another 50,000' Verena Buser, 'Displaced Children 1945 and the Child Tracing Division of the United Nations Relief and Rehabilitation Administration', in *The Holocaust in History and Memory*, vol. 7: *70 Years After the Liberation of the Camps*, ed. Rainer Schulze (University of Essex, 2014)

370 'Whether through' Zahra, op. cit., p. 45

'The Red Cross' Dorothy Macardle, *Children of Europe* (Victor Gollancz, 1949) p. 305

'In the final' Michelle Mouton, 'Missing, Lost and Displaced Children in Postwar Germany: The Great Struggle to Provide for the War's Youngest Victims', *Central European History*, vol. 48, issue 1 (March 2015), p. 54

'In the Soviet zone' ibid., p. 61

'As early as 1943' ibid., p. 54

'But when the time came' ibid., p. 56

'In setting up' ibid., p. 55

'Many families' ibid., p. 57

371 'Children arriving' ibid., p. 63

' "From experience" ' Hans Szperlinski, the founder and head of the German child search agency Kindersuchdienst, cited in ibid.

'While the Allied authorities' ibid., pp. 55–6

'The majority had' ibid.

375 'But the children' Robert Foster, unpublished memoir, undated, private family archive

40

377 'Ilse's teenage years'   Ilse von Hassell, unpublished memoir, undated, private family archive
'Like so many'   David Stafford, *Endgame 1945* (Abacus, 2008), p. 461

Epilogue

393 ' "As a teenager" '   Corrado Pirzio-Biroli, conversation with author, November 2016

395 'While there'   Peter Hoffmann, *Stauffenberg: A Family History, 1905–1944* (Cambridge University Press, 1995), p. 281
'After his release'   ibid.
' "He was a true" '   Dr Gudula Knerr-Stauffenberg, correspondence with author, 8 March 2018

396 ' "It is not" '   Marie-Gabriele Schenk Gräfin von Stauffenberg, *Aufzeichnungen aus unserer Sippenhaft 20. Juli 1944 bis 19. Juni 1945* (Haus der Geschichte Baden-Württemberg, Der neue Blick, 2015), p. 129
' "The tour" '   ibid., p. 231
' "A society" '   Isa Vermehren, lecture at Ravensbrück, 1993

397 'He left'   Peter Longerich, *Heinrich Himmler* (Oxford University Press, 2012), p. 735

398 'Here, according'   Werner Grothmann, Preliminary Interrogation Report 031/Misc 19, 24 May 1945, WO 208/4431, The National Archives
'The river'   Peter Witte and Stephen Tyas, *Himmler's Diary 1945: A Calendar of Events Leading to Suicide* (Fonthill Media, 2014), p. 207
'They spent'   ibid., p. 210
' "Himmler was" '   Interim Report of Werner Grothmann, 13 June 1945, WO 208/4474, The National Archives

399 '. . . the British'   ibid.
' "At that time" '   statement by Captain T. Selvester (undated), WO 32/19603, The National Archives
' "The first man" '   ibid.

400 ' "At 22.45" '   'The Diary of Major Norman Whittaker', quoted in Witte and Tyas, op. cit., p. 218

'. . . "saw a small" '   Colonel Murphy, quoted in Roger Manvell and Heinrich Fraenkel, *Heinrich Himmler: The Sinister Life of the Head of the SS and Gestapo* (Frontline Books, 2017), p. 248

' "My God!" '   'The Diary of Major Norman Whittaker', quoted in Witte and Tyas, op. cit., p. 218

'Immediately'   Manvell and Fraenkel, op. cit., p. 248

' "The dramatic" '   Captain C. J. 'Jimmie' Wells, quoted in Paul Van Stemann, 'Himmler's Night of Reckoning', *Independent*, 21 May 1995

401 ' "This evil thing" '   'The Diary of Major Norman Whittaker', quoted in Witte and Tyas, op. cit., p. 218

' "These four" '   Second Army Defence Company War Diary, WO 208/4474, The National Archives

'During the six'   Janina Grabowska, *Odpowiedzialność za zbrodnie popełnione w Stutthofie. Procesy* [*Responsibility for the Atrocities Committed at Stutthof. The Trials*], KL Stutthof, Monografia

404 'In 1948'   Dorothy Macardle, *Children of Europe* (Victor Gollancz, 1949), p. 296

Index